WHEN MONTANA OUTRACED THE EAST

WHEN MONTANA OUTRACED THE EAST

THE REIGN OF WESTERN THOROUGHBREDS, 1886–1900

CATHARINE MELIN-MOSER

UNIVERSITY OF OKLAHOMA PRESS : NORMAN

This book is published with the generous assistance of the McCasland Foundation, Duncan, Oklahoma.

Library of Congress Cataloging-in-Publication Data

Names: Melin-Moser, Catharine, 1959– author.
Title: When Montana outraced the East : the reign of Western thoroughbreds, 1877–1900 / Catharine Melin-Moser.
Description: First edition. | Norman : University of Oklahoma Press, [2025] | Includes index. | Summary: "The untold history of when Montana horses dominated the eastern thoroughbred racing establishment"—Provided by publisher.
Identifiers: LCCN 2024032819 | ISBN 9780806195315 (hardcover)
Subjects: LCSH: Armstrong, Noah. | Daly, Marcus, 1841–1900. | Larabie, Samuel E., 1845–1914. | Race horses—Montana—History—19th century.
Classification: LCC SF338 .M45 2025 | DDC 636.1/209786—dc23/eng/20241212
LC record available at https://lccn.loc.gov/2024032819

The paper in this book meets the guidelines for permanence and durability of the Committee on Production Guidelines for Book Longevity of the Council on Library Resources, Inc. ∞

For Pearl.
I hardly knew you.

Contents

Preface

My grandfather Axel Melin followed both Thoroughbred and Standardbred racing. On an afternoon in 1968, he took his little granddaughter to the Maywood Park racetrack in Chicago. My memory is of standing with him at the track rail where, every time the trotters swept past, I heard and felt the sweep of hooves skimming the dirt. Half a century later, I believe that afternoon at the races instilled in me a lifelong admiration and affection for blooded horses.

The two favorites for the 1969 Kentucky Derby evoked a spirited debate between my grandfather and my mother in the days before that classic Thoroughbred race. Grandfather predicted Arts and Letters would wear the fabled blanket of red roses. My mother, Rae Melin, disagreed. She insisted Majestic Prince would go home with the blanket.

Mother got it right.

In the 1970s in Colorado, my family never missed the Triple Crown broadcasts. Sitting in front of the television in our family room, I watched the Thoroughbreds parade and cheered for my favorites. I always had more than one. In 1973, I watched Secretariat rout the Belmont Stakes competition by an unthinkable thirty-one lengths. When Ruffian broke down during her match race against Foolish Pleasure in 1975, I cried out in disbelief, "Oh, she's hurt!" All through my teens, I read biographies about famous racehorses, the likes of Exterminator, Count Fleet, Citation, and Native Dancer.

Through my work as a freelance writer in the 2000s, on assignment at a Montana ranch, what a thrill it was to pet a grandson of Secretariat. In researching my articles and combing through newspapers of the 1880s and 1890s, I found snippets that told of Thoroughbred horses from Montana winning important eastern races. It struck me that I had discovered a fascinating story about archival equines. It so happened in 2011 that Molly Holz, the editor of the Montana Historical Society's flagship magazine, *Montana, the*

Magazine of Western History, had asked me to peer-review an article about jerk-line freighting. On the day we finished our telephone conversation about the article, I screwed up my courage and gave Molly an off-the-cuff pitch about amazing Montana Thoroughbreds winning major eastern races. She was intrigued and recognized the subject as underrepresented in Montana sports history. I knew of only two books on the subject, Ada Powell's *Copper, Green and Silver* and Susan Nardinger's *Spirit Horse of the Rockies*. In 2014, my own groundbreaking scholarship complemented theirs. My article "In the Winner's Circle: How Montana Thoroughbreds Upset the Nineteenth Century's Racing Establishment" became the foundation for this book.

The book is not a history of nineteenth-century Thoroughbred horse racing in Montana. Rather, it is a study of Montana's influence on and contribution to American horse racing by way of three of her frontiersmen, Noah Armstrong of Twin Bridges, Samuel E. Larabie of Deer Lodge, and Marcus Daly of Anaconda. Their shrewd foresight, hustle, and sweat, along with a little luck, made them millions in the mining and banking industries. Still eager to speculate on tremendous possibility, they pursued a new enterprise in Montana—breeding and racing Thoroughbred horses. The men who were hired to train and ride the horses kept tapping me on the shoulder, letting me know that their stories were interesting, too. But the Thoroughbreds were what really drew me in. For a brief period from 1886 to 1900, magnificent Thoroughbreds representing Montana notched one famed race after another, even setting new track records, on the hallowed grounds of eastern racetracks.

I hypothesized that Armstrong, Larabie, and Daly must have interacted in a loose alliance of breeding and racing their horses. Archival documents such as *Index: Thoroughbred Stock* at the Marcus Daly Mansion and nineteenth-century newspapers told me that they had. My greatest triumph—and most memorable moment—was to discover the fate of 1889 Kentucky Derby winner Spokane, Montana's most famous racehorse. "Whatever happened to Spokane?" had been a great mystery and source of folklore. The answer had evaded historians and sportswriters for well over a century. I, too, made repeated searches. Then, on the night of November 29, 2019, I found it, in a New Jersey newspaper. In two sentences.

Even after fourteen years (as of this publication in 2025) of research and writing about the subject, I never tire of the implausible stories of the men and horses I have come to know so well. I have visited the grave site of

Samuel Larabie in Deer Lodge and that of Noah Armstrong in Seattle. My intimate knowledge about the life of Belmont Stakes winner Scottish Chieftain, my favorite flyer, landed him a berth in the Montana Cowboy Hall of Fame. Each horse, from quick-wired sprinter to weight-hauling iron horse, made his imprint during a classic period that had American and Montana horse racing deeply intertwined.

And it all began with the simple act of horses raced over a landscape of unfenced bunchgrass.

CHAPTER 1

"The Verist Madness"

On a plain of bunchgrass in the Deer Lodge Valley, a long straightaway is recognized as Montana's earliest racetrack. According to local lore, that is where Native Americans once raced their ponies. Horse racing was also a favorite pastime among frontiersmen. Tongues wagged faster than the speed of their horses with claims of "My horse is faster than yours." The dispute had to be settled, and the race set to decide the matter induced wagering of precious furs or gold dust. The frontier racehorse was typically a cayuse captured off the range, a homegrown cow pony or saddle horse, or a mix of all three. Across the unfenced frontier, all sorts of mismatches were conceived, mostly at the discretion of the horses.

Frontiersmen brought horse racing to the towns of Deer Lodge, Virginia City, and Helena. At Helena, a straight course of six hundred yards was built in 1867. The following year, second and third racetracks came into existence. The Widow Durgen oversaw the building of a half-mile straight course on her property, and Madam Cody, or Coady, opened a one-mile circular course at her home. Cody's selection of a name, Fashion Course, possibly borrowed from the famed racecourse in New York, did not go over well. "Too high strung for the boys, who thought 'Madam Cody's track' was good enough," said Bobby Graham, a frontier jockey in his youth. "Every miner owned one or two horses, and each thought his cayuse was a racehorse. Sunday was the day upon which all the disputes in this respect were practically argued and settled, and from 300 to 500 men attended the track, . . . the owners generally riding their own animals."[1]

Frontier jockey George Miller said that the only saddles available were the large California saddles. Their deep seat and high peaked pommel, and their weight, were unsuitable for racing. The boys improvised. "We just threw a surcingle around the horse and when we got on, stuck our knees through it until sure we could stay on and then wrapped our legs around the pony or dug our heels into his side and clung on like grim death till the race was over. We had no boots in those days and as a rule, wore nothing but our underclothes when starting for a race."[2]

Enthusiasm for the First Annual Territorial Fair in October 1868 included the first organized horse racing program in the Montana Territory. As many as 150 "flyers" or "bangtails," as racehorses were affectionately called, competed at Madam Cody's track and entertained delegations of frontiersmen traversing the mountains to reach Helena. Buckskin bags filled with gold dust were all over the place but perfectly safe. Bobby Graham explained the security measures in place as "too many handy trees in the vicinity for anyone to think of stealing gold in those times."[3]

Bags of gold dust were likely all over the place in Deer Lodge on November 16, 1870, marking the historic Sixty Miler horse race. Colonel John C. Calhoun Thornton, a distinguished cavalry officer who served for the Confederate States of America, and livery stable proprietors Henry Valiton and James Talbot argued over the merits of their horses. Valiton and Talbot were the proud owners of a little horse named Lizard. They proposed "a single dash of sixty miles" against Colonel Thornton's horse, Billy Bay. Details were agreed upon, and each side posted $1,000. Multiple riders were secured for the contest, to change as often as they liked. Side bets were encouraged.[4]

Lizard and Billy Bay were prime examples of horses found in western hamlets who shared a similar ancestry. Both were Deer Lodge Valley homebreds and through their shared sire, Papoose, were half brothers. Legend has it that Papoose, a "thoroughbred Kentucky horse," was stolen as a colt from Mullan Road travelers by an unspecified native tribe in 1858 or 1859. If this is true, Papoose likely was the first full-blooded Thoroughbred to set hoof on Montana soil. The stallion fell into the hands of Indian traders and was sold to a Deer Lodge man in 1863.[5]

The *New North-West* newspaper in Deer Lodge published profiles of each horse, allowing the locals to gauge each animal's chances. Lizard, long in body and light in flesh, was introduced as "hound-built." At six years old, he stood slightly more than thirteen hands high—one hand is equal to four inches—and weighed about 690 pounds. Three years of racing had made him a famous little nag, and though his speed was not necessarily blistering, Lizard was of exceptional stamina for so slight a horse.[6]

Conversely, Billy Bay's merit as a racehorse was unknown. The Sixty Miler would be the ten-year-old's first competition as a racehorse. A bay in color, he stood fourteen hands and weighed 900 pounds. His acclaim as an extraordinary saddle horse with great endurance was warranted from arduous trips in mountainous country through which he carried heavy riders. The betting, generally fearless, involved gold dust or horses. Most wagers favored Billy Bay, on the popular belief that the sturdy saddle horse would wear down the slim racehorse in the last ten or twenty miles.[7]

On race day, frontiersmen streamed toward Olin's Track on the outskirts of Deer Lodge to watch two horses circle a one-mile oval sixty times. At eleven o'clock and amid eager shouts from close to three thousand predominantly male spectators, Billy Bay leaped into his stride with sixty-nine-pound Bobby Graham on his back. Eighty-two pounder Tommy Woods held Lizard a length behind the loping Billy Bay. By Mile 2, the lead had changed.

At Mile 7, with Lizard ahead by half a mile, Woods pulled him up to change riders. Billy Bay loped on, and in the minute needed to switch riders, Billy Bay gained back a quarter mile. At Mile 8, Graham jumped off Billy and a new rider jumped on.

By Mile 15 and "down to steady work," both horses were sweating profusely. Lizard's slender legs continued to outwhip those of Billy Bay, and by Mile 22, Lizard's lead was half a mile. Billy Bay was not giving up the race yet. His powerful hind legs gathered, stretched, and sprang, and his forelegs pulled him forward in a desperate bid to catch Lizard. His hard effort proved to be for naught. By Mile 48, he wanted off the track. Then, at Mile 55, he flat out quit. Lizard clipped along, four miles ahead. Colonel Thornton had seen enough. He waved Billy Bay off the track and the horse was led away.[8]

Lizard, with less than a mile of soil to cover, circled the remaining distance at a trot. He finished the Sixty Miler as the wintry sun sank and the temperature chilled. The little horse had circled Olin's Track for four hours and twenty-eight minutes. Cheers erupted from the frontiersmen who had waited to see the race out. More than $10,000 exchanged hands over the horse race, recorded as the longest and most lucrative in Montana history.[9]

The next landmark horse race in Montana, the Pioneer Stakes, was held on September 7, 1880, in Helena. It featured full-blooded Thoroughbreds, and four of the six were Montana bred. This unprecedented occasion during the Eleventh Annual Territorial Fair "excited more than ordinary interest and brought many an 'old timer' to stand to witness the first race among native Thoroughbred horses," the *Butte Weekly Miner* reported. The start was clean for the three-quarter-mile dash. The result stayed in doubt until the charge down the homestretch, where Neva Winters, a filly from California, outdistanced the natives.[10]

◼

When a reconnaissance tasked with determining a future route for the Northern Pacific Railway surveyed the Montana Territory's valleys and mountains, it reached the Deer Lodge Valley in 1869. Crew member Samuel Wilkenson wrote about the grass covering every bench, foothill, and mountainside:

> The fattening and strengthening properties of the grass in midwinter are precisely what they are in midsummer. I have seen mules and horses at the end of a severe season of packing through the Rocky Mountains as smooth and round as seals. They had been fed exclusively on the grass. I have seen "Cayuse" ponies avert from oats to bunch grass. I have seen Wells, Fargo & Co.'s stage horses kept in perfect condition on the range with the added allowance to some of the animals, of two quarts of oats a day, and no more. The "Bunch" grass is unquestionably the sweetest and most nutritious in the world. And here is a rolling ocean of it. . . . In the Deer Lodge Pass of the Rocky Mountains, I measured it twenty inches. Our horses when unsaddled and turned loose went at it ravenously, though to the hand it was as dry as a powder-horn and to the eye was dead.[11]

More than one frontiersman who raised stock said that the bountiful grass was more valuable to the territory than its minerals. On that point, territorial governor Benjamin F. Potts expressed his sentiment in April 1872, saying that the supply of bunchgrass was "worth more to the Territory than all her gold and silver mines, rich as these are." He then explained, "This peculiar grass, more nutritious than Ohio timothy, starts up in early spring, reaches maturity in June and then cures where it stands, retaining all its nutritive qualities and constituting the finest autumn and winter feed for cattle that nature has anywhere provided."[12]

The suite of native perennial grasses was generally known as bunchgrass. Some grasses grew tall and slender; others were short, fat, and tufted. Cool-season plants peaked in May and June. The warm-season species peeped out in June and thrived through August. The self-cured grass was remarkably nutritious throughout winter. To the west of the Deer Lodge Valley, in the neighboring Bitterroot Valley, grasses grew so tall and waved so thickly in lush profusion that, purportedly, "a horseman riding through it long after sunrise would have his boots dripping with the dew ere he had traveled a hundred yards."[13]

The sea of grass fated frontiersman Carsten Conrad Kohrs to raising cattle. Arriving in the Montana Territory in 1862, the twenty-seven-year-old German immigrant in pursuit of gold was quick to discover that more money was to be made selling meat to his fellow fortune hunters. Kohrs switched his profession from gold seeker to butcher but lacked consistent supplies of beef until he purchased four hundred head of "poor" cattle in 1864 at a Virginia City auction. His next purchase of four hundred head of "fine" steers was trailed from Walla Walla, Washington Territory, in 1866. He adopted the customary method of branding the herd and turning it out on the open range, rounding it up in the spring, branding the calves, selecting which animals to sell, and turning them out again. Kohrs wintered his herds in the Deer Lodge Valley, where, according to his notes of February 12, 1866, "Even then the young grass among the bunches of old grass on the south side of the hill was from four to six inches high." The animals were "in fine condition and heavy."[14]

Some frontiersmen tried their hand at raising blooded horses, as Thoroughbred and Standardbred breeds were commonly called. Charles Williams imported a Kentucky-bred Thoroughbred stallion named Cariboo. The six-year-old bay was well bred and described as "an old veteran of the racecourse, having fought many hard battles." News of the sale enthused the *Helena Independent* to track Cariboo's journey. Starting at the point of the sale, Saratoga, New York, weekly updates put Cariboo on the road to Corinne, Utah, then to Montana, arriving "from the states" in September 1876. Next, with the business at hand to breed Cariboo, the *Independent* in April 1878 reported exciting news of an important birth by a local mare: the Thoroughbred Bessie Douglass had foaled a chestnut filly sired by Cariboo. Named Peekaboo, she was accorded the distinction of being the first full-blooded Thoroughbred foaled in the Montana Territory.[15]

Meanwhile, another Thoroughbred stallion had been brought to the territory. On a cattle-buying trip in 1877, Conrad Kohrs was in West Liberty, Iowa, when he purchased a retired racehorse named Regent, who had won more races than he had lost on racetracks in Ohio, Tennessee, Illinois, and Wisconsin. Kohrs also purchased a second Thoroughbred stallion, Strideaway. The stallions were shipped from Ohio to a railhead at Franklin, Idaho, from where they were trailed to his Deer Lodge Valley ranch. Kohrs publicized Regent as "The Best Stallion West of the Missouri" for several weeks in 1879, relating Regent's pedigree and race record. Ohio bred and bay in color, Regent had fine breeding, including his sire, English-bred Bonnie Scotland, imported in 1875 to America. Bonnie Scotland sired winner upon winner. The dam was Lady Lancaster, a daughter of English-bred Monarch, also relocated to America and proving himself an exceptional sire of Thoroughbred broodmares. Kohrs charged fifty dollars to breed a mare to Regent. Neighboring horseman Samuel E. Larabie dropped off his highly bred Thoroughbred mare, Christine, for a mating. Kohrs's horse breeding enterprise established with his half brother John Bielenberg made them the earliest Montana breeders of Thoroughbred horses. They would, however, be best remembered in state history for their powerful partnership as cattle barons.[16]

The most serious blooded horse breeders typically imported Thorough-bred stock from Kentucky. Owing to steel-blue grass growing on top of soil flecked with limestone and fed by plenty of good water, the region known as Bluegrass Country was exceptionally suited for horse breeding. Kentucky horse breeders were passionate about Thoroughbred horses and bred the finest stallions to the finest mares. The average Thoroughbred, aside from his obvious swiftness, is long, lean, and leggy, stands fifteen to sixteen hands high, and is symmetric in conformation, pleasing to the eye, and of athletic build. His rear legs as they bend and straighten act as springs to propel him into flight and supply tremendous power that launches him forward as his front legs pull him over the ground. His neck and head move in unison with his forelegs, the rhythm aiding forward motion and extending the time airborne. He will withstand the equivalent of one hundred times the force of gravity on each hoof, which is the force exerted at full speed.[17]

The modern Thoroughbred traces his ancestry to three foundation stallions exported from the Mediterranean Middle East to Great Britain early in the seventeenth century. They were the Darley Arabian, Byerley Turk, and Godolphin Arabian, with the Byerley Turk arriving as early as 1689, and all bred to native mares. Arabian horses were prized for their speed, spirit, and

Willow Run Stock Farm lithograph. It is believed that Conrad Kohrs and John Bielenberg's success at breeding blooded horses in the Deer Lodge Valley influenced Samuel Larabie, their neighbor, to do the same. Larabie would establish the Willow Run Stock Farm. Courtesy of M. A. Leeson, *History of Montana, 1739–1885* (Chicago, Warner, Beers, 1885), 159.

endurance. The term "thoroughbred," formally defined in 1755, was originally applied to "completely educated; completely taught" people.[18]

As long ago as 1730 in Virginia, where American Thoroughbred breeding arguably began, a Virginian imported America's first Thoroughbred stallion, Bulle Rock, from England. Colonists in Charleston, South Carolina, formed America's first racing association, or jockey club, in 1734. In July 1759, Andrew Burnaby, an Anglican minister, remarked about Virginia racing that "the horses are fleet and beautiful; and the gentlemen of Virginia, who are exceedingly fond of horse-racing, have spared no expense or trouble to improve the breed of them by importing great numbers from England." Virginians and founding fathers George Washington and Thomas Jefferson were avid horse racing enthusiasts. Then, as the Civil War raged, Virginians,

Kentuckians, and southerners in general watched both armies deplete their Thoroughbred stock.[19]

The Commonwealth of Kentucky was the yardstick by which to measure exceptional Thoroughbred horse breeding. In 1883, the *Rocky Mountain Husbandman* editor at Diamond City, Montana, dared to put his home territory on a similar footing, writing, "Now if these qualities [water, soil, grass] be the secret of success of raising fast horses, Montana may well claim to be the equal if not a superiority over Kentucky. Nowhere on earth can there be found purer water than courses in our mountain streams and brooklets . . . the soil of many of our valleys is so strong of lime. . . . And the superiority of our wild grasses over the regular bluegrass is readily admitted by all Kentuckians who have had an opportunity of testing its qualities."[20]

The following year, with the *Husbandman* stating, "The time will come when Montana bunch grass will be matched against Kentucky blue grass, and we will wager our last nickel that bunch grass will win," the Deer Lodge Valley was, in fact, turning out some pretty good colts. The likes of Bonnie Australian, bred by Samuel Larabie, and Jocko, bred by Kohrs and Bielenberg, were winning in San Francisco, Lexington, Chicago, New Orleans, and in New York and New Jersey. This rapid uptick rated an article in the *Spirit of the Times*, a highly regarded national sports weekly routinely covering horse racing. The *Husbandman* reprinted the article alerting the nation's turfmen to Montana's ascent in American horse racing. "The peculiar advantages of Montana as a stock breeding setting are already making themselves felt," and, *Spirit* ventured, "in fact, the advantages of climate, pasturage and the cheapness of land are beginning to attract general attention toward Montana as the coming breeding section of America, and the day is not far distant when it will rival the worlds of old Yorkshire and the Blue-Grass region of Kentucky in the fame and celebrity of its racehorses."[21]

Yet most Thoroughbred traditionalists in the East and South stood firm: breeding Thoroughbred horses in Montana was a doomed experiment. Some even predicted dwarfs as the outcome. With Thoroughbred horses firmly implanted in the histories and traditions of the East and South, little wonder that the revolutionary idea to breed and rear an exquisite breed on vast landscapes of native bunchgrass and under wide skies at high altitude in "that nowhere of the West" was thought to be "the verist madness."[22]

CHAPTER 2

Noah Armstrong

Silver-Mining Lion

At Churchill Downs in Louisville, Kentucky, Noah Armstrong waited restively for the ninth running of the Kentucky Derby, in which he had entered his prized racehorse, Lord Raglan. All day long on May 23, 1883, an uncomfortably warm day, turf scribes had tailed him. They did not know much about his history, but he was a sixty-year-old silver-mining lion from the Montana Territory, still very much a frontier, and he was breeding Thoroughbred horses there. This was highly irregular and exciting. Tall and weedy framed, Armstrong wore a long beard forked like a bird's tail. The gray whiskers made him look grandfatherly, approachable. The turf scribes waded in, asking, "What horse do you like, Mr. Armstrong?" He answered with his standard quip: "Whiskey and Sugar."[1]

A newcomer to the American turf, Armstrong was nearly thirty years a newcomer to America. He left his birthplace of Kingston, Ontario, in an unknown year. He renounced his Canadian citizenship in 1855 and wed New York–born Hannah Howd. Three years later, the couple farmed 123 acres in Blue Earth County, Minnesota. Life was probably pretty good, but Armstrong was restless and felt a sense of urgency as gold seekers by the thousands rushed to California, or the Pacific Northwest, or the Rocky Mountains, upon news of gold strikes. In the Idaho Territory in July 1862, bonanzas were struck at Grasshopper Creek and Alder Gulch. Armstrong at age forty or forty-one decided to forgo farming in exchange for adventure in the West's roaring mining frontier. He would later move Hannah and the three children to be with him.[2]

Armstrong engaged in the dirty, backbreaking business of placer mining. A pick, a shovel, a pan, an ax, and a whipsaw for constructing a wooden sluice box were all the tools needed. A few bucks paid the fee to record a claim. A simple enterprise, it required but little capital. Mining camps in the Idaho Territory abounded, including those of Bannack, Virginia City,

Nevada City, and Helena. Each had its own brand of madness, but the madness warranted the creation of the Montana Territory on May 26, 1864.[3]

During summer 1872 in the Pioneer Mountains, Montana Territory, prospector Jerry Grotevant and three partners set out on an expedition to trap furbearing animals and relocate a silver lode. On the morning the men awoke and found themselves without horses, Grotevant in search of the wandering animals traversed Trapper Hill, where he spied a small boulder and, booting it, saw that the underside gleamed. He picked up the rock, heavy with silver. The horses forgotten, Grotevant's search for the lode led him to a quartz outcropping studded with silver. His partner Bill Hamilton tried to go undetected when entering Bannack to record the discovery, but he was spotted and immediately aroused suspicion. Every miner camp was alert for signs of a new discovery, and a horde of men tailed Hamilton back to where he came from. And so, at the rich Trapper lode, the camp of Trapper City sprang to life.[4]

Noah Armstrong moved his prospecting crew to the vicinity of Trapper Mountain. At Lion Mountain, described as an upthrust of bald, white rock rising above timberline, he struck multiple high-grade silver lodes. He now needed capital to develop mines. The recovery of silver ore, less lucrative than gold and far more difficult to extract from its source, was in those days a sophisticated, labor-intensive, and costly venture. It commanded multitudes of miners and enormous capital to tunnel into the earth and extract the mineral from hard rock. That was half the proposition. Once the ore reached daylight, mills and smelters separated the silver from its protecting rock. And again, large amounts of capital were needed to front the cost of constructing mills and smelters. Access to wealth of that kind was scarce in the West.[5]

Armstrong's quest for an investor took him to Indianapolis and to industrialist Elias Atkins, who agreed to finance silver mining operations at Lion Mountain. The two men might have been aware of each other as early as the 1860s in the Idaho Territory goldfields. Atkins's firm, the Atkins Saw Works, was among the world's largest saw manufacturers, and his wealth financed Armstrong, Atkins and Company. Armstrong's education, more extensive than that of most men, brought to the table knowledge in pharmaceuticals, chemistry, economics, banking, and assay.[6]

Noah Armstrong prospected and mined minerals all through the Rocky Mountains, from Montana to New Mexico to Alaska, and in Mexico and South America. He claimed to have crossed the Great Plains five times, three times by ox team and twice with mules before the completion of the transcontinental railroad. As his silver mining interests expanded through the Pioneer Mountains, he founded the company towns of Lion City and Glendale. Photo courtesy of Jacoby Lowney.

At eleven thousand feet in elevation, Lion Mountain mining crews labored under arduous and dangerous conditions. Caverns inside the Cleopatra Mine were so frigid that regardless of their layers of heavy clothing, gum boots, and gloves, the two-man drilling teams had to hustle to keep warm. Pity the man twisting the drills. He was so numb after a fifteen-minute shift that he could hardly wait to restore his circulation by swinging a double jack. At the base of Lion Mountain, new settlements—Lion City, Glendale, and Hecla—thrived. Armstrong purchased the Trapper Mine in 1877, and why it was shut down one year later is unclear. Trapper City, doomed, watched its people and commerce pack up and move to Lion City. Five hundred to six hundred people populated the Armstrong company town of Lion City when at its zenith.[7]

Piles of high-grade silver ore extracted from the mines were loaded into wagons that groaned under the tons of weight before traveling over crude trails to the Melrose settlement. Every day more than one hundred horses, six to eight per team, pulled the wagons seventeen miles from the Lion Mountain mines to Melrose. There, jerk-line freighters and their teams of six or eight horses, mules, or oxen took charge. The outfits freighted the ore-laden wagons 450 miles overland to the railroad terminus at Corinne, Utah. The next leg had the ore transported by rail to San Francisco, and from there shipped to Swansea, Wales, for smelting.[8]

Despite the enormous costs, the venture yielded profit. Even so, Armstrong traveled to Virginia City, where he induced banker Charles L. Dahler to finance construction of a smelter. He reasoned that profits would be greater and flow into everyone's pockets more quickly if a smelter were erected on-site. The firm of Dahler, Armstrong, and Company erected a forty-ton-capacity smelter on Trapper Creek. With their objective met in 1877, it is believed that Dahler and Armstrong dissolved their partnership.[9]

The smelter rendered tons of raw ore into ninety-pound bars of base bullion. That was a godsend, but Armstrong rankled at the sight of thousands of gleaming bars stockpiled in the smelter yard awaiting transportation. The logistics must have been nightmarish, and the weather bedeviling. Instead of freighting pounds of Armstrong's silver ore, the jerk-line teams now freighted his silver bars to Corinne, from where they were shipped by rail to Omaha for final refining. Modes of transportation in the Pioneer Mountains remained aggravatingly rudimentary until relief and expediency arrived by way of the Utah Northern Railroad building a spur line to Melrose in 1882.[10]

The camp of Glendale encircling the smelting works at Trapper Creek was crude and violent. Sagebrush and prickly pear cactus were scraped from a hilltop to make way for the cemetery. Time passed, but, when nobody died, miscreants grew impatient and, in the words of one Montana historian, "killed a Chinaman and buried him." The regional newspaper, the *Atlantis*, aligned itself with other mining settlements ablaze with anti-Chinese sentiment. "An interpreter was in Glendale the other day, looking up Chinese to work on the railway grade. The very moment that a foreign corporation attempts to put Chinese coolies to work in herds in this Territory, the said peons should be treated as their kind are at Leadville, Colorado, and Storey County, Nevada; just driven right back over the line and given to understand that it will be rather an unhealthy climate for them; if they attempt to return to Montana."[11]

Through the 1880s, Glendale grew into a company town under Noah Armstrong's thumb. He owned the bank, co-owned the town's two stores, and was postmaster. At his assay office, the foremost job was to assay his minerals before anyone else's. Thirteen saloons sprang up, of which he owned none. Social activity for the 1,700 residents was otherwise a short list, according to pharmacist Jacob Miller. "The majority of people around here seem to think that a saloon is the next best thing to paradise and that foot races, dog fights, and horse races are the only subjects fit to talk about." The flamboyant, raucous element that had founded Glendale eventually gave way to coalescing civic-minded folk. Theatrical groups performed at the opera house. All-night dancing to the music of fiddles, banjos, drums, and mouth harps attracted everyone looking for a good time. Families roller-skated at the rink, and community horse races were run on a homemade track pounded out on flat ground behind the schoolhouse. On a Saturday in September 1885, a black horse and a gray horse squared off. The crowd was good sized and the atmosphere festive, leading the *Dillon Tribune* to enthuse that "a stranger entering Glendale last Saturday might have believed it to be a legal holiday." The black horse won.[12]

Armstrong, Atkins and Company reorganized in January 1877 as the Hecla Consolidated Mining Company, with seven new investors. Company assets were valued at $500,000. Armstrong and Atkins, equally invested at 23 percent, were the largest shareholders, with Armstrong appointed as the company superintendent. With capital at his disposal, all Lion Mountain properties not already under his ownership were purchased. His plans for multiple properties were to systematically update and expand existing infrastructure. The most ambitious of these rendered 1,100 feet of snow sheds, and the narrow-gauge rail tramway accessed mines almost as high as the clouds. Conveyances called ore boats transported the piles of extracted ore up and down. As one visitor recounted: "Samuel Barbour, Supt., put us under escort of his assistant, Byron Cook, who piloted us to the foot of the tramway leading to the Silver Quartz, where we took an ore boat, and as the one laden with ore came down, took ours containing two men up. The rope connecting the two boats is wrapped once around a wooden drum at the top of the dump, and both boats fairly fly past each other over 1,000 feet of seeming almost perpendicular track."[13]

The tramway reportedly had cost $96,000. That project and other expensive improvements made Hecla Company stockholders jittery, and when dispersal of dividends was smaller than expected in 1878, they ousted Armstrong as superintendent. Under his management, the Hecla Company mines had released more than one million ounces of silver annually and thousands of tons of lead and copper. Elias Atkins assumed the role of company superintendent, but his tenure was brief. On June 25, 1879, one of the company's two smelters burned. Atkins was blamed for the setback and ousted in January 1881. The Hecla Consolidated Mining Company also gasped under a debt of nearly $78,000.[14]

As much as the stockholders had confidence in the new Hecla company manager Henry Knippenberg, formerly the capable manager of Atkins's saw manufacturing firm, they balked at his request for $95,000 to stabilize the company. New investors fronted the cash. By the end of 1881, Hecla Company was reorganized, solvent, and showing a profit of $237,729. This must have warmed stockholders' hearts.[15]

The silver-producing giant systematically depleted stores of silver ore in the Pioneer Mountains throughout the 1880s. In 1893, Grover Cleveland ascended to the presidency and exerted his presidential authority to successfully obtain repeal of the Sherman Silver Purchase Act of 1890. The premise for the act was western Republicans wanting to strengthen the silver mining industry in their states and counterbalance losses resulting from drought-stricken crops and falling prices. The Sherman Silver Purchase Act required federal purchase of four and a half million ounces of silver monthly, redeemable in gold or silver. Following the repeal, silver prices plummeted. The ensuing Panic of 1893 toppled silver producers, but Hecla Company hung on. Another decade passed. From the outset of Knippenberg's tenure in 1881, to the permanent shutdown of operations in 1901, to company dissolution in 1904, Hecla Consolidated Mining Company extracted precious metals valued at $22 million. Dismantling the three company smelters was the final order of business. With that, Lion City, Glendale, and Hecla were abandoned.[16]

▬

Upon his ouster in 1878, Noah Armstrong entrusted his mining industry interests to his son, Charles. Free to pursue new activities, he began to study blooded horse pedigrees. Whether he was inherently fond of horses is a question unanswered, and the circumstances surrounding his indoctrination to the blooded kind are similarly unknown. Charles wrote extensively about his father's horse venture. In his narrative, written between 1890 and 1894, he characterizes Noah Armstrong as a man for whom "to think was to act, [and] he was not long in getting to work on plans for the consummation of his project." Noah engaged in his new pursuit with his usual passion and industry. The Thoroughbred and Standardbred horses he imported as early as 1880 represented "the most notable running and trotting horse families in the country," Charles noted. Noah was not averse to purchasing local blooded stock. William Raymond was the first horseman in Montana to import the Standardbred breed, doing so in 1876. From Raymond of Belmont Farm near Virginia City, Noah purchased Doncaster, described by Charles as "a splendid black." The stallion would be the foundation stud for the Standardbred horses Armstrong wanted to breed.[17]

He needed a suitable location to breed and rear his horses. Montana was up to the task. According to Charles, "In points of climate, soil, pasturage, and other natural accessories to his purpose, Montana was the equal, if not the superior of the best-known horse raising districts of the United States, not excepting even the highly extolled Bluegrass Region of Kentucky." Neither he nor Noah had ever lived in Kentucky, but Noah frequently visited there, and both father and son had farmed in Blue Earth County, Minnesota. Undoubtedly, they recognized fecund land when they saw it.[18]

They scouted Montana's southwest valleys, and they liked the Jefferson Valley, wedged between the Highland Mountains to the northwest and the Tobacco Root Mountains to the east. Charles described the soil as "deep, alluvial loam" supporting a "prolific growth of rich and nutritious grasses . . . a famous pasturage and feeding ground for horses, and stock cattle of every kind." The "mild salubrity of climate and uniformly equable temperatures" also recommended the Jefferson Valley. As luck would have it, Charles's wife, Elizabeth Bertha, owned property there. The acreage, nicely situated along the Jefferson River, was located just north of Twin Bridges, Madison County. In 1882, Noah purchased the property from his daughter-in-law for $5,000. With additional land acquisitions, the spread would expand to around four thousand acres. He settled on a name, Doncaster Ranch, in honor of his prized stallion.[19]

Noah's retooling of the ranch was to emulate the tony ones he had admired in the eastern and southern states. So, on a plain of bunchgrass in the Jefferson Valley, a large, circular red barn took shape. Armstrong himself designed the three-story structure tiered like a wedding cake. At completion, the barn stood seventy feet from ground to roof. Walls were three layers of lumber thick, and a coating of mineral oil fireproofed the roof. Fear of fire was not unwarranted—wooden barns filled with hay burned hot and fast. Stable conflagrations were common. Horses usually died.[20]

The barn's first floor, one hundred feet in diameter, provided ample space for a well, eighteen twelve-foot-square stalls, and a quarter-mile circular exercise track. The office was on the main floor, as were sleeping quarters and rooms for grooming, veterinary care, feed, and tack. The second floor, seventy-six feet in diameter, stored hay and grain. The third floor, thirty-six feet across, housed an eleven-thousand-gallon water reservoir. Armstrong himself engineered the ingenious water system. A windmill atop the barn roof pumped water from the first-floor well to the third-floor water reservoir. Upon release, gravity-fed water sped downward to replenish the first-floor water troughs. Five more barns of modest architecture and dimensions complemented the round red barn, or the Doncaster Barn, as it was called at the time. A half-mile outdoor exercise track for the horses was cut out of the bunchgrass.[21]

The amount of money invested into retooling the ranch into a state-of-the-art horse farm alarmed Charles, who wrote, "A good-sized fortune has already been expended in erecting the building and accommodations essential to the proper housing and handling of the valuable animals." Purchase of the horses and their importation represented a substantial investment of thousands of dollars. Management of the Doncaster Ranch, according to Charles, followed "with strict adherence to its founder's predominant ideas, i.e.: that the introductions and cultivation of the finest and purest strains of horse blood, intelligence and honestly pursued, would be a profitable investment." One day he asked his father about the spending; Noah was mum. Charles professed, "On this point, Mr. Armstrong maintained a modest reserve, which was impenetrable to the writer."[22]

His father got to the business of hiring men to run the spectacular yet functional horse-breeding establishment said to be unrivaled west of the

Doncaster Round Barn. Designed by Noah Armstrong, Doncaster Round Barn
landmarked Doncaster Ranch. Photo courtesy of Thomas Ferris.

Mississippi River. The hands were mostly cowboys who were not only well
versed in handling horses but could handle any chore. Cowboy Joseph
Redfern called the outfit "a show place," and people traveled "great distances to see the one-of-a-kind barn." Horseman Samuel E. Larabie of the
Deer Lodge Valley was intrigued. His praise of the barn after his inspection
of it delighted Charles, who wrote, "Mr. E. S. [sic] Larabie, of our lodge,
himself a distinguished patron of the turf and owner of some of the finest
racing stock in the country [upon] returning from an extended tour of the
eastern states . . . halted at Doncaster Ranch on his way home. . . . After a
critical examination of and scrutiny into the details of the establishment,
Mr. Larabie said: 'I am quite sure that, for elegance of design, convenience
in all its appointments and general adaptability, there is nothing equal to
it on any of the great horse farms in Kentucky.'"[23]

No matter from where in America a turfman hailed, entry into the world
of Thoroughbred horses was a speculative proposition demanding a
great deal of money and was typically the dominion of wealthy eastern

capitalists. As a rule, for every two horses raced, "a man and a boy had to be kept," and, on average, "kept" cost around eight dollars a week, as reported by the *Helena Independent* in 1891. The newspaper continued to tally. Feed was the finest quality and, of course, expensive. A racehorse needed shoes, four dollars a set, and needed multiple sets, as many as eight to ten during a single racing season. Each horse wore his own wardrobe of blankets and pads, and some wore hoods. Bridles cost eight to nine dollars, martingales about three dollars, saddles from twenty-five to fifty dollars, and racing silks from ten to seventy-five dollars. Jockeys and trainers, of which the best in the sport were salaried, received their pay whether horses won or lost. There were race entrance fees to pay, and for westerners, transporting racehorses cross-country by rail was extremely expensive. The figures recorded in the "expenses" column of a western racing stable accounting ledger "piled up mountain high." Those in the "earnings" column, not so much. Piles of millionaire capitalist money unstintingly financed and supported the East's principal racetracks and most lucrative races. The famous turfman John E. Madden was known for spouting epigrams, and one favorite summed up the Sport of Kings this way: "If wealthy, idle and tired businessmen will take up breeding of Thoroughbreds as a pastime, they will enjoy life, even though they die poor."[24]

Entry into the American turf was a means for newly monied millionaires to access exclusive social circles controlled by old-monied millionaires. From East Coast to West Coast, little else better signified copious wealth and gentility than entry into the "Sport of Kings," the phrase denoting the sport's centuries-long association with aristocrats. As American historian Dixon Wecter noted in his book *The Saga of American Society: A Record of Social Aspiration, 1607–1937,* "It was the mark of a gentleman to participate in the sport of horse racing." In this way, Noah Armstrong became a leading member within the Memphis Jockey Club, and in San Francisco, he attended the races with Senator George Hearst.[25]

The gist of racing high-strung, beautiful Thoroughbred horses has been described as electrifying, risky, and sometimes reckless, and Armstrong found his perfect complement in this sport. The *Farmer's Magazine and Kentucky Livestock Monthly,* an agricultural journal, introduced him in

1882 as he was embarking on his inaugural season of eastern racing, calling him "a new man to the thoroughbred camp" who was ready for "a good trotting as well as galloping fun." His group of eleven runners, or string, representing his newly minted Montana Stable, netted a $10,000 profit in its inaugural season. He must have grinned over that, and, importantly, the horses averted season-ending injuries. Born with a natural inclination to *run*, a Thoroughbred's four slender legs churn at thirty-five to forty miles per hour as he hauls one thousand pounds of body mass over varied distances and over dirt or grass. Endowed with strength, fluidity, and cat-quick reflexes, he can change his pace as fast as the action dictates, but a slight misstep could end his career or his life. If a bad step on the racetrack snapped a leg, a bullet ended his misery, or, as put by one observer, "his body [was] dragged out of sight as if he were a common truck horse."[26]

By most turf scribes' accounts, Noah Armstrong's entry on the American turf was simply one more idle, wealthy capitalist indulging in a pastime. As the *Louisville Courier-Journal* stated, he pursued horse racing for "sport and pleasure only," and to those who said otherwise, "such is not the case. He is a gentleman on the turf, and he runs his horses as gentlemanly amusement and because he has nothing else to do in the summertime." While the *Courier-Journal* was in step with the conviction that wealthy capitalists partook in the sport for leisure and recreation, Armstrong was an exception. Racing his expensive, royally bred horses was a matter of dollars and cents, of profit and loss, of quick execution and returns, or, as Charles Armstrong stated, "a profitable investment."[27]

Early in 1883, the *Spirit of the Times* published a letter written by General Abraham Buford II. This respected eastern turfman informed *Spirit* that Noah Armstrong was in Louisville, where he stabled three of his runners. Of the three, Buford was most impressed with three-year-old Lord Raglan. The colt was sired by Ten Broeck, who dominated 1870s racing. The dam, Catina, foaled Lord Raglan, probably in Kentucky. The scribes soon fell in love with Lord Raglan. At one sloppy, waterlogged racetrack, Lord Raglan reportedly "danced about and spattered the mud in every direction, apparently as happy as a bare-footed boy in a puddle." He plowed through puddles and mud and won his race. They said he was a "magnificent mud horse" or, in horse racing vernacular, a "mudder." Those mudder hooves next hydroplaned over the messy surface at the Phoenix Hotel Stakes, regarded as a credible precursor to the Kentucky Derby. He won that one, too.[28]

Three days before the ninth running of the Kentucky Derby, rain battering Louisville forced postponement of the race by one day, to May 23, 1883. When morning dawned with sunshine and dry air, the sight belied the wet, heavy track at Churchill Downs. Historically, the spring day would mark the first use of Churchill Downs to landmark the track. Given the surface conditions, Armstrong must have felt good about Lord Raglan's chances. But many of the more than ten thousand racegoers preferred Ascender and backed him as their first choice. The old-time Kentuckians likely reminisced about how horse racing had limped along in their state while the Civil War was being fought. The sport's predicament worsened in 1870, the year Louisville's last surviving racetrack, Woodlawn, closed.[29]

Two years after the sport had completely been abandoned, Colonel Meriwether Lewis Clark Jr., grandson of William Clark, traveled to England and went to the races. Upon returning to his Kentucky home, Clark was a man inspired. Leasing land from uncles John and Henry Churchill, he built Churchill Downs. Next, he organized an event similar in style to England's prestigious Epsom Derby. Clark's imitation was the Kentucky Derby, a mile-and-a-half contest for three-year-olds. The inaugural race went off on May 17, 1875, as a minor midwestern event won by a chestnut colt, Aristides. Since then, the Kentucky Derby has bundled three centuries of historic racing and rivalries, tradition and pageantry. The Kentucky Derby is our nation's oldest continuous sporting event.[30]

Armstrong must have relished the sight of Lord Raglan on parade at Churchill Downs. The jockey astride the colt wore a blue jacket with orange sleeves, the colors signifying the Montana Stable. The starting official at the post, or starter, directed the jockeys to form a horizontal line and then walk their mounts forward. At the tap of the drum, the horses broke in a straggling start. Drake Carter jumped ahead but quickly lost the lead to Leonatus. In the slipstream of those two, Lord Raglan followed. In this order, the three horses moved through three-quarters of their muddy journey. Leonatus edged farther ahead and opened a two-length lead. By that margin he reached the final turn and rounded into the homestretch. Lord Raglan tore after Leonatus and Drake Carter, but at the sixteenth pole he veered halfway across the track before his jockey could right him. Lord Raglan hung on to third, Drake Carter was second, and Leonatus won his race by a commanding five lengths. Watching all this, Armstrong must have been disappointed with the result.[31]

Six weeks later, his life took a long, dark turn. The three children born to Charles and Elizabeth Bertha were stricken with what was probably diphtheria. Harry, age three, died on July 7, 1883. Two-year-old Nellie followed her brother nine days later. One-year-old Ethel succumbed in September.[32]

The fourth tragedy to strike that summer had Lord Raglan "cut down" at the Saratoga Racecourse in Saratoga, New York. The gist of the four-horse collision on August 13 was that Lord Raglan severely injured his leg when he struggled to free himself from the pile. In December, the *Helena Independent* reported the upbeat news that Lord Raglan's future was use as a stud. Brought to Doncaster Ranch, he did not recover from his injury as well as was hoped. A surgeon was summoned from Salt Lake City. The horse survived the surgery, but something else must have gone awry. On January 5, 1884, the *Dillon Tribune* reported heartbreaking news: "Lord Raglan, Noah Armstrong's famous racehorse, is dead."[33]

The following September, all of Helena was eager for the Seventh Territorial Fair and the featured horse races. An influx of turfmen with their flyers descended on the town. On Main Street, Dan Lawrence from Doncaster Ranch herded "six fine horses for the races," the *Helena Weekly Herald* reported. People on the sidewalks paused to watch the "noble animals as they passed in review." On the avenue was two-year-old Grey Cloud, whose smoky-colored coat always drew attention.[34]

Armstrong had purchased Grey Cloud as a yearling from the Meadows Farm near Carlinville, Illinois. According to local lore there, General Richard Rowett, master of the Meadows, sought a replacement Thoroughbred stallion. Rowett was set on owning a son of Leamington, an exceptional sire in the Meadows Stud until his death in 1878. Rowett's determination to find that horse led him to Pennsylvania-bred Hyder Ali. During a brief career as a racehorse, Hyder Ali was characterized as "fast as an arrow and game as a bulldog," but an "unlucky good horse." At three years old and broken down, he had been exiled to stud duty in Toronto. Legend also says that Rowett had dinner with a Mr. Lyon, who owned Hyder Ali. The two men sipped champagne and smoked cigars and Rowett convinced Lyon to sell him Hyder Ali for $750. At the Meadows Stud, Hyder Ali nicked with Interpose, an exquisitely bred, striking gray broodmare. Interpose foaled their son, Grey Cloud, in 1882.[35]

At the Territorial Fair races on September 10, Grey Cloud made his start as a maiden in the Pioneer Stakes. (A racehorse without a win is a maiden and stays a maiden until he wins a race.) He finished third in the five-horse race. On September 17 in a three-horse contest, Grey Cloud finished first and broke his maiden. The two races completed his two-year-old season.[36]

On the eve of the 1885 racing season, Noah Armstrong and Samuel Larabie worked together to arrange transportation for their racehorses to the eastern racetracks. Grey Cloud's campaign was spread across Latonia, Chicago, St. Louis, and Louisville. All told, the gelding won four of thirteen starts and finished in the money six times, a pretty good record. At four years old in 1886, he raced five times and came home a winner twice. Charles Armstrong complimented Grey Cloud, noting in his narrative that the gray gelding delivered a "brilliant season of success." When Armstrong wished to sell the horse in 1887, the buyer, Dan Honig, paid $1,000. Grey Cloud went on to race four more seasons, for multiple owners. Twentieth-century turf historian John H. Davis saw Grey Cloud as a horse who rarely lost when the going was "to his liking." He added, "Much might be said regarding this celebrated horse, but Gray [sic] Cloud was a good one and was able to impress the beholder wherever he was raced."[37]

No wonder that Armstrong made a return trip to the Meadows Farm in 1885 for the express purpose of purchasing Interpose, in foal to Hyder Ali a fourth time. The price was $1,000 for the mare, her unborn foal, and the suckling filly at her side. At an Illinois depot, railroad workers carefully entrained the pregnant mare and her pretty filly. Satisfied that the little family was comfortable and secure, the workers heaved the stockcar door shut and the train chugged west.[38]

CHAPTER 3

Spokane

"Bunchgrass Fed Horse from Way Out West"

Henry Wetmore might have been the cowboy who met Interpose and her filly at the depot in Dillon, Montana. He walked them twenty-eight miles north to Doncaster Ranch. Wetmore's job was foaling man, and for it he bore the worry of assisting pregnant mares. Ideally, both the mare and foal survived the ordeal of birth. Interpose's bloodlines exemplified aristocratic breeding on which racing stable empires were built. Under his care, the mare might have put Wetmore more on edge than usual.

The day came in 1886 when Interpose lay down in her stall and bore her colt. The newborn drew his first breaths and opened his eyes. She began licking him, the equine way to learn each other's scent and sounds. Wetmore helped the colt, snug in a bed of straw, to stand on four birdlike legs. His coat gleamed like copper, but chestnut was the true color.[1]

Noah Armstrong learned the exciting news of the birth while attending to his mining interests in Spokane Falls, Washington Territory. The cowboys needed a name. Armstrong's choice, Spokane, honored the region's native inhabitants as well as the Spokane Falls settlement. "Spokane" translated to the poetic "Children of the Sun" of the Spokane Tribe. A tribal narrative told the story about the Great Spirit promising a wounded warrior a wondrous Spirit Horse. Endowed by the Great Spirit with unearthly speed and stamina, that Spirit Horse, Spokane, would conquer all earthly horses.[2]

In the Jefferson Valley, the long-stemmed bunchgrass brushed Spokane's slender legs as he trotted alongside Interpose. The air he breathed at the foot of the mountains was thin and clean, and the water he drank pure. His coat darkened to deep chestnut. Training for young racehorses moved at a deliberate, stepped pace at Doncaster Ranch. The horses calmly took in stride strange faces and hands, and people marveled over it. One visitor remarked, "Anyone can go into the stable and by putting his arm around the neck of a colt can lead it where he chooses." Joseph Redfern was given the job of breaking the colt. One day he gently placed a saddle on Spokane's back. "Didn't have too much trouble, broke him without spur, and with a pancake [racing-type] saddle," Redfern said. That was well and good, but the young racehorse could be lazy. "He'd run like all get out when he had to, but sometimes he had to be forced." Spokane's disposition was somewhere between affectionately shoving his nose into the "bosom" of those he liked and taking a nip at a stranger's arm, but he was not mean.[3]

Training and exercising Thoroughbred horses suited cowboy Bill Dingley perfectly. He had been riding rough frontier racehorses as early as 1880, the year the census taker for Butte City, Montana, recorded the twelve-year-old boy's occupation as "Jockey Rider." At the 1884 Territorial Fair, Dingley had stretched flat along Grey Cloud's back for the horse's two races there. When Grey Cloud went east for his 1885 and 1886 campaigns, Dingley was his jockey. Dingley advanced in his profession of a frontier jockey who earned prestige on the eastern racetracks. Returning to Montana as a celebrity, young Dingley was "very popular with the Beaverhead County young ladies," as the story goes.[4]

Dingley and his pal Henry Wetmore were nervy, hell-for-leather riders. Wetmore owned a lightning-fast quarter horse named Cap, and Wetmore astride Cap and Dingley astride Spokane raced. Cap, with explosive early speed, outran Spokane the first quarter mile, but Cap thereafter "took a back seat, for [Spokane] was the winner before the mile was reached," said Henry's son, Cecil Wetmore.[5]

On a warm day in March 1888, Noah Armstrong selected the string of horses he wanted to represent the Montana Stable in eastern racing. Spokane and nine stablemates were walked from Doncaster Ranch and entrained at the Dillon depot. Armstrong hopped aboard a passenger car. The Montana Central locomotive made a stop at Great Falls, Montana. A newspaper reporter on the spot noted that the customized stockcar in which the horses rode was "as comfortable as if in a stable" and wished the flyers "many good wishes, in parting with Mr. Armstrong."[6]

Spokane debuted as a maiden at Washington Park Racecourse in Chicago on July 5, 1888. Stepping onto the brown oval for the Hyde Park Stakes, open to two-year-old maidens only, he paraded with four more maidens. The starter's flag twirled. Spokane was slow to start and broke last. His position did not improve despite his jockey whipping him the entire distance of six furlongs (one furlong equals an eighth of a mile).[7]

Armstrong ordered three more months of training. It is unclear who trained Spokane in 1888, but Armstrong claimed to have trained the colt for part of the season. His partner in racing, Colonel William B. Hundley, was a prominent horseman and the proprietor of Meadow Brook Farm near Helena. Although the men co-owned the Montana Stable, each man raced his own string of racehorses.[8]

Spokane made his second start on September 25 at Churchill Downs and earned ninth. At Latonia on October 2 over a wet, muddy racetrack, Spokane delivered a "remarkable" performance in the Maiden Stakes, according to the *Cincinnati Enquirer*. "He got off absolutely last in a field of fourteen, and by wonderfully good running passed one after another, and won as he pleased. He did not get to the front until in the last furlong, then he went up on Sportsman, took the lead, and left all the others as though they were tied up."[9]

The *Enquirer*'s summary pegged Spokane as a "closer." In the parlance of horsemen, "closer," "speed," and "pace" horses characterize the common racing styles. Speed horses break lightning fast and want to be the front-runner wire to wire. Pace horses, or "stalkers," settle in at midpack, and about midrace they make their charge and pick off the front-runners. "Closers" are positioned behind the pack before unleashing searing speed and making a mad dash through the closing furlongs. The closer style is chanciest because jockeys are more prone to err. The jockey must pick the precise time to urge his mount to maximum effort. If he asks too early, his mount might tire during the stretch run. If he asks too late, maybe his mount will catch the front-runners, maybe not.

On October 11, Spokane raced at Latonia Racecourse, finishing sixth. A heavy racetrack and an increase in the weight he carried likely contributed to his losing. While 118 pounds of impost was not excessive for a healthy two-year-old to manage, it was substantially heavier than the feathery 100 pounds he had shouldered in the Maiden Stakes. Racetrack handicappers, in the past as well as today, allocate the weight, or impost, a racehorse must carry when he races. Impost includes the weight of the jockey, tack, and lead slabs inserted into the saddle if necessary to make the required weight, say 118 pounds.

Weight is adjusted according to age, and fillies receive an allowance from colts. Weight carried is also based on past performances. Superior performers are penalized for the victories they garner by having to carry higher weight in future races. Theoretically, if weight were perfectly distributed across the board to greater and lesser performers, all races would end in dead heats.[10]

Spokane's two-year-old campaign closed on October 23, 1888, at rain-soaked West Side Park in Nashville. Showing complete disregard for the unpleasant conditions, he picked off six rivals. A $300 purse capped off a moderately successful season of five starts and two wins. Armstrong kept the colt in the East, resting and overwintering him in temperate Nashville.[11]

The groundwork Armstrong put in place for the 1889 season included John Rodegap, a well-established and respected trainer. Rodegap sent Spokane postward on April 24 for the Peabody Handicap at Montgomery Park Race-course in Memphis. At a mile and an eighth distance, and open to colts and fillies of all ages, the race would be Spokane's longest to date. He was the youngest of seven entries, and the older veterans would test his three-year-old mettle. At sixteen hands and, according to one observer, of "big frame, fine bone and an abundance of muscle and clean cut as a greyhound from muzzle to heels," Spokane looked a worthy competitor. A feather-light impost of 100 pounds would be his friend.[12]

The Peabody favorite was Strideaway, breaking crisply and rushing to the front. The lead switched back and forth—Strideaway, Endurer, Strideaway, Endurer—but Strideaway led the pack down the homestretch. Spokane challenged through the last sixteenth but finished runner-up to Strideaway, two lengths the winner. Armstrong, pleased with the performance, instructed Rodegap to prepare the colt for the Kentucky Derby.[13]

Meanwhile, in Bluegrass Country, everyone was swooning over Proctor Knott. His arrival in Louisville as an entry for the Kentucky Derby created a sensation. He was owned by stout, red-faced, red-haired Sam Bryant, who more than once pointed to his blaze-faced chestnut and declared unabashedly, "That's the greatest hoss that ever looked through a bridle."[14]

His forty years of luck as a horseman were "phenomenally bad," according to one scribe. "Horse after horse has gone wrong for him . . . diseases, lame, blind and spavined." Then, on a summer day in 1887, Bryant had to be America's luckiest turfman. The annual horse sale at Belle Meade Plantation, Davidson County, Tennessee, was always a grand occasion for America's turfmen. The plantation, renowned for breeding winners, was also admired as Tennessee's largest blooded horse farm. That year, Bryant plunked down $450 for the shiny chestnut yearling he would own in partnership. Needing a name, he chose that of a politician he admired, James Proctor Knott, the sitting governor of Kentucky.[15]

The sire of Bryant's new colt was Tennessee-bred Luke Blackburn, also named for a Kentucky governor. When raced as a three-year-old in 1880, Luke Blackburn won fifteen consecutive starts and rewrote American turf records. The dam was Tallapoosa, a Belle Meade native. She was unusual in that she was not very attractive, and even less so in the company of Belle Meade's otherwise comely broodmares. Sam Bryant took Proctor Knott home to Louisville. The yearling grew to be massively muscled in girth, chest, shoulders, flanks, and legs. His head was big, broad, and heavy, and someone said his nostrils were wide enough for a man to stick his fist.[16]

In the matter of male racehorses, Sam Bryant advocated emasculation as "the best means of promoting qualities." Proctor Knott, gelded, delivered multiple swashbuckling performances in 1888. The best was at Sheepshead Bay Racecourse on September 3 in a newly minted race, the Futurity Stakes, for two-year-olds. Knott and his jockey Shelby "Pike" Barnes swooped through the field of fourteen, dug into the homestretch, and pounded out a dramatic victory. In barely more than a minute, America celebrated two new turf stars.[17]

The winner's share of the Futurity purse delivered an unheard-of $40,900. The Futurity would stand as American horse racing's richest event for several years. Winner's purses rarely exceeded $10,000. For comparison, first money for the 1888 Kentucky Derby, Preakness Stakes, and Belmont Stakes paid $4,740, $1,185, and $3,440, respectively. Proctor Knott triumphed in the 1888 Junior Championship, and the purse paid out $20,786. After that victory, Governor Knott was moved to pardon some of Bryant's gambling friends. Making nine starts in 1888, Proctor Knott produced six wins and earned $69,780. Sam Bryant no longer had to operate his quaint Louisville farm on a shoestring.[18]

He was besotted with Proctor Knott. Bryant slept in the stockcar in which Proctor Knott rode; he slept in a small bed placed inside Knott's stall at racetrack stables. When he absolutely had to leave the gelding's side, Mrs. Bryant stood guard. Surely *New York Times* readers fell in love with Proctor Knott even more on Christmas Day 1888 upon reading the *Times* story about the young racehorse frolicking at the Sam Bryant farm.

> The animal seems as fond of the members of the family as they are of him. . . . He is very gentle and playful, and when a visitor comes into the lot to see him, he usually kicks up identical heels and with a snort, gallops over to the fence at the farthest corner and amuses himself by poking his nose through the space between the pickets and consulting with the common horses in the adjoining field. He shows a great fondness for apples, and about the best way to get in his good graces is to bring him one properly peeled, and he will consent to press his pretty nose against one's hand while he munches the fruit with evident relish.[19]

On the morning of May 9, 1889, the Kentucky Derby was the main draw for opening day of the Louisville Jockey Club's spring meeting. Proctor Knott was unquestionably the eight-horse field's most accomplished racehorse. It would stand to reason that he would carry the heaviest, or near heaviest, impost, but that was not the case. The colt was accorded the "old scale" of weights of a three-pound gelding allowance, meaning that he would carry 115 pounds to his rivals' 118 pounds. The advantage in weight was immaterial in the minds of the Proctor Knott faithful because of his speed and strength, these being so insurmountable that no earthly horse could catch him.[20]

The throng of turf scribes mixing it up with sixteen thousand spectators did not tail Noah Armstrong as they had in 1883, the year he ran Lord Raglan. This time around it was his horse, Spokane, foaled and reared in the land of "the tepee and tomahawk," who was captivating the scribes. Perceptions held by America's non-western population about Montana in 1889 were generally realistic in that the expansive, remote, largely unpopulated region had horses, but few were Thoroughbreds, fewer had ever stepped on an eastern racetrack, and fewer still had ever won.[21]

Churchill Downs racegoers wanting to wager could bypass the customary choices of auction pools and bookmaking stands. If choosing an auction pool, an auctioneer on his stand put up for auction every horse in the field. Bettors bid on the horse, or horses, on which they wished to wager for a particular race. The highest bidder "won" the horse, and after every horse had been auctioned, the winning bids were placed into a winner-takes-all pool box. The bettor who purchased the winning horse won the pool, with the auctioneer retaining a percentage. Bookmaking stands appeared at racetracks around 1866, and from each stand a bookmaker shouted the odds he offered. An assistant at the elbow of each bookmaker recorded bets as fast as bets were made, and a second assistant accepted and counted the paper bills handed over.[22]

Bettors at Churchill had a third option of pari-mutuel betting. The curious pari-mutuel machines had been imported from Paris by Churchill Downs founder Colonel Meriwether Lewis Clark Jr. It was said of the machine's inventor, Joseph Oller, that he had grown weary of losing his shirt to corrupt auction pools and bookmakers. In pari-mutuel wagering, interpreted as "betting amongst ourselves," the money is deposited into a common pool. The machine dispenses a ticket, and all winning ticket holders split the money in the pool, less a percentage taken to cover racetrack expenses. In use at Churchill from 1878 to 1889, the machines failed to catch on. After 1889, they were stored away and forgotten until an anti-gambling sentiment gripped the nation several years later.[23]

The Churchill betting shed was overstuffed with males wriggling, shoving, swearing, and fighting their way to one of thirteen bookmakers. Upon exiting the building, the men spread the exciting news—Frank James was in there! The turf scribes, alerted, tailed the pardoned outlaw. If one could get a good, close look at his face, shaded by his "soft white hat of the brigadier pattern," one could see his "keen, shrewd, dangerous looking eye." They jotted down other observations: "spare-built, but sinewy," "rather sandy mustache," "thin face," "long nose," and "bets freely." James's remarkable ability to pick winners at long odds was accorded to "judgment of horseflesh which he acquired during his professional career to much effect."[24]

James was a heavy "plunger," someone who unflinchingly wagered a lot of money on a horse because he believed he had accurate information about the animal's chances. Plungers loved matching wits with bookmakers equally as shrewd. In the cat-and-mouse game they played, the plunger speculated on a horse's likely success by playing the odds the bookmaker laid against the horse, whereas the bookmaker speculated on its defeat. Plungers often waited for odds to lengthen on the horse they wanted to play and would wait until the last possible moment to make a bet. James approached a bookmaker and asked about the odds laid on Spokane. "Ten to one," the book replied, "the sky's the limit." James handed over a wad of bills. "There's $5,000."

Said the bookmaker, "As far as I'm concerned, that's the sky."[25]

The afternoon grew hotter, sultrier. The entire populations of Kentucky and Tennessee seemed to have wedged themselves into the Downs to see Proctor Knott smear seven rivals over the mile-and-a-half track. They flowed into the grandstand, fanned across the lawns, and crowded the beer counters. Spokane at ten-to-one odds was the fourth pick, and Proctor Knott, at one to two, was the favorite. Colonel Meriwether Lewis Clark Jr. rang the saddling bell. Bettors' talk shifted from what odds they had gotten to the horses and jockeys now pointed postward. Cassius pranced at the head of the parade, followed by Outbound, then Spokane, who gleamed like copper in the sunlight. Hindoocraft stepped out, and Sportsman, and Proctor Knott, whose sun-warmed chestnut coat glistened. Jockey Pike Barnes donned the Sam Bryant silks of "gaudy game chicken," a combination of garish purple and canary yellow. Bryant at one time had avidly engaged in cockfighting; hence he was the "game chicken turfman," and for this, a "marvelous" rooster "spurred for battle" was embroidered on the back of his racing jacket.[26]

Knott had no sooner stepped onto the firm russet soil than he kicked out his stockinged hind legs and tugged at the bit with such force that he half lifted Barnes from his seat. The fiery display of spirit delighted Tennesseans and Kentuckians, whose thunderous whoops and cheers in response sent frightened birds and rabbits scurrying across the grounds. Bootmaker and Once Again, the last two horses to parade, had to follow that.[27]

Starter James B. Ferguson had a miserable time trying to do his job. The zealous commotion out on the lawns and in the grandstand agitated Proctor Knott, who broke from the post before Ferguson had a chance to start the race. Knott broke away twice more in "false" starts and galloped almost a furlong down the bone-dry track deep with dust. Pike Barnes had a time of it, hauling back on the reins to stop the colt, who nearly slung him to the dirt, and forcing Knott back to the post.[28]

Marshaling racehorses and jockeys to a fair start was often frustratingly difficult and thankless. Once the jockeys and mounts assembled at the post, the starter directed them to move to their respective positions and form a line even with the starting post. A starter had the authority to admonish, fine, or suspend jockeys, barking orders and taking careful measures to ensure that all contestants had a fair start. He started the race from the starter's box, positioned against the inside rail. In the "flying" starts of the day, once the jockeys and horses were facing the post, the starter ordered them to turn their mounts in the opposite direction, hold the line, and walk. The starter followed behind. After the line was walked a "sufficient" distance, the starter ordered them to turn around and face the post. When he gave the word *Go*, the jockeys walked their mounts toward the post. The starter, still well behind the line, hoped for the line's uniform approach to the post. A drum tap might start the race, but more commonly two flags were used, one in the hand of the starter, the other held by an assistant whose only business was to keep his eye on his superior. When the starter lowered his flag, the assistant, positioned about a hundred yards ahead of the post, lowered his, and it was his flag that signaled the start.[29]

Overeager horses and jockeys were responsible for "false" starts whereby horses left the post and ran down the track, only to be returned to the post for the next attempt at a fair start. Tedious delays unnerved and exhausted the horses. While jockeys and horses were both problematic, most culpable was the flying-start method, alternately called "walk-up" or "walking." Experimentation to improve the method included webbing or a rope "ladder" stretched across the track as a barrier. In this scenario, jockeys walked their mounts toward the webbing, and if the starter liked what he saw, he released the barrier, which flew skyward and angled above the horses' heads. Starting stalls would not be introduced and adopted until the 1920s. Stalls with magnetically held spring gates would not debut until 1939.[31]

It is not a stretch to say that as many nineteenth-century horse races were won or lost at the starting post as at the finishing post. More than anyone liked, attempts to start a race fairly were scarcely more orderly than a roundup on the open range. At the 1893 American Derby, as an example, the beleaguered starter, after an hour and thirty-five minutes and twenty-five to forty restarts, finally got the field off. The crowds were never sympathetic and were not always fair. "Don't rail the starter because he refused the break . . . he is having trouble of his own," advised one etiquette tip in *Going to the Races*.[30]

Starter Ferguson marshaled the horses and jockeys forward a third time. They walked straight as a ruler toward the post. The drum tapped. The line surged forward to a perfect start. Hindoocraft sprang to the front, with Bootmaker lapping at his side. Spokane was along the inner rail, third, and almost immediately Proctor Knott, fast as a meteor, passed them all as if all were standing still. Barnes hauled back on the reins for all he was worth to slow Knott down and conserve speed, but the colt overpowering the jockey steamrolled his muscular, pumping legs, forcing a terrifically hot pace. Making the first grandstand pass, Knott led by five lengths. Sportsman, Hindoocraft, Bootmaker, and Spokane, in that order, chased him through the backstretch, where they narrowed the gap. Spokane and jockey Thomas Kiley gained ground on Knott not because Spokane was quickening his stride but because Knott was cooling off. After one mile, the field had cut his lead to two lengths.[32]

Kiley's voice and hands urged Spokane to pick up speed. The colt flattened his head and body even lower to the ground before rushing ahead of Hindoocraft. Arcing around the final turn, he trailed Knott by a length. At a furlong to go, shouts of joy from the grandstand that urged Knott to run faster turned to shrieks the instant he veered toward the outside. Barnes straightened him within seconds, but nearly all the horses had flown past, and Spokane had the lead. Then he erred when wobbling to the outside. Kiley steadied him, but Knott, reengaged in his sweeping, rhythmic stride, was now nearly even with Spokane down the homestretch. Kiley swung his whip and lashed Spokane. Barnes answered by rapping Knott, and Knott on the outside and Spokane on the inside went at it stride for stride, their necks thrust out and pumping, heads bobbing out of time and trading the lead. Sixteen thousand voices yelled hoarsely as the two horses passed the wire as one.[33]

The timekeepers stopped their watches. The watches stopped at 2:34 ½, record time, but the keepers were not sure which horse had won. The crowd was unsure, as were the three judges perched on their stand above the finish line. The decision rested with the trained eyes of the judges. After considerable deliberation, they ruled that Spokane had outbobbed Knott by "the shortest of heads." Happy people swarmed into the winner's circle to

Portrait of Spokane with jockey Thomas Kiley by Henry Stull. Thomas Kiley would jump into national prominence after three consecutive victories aboard Spokane. Equine artist Henry Stull recorded Spokane and many more of America's greatest racehorses with his palette. His flattering horse portraits, highly accurate in musculature, attracted the attention of wealthy turfmen who became his patrons and clients. In fact, Stull studied horse anatomy at a veterinary college. Courtesy of Jacoby Lowney.

congratulate Thomas Kiley and Noah Armstrong, with Armstrong accepting the trophy and purse valued at $5,560. Spokane made out pretty good, too. When he was led back to the paddock and intercepted by a Bluegrass belle, she impetuously kissed him.[34]

In Helena at the *Helena Independent* office, the newspapermen printed Kentucky Derby bulletins and distributed the pages to the waiting crowd outside. Cheers erupted and rolled like waves. The election under way was suddenly forgotten. The next day, newspaper headlines across the territory told of Spokane: SPOKANE'S GREAT VICTORY or SPOKANE'S TRIUMPH or ARMSTRONG AT 'EM! The *Helena Independent* headline chimed MONTANA'S PRIDE, and the newspaper extended invitations to Noah Armstrong and Colonel Hundley to "feast at a banquet at Helena's expense." At the Doncaster Ranch,

Henry Wetmore pasted into his scrapbook clippings about the racehorse he had helped foal and train, and cowboy Joseph Redfern bragged, "Knew the minute I got aboard that animal I was sitting atop a future Derby winner." Even when an old man, Redfern relished retelling the story of Spokane, and from 1954, "Spokane wasn't given a chance. It wasn't in the cards that a bunchgrass fed horse from way out West could run in the same circles with the blue-grass region entries, but that bunch-grass-fed chestnut, 16 hands high, and 1,100 pounds of energy beat the best from the Bluegrass country and did it in record time."[35]

Commentaries about the rising presence of Montana Thoroughbreds in American horse racing appeared overnight, including this from the *New York Times*:

> When a year ago Noah Armstrong brought his Montana-bred horse from his mountain ranch and declared that he would win the Derby, Kentuckians laughed at a man who could carry such a delusion. Now they doff their hats to the owner who came to the famous Churchill Downs and beat the bluegrass bred ones out of sight, save one [Proctor Knott]. Such a victory is the most fortunate thing possible for the horse ranches in the extreme Northwest. The new industry of raising horses for the markets of the Eastern States and of Europe promises to be a considerable source of national wealth.[36]

While the race was praised by many as the "greatest, fastest and best Derby ever run," a correspondent for the *San Francisco Examiner* wrote about the disappointed people. "The result was almost sickening to the vast throng of spectators. Most of them would rather have seen Spokane break his neck than break the record, and, least of all, win the Derby from Proctor Knott." Nobody at that time knew of the dilemma to come. The nation's turfmen later debated whether the Kentucky Derby mile-and-a-half distance was too taxing for three-year-olds so early in the year. Churchill Downs officials decided in 1896 that it was, and so, shortening the race to its present-day mile and a quarter forever secured Spokane's track record at a mile and a half.[37]

Sam Bryant was drubbed for giving jockey Pike Barnes the mount in the first place. Bryant responded, "Was I disappointed? Well, I should say I was. Mind you, I haven't any fault to find with Barnes, because the boy did his best, and an honester rider and a better lightweight never lived. But see

here, you know as well as I do that Barnes was too light to ride my horse."
Bryant's attempts to engage a different jockey had been unsuccessful, and
he was left "to do the best I could. Would [Knott] have won with a strong
jockey in the saddle? Don't talk to me that way when you know as well as I
do that he couldn't have lost."[38]

Pike Barnes's performance in the Kentucky Derby was conceivably his
worst in a long time. In an era when Black jockeys dominated the sport,
Kentucky-born Barnes was the first jockey to straddle more than 200 hundred winners in a single year, accomplishing the feat in 1888. Notching 206
wins on 616 mounts, he was then only sixteen years old and at the top of
his profession. The statistic becomes more impressive given that the second most frequent winner, George Covington, who was white, counted 95.
In the interceding six months between Barnes winning the 1888 Futurity
with Knott and losing the 1889 Kentucky Derby, the slightly built teenager
could no longer control the colt who had grown into an incredibly powerful animal. Despite the Kentucky Derby hiccup, Barnes accrued 170 wins
from 661 mounts in 1889 and repeated as North America's leading jockey.[39]

Pike Barnes's poor ride was one unfortunate circumstance southerners
pointed to when calling Spokane's victory dumb luck. One question repeated
ad nauseam was "Would Knott have won if he hadn't swerved?" Theories
were advanced, and Noah Armstrong reminded them, "You see, Spokane,
collared him at the head of the stretch, and Proctor Knott was beaten right
there. . . . Everybody who saw [the homestretch drive] will never forget
Knott's rattling pace down that path to the grandstand. He made up a
lot of ground, but not enough to win the race."[40]

CHAPTER 4

"Plater," "Pigs," and "Cur"

Kentuckians and Tennesseans alike were eager for the Clark Stakes at Churchill, a mere five days after the Kentucky Derby. Proctor Knott would whip Spokane in that one. Westerners' retort was that it would be the other way around. One sidelined easterner observing the squall was Michael Nolan, a New Yorker, who was keen to secure Spokane for his Beverwyck racing stable. Nolan's attractive offer to purchase the horse with only one minor stakes to his credit put Noah Armstrong in a quandary. On May 12, 1889, he wrote to Charles, "I am offered $25,000 for him. This is quite a good price for a colt and is quite a temptation. I could make more than that with him this season and have the horse left, providing he met with no accident or mishap, but there is the rub. I have until tomorrow at noon to think the matter over. I wish I had time to get advice from you . . . as I wish to do what's best and find it hard to decide what that is."[1]

Noah Armstrong kept his prized racehorse home.

On May 14, the six thousand racegoers at Churchill Downs favored Proctor Knott as the horse to take home the Clark Stakes winner's purse worth $3,510. In this race, Knott and Spokane were equally weighted with 118 pounds of impost. The Clark, a shorter distance of a mile and a quarter, better suited Knott's speed horse racing style. On the other hand, the big colt did not run well on wet, heavy surfaces, and Churchill Downs was damp with rain. The small field of four reached the post. Once Again waited patiently as rivals Come-to-Taw and Spokane were wheeling back and forth. Proctor Knott joined in, and his new jockey "Ritchie," a stable boy plucked from the Bryant stable, had to work hard to keep the gelding under control.[2]

They settled down after a ten-minute delay. Starter Ferguson waved his flag. The foursome bolted. Come-to-Taw in the lead sped at a checked pace through the opening quarter. Moving through the second, Ritchie's release of a bit of rein signaled *Go!* Proctor Knott, now running wildly, surged past Come-to-Taw on the first pass through the backstretch, but Spokane clung to Knott's side like a lion on a gazelle. At three-quarters covered, Spokane was driving hard and closing, and Ritchie, seeing this, spurred and whipped Proctor Knott. The soft, clinging mud in which Knott's legs sank tapped his speed and power, and these depleted when, reaching the homestretch, the gelding surrendered the race. Spokane whisked away like an airy swallow skimming the surface of a placid lake. "Spokane wins!" came the roar, with Knott two lengths behind, Once Again was third, and Come-to-Taw last. Thomas Kiley had a time of it curbing his colt, still fresh and full of go. Noah Armstrong met the victorious pair in the winner's circle.[3]

Sam Bryant walked away from that commotion. He sought a quiet spot, sat down on a plank and faced the turf scribes. He said his horse was as fit as ever. Ritchie rode him the best he could. Knott had been defeated fairly. As Clark Stakes Day later waned to twilight, a scribe for Nashville's *Daily American* imagined a sad night for Proctor Knott. "The once great son of Luke Blackburn and Tallapoosa, who after his splendid race in the Derby had more and stauncher friends than ever, stands in his humble stall to-night with no one to caress him, no one to love. Not even his faithful owner, Sam Bryant, can say a word in his behalf for he was beaten to-day, and beaten as if he were an ordinary selling plater." "Plater," used to describe a medium-quality or low-class racehorse, was a dirty word among horsemen.[4]

Distressing news on May 18 rattled the Bluegrass Country. Proctor Knott had not eaten since four days before. Sam Bryant startled turfmen further with revelations blatantly contradicting earlier assurances of the gelding's good health. He now said that Knott was "hardly fit" for the Kentucky Derby and "almost a corpse" in the Clark Stakes. According to the *Daily American*, Proctor Knott lost the Clark Stakes because of Bryant's handling. The owner-trainer had worked the gelding "at a kill pace" two days before the race. Bryant himself had "hammered" Proctor Knott, and the "boys on his back have seesawed him until the great gelding has lost his courage and won't try when the time comes." The horse was now "bodily ill" and "track sick." Four days later, May 28, Bryant angered turf scribes and turfmen again when he sent Knott postward for the Himyar Stakes at Latonia.

Reports had said he was "in very bad shape," foreshadowing his last-place finish in a three-horse race.[5]

▮▮

During the hullabaloo over Knott's health crisis, Noah Armstrong was at Latonia, strolling the grounds day after day. All his runners stabled there were racing except Spokane, who was resting. He began to notice that people were stopping to stare at him. One of them was a turf scribe who later wrote, "The gentleman, perhaps 50 years old, dressed in black clothes, with a black overcoat, leaning on a black cane with white points on it, was the object of talk on the quarter stretch. It was Noah Armstrong, the owner of Spokane."[6]

He moved his string to Washington Park. Intermittent rainfall made the racetrack surface heavy. Keeping racehorses well conditioned was difficult for the trainers. Spokane was sparingly exercised, and his workouts seemed sluggish. John Rodegap sparred jocosely with Chicago's scribes. "He's lame, I know. At least they all say he is lame, but he is no more lame than he was when he won the Kentucky Derby and Clark Stakes. In trotting he goes clumsily at first, having a sort of a flop, and every time he is seen at it, away goes the report that he is lame. The morning before he won the Clark Stakes, he was noticed flopping along, and trainers and owners began touting him as dead lame and having no chance to win." At the distance of about one hundred yards, the flop surrendered to the fluid stride of a winning Thoroughbred.[7]

Armstrong, too, joked with the newspapermen. Grabbing a feedbag and reaching his hand inside, he pulled out a handful of lustrous feed. "We got some good oats for [Spokane] from Montana," he said. "Just look at them and feel their weight. I don't see how they can beat him now. Ain't he a fine-looking horse?" Meanwhile, reports about Colonel Hundley's whereabouts placed him at the Washington Park stables. He was even sleeping there. Wary of harm, Hundley guarded Spokane with "great vigilance."[8]

Opportunity to salvage the 1889 season was an avenue narrowing for Proctor Knott, desperately in need of a victory in the American Derby to restore his reputation. But his ribs were visible and his body bony, although he looked better than he had in the Himyar. Sam Bryant was cautionary, saying he doubted his horse could win the mile-and-a-half event attracting the nation's best three-year-olds. The nation's famed turfmen all wanted to win an American Derby. No other race for three-year-olds was comparable to it in prestige or as rich. The lucrative winner's purse for the 1889 running was valued at $15,440.[9]

Meanwhile, in Spokane's namesake town of Spokane Falls, Washington, westerners ought to capitalize on the colt's overnight celebrity, or so reasoned the community's leaders. Mr. Herbert Bolster brainstormed a marketing plan to honor the racehorse and his municipality simultaneously. The city fathers paid $5,000 for what was reportedly the most expensive equine wardrobe in existence. Handcrafted from blue silk plush and lined with pale blue eiderdown, the blanket and matching hood trimmed in satin also featured "Japanese gold" inlays. Raised letters of orange-gold coloring were appliquéd to the blanket: "Spokane, presented by the citizens of Spokane Falls, W.T." City fathers packed up the wardrobe and traveled to Chicago. There, at the Richelieu Hotel on the evening of June 19, 1889, Noah Armstrong accepted the luxurious blanket and hood.[10]

Chicagoans celebrated the race short of a public holiday. Every American Derby Day, shops of all sorts, the chamber of commerce, and even the Chicago Board of Trade closed by noon. Within the metropolis and surrounding areas, trains transported thousands of people eager to see the race. Those who were too poor to pay the fares walked through Chicago neighborhoods. Conveyances of all kinds were abroad in the streets—the coach, surrey, road cart, dray, T cart, hack, cab, even the bicycle. One estimate placed between three and four thousand vehicles congregated at Washington Park, Chicago's premier horse racing venue. The park was founded in 1883 by five hundred prominent citizens organizing as the Washington Park Jockey Club, with General Philip H. Sheridan as president. Two tracks were constructed, and inside the handsome clubhouse an elite membership circulated. Washington Park's inaugural season of 1884 presented the American Derby. Now, five years later, thirty thousand people filled the grandstand, the rooftop, and the lawns for the sixth running. A cloudy day dimmed the grounds to gray, but color pulsated in the paddock where jockeys hastened in varicolored silks of green and yellow, white, red, checkered, or garish purple and canary yellow.[11]

Thomas Kiley, back for his third ride on Spokane, wore the Montana Stable orange and blue. Owing to the Kentucky Derby and Clark Stakes victories, Spokane showed as the six-to-five favorite. Some bettors loyal to Proctor Knott made him the two-to-one second choice, since his prospects for an American Derby victory had improved by way of weight carried, 115 pounds, the lightest impost in the seven-horse field, and astride the horse sat highly regarded William Fitzpatrick, or "Daredevil Fitz."[12]

The bugler sounded "Boots and Saddles." The sight of Proctor Knott and Fitzpatrick making their entry enthused rounds of applause, but Chicagoans erupted into wild roaring and hooting for Illinois-bred Spokane and Illinois-born Thomas Kiley. They were the native sons. But the lovely, orderly promenade on the racetrack disintegrated into fifteen minutes of delay at the post. On the first attempt to get the horses under way, Proctor Knott and Long Dance broke from the line early. On the next try, the field leaped into their strides but without Sorrento, who refused to budge. Proctor Knott had galloped a good distance before Fitzpatrick could stop him and turn him back. The third try was a repeat: Sorrento stood still; Knott ran off. On the fourth, the flag flashed down. The spectators cheered for the beautiful start.[13]

Once Again was streaking ahead until arcing around the first turn, where Proctor Knott in a frantic charge thundered past. Fitzpatrick's strong arms checked the horse, but not before Knott opened a four-length lead through the first quarter. The tight-knit trailers were barely able to chip away at it. The first mile peeled away. At half a mile to go, Spokane and Kiley darted through lanes and broke clear of the trailers. Kiley cued for more speed. Spokane's quick acceleration ran down Once Again. Knott rounded into the homestretch and was losing ground despite Fitzpatrick's frantic whipping. Spokane, pulling even with the big gelding, shadowed him for a few strides before spinning off ahead. Knott was likely beaten, but Kiley knew his horse could turn sluggish in the final yards. He raised his whip and smacked. Spokane lunged so violently he skewed sideways. That opened the door for Sorrento, who swooped by in the millisecond Kiley took to correct his horse. The wire was closer, and Sorrento almost to it. Spokane mauled the homestretch dirt and hurtled himself in front of Sorrento, gaining the scant length that won him the American Derby.[14]

Thomas Kiley circled Spokane back toward the grandstand and rode him to the winner's circle. Onlookers flooding the racetrack pressed forward, wanting to touch the colt. After Kiley dismounted, Spokane was unsaddled and robed in his beautiful blanket. His handlers presented him to the judges. Somebody important placed the celebratory saddle of yellow roses on his back. The scribes who encircled Noah Armstrong wanted to know whether he had backed Spokane, and for how much.

"I had about $600 or $700 on him."

At what odds?

"About eight for five. I must have won close to $2,000 on the side."

Would he name a price for Spokane?

"I wouldn't take less than $50,000 for him. He's a pretty good horse, you know."[15]

At a spot less boisterous, Fitzpatrick leaped off Proctor Knott. The handful of people nearby overheard the jockey, who spat, "That's the worst cur I ever threw a leg over." Sam Bryant's face glowed as red as his hair while he silently ran his hand over the quivering horse, whose sides were bleeding from whip and spur. Proctor Knott had finished last.[16]

American Derby fever continued overnight and into the next morning. The *Chicago Tribune* declared the day after the race as "Illinois Day." Using an Illinois thread, it dove into American Derby coverage: "An Illinois bred colt wins the great Illinois race. An Illinois jockey pilots him to victory. Illinois money makes him favorite over a field representing the proudest blood of the turf from California to the Gulf and to the Atlantic Coast. Thirty thousand loyal Illinoisans see horse and rider pass under the wire, and 30,000 ecstatic sons and daughters of the Prairie State raise such a shout of exultation as only such a scene and hour and deed can call forth."

For the third time in six weeks, Spokane was the wayfarer from the West who came to town to upend American racing. On Proctor Knott's home ground, the *Memphis Daily Appeal* related to Tennesseans the magnitude of Spokane's accomplishment in a mere fifty days: "The Memphis-trained horse has added one more victory to his crown of laurels, making the unparalleled achievement of winning three classic events in one-two-three order—the Kentucky Derby, the Clark Stakes, and the American Derby. This has never been done before, and probably will never be done again in a hundred years to come. Hurrah for Spokane!" The *Courier-Journal* in Louisville urged both Kentuckians and Tennesseans to "gracefully acknowledge the superiority of the Montana colt, since it has been proven in three exciting duels of speed. If our own representative had to be beaten, we prefer that Spokane should have been the winner, since he is half a Kentuckian himself, for, although not born on Kentucky soil, he is of pure Kentucky blood, and dates his descent from the Bluegrass."[17]

Noah Armstrong was repeatedly asked, "Where is Spokane's home?" He would laugh before reciting, "Kentucky, Illinois. Tennessee. Washington, Montana. All put in claims to be Spokane's home, but Montana was his birthplace and home." Several national newspapers printed inaccurate stories about Spokane's life in the West, and some reports were grossly exaggerated. The *New York Sun* misidentified his birthplace as the Meadows Farm. It also played loose with the Meadows master, General Richard Rowett, claiming that Rowett had eyed over the "puny and out of proportion" colt and declared, "The youngster must be shot!" Romanticized fables told of Interpose foaling her famous son on the isolated, windswept Montana prairie instead of the snug comfort of the Doncaster Barn, and, sinisterly, a mountain lion had attacked and killed her just days after the foaling. The cat had jumped Spokane, too, and claw marks marring his copper-colored coat could be seen to this day.[18]

On Spokane's home ground, newspaper editors giddy in anticipation of statehood talked up Montana's superlative Thoroughbred horses. The *Stock Growers Journal* in Miles City enthused, "The Montana horse leads America! This is the verdict now. The victory of Spokane, the Montana-bred horse, is not only a reason why Montana people should point with pride to him as a single animal that has vanquished the best horse in Kentucky. In addition, the horse growers can safely rely upon Spokane's performances as final and conclusive proofs of what has been for a long time claimed, viz: that for speed, health, endurance, wind, bone and all that goes to make a good horse, our Montana bred and raised horse is the superior of all others."[19]

Sam Bryant blamed himself for Knott's toppling. He now regretted running the horse when the horse should have been resting. The scribes asked about Knott's future. "Proctor will go East and very shortly now," Bryant told them on June 24, two days after the American Derby. "He will have a long rest, just what he needs, and by the time Sheepshead Bay opens for its fall meeting, he will be in shape to beat anybody's horse." A long rest was ten days. Bryant's closest associates were worried. They feared their "rattled" friend would ruin Proctor Knott "for good and all."[20]

The Sheridan Stakes on July 4 at Washington Park staged a fourth meeting between Proctor Knott and Spokane. Proctor Knott leaped to the front

PROCTOR KNOTT
BY LUKE BLACKBURN, DAM TALLAPOOSA

Proctor Knott lithograph painted by Gean Smith. Near the end of Proctor Knott's career, Colonel William Hundley of Helena likened the colt's mental and physical depletion to "about the same [poor] condition" as Spokane's, but their futures off the racetrack would be diametrically opposite. Hundley said that Spokane was "valuable as ever," but Proctor Knott, gelded, was "not worth six bits." Courtesy of Library of Congress. Currier & Ives, Lithographer, and Gean Smith. *Proctor Knott by Luke Blackburn, Dam Tallapoosa* / / Painted by Gean Smith, Chicago, 1888.

of the seven-horse field. Spokane leaped out behind him. During the first pass over the backstretch, the gap separating the two front-running rivals widened by two lengths. Thomas Kiley urged on his colt, but Spokane's game effort to run faster amounted to nothing more than a chase. Proctor Knott led the entire way for a wire-to-wire win. Knott's ice-cold revenge over Spokane, runner-up, must have had Sam Bryant smiling in smug satisfaction. Everyone else puzzled over Spokane's misstep. Explanations abounded. Too much weight. Too far to run. Too heavy a surface. All were valid points.[21]

After seesawing with his Bluegrass rival in his last four starts, Spokane found relief from Proctor Knott in the one-mile Drexel Stakes on July 9. Yet 125 pounds of impost sank him to fifth in that seven-horse race at

Washington Park. Registering an unplaced finish was a first in his six-starts-long career. The stakes also marked Thomas Kiley's final ride. All of his engagements to ride the colt were met.[22]

Spokane had lost back-to-back races, a fact to be casually overlooked by one influential man on Spokane's home turf. The Montana Territory was nearing statehood, and the Honorable William A. Clark, rising player in politics and president of the Constitutional Convention, was in Great Falls on July 14, 1889, to address an audience of other influential men. "I might speak of other things in which Montana excels," Clark said. "I might refer to the fact that we have the most beautiful women that can be found anywhere. I might mention another fact, that next to beautiful women, in the estimation of all well-educated gentlemen, a fine horse is next in order, and haven't we got Spokane? Spokane, the prince of the turf, beat the great blood of the Bluegrass regions of Kentucky. Gentlemen, we are going to have a great state here."[23]

Spokane had been soundly beaten. Colonel Hundley was alarmed. The horse needed rest. Hundley advocated rest, but Armstrong wanted nothing of the kind. Spokane was to stay on the racetrack for the benefit of his fans. But after tangling with Hundley and John Rodegap, Armstrong acquiesced. Spokane rested six weeks. The campaign picked up with the Pelham Bay Handicap on August 31 at the Morris Park Racecourse in New York City. For the third time in as many races, Spokane's march to the post included a load of 125 pounds. Hotshot jockey Edward "Snapper" Garrison was in the saddle, and the result of his one and only ride on Spokane was to finish third.[24]

Meanwhile, an auction at the Sheepshead Bay Racecourse on Coney Island on September 2 rattled the ever-changing ownership of America's Thoroughbred horses. Proctor Knott was sold for $17,100 to George Scoggan, former racing partner of Sam Bryant. The next day on the Sheepshead Bay oval, Knott carried the Scoggan stars and stripes silks.[25]

Knott was pointed postward for the Twin City Handicap. He finished fifth in a field of ten. It was worse for Spokane, seventh. Veteran horsemen who witnessed the race said it was a sorry day for American horse racing, starting with Knott, who they said looked "unfit." His ears were constantly pinned back; he was combative with his jockey. The horse clearly communicated "strong dislike" for what he once was eager to do. Spokane looked little better off. His action around the racetrack was "stiff and halting," and this hand in glove with the stiff and hard condition of his coat.[26]

Spokane was retired for the season and stabled in Louisville. Despite a losing season, he was still wildly popular with the public. As one bystander observed, "Hardly anyone ever visits the Downs without taking a look at Spokane . . . he stands quietly in his stall munching his hay and nabbing at the sleeves of too curious visitors who come within reach." The place where Noah Armstrong chose to spend the winter is unclear—Bluegrass Country; Seattle, where he was investing in property; or Doncaster Ranch. If at Doncaster, he would have seen the Montana Territory pass to the ages. On November 8, 1889, the Union admitted Montana as the forty-first state. The history-making day had Montanans in heated debates as to which of two events was more thrilling: statehood or Spokane's three glorious trips to the winner's circle.[27]

They were feeling optimistic about their new state swelling in population and commerce. The number of people populating Montana increased through the 1880s, from 39,150 to 132,159, a jump of 237.5 percent. America, too, reached a historic milestone in the census year of 1890. A report by the US census superintendent stated that he could no longer locate a continuous "frontier line" where population thinned to less than two people per square mile. On this, historian Frederick Jackson Turner penned his landmark thesis, "The Significance of the Frontier in American History," in which he stated, "The frontier has gone, and with its going has closed the first period of American history."[28]

Noah Armstrong found himself at a new juncture early in 1890. He had parted ways with Colonel Hundley and John Rodegap, the colonel admitting that his rift with Armstrong had involved Spokane. The colt, he said, was in peak form for the American Derby but was overworked afterward. Armstrong did not think so. The opposing mindsets in place, the partnership had ended. The split from Rodegap was "ill-advised," according to one New York scribe, who added, "Mr. Armstrong's ambition was to win a Derby. Well, he won two of them, but, [sic] like many another, he could not stand the defeats that almost alternates with successes on the turf. Such has been the history of American racing ever since the first thoroughbred was saddled in this country, and Dame Fortune did not make any exception in the case of the Montana Stable."[29]

In January 1890, Armstrong assured a Seattle correspondent that Spokane was in perfect health. The colt's earnings of $28,000 in 1889 were, according to Armstrong, "a large sum of money, to be sure, but it would have been greater had not my horse gone lame." He did not disclose "gone lame" details. The horse was as "sound as a new dollar, as playful as a kitten, and has the speed of a cannon ball," and further, "I expect him to win all the races in which he starts and shall scratch him whenever he appears to be at all out of sorts or unfit to run and win." Yet in the next breath he said, "Spokane will be at the Twin City Jockey Club meeting [in St. Paul] unless he falls dead in his tracks."[30]

Despite assurances of good health, reports circulated to the contrary that Spokane, in truth, was close to breaking down. Armstrong probably sighed an umpteenth time when he described his horse as "rugged, hardy . . . never sick a day in his life." But then came the May 25 report. Spokane had fallen sick with a lung infection. The veterinarian advised rest, but for what duration was not reported. Perhaps the recommendation was shorter than two weeks. On June 7, Spokane started as a four-year-old. Though inconsequential, the sweepstakes at Latonia was the stage for the sixth, and final, showdown with Proctor Knott. Both horses ran miserably: Spokane was fifth, and Knott sixth, in the seven-horse race.[31]

The scathing commentaries that followed included this from the *Cincinnati Enquirer*: "The most sensational event of the day was the downfall of the two cracks, Proctor Knott and Spokane . . . both [are] fat as prize pigs and had no business on the track." The *Daily American* characterized the race as "a queer proceeding" and questioned Latonia officials' decision to allow the two horses to race in the first place. Spokane, after all, had recently battled back from a severe attack of "lung fever" and "all well-informed people know that Proctor Knott is not up to a bruising race yet, if indeed he will ever be again." The *Daily American* scribe continued, "The club managers certainly knew these facts, or ought to have known them. The writer does not believe that Noah Armstrong, the owner of Spokane, or Scoggan Bros., who own Knott, would be guilty of any rascality, but he does believe that they were persuaded to allow these horses to run when they knew they were unfit to face the flag." The swift decline of two champions elicited snickers of "plater," "pigs," and "cur." Proctor Knott was alternately reported as lame, sick, or "poor broken down, fallen Proctor Knott." Within a fortnight of the commentaries, Knott was whisked away to a veterinary hospital to undergo a "fire and blistering" procedure. In other words, a cauterizing technique that treated the bones in the hock joint of horses raced beyond the structural limits of their bone and sinew.[32]

At the equine hospital where the gelding was being treated, amid smells of liniment, ammonia, and straw bedding, the bandages were unwrapped from Knott's forelegs. A *New York Tribune* writer on the scene described the effect: "The brand of the white-hot iron was visible, exhibiting in a painful light the desperate measures taken to patch up an almost hopeless cripple and get him once more to the starting post." The attending veterinarian was optimistic for Knott's future, saying that the roughed-up gelding would "stand training next year."[33]

At the start of 1891, "patched up," Proctor Knott won his first race, finished third in the next, and in the two-horse race against Dr. Nave was trounced by five lengths. Surely Knott had hurt that day. An ulcerated mouth had bothered him for longer than a week. He could barely eat. He had no business being on the racetrack, horsemen agreed, but they stopped short of criticizing George Scoggan or trainer Peter Wimmer. Later, when Wimmer was older, wiser, and highly regarded as a trainer, for him to run an unhealthy horse would be uncharacteristic.[34]

Knott raced twice more before catching cold and becoming very sick. At Horse Haven hospital where he was being treated, on the morning of August 6, 1891, Proctor Knott died. Sam Bryant, with him in his stall, wept. Knott was only five years old.[35]

He made twenty-six starts, won eleven, and finished runner-up in six. His earnings had reached $80,350. Knott squared off with Spokane in six of his starts. He outdistanced Spokane once. Spokane prevailed in three. They were both unplaced in two. Knott's victories and disappointments would resurface in the weeks before Sam Bryant's death. One last wish was to see the American Derby. This being granted on June 21, 1902, Bryant watched Kentucky-bred Wyeth win the prize. Bryant died one week later at his Louisville home. In a lengthy tribute to the "unlettered and uncouth" and "old-time, ante-bellum" Sam Bryant, the *Courier-Journal* recounted Knott's startling loss to Spokane in the 1889 Kentucky Derby. Bryant, who "never felt so sore about anything," always maintained the judges got it wrong.[36]

◼◼

After the "plater," "pigs," and "cur" debacle at Latonia, in the next three starts Spokane finished second, second, and third against lesser competition. He had not won a race in more than a year. All the while, rumors of ill health had persisted. The *Helena Independent* reported on Spokane's predicament on June 27, 1890, as related by Ben C. Kingsbury of Butte. The well-known turfman had gone to the races at Washington Park, and, looking in on Spokane, he found an animal "stale and overworked." His coppery coat was dull and lacking the "bright glossy appearance" of good physical condition and training. In Kingsbury's opinion, Spokane had been run to death.[37]

Armstrong was on record in 1889, 1890, and 1891 stating that Spokane had suffered multiple leg injuries. When relating the circumstances, he assigned culpability to two trainers, a jockey, and a stable boy. In the instance of the jockey, that injury occurred as early as the maiden race in 1888. Spokane had been repeatedly spurred and, trying to escape the punishment, the horse misstepped, and "this was the time his leg was hurt." Armstrong was also in "wonder" that Spokane had not been "completely ruined" after that ride. Yet he continued to race a two-year-old colt that he knew was injured. It is likely that Spokane raced lame all three seasons. In July 1890, Armstrong uncinched Spokane's racing saddle for good. A career record of seventeen starts in three campaigns had earned $26,805.[38]

Everyone wanted to know about his future. Armstrong had disappointing news for Montanans: Spokane would stay in Kentucky. Owing to "subnormal fertility problems," he would pass through multiple stud farms. The filly Spirituelle was the only offspring to save him from complete failure as a sire. At two years old in 1898, she launched an explosive season, winning eleven of sixteen and finishing as runner-up in the rest. At age three, however, she was on the descent.[39]

◼◼

A large sale of blooded horses took place at Doncaster Ranch in April 1891. The striking black Standardbred stallion Doncaster was sold to Marcus Daly, who was breeding blooded stock in the neighboring Bitterroot Valley. Armstrong sold Doncaster Ranch in 1900, but he had already left Montana for good. Gold mining ventures in Alaska would occupy his final years. The silver mining lion died in the Seattle home of his son, Charles, on April 21, 1907, at age eighty-four. Burial was in Lake View Cemetery, Seattle. Charles died at age fifty-six on May 4, 1914, in Sedro-Woolley, Skagit County, Washington. Hannah Armstrong, to whom Noah was wed for more than thirty years, predeceased her husband on June 4, 1885, and was buried in the Glendale cemetery.[40]

The famed three-story red barn that had alarmed Charles because it was so expensive to build stands north of Twin Bridges. Known today as the Doncaster Round Barn, it is among Montana's most beloved barns and is listed on the National Register of Historic Places, earning an induction into the Montana Cowboy Hall of Fame and Western Heritage Center. The royal blanket and hood Spokane wore after his American Derby victory are in the care of the Northwest Museum of Arts and Culture in Spokane, Washington.

Montanans wondered about Spokane's fate, but, unable to find anything conclusive, some claimed to have solved the mystery. Homer Faust wrote for the *Circle Banner* in the 1930s. He might have been the first to bring Spokane home to Montana. In an article dated May 19, 1932, he wrote, "Horsemen from every corner of the state journeyed to Twin Bridges to do him honor." In 1974, George Hungerford contended that when a child in 1914, he had received Spokane as a gift. Under his ownership, Spokane lived to the ripe age of thirty. Grace Roffey Pratt, in her June 1976 article for *Western Horseman*, returns Spokane to Doncaster Ranch, where he lived peacefully as a pensioner. Sportswriter Ralph Bidwell, writing for the *Great Falls Tribune* in 1977, placed Spokane in a stockcar clattering toward Doncaster Ranch at the end of 1889. Spokane's injuries from racing were aggravated during the journey, to the extreme of having to destroy him near Miles City. Bidwell was evidently unaware that Spokane had raced in 1890. Spokane biographer Susan Nardinger thoroughly researched Spokane's life, but even she could not determine his fate. In her 1988 book, *Spirit Horse of the Rockies*, she simply states, "The truth is that Spokane's fate remains a mystery."[41]

New discoveries made by the author of this book expand Spokane's life history. At a Lexington horse sale on December 2, 1898, a Kentucky newspaper reported that Spokane had "hobbled up to the auctioneer's block" and "amid laughs" sold for $170. Less than a year later, according to a New York paper, Spokane reappeared in a Lexington sales ring. He sold for $100 in that auction. The new owner was J. Hume Carter, a prominent New Jersey veterinarian. Carter and Spokane appeared together in November 1900 at the National Horse Show at Madison Square Garden. In the show ring and on exhibition in the "in-hand class" for Thoroughbred stallions, they competed against six more stallions and masters. Fourteen-year-old Spokane took second place. Carter pocketed $100 in prize money. The next year they were third. Carter pocketed $50.[42]

Spokane's extraordinary life would end in late 1904. He was then fifteen years old. On December 3, two sentences tucked inside the pages of a Camden, New Jersey, newspaper related Spokane's death: "After a long and useful career, the stallion Spokane, owned by Dr. J. Hume Carter, has 'passed in his checks.' He was the only horse that was twice a Darby [sic] winner."[43]

CHAPTER 5

Samuel E. Larabie

"Old-Time Banker"

A young store clerk in Omro, Wisconsin, faced a crossroads in 1863. He could either throw in with his employer and head for the goldfields in the Montana Territory or remain in Omro and continue clerking in the dry goods store. The proposition perplexed eighteen-year-old Samuel Edward Larrabee because he loved his mother very much. He was born to Mary Ann and William Larrabee on June 16, 1845, in Portville, New York. William would desert his family, and Mary Ann, faced with raising five-year-old Samuel and his older brother, Charles Xavier, moved to Omro to be near her parents. Samuel, or Eddie as he was called as a boy, attended school until age fourteen. Why he quit his schooling is unclear, but possibly he took a job to help support Mary Ann. Deciding that adventure in the West sounded a whole lot more exciting than clerking in a store, Samuel left Omro.[1]

━

In Council Bluffs, Iowa, he took charge of an ox team and followed the Platte River west. Along the way, the spelling of his last name changed to Larabie, attributed to Fort Laramie in Wyoming. The change was one way to avenge his father's desertion. By winter 1864, Larabie and a partner, William A. Clark, were engaged in gold mining at Alder Gulch, Montana Territory. Floods ravaged the claim the following spring. Without the capital needed to restore the claim to working condition, the partners sold the claim for "a trifle."[2]

Larabie drifted to the Blackfoot mining camp, but grubbing for gold lost its luster. Falling back on his dry goods experience, he purchased a stock of goods on credit. His little grocery became a success, but he sold it and moved on. In 1866, Larabie was manager of the Tutt and Donnell grocery in Deer Lodge. Co-owner Robert W. Donnell offered Larabie an interest in the grocery, but Larabie was cautious about incurring debt. He needed his full $150 monthly salary to support Mary Ann. Donnell voluntarily increased Larabie's salary by $100 a month. The young clerk who saved a little money purchased an interest in the grocery in 1869. At around this time, William A. Clark reappeared. He, too, invested in the grocery.[3]

Meanwhile, the business of gold mining pushed on furiously in the mountains skirting the Deer Lodge Valley. The partners renamed their firm Donnell, Clark and Larabie and expanded into the lucrative business of buying and reselling gold dust. Larabie became an expert assayer. They next tried their hand at banking. The financial institution built by the partners on Main Street opened in 1869.[4]

Now that they were established as bankers, they sold the grocery. Donnell relocated to New York, where his connections in banking financed the building of an elegant bank building in Deer Lodge. On December 23, 1870, the Donnell, Clark and Larabie bank on Main Street opened its doors. Shafts of morning sunlight streaming through the brick building's tall windows illuminated the spacious high-ceilinged lobby where Clark and Larabie stood ready at the counter. Important discussions about lending and investing were conducted over polished wooden counters and desks. "They have, we believe, unexceptionably, the handsomest and neatest banking house in the Territory," the *New North-West* praised. The purchase of gold dust during the first two years of business averaged $1 million per year.[5]

In early 1875, twenty-nine-year-old Larabie arranged a trip to Lexington, Kentucky. On February 16, he wed nineteen-year-old Miss Julia Woolfolk. Just how the frontier banker from the remote Bunchgrass Country of the Deer Lodge Valley became connected with the Woolfolk family of Bluegrass Country is unclear. Making visits to the region's venerable horse farms, Larabie bought two horses of mixed blood and ten highly pedigreed Standardbreds. The lot would ship to Deer Lodge the following summer. The couple toured several states as they traveled west. Upon their arrival in the tiny hamlet, the Deer Lodge Brass Band picked up instruments and serenaded the newlyweds. The local newspaper described their home as a "hospitable mansion."[6]

The firm of Donnell, Clark and Larabie grew exponentially. In 1877, the company opened a branch in the booming silver camp of Butte, southeast of Deer Lodge. Upon Donnell retiring from the partnership in 1884, the banking houses both succeeded as Clark and Larabie. Then, on January 7, 1890, the firm cited "varying interests" as the reason for its dissolution. Clark assumed full ownership of the Butte institution, renaming it William Clark and Brother. He and Larabie would remain friendly the rest of their lives. Larabie took ownership of the Deer Lodge branch and did not cast his net far for a new partner. His older brother, Charles Xavier, making millions from copper mining interests in Butte but now relocated in Portland, Oregon, became an absentee partner.[7]

Samuel Larabie renamed his institution Larabie Brothers Bank and conducted business in his preferred style of relaxed banking regulations. After seating customers in his office, generally miners, merchants, and stockmen, he listened intently as they explained their needs. They, too, relaxed. Larabie's urbane manner perfectly complemented his appearance, described as "typical type of old-time banker, very stately." The people in the Deer Lodge Valley also commended him for his inclination to lend money on the grounds of a man's integrity rather than on what he owned.[8]

Regardless of the fast-occurring changes in his life, Larabie had remained very close to his mother, Mary Ann. For one year at least, Mary Ann lived with her son and daughter-in-law. After her death in 1881, Samuel commissioned the casting of a six-hundred-pound bell and presented it to the Deer Lodge Presbyterian Church. An inscription expressed his sentiment for her: "In loving memory of Mary Ann Larabie, by her son S. E. Larabie."[9]

At some point, Larabie recognized the Deer Lodge Valley as a place well suited to breed blooded horses. At sixty miles long and as much as ten miles across, the valley had crystal-clear streams that cut through the sweep of deep green, blue-green, and pale green bunchgrass. Mild winters were typical of the moderate altitude. Long before Larabie's blooded horses indulged on the grass, white-tailed deer grew fat on it. Sprinklings of salt at a thermal spring also drew them in. To the Native Americans, the valley was Soo-ke En Carne, or "Lodge of the White-Tailed Deer." French trappers translated it as La Loge du Chevreuil, or "The Deer Lodge." Frontiersmen snipped it down to Deer Lodge.[10]

Larabie's initial blooded horse purchases of 1875 favored the Standardbred breed. He came around to the Thoroughbred in 1878. Like most Montana breeders, Larabie drew largely on Kentucky for breeding stock. The five horses he imported in 1878 traveled in the confined space of a clattering stockcar. The mare Christine had the worst of it. In foal to War Dance, she bore the added misery of her belly growing larger and rounder every day. There was nothing humble about Christine's breeding. Bred at the Fleetwood Stables, Franklin County, Kentucky, she was foaled there in 1871 and, according to local lore, named for a popular Franklin County belle. Christine's dam was La Grande Duchesse, a daughter of the famed Lexington, America's 1870s leading sire of winning Thoroughbreds. Christine's sire was an imported English bred named Australian. A first-rate sire in his own right, he would always be overshadowed by Lexington.[11]

Christine gave birth to her first foal on April 25, 1878, either inside a stockcar at an unknown location or on the trail to Deer Lodge. She and her chestnut filly, Gypsy, had a long walk. Gypsy was only ten days old when Larabie sold her, a too quick sale that he would later regret.[12]

<hr/>

Five months after Christine's arrival in Montana, gatekeepers at the Montana State Fairgrounds in Helena welcomed fairgoers to opening day of the Ninth Territorial Fair on September 23, 1878. The horse races drew fairgoers' almost exclusive interest, leaving the other fair departments feeling slighted. The *Bozeman Avant Courier* rankled: "There is no disguising the fact that our Territorial Fair, like most of similar institutions west of the Missouri river, is gradually but surely degenerating into a jockey club."[13]

Fairgoers filling the grandstand cheered and whooped for the race mare Christine and five more contestants at the post. At the tap of the drum, they cried, "They're off!" Christine and Sorrel Mike smoked to the front. With only yards left to cover before the finish, Christine fell off her pace. Mike drew ahead and beat her by a neck. The *Helena Weekly Herald* spread the sad news: "The beautiful mare, Christine, owned by Mr. Larabie of Deer Lodge, was injured, and we understand will be withdrawn from further contests."[14]

Samuel Edward Larabie. The Larabie Brothers Bank in Deer Lodge became a trusted institution that Montanans regarded as "sound and secure as the Rock of Gibraltar." Little wonder the Deer Lodge County Bible Society installed Larabie as treasurer. Photo courtesy of First Presbyterian Church, Deer Lodge, Montana.

Meanwhile, Larabie's expanding horse herd outsized his modest stable. In search of acreage near Deer Lodge on which to build a proper horse farm, Larabie picked an eight-hundred-acre parcel. A small brook fringed in willows and bubbling through the property provided a name, Willow Run Stock Farm. Over the years, Larabie would expand Willow Run's acreage. He broke ground around 1882 and built a spacious colonial-style house. Avowing to always keep his horses sheltered, Larabie oversaw the building of multiple stables outfitted with modern conveniences.[15]

The circumstances that brought grocer John Augustine "Gus" Eastin of Lexington, Kentucky, to Deer Lodge in 1882 are unclear, but they led to a fortunate meeting with Samuel Larabie. Eastin, too, admired blooded horses, and Larabie, so proud of his foundation Thoroughbred broodmare Christine, instructed a stableboy to march her around so Eastin could admire her. Larabie said to Eastin, "That mare is too good for the country out here. . . . I want you to take her to Kentucky and keep her for me." If Christine were in Kentucky, Larabie reasoned, she would have access to America's best sires. Eastin agreed to accept stewardship of the mare, who was already in foal to a local Thoroughbred stallion, Regent, owned by Larabie's neighbor Conrad Kohrs. Eastin soon found himself rocking in a stockcar with Christine.[16]

In spring 1883 in Lexington, Christine foaled her third colt. Larabie, wishing to express his gratitude, offered Eastin half interest in the chestnut-colored colt, named Montana Regent. "If you do not think well of him," Larabie wrote, "I will send you a jack-knife instead." Choosing the half interest, Eastin laid the cornerstone for their breeding and racing partnership, founded as the Eastin and Larabie Stable.[17]

Larabie's role as partner was to furnish broodmares and direct the entire operation from Willow Run. Eastin, already accomplished as a turfman, would select the stallions and train the foals. When eastern traditionalists learned of the unconventional arrangement, many shook their heads in disbelief, for good reason. For one, spotty communications between the East and West posed challenges. Next, more than one thousand miles separated Willow Run mares from the East's highly bred stallions. Further, transporting valuable horses across the country by rail was expensive, risked injury to the animals, and was stressful. Space was tight in a standard slatted stockcar. The journey was noisy. Blizzards stopped trains in their tracks for hours, even days. Equine nerves frayed. One solution for owners who could afford it was to purchase an Arms Palace Horse Car. The "stable on wheels," recognizable by its rich yellow color, was the brainchild of livery stable proprietor Harrison Arms of Toledo, Ohio, who founded the Arms Palace Horse Car Company in 1885. The company advertised a "well and substantially built car for the convenient, safe, humane and economical transportation." Prized horses not only traveled safely and comfortably but rode in a "finely appointed stable." Palace car windows provided ample ventilation and abundant light. Cars could be custom built, but the typical car, at forty-six feet in length, furnished eighteen stalls and space for a bale of hay and an attendant. Eastin and Larabie purchased an Arms Palace Horse Car.[18]

John Augustine Eastin. When Eastin was twenty-seven years old, he enlisted in Company D, Second Kentucky Cavalry Regiment, Confederate States of America, as a private on September 6, 1862. The unit was formed from the remnants of John Hunt Morgan's cavalry squadron, the "Lexington Rifles," soon after the Battle of Shiloh, in early 1862. The Company D soldiers active in Tennessee, Kentucky, and Ohio were noted for fighting on foot as well as on horseback and for their discipline under fire. Photo courtesy of Keeneland Library General Collection.

Owing to fine breeding and the nourishing qualities of bluegrass, Montana Regent at three years old displayed exquisite symmetry suggesting "speed in every line," said his admirers. His coat darkened to rich chestnut, and he stood at slightly more than fifteen hands. Montana Regent made four starts before he broke his maiden in the fifth, a $500 purse race at the St. Louis Fair Grounds racetrack. Eastin, as trainer, tried him in three more starts at the Fair Grounds. After going unplaced, he won the next two.[19]

The racing season rolled through July. Montana Regent heated up and fired off consecutive victories in the Hotel Richelieu Stakes, Maiden Stakes, and Woodlawn Stakes, in eight days. During this whirlwind time, Montana Regent advanced the Eastin and Larabie Stable to the forefront of American racing. One impressed turfman offered $5,000 for the topflight colt. Eastin, cleared to act on behalf of his partner in such matters, refused to sell. Next, on September 16 at Churchill Downs, a cooled-off Montana Regent ran third in the Cash Handicap.[20]

Under the autumn skies of September, Samuel Larabie made a rare trip east to see Montana Regent carry the Eastin and Larabie silks of red jacket and white sash, with a blue and white cap. On October 2 from the Latonia grandstand, Larabie waited for the five-horse Springbok Stakes. The entry Silver Cloud, the favorite, as expected sprang into a fierce pace in an instant. Montana Regent stuck to Silver Cloud like a shadow as they circled the course and into the homestretch for a showdown. There, Montana Regent's frantic charge scored a one-length victory over Silver Cloud.[21]

Five days later, Montana Regent was set to start in the Falsetto Stakes at Latonia. Turfmen Elias J. "Lucky" Baldwin and R. P. Ashe, faced with the prospect of a superior horse on the track, conspired to defeat Samuel Larabie and his Montana Regent. When in this predicament, one trick turfmen employed was to run two horses and sacrifice one as the "rabbit." The work of the rabbit is vital yet largely unheralded. He immediately takes the lead and runs insanely fast, forcing the whole field to maximize their speed much earlier than most of them want to. The rabbit is sacrificed for the benefit of his preferred stablemate, who, in exemplary style, swoops through the final furlongs to steal the race from the gassed front-runners, victims of the rabbit.[22]

Baldwin's two entries were Silver Cloud and Mollie McCarthy's Last. Ashe's entry was Guenn. With Silver Cloud appointed as the rabbit, surely Guenn or Mollie McCarthy's Last would outgun Montana Regent.[23]

Silver Cloud burst to the fore. Montana Regent, second, ran crazy fast to stay with him, with Guenn third, and Mollie McCarthy's Last, fourth. In that order the foursome covered a mile and a half. Silver Cloud then slowed his pace, and the moment new front-runner Guenn took to suck in a few breaths, Montana Regent streaked by like a chestnut-colored vortex, winning the Falsetto by two lengths. "There is the best animal I ever straddled," said his jockey, Godfrey, "and I make no exception to anything either east or west, and over a distance of ground he has no equal regardless of sex or age."[24]

Montana Regent raced twice more, a runner-up both times, before his three-year-old campaign ended. Larabie returned to Willow Run in late October, at a time when his horse was talked up as the "famous Western horse" and "one of the best long-distance performers of his age." The Eastin and Larabie Stable, existing only four years and unorthodox in operations, was rather amazingly quick to produce an extraordinary racehorse in Montana Regent, the first Montana Thoroughbred to reach American turf star status.[25]

There was bad news, however. The colt had raced lame part of the season. Lameness might have swayed Larabie to sell the colt in February 1887, although the $10,000 that Colorado mining millionaire John D. Morrissey paid surely did not hurt. The 1887 season was under way, and in twenty-one days Montana Regent won three of four, including the prestigious Louisville Cup. But, injuring his leg in one of those races, he was retired for the season. Morrissey had invested $600,000 in his turf venture only to see it flop. Having had enough of that, he commenced the dispersal sale of his racing stable in September 1888. Montana Regent, reportedly looking "bad" in the auction ring, "went cheap" for $950. Three months later, Morrissey, apparently regretful, bought back Montana Regent. Sent to New Jersey for winter racing at the Guttenberg Racecourse, the horse was unplaced in three starts. Then, in September 1889, he raced in Portland, Oregon, losing his only start there. The following spring, May 1890, Morrissey sold seven-year-old Montana Regent as a sire prospect to a Denver man. How the stallion fared thereafter is unknown.[26]

In the blue-hazed hills of Woodford County, Kentucky, Christine gave birth to her fifth foal on May 17, 1885. Larabie, to honor his wife, named the filly Julia L. He liked to name promising youngsters in honor of his family, friends, or famous Americans. By two years old, Julia L. was the picture of Christine in symmetry, but her brown color and the tapering white stripe on her slender face told of her sire, Longfellow, an 1870s winning racehorse and now a leading sire.[27]

Practicing the exact methodology that had proved effective with Montana Regent, Eastin, who trained the filly, sent her racing under the Eastin and Larabie silks at age three. On May 11, 1888, Julia L. walked onto the

Lexington racetrack for the Ashland Oaks, her maiden race, which she finished runner-up. She was then runner-up in the Latonia Oaks. Her third race was an important one for America's fillies, the one-mile Englewood Stakes at Washington Park. On the afternoon of June 30, Julia L. was on display in the paddock, and the Montanan who was on scene insisted she was "the handsomest animal" of all. She showed well in the betting, too, second favorite to Winona.[28]

The jockeys shuffled their fillies into a line. The drum was tapped, and Winona struck the pace. At the half-mile pole, Zuleika sped ahead of Winona, and Zuleika seemed the winner until Julia L.'s speed to the wire outclassed that of her opponents. She won the Englewood Stakes by three lengths. On July 14 in the Finality Stakes at Washington Park, matched against Bohemian and Falcon, Julia L. bobbed nearly in unison with the two colts until the final turn. Her pace slackened, and although she ran as hard as she could over the homestretch, she could not catch the colts. The filly rebounded in September, winning the Cash Handicap and the Merchants' Stakes at Churchill Downs. Of the six starts in 1888, she won three and was never unplaced. The filly's ascension in American racing came soon after those of Montana Regent and Grey Cloud, in the short four years of 1885 through 1888. "Montana will yet become the home of the racehorse of America," remarked *Turf, Field and Farm*, a journal devoted to racing, trotting, and other subjects.[29]

While the accuracy of the pedigree and birthplace of a racehorse mattered to the sport's most fevered aficionados, the detail was of slight interest to the public. When the *Helena Independent* relayed news of a Julia L. victory, the headline read, A MONTANA WINNER, and the *Bozeman Weekly Chronicle* used MONTANA FLYERS to head an article about the "Montana mare." Julia L. was bred and foaled in Kentucky, but figuratively she was a "Montana horse," or, as the *New North-West* explained the misnomer, "[She] is a true daughter of the Bluegrass State, but we feel a real interest in the mare and her success, since she is the property of one of Montana's most thorough and successful breeders." This pretense of ownership would extend to future Montana runners who, like Julia L., would not be reared on bunchgrass but rather on bluegrass.[30]

She was in training in April 1889. Larabie received a telegram from Eastin. As he read the contents three words jumped out—"hopelessly broken down"—the dread of all turfmen. A workout had gone haywire; Julia L.'s racing career was over. Eastin would say for the rest of his life that she was one of the best he had ever owned.[31]

━

Augustine Eastin and Samuel Larabie operated their racing stable peculiarly but adhered to the customary practice of engaging the best riders. America's top-sawyer jockeys Fred Taral and "Alfred" Monk Overton had piloted Julia L., and Pike Barnes directed her to victory in the Englewood Stakes. Barnes and Overton, together with "Black Demon" Anthony "Tony" Hamilton, Isaac Murphy, and John "Kid" Stoval represented America's famous band of Black jockeys, or as one newspaper put it, the "colored division." The era's turf scribes commonly projected skin color into their writing about Blacks. The shade might be "very black," "chocolate-colored," or "bright mulattos." In the white ranks, ethnicity was the ogre. A well-known Kentucky turfman

This photograph, taken at the Coney Island Jockey Club in 1891, features several of the era's most famous jockeys. Front row (left to right): Fred Taral, Anthony Hamilton, Thomas Kiley, Martin Bergen. Middle row (left to right): Isaac Murphy, Willie Simms. Standing (left to right): Fred Littlefield, George Covington, Charles Miller, S. Taylor, Pike Barnes, Billy Hayward, Chippie Ray, J. Lambley, Tiny Williams. Photo courtesy of Keeneland Library Hemment Collection.

quoted in 1890 supplied an example of white jockey prejudice: "Sam Bryant thinks more attention should be paid to breeding jockies [sic]. He says the cross should be sire Irish, dam English to stay, and Jew for cunning. All the dare-devil riders are Irish, the English are bull dogs for hanging on, and fortune favors the Jews."[32]

The Black rider was integral to the history of early American horse racing. From colonial times until the start of the Civil War, the racehorse in the southern states was generally cared for, ridden by, and sometimes trained by enslaved Blacks. Prominent turf scribe of the 1890s Charles Trevathan shared what he knew about Blacks at work in the racing stables: "It is a curious fact, but colored boys are much more apt about a racing stable than white boys. They learn more quickly and get along better with their mounts, whether in exercise or actual racing. Any trainer will tell you that a midget of a negro will learn more about a stable in a week than a white boy will learn in a month." The 1826 founding of the Kentucky Association was to promote Thoroughbred horse breeding and racing and in hand advanced Black horsemen from stableboys or grooms to jockeys. By 1875, fourteen of fifteen jockeys competing in the inaugural Kentucky Derby were Black. The winning jockey, Oliver Lewis, was Black.[33]

The conventional wisdom that racehorse owners and the betting public had long held close was that the best horse won regardless of the nimble man perched atop. By the 1880s, however, owners and trainers began to understand the importance of a small, slight, wiry rider who could coax, or prod with whip and spur, his mount past the finish line first. The sport of racing horses was one of speed, positioning, and shifting momentum; the riders blessed with an innate sense of pace, timing, and positioning mastered the homestretch run. When strategizing a trip over the course, the best jockeys constantly calculated their ride based on knowledge of their mount's strengths and weaknesses, and their knowledge of the competition. An exceptional jockey could judge how much speed, or how little, his mount could expend in order to reach the wire first, and he could also judge the speed at which rivals traveled. Physically, he had to have the blended athleticism of balance, coordination, blink-of-an-eye reflexes, strength, and extraordinary endurance to control a one-thousand-pound animal. Jockeys competed in several races each day. Occasionally they won every race in which they rode, like Monk Overton managing the feat on July 10, 1891, when he won six at Washington Park. One of his mounts that day happened to be Poet Scout, a plucky colt representing the Eastin and Larabie Stable.[34]

Entering the 1890s, America's highest-paid and wealthiest athletes were the money riders, or the select jockeys whose lucrative contracts were attached to large, wealthy racing stables. This elite group of Blacks and whites nego-tiated lucrative retainer fees for first and second call on their services in addition to a percentage of purses won. In 1891, Anthony Hamilton, for instance, earned $15,000 for first call. The stable owner with first call could count on Hamilton's availability for all races. An owner with second call services would be guaranteed Hamilton's services if the jockey was not riding for the owner with first call. Another fast-rising jockey of 1891, Fred Taral, commanded $12,000. Also in 1891, Isaac Murphy, regarded by many turf historians as America's best nineteenth-century jockey, was thought to have amassed $125,000 during his career. Considered almost equal in tal-ent to Isaac Murphy, Pike Barnes garnered wealth estimated at $40,000. By comparison, a US senator in 1891 earned $5,000 annually. Few jockeys saved or invested their earnings. Wealth and fame that came fast was perplexing for uneducated and unsophisticated young men. At best, their career might last three to five years, about as long as that of a good racehorse. Black or white, famed or not, nineteenth-century jockeys often found themselves stone broke at the end of their lives.[35]

In exchange for wealth and celebrity, they endured physical and mental torture to keep their weight unnaturally low. Unlike in other sports where young players developed naturally and were not exasperated by growth spurts to manhood or weight gain, jockeys abhorred them. They resorted to crash diets, intensive exercise, sweat baths, and other pernicious meth-ods for "training down" to their riding weight, which was abnormal. Isaac Murphy took long walks and simply went without food until he reached his desired weight. Only then might he nibble fruit and small pieces of meat. Monk Overton was known to soak in a steam bath for fifteen hours. He then drank a cup of tea and ate a piece of toast before going to the scales to weigh in. As one jockey remarked, "Of course, to keep from getting too weak or losing all one's strength we have to take occasional rest and nourishment, while having as much horror as getting back a few ounces of weight as you would of catching smallpox." Yet these skinny young men could pilot half-ton, high-strung racehorses over dirt or grass and win.[36]

Radical reducing was one necessary peril. Recklessness was another. The clutch riders rode with ice in their veins and could smell their way through the hotly contested races exploding with intense, erratic action and reaction. Displays of equanimity seemed, at times, unearthly. A serious injury was a matter of "when," not "if." Mortal injuries were common.

Horrific mishaps had mixed outcomes. On June 26, 1891, at Sheepshead Bay, Anthony Hamilton was astride Portchester. Driving down the homestretch, in a blink the shifting field had them boxed in. Hamilton needed to act fast. His sharp pull on the reins confused Portchester, who crossed his legs and pitched forward into a somersault. Hamilton tumbled underneath. Shrieks of horror erupted from the grandstand. It took a few moments before the jockey picked himself up and trotted off the track. The crowd, incredulous, erupted into wild cheering. Hamilton's escape was, according to the *New York Times*, "almost miraculous": "How it happened that he was not killed is something that neither he nor anyone who saw the accident [could] explain."[37]

Despite the perils, few jockeys who achieved fame and wealth could walk away from the money, the intoxicating melodrama of mastering strapping, lightning-fast Thoroughbreds, the thunderous finishes that spiked adrenaline, or the resounding cries of adulation from the grandstand. The egotistical jockey sated his need for idolatry with personal entourages serving his every whim.

Even a celebrity jockey bounced in and out of public favor. Adored one day for a spectacular finish, he could bungle the next one and have to weather criticisms that could be cruel and unjustified. "Jockey worship" was, in the words of one Chicago writer, "one of the most common forms of dissipation on a racetrack." And from a writer in Cincinnati was this somber perspective on the life and times of the boys suited in colorful silks: "In a little time, they can no longer ride winning races, and none wants them."[38]

◄►

At the Eastin and Larabie Stud in Kentucky in 1892, Julia L., recast as a broodmare, gave birth to her third foal. He was Halma, named for the parlor game played like checkers. At racing age, Eastin sized up Halma as "one of the best shaped horses" he had ever seen, the "living picture of his sire Hanover." The exception was color. Both parents, Hanover and Julia L., were chestnuts, but Halma's paternal grandsire, Virgil, had shone coal black. Halma's three white-stockinged legs and long blaze extending from forehead to upper lip sparkled on his midnight coat. Curiously, irrespective of the colt's illustrious pedigree and near-perfect symmetry, Eastin searched for a buyer. On November 24, 1893, he messaged Larabie: "Sold Halma to Byron McClelland for six thousand dollars."[39]

McClelland sent two-year-old Halma to the races in 1894 for a moderately successful campaign. On the racetrack in 1895, Halma delivered back-to-back record-breaking performances before his third start in the Kentucky Derby on May 6. Racegoers at the Churchill Downs paddock admired the charismatic leggy black, standing nearly sixteen hands. "He was truly an animal fair to see, and every turfman who saw him fell in love with him," gushed one turf historian. Jockey James "Soup" Perkins got a leg up on the colt. The young Black jockey's professional engagements began under the tutelage of trainer Peter Wimmer. Perkins developed into a confident rider who judged pace accurately and scored strong finishes. Perkins's mother made the trip from Lexington to see her son ride, but upon reaching the entry point into the Churchill Downs grandstand, she was refused entry because she was Black. If she were a white person's attendant, however, she could enter. Mrs. Perkins approached an elderly white woman who looked to be alone and explained her predicament. The two women entered the grandstand together.[40]

Action in the Kentucky Derby unfolded as expected: Halma burned to the front, led wire to wire, and beat outclassed rivals by four lengths. Victorious Halma pranced in front of the grandstand and shook his black head "with the air of a king," a display cheered wildly by his subjects. Mrs. Perkins shouted for joy for her fifteen-year-old son and wept when she saw the people swarming around him in the winner's circle.[41]

One week after the derby, Halma and Perkins rolled over the Clark Stakes competition at Churchill Downs. On May 23, 1895, Halma set his third track record upon winning the Latonia Derby for his new master, turfman Charles Fleischmann. When the colt lost the Himyar Stakes, murmurings about problematic legs circulated. The Fleischmann stable refuted that he was lame, but training was suspended indefinitely. After missing all of 1896, Halma started twice in 1897, earning third and first in purse races before Fleischmann permanently retired the stallion. Making sixteen career starts, Halma won seven, was second twice, and three times third. His earnings were $15,885.[42]

Halma's name resurfaced on July 11, 1901, upon his sale to William K. Vanderbilt for $25,000. Straightaway, the millionaire turfman exported Halma to the Vanderbilt Stud in France. Halma while overseas made American turf history as the first Kentucky Derby winner to sire a Kentucky Derby winner. His flashy, white-legged chestnut son, Alan-a-Dale, won the contest in 1902. Vanderbilt later gave Halma to the Jockey Club in New York for placement in its Bureau of Breeding. Rural horsemen in upstate New York now had access to a highly bred champion. The fee they paid to breed their mares to Halma was nominal.[43]

The coal-black beauty died at age seventeen in June 1909 from an attack of colic. Perhaps his greatest legacy was to reach the number-one spot on the winning sires list in France. In Europe as in America, a stallion owed his ranking on the winning sires list to the prize money his progeny earned in a single season.[44]

The Eastin and Larabie Stable's remarkably quick ascension in American racing rankled many eastern traditionalists. Cool indifference in the East for western horse breeding in general was occasionally flamed by eastern newspapers. A perfect opportunity for ridicule presented itself in 1891 when Samuel Larabie purchased the famous high-class broodmare Megara at an eastern sale, only to have the mare die overnight. The New York Tribune was quick to jump on Larabie's misfortune, mocking, "[Megara] was disgusted at the idea of going to Montana. So, she lay down and died in the paddock that night. The deal is off." The Tribune, however, elided Megara's advanced age of twenty-one years.[45]

Of course, the value of a broodmare at any age was uncertain until her foals raced. Larabie's good fortune with broodmares was quick, notably with Christine. He now regretted the hasty sale of her first foal, Gypsy, and had lost track of her. He found her in 1886, on a farm in Granite County, Montana. To buy her back, Larabie shelled out more than the $400 he had sold her for, but he did not mind. Gypsy, he said, was "a fair investment as very few mares in America are bred like her, she inbred to old Lexington."[46]

Larabie sent Gypsy to Eastin in Lexington, and Eastin took the mare to Nantura Stock Farm, Woodford County, Kentucky, for breeding. She was mated to Longfellow. At seventeen hands, he was a giant. The story goes that owner John Harper, when asked whether he had named the horse for poet Henry Wadsworth Longfellow, responded, "Never heard much of that feller, but that colt of mine's got the longest legs of any feller I've ever seen." Renowned handicapper and racing turf historian Walter Vosburgh was rarely prone to superlatives when evaluating great racehorses, but Longfellow was "sensational," and the historian related that in the 1870s, "extravagant stories of his prowess were frequent, and people seemed to regard him as a superhorse." Turf historian John H. Davis, who, like Vosburgh, bridged two centuries of American racing, also paid homage, writing, "A horse that traces his lineage to Longfellow is certainly bred in the purple and has a claim to equine royalty."[47]

Samuel Larabie must have felt unusually joyous on December 23, 1887. Gypsy and Christine, both in foal to Longfellow, were safely returned to Willow Run. That evening, when the low-angle sun submersed his farm in twilight, Larabie bade the mares good night and quietly closed the stable doors.[48]

CHAPTER 6

Native Sons of Montana

The healthy births of two bright bay colts were only weeks apart in 1888. Choosing High Tariff as the name for Christine's colt, Samuel Larabie had borrowed from a political hot potato. The preceding December, President Grover Cleveland, the nation's first Democratic president since the Civil War, called for high tariff reductions.[1]

When naming the colt Gypsy had foaled, Larabie exercised a favorite custom of selecting names of people he admired. His choice, Poet Scout, was to honor his friend John Wallace "Captain Jack" Crawford. A famously colorful storyteller and poet, Crawford was known otherwise in America as the "Poet Scout." Larabie took a deep breath the day he watched railroad workers entrain the two colts and their mothers. The locomotive rumbled east. Upon their arrival in Lexington, he exhaled. Augustine Eastin received the four horses, all safe and healthy.[2]

Gypsy and Christine were placed in the Eastin and Larabie Stud. High Tariff and Poet Scout were sent to trainer John W. "Doc" Marr, whose preoccupation with horse moods, motions, likes, and dislikes was no less than a parent nurturing "petted children." Eastin would say, "Doc Marr is the slowest trainer, I suppose, in the world. He can't be pushed." Marr's approach to his job exasperated more than one impatient owner.[3]

The blood brothers matured differently. Marr spoke of High Tariff as "rugged" at age two, mentally and physically equipped for the rigors of racing. Or so Marr thought. Making four starts in 1890, High Tariff ran third, seventh, thirteenth, and seventeenth. As one Kentucky turf scribe understated, "His performances did not attract the attention of the racing world."[4]

High Tariff tightened down, however, from loose-jointed two-year-old to solid three-year-old at slightly over fifteen hands. Under the play of dappling sunlight, his bay coat deepened to dark brown. His hind legs gleamed with white stockings, and the white star on his forehead glistened when he tossed his head. A "fiery eye" and "finely chiseled nostril" dignified his beauty, according to admirers. He could captivate by simply arching his tapering neck.[5]

After six starts as a three-year-old, High Tariff had lost all six and was still a maiden. Doc Marr tried him at Churchill Downs in the Clark Stakes. The field of seven was considered equal in talent, and each horse carried 122 pounds of impost. Picking a winner for the mile-and-a-quarter contest was anyone's guess.[6]

Hart Wallace had the first crack at winning it. He broke fast as lightning and swept up the lead. High Tariff, trailing, was in last place. After the first half mile was run, jockey Monk Overton urged High Tariff to close on the leaders. Peeling off more speed, the colt was quickly side by side with the pack. All seven flyers swung through the final turn and fanned across the homestretch. Hart Wallace was too weary to answer challenges from High Tariff and Dickerson, running stride for stride. Those two burned through the last furlong, but Dickerson could not outlast High Tariff, who locked up the Clark Stakes by half a length.[7]

Thunderstorms battered the region surrounding Covington, Kentucky, the day and night before the Latonia Derby. At sunrise on race day, May 23, puddles of water on the racetrack reflected the gray sky threatening to drop more rain. After his examination of the surface, Doc Marr without explanation withdrew High Tariff from the Latonia Derby.[8]

Poet Scout stood in his stablemate's stead, head held high, ears pricked, eyes alert. Marr's development of that colt into a racehorse required slow and deliberate schooling. As Doc Marr put it, Scout was "delicate" and a typical representation of his sire's slow-to-mature progeny. At three years old, Poet Scout stood sixteen hands and was remarkably improved in his training. With each fidget, his bay-colored coat glistened with glints of cinnamon and saturating brown. A wide blaze covered nearly all of his face. White stockings striped one foreleg and both hind legs. His tail, thick and black as crow wings, hung so long that it brushed the blue-tinged grass.[9]

The Latonia Derby was an unusually high-profile race in which to debut a racehorse, and if a Cinderella ending was to be granted to Poet Scout in his maiden start, he would come home a winner. The hard-fought race through mud and pooled water included a terrific homestretch drive, but coming up short, Poet Scout earned third.[10]

Doc Marr and his contemporaries well knew that a champion Thoroughbred was one likely to be born, sometimes made. The secret of winning with a good horse rested not only in the method of training but in an intuitive ability to "class" a horse. "Class" could not visibly be seen or precisely described. Trainers simply knew it when they saw it. The term was also applied to the racetrack, in a literal sense, as one turf handbook offered: "Class is determined by the public performance of a horse in any former contest or trials of speed." From another turf expert, "class" was a catchall measuring speed, courage, endurance, good disposition, and the ability to carry weight. A "first-class" horse implied that he showed all those desirable qualities on a level superior to his competition.[11]

A trainer's job was as much to manipulate excellence as to circumvent faults, but a slight miscalculation could derail the horse's chances of winning thousands of dollars. He bore the brunt of the owner's disappointment and impatience and walked a tightrope of trust. The job taught self-denial and how to wear a tough skin. Ranked above the jockey in authority, the trainer instructed the jockeys, had the last word on horses' welfare, and ensured that stable workers did their jobs properly. Trainers typically earned two or three dollars a day for each horse trained. High-strung Thoroughbred horses required unending patience to make them successful. Trainers were typically eccentric and likely to be misunderstood. Some became wealthy, and some were as well known as the sport's flamboyant jockeys and horse racing tycoons.[12]

Doc Marr started High Tariff in the Ripple Stakes at Latonia. Springing from the post "game as a fighting cock," High Tariff tucked behind front-running Hueneme all the way to the final turn. Rounding into the homestretch, High Tariff accelerated, passed Hueneme, and won the Ripple, outdistancing the field by two lengths.[13]

The nation's newspapers printed the buzz coming out of Chicago days before the American Derby. Turfmen with name recognition extending from New York to California were converging on Washington Park with the hope of pocketing the $18,610 winner's purse. The rich and famed event likewise beckoned a select club of jockeys rarely seen in a single day. On the morning of June 20, 1891, American Derby Day, the star-studded roster featured Thomas Kiley, Snapper Garrison, George Covington, Fred Taral, Daredevil Fitzpatrick, and Monk Overton. Kiley, Covington, and Taral, all Illinois born, were Chicago favorites long before any were famous. The general belief was that all ten jockeys were as evenly matched as were the ten mounts they would ride. Overton accepted Poet Scout as his mount, and Kiley, picking High Tariff, was in for the ride of his life.[14]

Doc Marr's decision to send both colts to the post meant that one had to be sacrificed for the sake of the other, and Marr was not starting High Tariff to purposely lose. He would run Poet Scout as the rabbit. Throughout the day, fifty thousand people walked into Washington Park. The morning rain showers had stopped, but the cutting wind twirled ladies' parasols under a cold Chicago sun. The betting ring, full of men who surged, pushed, elbowed, and shoved money in bookmakers' faces, was not a proper place for "pretty summer girls" or respectable matrons. Women represented a large part of the American Derby crowd. The nation's predominantly male turf writers turned chivalrous when covering the season's most famous races. They wrote of ladies with beautiful faces who were dressed in tasteful gowns made of yards of fabric and who accessorized with pretty things. Two years in the future, 1893, a Chicago woman would task herself with describing the women she observed at Washington Park on American Derby Day. She, too, emphasized beauty and dress. The unnamed woman's narrative appeared in Chicago's *Inter Ocean*:

> The sloping lawn was picturesque with striking costumes, as were the broad verandas filled with varying color. Wealth, taste and all the subtle blandishments that are the arts of womankind, helped to add interest to the scene, and, indeed, "Who will win the Derby?" was a secondary consideration to the momentous question, "Who shall hold the palm for beauty?" Seldom . . . has there been such unanimity of opinion that at Washington Park on Derby day is always to be found the most beautiful galaxy of women in all the land. The ladies spread about the green turf until it became a mere frame of the loveliness of the picture. There was holiday in the air, and there was pleasure stamping itself indelibly, for the day at least, upon the faces of the fair ones and their gallant companions.[15]

Strathmeath ascended quickly as the betting favorite. Curiously, High Tariff and Poet Scout, coupled as a single unit in the betting, showed no better than fifth choice. High Tariff, after all, had easily outfooted the competition in the Clark Stakes and Ripple Stakes, and Poet Scout had delivered an impressive performance in the Latonia Derby. The modest ranking illustrated the confidence bettors attached to the first four choices of Strathmeath; Pessara and Snowball, coupled; Kingman; and Michael. At seven minutes before four o'clock, the bugler stepped onto the racetrack and picked his way around pooled water. Finding a dry spot, he stopped, lifted his bugle, and blew the notes to summon jockeys and horses. The mile-and-a-half journey over a soaked, muddy racetrack was sure to grind down the field's speed, strength, endurance, and heart.[16]

After three false starts, the horses sprinted away in a cluster. Poet Scout and Monk Overton, sixth, worked the first half mile by threading through the shifting field. They improved to third. High Tariff and Thomas Kiley held the fifth spot but slipped to ninth over the next quarter. At three-quarters of a mile, halfway, not a single horse was out of contention. Kiley started riding High Tariff hard. The game colt plowed through the fetlock-deep mud, passed two rivals, and was rolling past a third when Kiley felt an abrupt shift in stride. High Tariff unraveled within seconds. His legs flailed wildly, queerly, over the wet loam. Kiley frantically yanked back on the reins. The panicky colt lunged upward, landed on his feet, and tried to run but could not gather his legs. High Tariff, confused, half ran, half staggered after the field thundering away without him.[17]

As High Tariff slumped into the mud, Poet Scout reeled down the racetrack with the lead. He had Michael and Strathmeath staved off by a neck when rounding the turn for home. "Strathmeath! Strathmeath!" cried the crowd, watching him closing fast on Poet Scout. They jumped to their feet to watch Strathmeath barely outblitz Poet Scout at the wire. Eyes then darted from the finish to the backstretch, where Thomas Kiley, miraculously unscathed, knelt beside High Tariff prostrate in the mud. Reaching out his hand to touch the colt, he realized High Tariff was dead.[18]

During the rest of the afternoon, Poet Scout paced and fretted in his stall. His grooms tried to soothe him with buckets of feed. He took a mouthful and then turned to the stall's half door and stared outside. He was very bonded to his brother. Since their births at Willow Run, they had rarely been separated. They frisked in the same paddock and enjoyed adjoining stalls, with a board removed so they could see each other. As afternoon in Washington Park turned to gray dusk, Poet Scout began to whinny. The throaty sound carried through the hushed, dark shed rows at moonrise. He whinnied at daybreak and the entire next day, and the next, and the next. Poet Scout, said his grooms, grieved "as much as any human being ever grieved at the death of a brother."[19]

▶◀

On the Fourth of July in Chicago, the big race on the Washington Park card was the mile-and-a-quarter Sheridan Stakes. Doc Marr kept fussing with Poet Scout, making sure every leather strap of tack was perfectly fitted, buckled, and latched. When he was satisfied, Monk Overton got a leg up. At the post, Overton leaned forward in the saddle. The starter's red flag cut through the wind. Poet Scout gathered his hind legs and pushed, his forelegs springing forward and his body lifting into flight. All five horses broke like thunder. Making the first pass of the grandstand, Poet Scout's nose pushed out in front of Pomfret's. Spectators yelled wildly for Poet Scout, who took command of the race. Unquestionably, he was their favorite. The crowd of twenty-five thousand jumped up and down and waved their arms for Scout in the moments before he won the Sheridan Stakes. The race was over, but cheers and roars grew louder. The old-timers could not remember an ovation more deafening or emotive, nor could a Chicago turf scribe who took it upon himself to offer an explanation. The extraordinary delirium as wholly emotional, partly a "royal tribute to the hero of the Sheridan Stakes" and partly homage to owners Augustine Eastin and Samuel Larabie, respected as "true sportsmen." Most poignantly, Poet Scout's victory was the means to acknowledge and honor the tragic death of his brother, High Tariff.[20]

On July 10, Scout accepted 122 pounds of impost, seven pounds more than in the Sheridan, for the mile-and-an-eighth Maiden Stakes. With Monk Overton in the saddle, he won the Maiden by two lengths. Overton had barely begun his afternoon of work; he won the next three races. Landing those three mounts as winners looked easy for the "remarkably broad-shouldered, erect, manly-looking, coal-black negro," the *Daily Racing Form* noted. At the *Chicago Tribune*, Overton was the "strong and honest black boy" to set off the raid in the Washington Park betting ring. Before the last three races were run, bettors wagered on his mounts. Overton went on to win those three, and his gleeful backers went home with a lot of money. Monk Overton's feat of six for six in a single day was historic. He was first to do it on the American turf. For years to come, newspapermen would periodically remind readers about Overton, the "best left-handed whip that ever sat in the saddle," and his historic day.[21]

Overton stayed at Washington Park. Doc Marr shipped Poet Scout to the Morris Park Racecourse in New York City. At nearby Coney Island, the Brighton Beach, Sheepshead Bay, and Gravesend courses operated. All four venues drew large crowds, and racing was available to New Yorkers every weekday as well as weekends. The state of New York was accorded the distinction of being the birthplace of formalized racing, with America's first formal racecourse laid down in 1665 on Long Island. By the 1890s, New York, particularly the New York City metropolis, was indisputably the epicenter of American horse racing. The sport's national governing body at the time, the Board of Control, was headquartered in the city. National sporting publications that covered Thoroughbred racing, the likes of *Spirit of the Times* and *Goodwin's Turf Guide*, were published in New York City. The *Goodwin's* books were "indispensable to turfmen," said *Turf, Field and Farm*, also published in New York City.[22]

The sport that was once scarcely more than colonists racing their swiftest horses through village streets had opened the way for a national multimillion-dollar industry. From the desire to breed the next winner of the Futurity Stakes or American Derby, acres of land and millions of dollars were committed to breeding Thoroughbred horses and developing the tracks on which to race them. The popularity of the sport and its rapid expansion accounted for more than six thousand races run in 1891, and according to the San Francisco–based *Breeder and Sportsman*, "500,000 men and boys find employment in various ways on the tracks, in the stables and in the pool rooms and betting rings, and 25,000 persons often witness a great contest." Meanwhile, each racing association, or jockey club, was a law unto itself. Several New York jockey clubs would unite to provide uniformity in meets and rules, and to stem corruption. This authoritative body and precursor of today's Jockey Club was the Board of Control, organized on February 16, 1891. As this governing body matured, it oversaw the administration of the tracks it sanctioned. Jockeys and trainers, for instance, had to be licensed annually. If they, or a horse owner, refused to comply with Board of Control rules, they were banned from the Board of Control sanctioned tracks.[23]

On August 18, 1891, by way of the Omnibus Stakes at Morris Park, Doc Marr introduced Poet Scout to New York racing. The colt ran third but delivered a brilliant performance in the twelve-horse race. In fact, billows of racetrack dust had scarcely settled before Augustine Eastin was fielding an offer. The prospective buyer's identity was not revealed, but likely it was Green B. Morris. The trainer's first offer to buy the colt was tendered back in June, for $17,000. Now he offered $20,000. Acting on behalf of his partner, Eastin declined to sell the colt.[24]

At Gravesend Racecourse on the morning of September 17, Poet Scout seemed off a tick. Doc Marr ran his hands over joints, tendons, and feet and checked the mouth. Not finding a concrete reason to scratch Scout from the Fulton Stakes, Marr pushed his worry aside, and Scout paraded to the post. Six horses sprang from the start. Poet Scout slipped in behind Pessara and dogged the front-runner all the way to the homestretch, where something went wrong. Scout decelerated like an arrow skidding into the dust. The crowd, agape, watched the jockey go to work, but his urging failed to rouse the colt. Scout was a "bad" fourth to Pessara. Accusations flew. Doc Marr was in the cross hairs. Critics blamed him for the loss. Marr insisted something sinister had been at play, that possibly somebody had "dosed" his colt. He never wavered from his belief.[25]

The Jockey Club, after absorbing the Board of Control in 1894, drafted and adopted a rule to end "the reprehensible practice of 'doping' horses." Doping, as the Jockey Club defined the practice in 1897, consisted of injecting under the skin of a horse a liquid or an opiate, such as caffeine, morphine, strychnine, cocaine, or heroin. The extent of drug testing in the day was no more sophisticated than a visual inspection. Cruder methods employed to secure a defeat included shoving a sponge up a nostril to impair the horse's ability to breathe, or overfeeding or overwatering the animal during the hours before the race. Efforts by the club to outlaw doping, according to contemporary turf writer Ryan Goldberg, were more about dishonest gambling than concern for horse or jockey welfare. The club was largely under the thumb of wealthy turfmen who had so much money they did not blink an eye at wagering thousands of dollars on a race, but they minded very much unfair contests affected by doping and other dishonest practices.[26]

All season long Doc Marr had guardedly developed Poet Scout for the purpose of starting him in the Hickory Stakes, the event his bosses Eastin and Larabie wanted most to win. The Hickory, last of the rich stakes for three-year-olds in 1891, would dole out $17,000 to the victor. As race day neared, Marr's intimates, well apprised of his guarded work with Poet Scout, surreptitiously wagered on Scout at long odds.[27]

On October 10 at Morris Park, racegoers made good on the opportunity to see not one, but two racehorses representing the young state of Montana in the mile-and-a-half Hickory Stakes. The crowds breezed through the saddling paddock, where Poet Scout on view looked every inch a racehorse. When all eyes turned toward the other horse from Montana, a bay colt eponymously named Montana, the hubbub of voices nearly stopped at the sight of the gangliest, ugliest colt footing America's racetracks. Worse, he was unplaced in his last four starts.[28]

The "bright-eyed" ladies looking over racehorses they knew nothing about gave their escorts "no peace" with questions about this and that, exactly as expected of sheltered ladies. The scene was a typical one at the track. The escorts, as expected, good-naturedly indulged the ladies with information and recommendations as to which horse they should bet on. Still, after viewing the horses and hearing recommendations, the ladies made their selections based on the "fancies they formed for any particular names," noted the scribe writing for the New York Sun.[29]

The escorts hurried to the betting ring pulsing with hundreds of other males. Strathmeath was the top pick at nine to five. Poet Scout, having lost his last two races, showed at eight to one, or fourth favorite in the eight-horse field. Montana was the twelve-to-one fifth choice. The imposts allocated were not extreme. Poet Scout, Montana, Strathmeath, Russell, and Rey del Rey were equally weighted at 122 pounds. Reckon, Kildeer, and Equity each shouldered 119. The jockeys suited in their smartly colored silks included big guns Fred Taral, George Covington, Pike Barnes, Isaac Murphy, and Anthony Hamilton. Inside the paddock, saddles were lifted, squared, and cinched. The bugle sounded; the field fell in file from the paddock to the racetrack.[30]

The keyed-up crowd roared in approval for the burst of flashy colors flattened atop the racehorses thudding away from the post. Kildeer in the lead ignited a scorching pace, with a band of runners ripping behind her. Poet Scout was in the rear, as was Montana, already struggling to keep pace. He would fall back to seventh, where he would finish. Kildeer was trying to shake Russell off her tail as she streamed through the backstretch on the first pass. Anthony Hamilton astride Poet Scout went to work, urging the colt to catch the leaders. Hamilton positioned Scout within striking distance and held the colt steady.

At a quarter mile left to cover, Kildeer and Russell tired and were soon hopelessly beaten. Strathmeath and Equity felt Poet Scout lapping at their heels. Dust spewed, whips sang, and spurs cut. Arcing around the final turn, Hamilton wanted more speed and fight. He chirped, and from beneath his seat he could feel Poet Scout wind up, release, and whirl his four legs like firing pistons. In six long, swinging strides, Poet Scout was alongside Strathmeath and Equity.

POET SCOUT
The famous race horse that will figure prominently in the picnic of the
Irish societies at Anaconda to-day.

At age sixteen, Poet Scout hardly looks like the dominating force he exemplified
in the 1891 Hickory Stakes. "His victory in Hickory Stakes stamps him first-class,"
said eminent New York turfman James L. Carrigan. "He is a slashing big fellow
with a good way of going." Photo courtesy of the *Anaconda (MT) Standard*, July 24, 1904.

In six more he was ahead, his speed having completely overwhelmed them. In this way, Poet Scout steamrolled the Hickory Stakes by a five-length margin.[31]

After the exciting race, Augustine Eastin relaxed on the Morris Park grounds with a glass of wine. Joining him for conversation was turfman Fred McLewee, whose firecracker filly, Yorkville Belle, had won the Nursery Stakes for two-year-olds. The men were interrupted by a *New York Tribune* reporter, and Eastin always treated people courteously. The reporter said he thought that Poet Scout was a curious name. How did the colt get it? Eastin explained that his racing partner liked to name horses in honor of people. Eastin elaborated, "General Custer once had in his employ a scout who was distinguished not only for his skill on the trail, but for his learning. He was a clever poet and became known far and wide as 'the poet scout.' My partner, Mr. Larabie, who lives in Deer Lodge, Montana, was his intimate friend, and we named him in his honor, 'Poet Scout.'" Eastin misspoke on one point, or perhaps he was embellishing. Captain Jack Crawford, the Poet Scout, was in fact a scout, but for Colonel Wesley Merritt of the Fifth Cavalry. Crawford never scouted for General George Armstrong Custer of the Seventh Cavalry.

The reporter had more questions.

Was Poet Scout's win a surprise?

"No. He had been carefully trained and was very fit. We thought he should have won the Omnibus," Eastin said.

Had Eastin bet on Poet Scout?

"A little. But you know we are not betting men."

Perhaps Eastin was unaware of Samuel Larabie's $5,000 side bet with his Bitterroot Valley neighbor Marcus Daly, who was the owner of the colt Montana. Moreover, according to the *Chicago Tribune*, Larabie as well as Eastin had wagered on Poet Scout at "comfortable" odds and pocketed several thousand dollars.[32]

The colt's commanding performance in the Hickory failed to impress all turfmen. Some who were prominent in eastern racing circles publicly stated that Poet Scout was not worthy of matching strides with any of the East's top colts. Joining that bandwagon was a pessimistic eastern turf scribe who wrote, "A thoroughly representative lot of this year's three-year-olds faced the flag [in the Hickory]. There was Montana, Russell, Reckon, Kildeer, Equity, Poet Scout, Strathmeath and Rey del Rey . . . and what [a] poor lot they are, to be sure! . . . Poet Scout is an enigma, and his name ought to be changed to Pirate Scout. . . . It was fitting that the Hickory should be won by Poet Scout. Of all the horses entered, his recent form has been the worst." More of his denigrating remarks were leveled at Montana, or the "Big Brown Jug." The worst of the insults was this: "A gang of Guttenburg [sic] selling platers could not furnish more inconsistent performances." Except for horsemen who did Guttenberg's bidding, everyone else connected with American racing despised that outcast racetrack operating in New Jersey.[33]

In February 1892, Doc Marr moved the Eastin and Larabie runners from Lexington to Louisville. Spring training started. Marr was feeling sweet about four-year-old Scout, saying, "There may be some that will head him, but I doubt it." Marr must have been doubly disappointed when Poet Scout lost his first two starts, the Decoration Handicap on May 30 and the Suburban Handicap on June 18.[34]

On July 12, racegoers at Monmouth Park Racecourse at Long Branch, New Jersey, withstood sweltering heat as they predicted an afternoon of racing just as hot. On the wings of the breeze, stifling, oven-hot air sagged over seven horses saddled for the Shrewsbury Handicap. Jockeys wondered how masterfully they would manage a long mile and a half in the sultry heat. One of them was Snapper Garrison, who had first laid eyes on Poet Scout nearly one year before and reportedly was "much taken with the Montana colt." Although Garrison was under contract to Marcus Daly in 1892, the boss was not running a horse in the Shrewsbury, leaving Garrison free to make his only ride on Poet Scout. Greenbacks came in fast on the Garrison–Poet Scout ticket. Odds dipped to even money by post time. Poet Scout had lost the Suburban Handicap three weeks earlier, but the bookmakers were fully aware of the colt's strong homestretch run. Now that he was teamed with arguably the nation's greatest jockey at the time, the books did not want any part of the pair.[35]

The starter glanced over the seven flyers in an orderly line and dropped his flag. Garrison guided Poet Scout away from traffic and settled him in seventh. At three-quarters of a mile, the halfway point, Garrison and Scout keyholed through the pack and improved their position. Rounding the final turn and meeting the homestretch, Scout, Raceland, and Demuth gunned their way to the front, and Scout and Demuth, throwing longer strides than Raceland, soon had that colt outdistanced.[36]

Garrison locked himself into that funny-looking position he was famous for, curling his back into a hump, crouching over his mount's neck like a wildcat ready to strike. Spectators cheered for Garrison, who was famous for his seemingly superhuman ability to willfully lift his mounts from the ground into the air and land them over the finish line. Garrison did exactly that, with one arm whipping and the other ostensibly lifting Poet Scout in front of Demuth by the margin of a head. The time was close to record breaking and was lauded years later as "one of the best performances on record at that time for a stallion at that distance and weight."[37]

At the Freehold Stakes on August 6, a freewheeler named Banquet laid a crooked trail. The four-horse field had spilled out over the Monmouth Park homestretch. Three horses, Banquet, Locohatchee, and Poet Scout, came away together for the stretch run. Banquet bored into Locohatchee once, then again, and the second slamming walloped Locohatchee so forcefully that jockey Martin Bergen hauled back on the reins to avert a collision. Banquet then ricocheted into Poet Scout, nearly knocking him from his feet. Jockey Fred Taral corrected Scout and got him back on stride. Banquet rambled on and won the race. Moments after Locohatchee, second, passed the wire, Bergen flung himself from the saddle and bulled his way to the stewards' office. The stewards said he rightly claimed interference. Upon Banquet's disqualification, Locohatchee and Poet Scout were accorded one-two in the Freehold Stakes. After that wild contest, Scout made one more start in his 1892 campaign, the Champion Stakes, in which he finished fourth.[38]

◼

With a new crop of foals on the way every spring and yearlings to sell, Samuel Larabie compiled his annual catalogue publicizing Willow Run stock. The pages tabulated pedigrees and race records and cited noteworthy offspring. An earlier catalogue published in 1888 explained his approach to breeding blooded horses and what he hoped for as an end result. "No man believes more strongly than I in pedigree, but I want it to come directly from animals whose blood has been found by actual test to produce a high rate of speed, and the soundness and courage to carry that speed for a long distance; from animals of fine appearance and whose families have, as a rule, produced horses of fair size and symmetrical proportions. In a few words, my aim is to get horses suitable for the track, road, and stud." Larabie's choice of a title for his newest book was *The Poet Scout Catalogue of Thoroughbreds for 1893.* Appropriately, Poet Scout was honored with the first entry. The book's title and its first entry suggest Larabie's optimism for his most famous race-horse at the time. He probably figured the horse would perform no worse than he had in 1892.[39]

But as 1893 clipped along, Scout, with Eastin as his trainer, was losing. The five-year-old veteran seemed to have lost his speed and stamina, but then he roused a winning drive in a race at Latonia. Next, on October 3 at Latonia, torrents of rain doused the six horses parading for the Queen City Handicap. Hooves sank into mud fetlock deep, and Poet Scout's added burden was a top weight of 120 pounds, conceding 9 to his opponents. The crowd, apparently unconcerned by the rain, mud, and weight that would make Scout's mile-and-an-eighth journey seem like an eternity, made him the favorite. From the instant the race started, his backers must have cringed as they watched La Colonia ramp up her speed and roil the sea of water and muck. She was leading through the last sixteenth and had her rivals outdistanced by a huge seven lengths. But when her speed began waning, it waned rapidly. Poet Scout swept past her, his long, wet tail snapping like a black whip as he slipped and strained and scudded past the wire a neck ahead of Buck McCann, second, and La Colonia, third. He remained at Latonia for his final start of 1893. Unable to duplicate the impressive effort he showed in the sweepstakes, he ran fifth in the Cincinnati Hotel Autumn Handicap.[40]

Poet Scout was in the stud for all of 1894, the year Edward Gardner Jones noted the Deer Lodge Valley in his 1894 book, *The Oregonian's Handbook of the Pacific Northwest.* Jones's praise for the "Lodge of the White-Tailed Deer" stated: "The land and climate here are especially favorable to the raising of fine stock, and during recent years Deer Lodge has become known through the East as the home of horses of notable reputation. Thoroughbreds foaled and raised at Deer Lodge have figured prominently in some class events of the American Turf. Deer Lodge is the home of Poet Scout, High Tariff,

Nevada, Eolian, Regent, and a number of other well-known thoroughbreds that have won laurels on the turf."[41]

The comeback season of 1895 was not fireworks. Scout was second twice, third, and unplaced in four starts. After the brief campaign, Samuel Larabie brought his aging racehorse home and placed him in the Willow Run Stud. In an unspecified year, James Ben Ali Haggin purchased Poet Scout for $40,000 as a stud prospect. Haggin's vast Rancho del Paso, a horse ranch in California, was teeming with highly bred broodmares. Yet if any of Scout's colts and fillies ever reached the winner's circle, they were few.[42]

Ⅰ◀▶Ⅰ

An anticlimactic stud career brought emasculation and a return to the racetrack. Poet Scout was owned by Haggin, but he campaigned under the Henry Byrnes and Company Stable at Butte. On July 2, 1898, Scout was the "red hot" entry for a $350 purse. He had not raced in three years. Little wonder the ten-year-old behaved badly at the post and delayed the start. He finished third and won $30. At the post six days later, he blasted Veloz with a kick before the start was made. Scout finished third and won $30. Poor Veloz was last.[43]

August rolled into the Deer Lodge Valley, and Tom McTague was going about his business as the warden of the Deer Lodge prison. The avid horseman was a close friend of John Mackey, who was Haggin's superintendent for Rancho del Paso. The *Anaconda Standard* related that Mackey had presented to McTague "the famous runner, Poet Scout," and Mackey's deed illustrated "the high regard which the veteran horseman has for the warden." With Scout in McTague's "good hands," the *Standard* predicted the aging race-horse would "be heard from later."[44]

It took three years, but McTague plucked Poet Scout from the bunchgrass and sent him over the mountain to race. This was the summer of 1901. At Butte, Scout made four starts, and if he was not last, he finished nearly last. At Butte in 1902, Scout lost both of his two starts. Even the scribe at the *Great Falls Tribune* winced over the ignoble predicament of a fourteen-year-old race-horse. "It was painful last summer at Butte to see this once great racer, which has thrilled the people of New York and Chicago with his best exhibitions of speed and gameness, beaten by 'dogs.' . . . But the ancient warrior will go to the turf wars no more but spend his remaining days on Mr. McTague's farm munching the best of grass, hay and oats. And if ever a horse had earned a life of ease and comfort it is old Poet Scout, scion of one of the best racing families in all America."[45]

◄►

On July 24, 1904, in Anaconda, five thousand Montanans gathered for a community picnic. The sponsoring United Irish Societies of Butte and Anaconda were raising money for a monument to posthumously honor Irish-born Francis Thomas Meagher, Montana's first territorial governor. The picnickers warmly welcomed Poet Scout, whose mane they festooned with green ribbons. Festivities paused when Tom McTague strode onto an improvised stage. After formally giving sixteen-year-old Poet Scout to the Irish Societies for their highly anticipated raffle, McTague recited Scout's pedigree and race record. He picked the victory in the 1891 Sheridan Stakes as the old boy's crowning moment. Scout had won seven of twenty-five races. His purse money topped out at $34,150. McTague then reached his hand into a basket and retrieved a ticket. The winning ticket holder, J. J. Conney of Butte, was Scout's new master. To the delight of the picnickers, their native son was paraded around Mountain View Park. His long black tail swept the grass.[46]

CHAPTER 7

Ben Holladay

Iron Horse

The Overland Stage Line operating under the thumb of Ben Holladay stood above all other stagecoach lines crisscrossing the West. Such sobriquets as "Stagecoach Ben," "Napoleon of the Plains," "The Stagecoach King," and "Old Hell-on-Wheels" were ascribed to the flamboyant transportation tycoon who pieced together the West's best-equipped stagecoach and freight company. At its peak, in 1862, the Overland employed 450 men, ran 1,750 horses and mules, and owned a fleet of 110 Concord coaches. Holladay grew weary of increasing conflicts with Native American tribes and foresaw railroads as the future in transportation. The $1.5 million he reaped from the sale of his Overland empire to Wells Fargo and Company in November 1866 would finance new ventures in railroad and steamship lines. Such notables as Abraham Lincoln, Brigham Young, Mark Twain, and Horace Greeley were said to have admired Ben Holladay.[1]

Samuel Larabie also admired Old Hell-on-Wheels and named a new colt for him. The place of foaling has long been accorded to Montana, but study of the chronology and architecture of Larabie and Augustine Eastin's breeding and racing operation indicates that Kentucky is likely Ben Holladay's birthplace, likely at Eastin's farm near Avon. Bay-colored Ben Holladay had a beautiful pedigree. His dam was Indiana-bred Mollie L., sired by Longfellow and foaled by Mollie McCann. Mollie L. was an exceptional broodmare. Several of her fillies distinguished themselves on the racetrack before distinguishing themselves as significant broodmares. In fact, Mollie L.'s death in 1902 left an orphaned filly described as "priceless." Ben Holladay's sire was Hanover, a Kentucky-bred horse who defeated his rivals over all distances no matter the hefty imposts he carried. There were many career highlights, but in 1887 Hanover ran the table by winning fourteen straight in a mere ten weeks.[2]

The big race at Churchill Downs on May 6, 1895, was the twentieth running of the Kentucky Derby. Halma won it, and after leaving the winner's circle, his jockey, Soup Perkins, changed into the silks of the Eastin and Larabie Stable before he reappeared for the next race. Perkins guided maiden colt Ben Holladay to the post. At the dip of the starter's flag, ten maidens bounded into their strides and futures. Holladay's career opened with a ninth-place finish. At his next start, June 26 at Latonia, with Perkins in the irons, he broke his maiden in the $400 purse race. In his next six starts, spread between the Oakley Racecourse in Cincinnati and Churchill Downs, he finished no worse than third. Back at Latonia for four races, the lone win was a $400 purse. All told, in twelve starts he won four and was unplaced once in his two-year-old season.[3]

The name of the man who trained Holladay in his inaugural season of 1895 is unknown, but Byron McClelland would train him in 1896. Soup Perkins was Holladay's regular rider. Perkins's ascent in 1895 was so fabulous that he finished the season as America's best rider. With Holladay in 1896, their eighteen starts were made at Churchill Downs, Oakley, and Latonia. Incredibly, they were unplaced only once. The highlight of this impressive record was "lightning time" in the Telegraph Stakes, which marked Holladay's first stakes victory.[4]

In mid-January 1897, the Eastin and Larabie Stable engaged a new trainer. Whether rain was falling at daybreak or the sun was shining, German-born Peter Wimmer worked by daylight instead of the clock. Wimmer had gone with the Confederate States of America during the Civil War. Habits adopted during his cavalry service were transferred to the racetrack. Always mounted, booted, and spurred, Wimmer looked the part of upstanding cavalry scout. Conspicuous at the racetrack, he received the sobriquet "Commander Cronje," in reference to General Piet Cronjé of the South African Republic. Exercise boys listened to his minute instructions prior to morning workouts. When the exercise was finished, the boys on their mounts formed a line in preparation for Wimmer's walk along the row, back and forth, inspecting each horse carefully, and the boys then walked their mounts. Wimmer watched for hints of lameness.[5]

His peers called him "Professor." An expert on Thoroughbred pedigrees, he had been storing knowledge on the subject since 1871, first in Mississippi, where got his start as a trainer. He worked his way to the top ranks. By 1889, he was training for eminent turfman Milton Young. They ran two horses in that year's Kentucky Derby, Bootmaker and Once Again, finishing third and eighth, respectively, to Spokane.[6]

With the intensity of a diamond cutter, Wimmer studied the Eastin and Larabie Stable prospects for 1897. Imposing four-year-old Ben Holladay was slow to break from the post because of his strapping musculature, broad chest, short back, and stout hindquarters. It took a while for him to gather and organize before launching into what was an exceptionally long, peculiar, "kangaroo-like" stride. When rounding turns, Holladay lost control of his stride more than anyone liked. One turfman, describing the horse's proverbial fault, said that it was "almost painful to watch him making turns." Holladay rarely reached full range of motion until well into the backstretch and thus was vulnerable at distances shorter than a mile and a half. He could otherwise run the length of the horizon.[7]

Pliant and sweet-natured Holladay was a handler's dream, but he had grown bored and restive with his routine. Wimmer then shifted exercise from the racetrack to jaunts of "road exercise" on country lanes. This harked back to his days as a cavalry scout when he had indulged in impromptu racing.[8]

Holladay's four-year campaign bounced from Churchill Downs to Latonia and to the Saratoga track in New York. At Saratoga on August 6, he started in a handicap of little regard but, importantly, on first asking won at New York racing. By virtue of that victory, on August 14 he was saddled with 125 pounds of impost, the weightiest of his career. He lost by a neck to Havoc, who shouldered one pound more. Sheepshead Bay was the next sampling of New York racing. Holladay won his first race there but was unplaced in the next.[9]

On the final day of the Sheepshead Bay autumn meeting, September 11, a flood of sunlight warmed racegoers doubly excited for the Great Eastern Handicap and the newly minted Autumn Cup. The fast condition of the racetrack and a windless afternoon foretold record-breaking performances, the expert horsemen said. The Great Eastern Handicap was reserved for America's crack two-year-olds, and spectators were eager to see Hamburg, the top colt of that age class. Loaded with 135 pounds of impost in the Great Eastern, an onerous amount virtually unheard of in the two-year-old ranks, Hamburg handily outraced thirteen rivals.[10]

The Autumn Cup at two miles was designed to test the speed and stamina of the veterans, three years or older. Ornament was the nation's most acclaimed three-year-old and correspondingly as popular with racegoers as Hamburg. Thus, Ornament was first pick for the Autumn Cup. Imposts were accepted. Ornament was fitted with 123 pounds. The second choice for the race, Dutch Skater, received 105, and Ben Holladay, third pick, was under 114. Five more lightly weighted contestants rounded out the field.[11]

The crisp start was perfect for Sunny Slope to strike a pace as scorching as the afternoon sun. She pushed her blistering pace fully a mile and three-quarters before cooling. Holladay, Rensselaer, Dutch Skater, and Ornament took charge, but Ornament and Rensselaer fell back into the brown haze spewed by churning hooves. Dutch Skater drifted sideways in the last quarter, and Holladay had his chance. He struck fast and by half a length brought home the Autumn Cup in the record-breaking time of 3:29 2/5, which destroyed the previous two-mile Sheepshead Bay course record of 3:31 ¼. New York newspapers carried reports of Holladay's commanding victory and Ornament's surprising defeat, with the New York Times calling Holladay's performance "extraordinary," adding that he "without any great effort defeated Ornament who is acknowledged to be one of the grandest three-year-olds the American turf has known."[12]

On two days' rest, Holladay raced at Gravesend and lost the Oriental Handicap. Seven days later at Morris Park, the Municipal Handicap field was well bunched for their final drive home. Dutch Skater mounted a challenge for the lead but found it fruitless against Holladay's rapid kangaroo strides, which won him that race. Upon the announcement of record-breaking time and in honor of it, the Morris Park band struck up "Hail to the Chief" amid the applause and shouted compliments serenading Holladay, who, according to the *New York Sun*, trotted "unconcernedly, as though breaking world records were an everyday occurrence with him." The 2:59 ¼ clocking eclipsed by a second and a half the previous world record time for the distance. "The ease with which this record-breaking performance was accomplished," the *Spirit of the Times* informed, "added much to his impressiveness and stamps Ben Holladay as the best stayer of the day." A "stayer" illustrated the admired characteristics in a racehorse: endurance, courage, and the ability to not "readily give in through weakness or a lack of vitality and energy," noted a 1894 turf handbook. The final start of 1897 came five days later at Morris Park. Earning third in a five-horse handicap over a mile and three-sixteenths, Holladay was under a career high of a 126-pound impost.[13]

In the highly competitive sphere of New York racing, Holladay's thirteen starts in 1897 produced four victories, and he was twice unplaced. His season was asterisked with two record-breaking performances. Trainer Charles Boyle, who noticed the horse's ascent, cornered Peter Wimmer at a New York racetrack and got right to the point: he wanted to buy Holladay for Canadian distiller Joseph E. Seagram. Wimmer, cleared to field offers for his bosses' horses, declined the $6,000 offer. A turf scribe in New York who noticed the Eastin and Larabie Stable trajectory in American racing wrote, "Every half dozen years this firm develops a good horse. Ten years ago, the stable boasted a fine three-year-old in Montana Regent, and some five years ago they came east with the colt Poet Scout."[14]

Americans were partaking in the sport of horse racing as never before during the decade of the "Gay Nineties." Characterized as a period of excess glitz and wastefulness, it included changing attitudes toward recreational pursuits as well. Pleasurable pastimes were viewed less and less as appealing only to shiftless people and as a squandering of time for productivity. Going to the races was likewise a popular pastime overseas. Across the Atlantic, for instance, the quintessential beautiful woman on the English stage was "Jersey Lily," otherwise known as British actress Lily (or Lillie) Langtry. Celebrated as the most desired woman of her era, Mrs. Langtry not only attended the races but also operated a racing stable under the male pretense of "Mr. Jersey." Said to be "as keen a trader and speculator as any professional in the [betting] ring," the English siren cast about for an American racehorse to buy in spring 1898. Ben Holladay was one of two she wanted—until she heard that Holladay finished a race lame. Though the lameness was thought to be temporary, Mrs. Langtry, "not dealing in lame horses," decided against taking a chance on him.[15]

Langtry's contemporary on the American stage was "American Beauty" Miss Lillian Russell. She sang and acted, but her flawless features and hourglass figure were what made her the most pictured woman in America. Russell and her theatrical counterparts frequented the racetracks, but she took her enthusiasm for the sport beyond being a mere spectator. As had Lily Langtry, Miss Lillian Russell organized a racing stable under a male pretense, "Mr. Clinton," the name borrowed from her birthplace of Clinton, Iowa.[16]

Peter Wimmer had four-year-old Ben Holladay conditioned to peak form for the 1898 season. Early in the campaign, the colt was fifth in the Metropolitan Handicap, second in the Brooklyn Handicap, and fifth in the Suburban Handicap. Wimmer must have been disappointed, but turfman William C. Whitney was not put off by the losses. Whitney offered $10,000 for the horse. Larabie refused to sell.[17]

With the campaign traveling to Sheepshead Bay, Holladay won a minor handicap there before his start in the Turf Handicap. Wimmer accepted 127 pounds for that one, the heaviest load Holladay had ever carried. If concerned about the weight adversely affecting performance, Wimmer watched his horse lead the field from wire to wire. Then, on the heels of that sterling performance, Ben Holladay "could not run a little bit," and his jockey, Willie Simms, "could not ride a little bit." That was how the *Brooklyn Citizen* characterized the effort in the Twin City Handicap. Simms and Holladay finished dead last.[18]

Morris Park offered three high-profile long-distance races on consecutive Saturdays in October. The series was open to horses of either sex, three years or older, and exemplified the high-quality racing Morris Park was known for. From the day the entrance gates first opened on August 20, 1889, under the auspices of the Westchester Racing Association, Morris Park was a prime example of late nineteenth-century jockey clubs building racetracks increasingly refined in design, complex in construction, and lavish in amenities. The entire 360-acre complex stood on a hill. The grandstand, accommodating fifteen thousand spectators, was America's largest. Spectators had unobstructed views of the Withers Course, the one-and-three-eighths mile oval; and the Eclipse Course, the three-quarter-mile straightaway that cut diagonally across the Withers. Because of the hilly terrain, the Withers Course undulated slightly, like a "Toboggan Slide," as New York's raft of wisecracking turf scribes dubbed the irregularity. The Morris Park stables stretched a mile and a half and could accommodate seven hundred horses. Built to "stand for a century," the stables were said to outclass all others at America's racetracks.[19]

The new racetrack drew fans from the New York City boroughs and beyond. As at all horse racing venues, common folk mingled with rich folk, but typically only rich folk could afford access to the fancy clubhouses. Inside the Morris Park clubhouse, all of five stories, the walls in the luxurious Ladies Parlor were covered in equal parts wallpaper and rich paneling. Large carpets with weaved patterns covered wooden floors. On chilly days at the races, the ladies could lounge near the fireplace while a lady played the piano.[20]

Peter Wimmer felt certain that Holladay could take down all three races, starting with the inaugural running of the Morris Park Special. On the morning of Saturday, October 8, a Morris Park gatekeeper described the racetrack surface as "heavy," but more accurately it was a sea of mud. Activity in the betting ring favored Algol over Ben Holladay. Both horses were under stifling loads of 130 pounds. Hauling weight like that over a waterlogged two miles was an especially bruising proposition for Holladay because of his iffy right foreleg. A tendon had ruptured earlier in the season, and the leg invariably swelled after every workout or race. Jockey Fred Taral got a leg up on Holladay, whose coat was slick with rain.[21]

Algol shot away to the early lead, with George Keene second, Ben Holladay third, and two more horses trailing. Setting the pace for nearly a mile and a quarter through a swamp, Algol grew leg weary. Seeing this, Taral chirped to Holladay, who through the last sixteenth gathered his large body tightly before releasing a get-up-and-go drive. George Keene, likewise keyed up, made a play for Holladay's lead. Taral's whip whirled and smacked. Holladay cut through the mud and pooled water. His lead grew to two lengths. By that margin he knocked out the Morris Park Special. The iffy right foreleg held.[22]

The next Saturday, a chilly and dreary October 15, Wimmer must have sighed in disappointment at the sight of another wet racetrack, but at least it was not a muddy sea. He was more attentive than usual to his jockey, Tommy Burns, when ticking off instructions to improve Holladay's chance of winning the Municipal Handicap in back-to-back years. The race was comparable in prestige to the Belmont Stakes or Withers Stakes. Burns, who was riding red hot that season, was making his first and only ride on Holladay. For the second time in as many races, the horse was under 130 pounds. At a mile and three-quarters, the race was a long one.[23]

At flag fall, the jockey riding long-shot Jefferson gunned him to the front because Jefferson's people thought he could win only if he led wire to wire. Lightly weighted, the horse skimmed over the track and, upon reaching the head of the homestretch a second time, opened an eight-length lead. Holladay, running effortlessly, as if five or ten more pounds on his back could not slow him, was the only horse likely to take Jefferson down. When he collared him, the crowd leaped to their feet. Thousands of screaming voices urged big Ben on. His lead over Jefferson widened to a length and a half, and Ben Holladay won his second Municipal Handicap.[24]

With two of the three Morris Park races won, Peter Wimmer expected Holladay to carry a huge block of weight for the third leg, the Morris Park Handicap. Maybe he winced when socked with 138 pounds. Surely the horse would feel the career-high weight on his back. He would concede no less than 41 pounds to four rivals and run an interminable two and a quarter miles. If Holladay could manage the weight and win his race, he would be America's first racehorse to accomplish the feat on a flat course, or in other words, on level ground without having to jump over obstacles, as in a steeplechase.[25]

Drenching rain had stopped on the morning of race day, Saturday, October 22, but the racetrack was an awful mess of pooled water and mud. Thousands of racegoers braved the wet and cold on the chance they might witness the making of American turf history. The crowd made Ben Holladay their favorite.[26]

Under the tremendous weight, Holladay lurched forward from the starting post, his hooves whipping pools of water. On the first pass of the grandstand, Fred Taral rode Holladay tucked in behind front-running Jefferson and Whistling Con. Holladay banked the first turn too widely, and the big sweep cost him ground and his good position on the inside. He was too big to deftly slip back inside, so Taral settled him on the outside, where sprays of mud no longer pelted their faces.[27]

On the second grandstand pass, the order was unchanged. Holladay was getting impatient through the second pass of the backstretch. He wanted to *Go!* and fought for his head. Taral's powerful arms strained to keep his mount in check until bending around the final turn. He let a link of rein slide and could barely control the accelerating horse on the fly. Whistling Con watched Holladay roll past. Jefferson was still in the lead but was tiring when arcing into the homestretch. Holladay leaped—one, two, three lengths ahead. He went charging past the finish and was tugging at his bridle, begging to keep running. Taral just let him go. Around they went, half a mile more, before Taral throttled the juggernaut down. Holladay kicked up his heels in play; he did not want the fun to end. Taral leaped off the horse and, flabbergasted, said, "Why he fairly ran away with me. My hand and arms are numb with holding him, and I could not pull him up after the finish . . . he is the greatest stayer I was ever on, and I don't know what weight would have stopped him today."[28]

Ben Holladay's racing season was over, and, with the horse racing season winding down across America, turf analysts began to write their reviews for 1898. Holladay was repeatedly mentioned, including this from one analyst:

> When the turf history of 1898 is written, the performances of no thoroughbred will receive greater praise than those of Ben Holladay, that is, if turf historians treat the subject justly. This horse proved himself not only a most consistent performer at all times, but his trio of victories during the fall meeting at Morris Park won the admiration and attention of lovers of horse flesh in all parts of the world . . . he is a horse that can undoubtedly hold his own at a distance against any animal on the turf to-day, no matter what country may claim a better. Had [he] lived in the days when long distance races were in vogue, he would have given the champions of that time a hard struggle for premier honors with the chances in his favor.

The Eastin and Larabie Stable relished its most successful year since its eastern racing debut in 1886. Holladay's career-high earnings netted $12,185 and were instrumental to the stable's historic year. The sum helped his famous sire, Hanover, reach the number-one spot on America's winning sires list

Ben Holladay. Only the greatest Thoroughbreds possessed the requisite speed and
strength to carry weighty imposts over long distances and make a titanic effort
look effortless. These preternatural weight carriers bulling around racetracks were
affectionately known as "stayers" or "iron horses." Iron horses like Ben Holladay were
all brute strength, stamina, and sheer will. They could cover the last furlong as swiftly as
the first. Iron horses were raced hard and were virtually unbeatable regardless of sore
legs and onerous imposts. Photo courtesy of USDA National Agricultural Library,
Beltsville, Maryland.

for a fourth year. Two more of Hanover's sons, Halma and Hamburg, were
regularly appearing in the winner's circle, too, earning thousands.[29]

Holladay turned six years old in 1899. He had reached turf star status at an
age when other famed Thoroughbred stallions were testing their genes as
sires. Samuel Larabie resisted that temptation. He was sure Holladay was up
for one more winning season. In early March at Churchill Downs, Holladay
recognized Peter Wimmer's voice coming from the shed row and, stretching
his head over the half door of his stall, frisked at his trainer. As Wimmer
affectionately stroked the horse's flannel-soft muzzle, he told a correspondent:

He's good and strong, and unless some accident happens to him in his training, he'll be fit as a fiddle when the eastern racing season begins. I am going to go slow with him and am not going to take any chance by pushing him too hard in his work. I don't think, though, that he is apt to meet with any mishaps in his work, as he's a horse that takes to training just like a duck takes to water. He's a great weight carrier and a good stayer of a distance of ground, besides having a nice turn of speed. . . . And as for gameness, they don't turn 'em out any better than this big fellow here.[30]

Wimmer added that his bosses were looking for a jockey. They had talked to several of America's best, but nothing had been decided. "Most of the boys want too much money and while we are willing to pay a good jockey what his services are worth, there's such a thing as overdoing it, you know," Wimmer said. "We want not only a good, strong boy, but one with a good head on him, a boy who is not easily rattled. That's the only kind of a boy fit to ride a big, strong horse, like Holladay." The bosses selected two. Fred Taral was engaged for Holladay's first four races, and "Iceman" Henry Spencer would then take the reins. The nervy Spencer was near the top of his profession in 1899, and the next year he would be at the top. For the first time since 1883 when the Eastin and Larabie Stable was founded, it would not be relying on a Black jockey. This was likely unintentional and simply a representation of the diminishing numbers of Black riders.[31]

⊷

The profession of jockey had long been viewed as unfit for even low-class white men. That perspective began to change around 1890. One prominent turf scribe of the era, Charles Trevathan, offered this 1900 perspective about putting whites in the saddle: "At one time existed in the south a strong prejudice against the employment of white boys in racing stables, a field of labor which was given over to the use of the negroes. That prejudice kept the white boys in the cornfields while the black ones went on, learned to ride races, and became great money earners. The passing of the prejudice mentioned probably accounts for the passing of the colored jockey." And it is likely that Trevathan's statement about Black jockeys' character raised eyebrows among the whites: "In the colored ranks are to be found jockeys of the most sterling honesty and integrity, and it is unfortunate that the same cannot be said of all the white jockeys."[32]

Contemporary turf historian Katherine Mooney writes in her book *Race Horse Men: How Slavery and Freedom Were Made at the Racetrack* that at many major racetracks, white jockeys "combined to intimidate and defeat black riders." She continued, "When wrapped up in a pack of flying horses on the backstretch, they tried to unseat black competitors, box them in, injure or kill them or scare them so badly that they quit racing." Mooney asserts further that whites deliberately intimidated owners and trainers who persisted in hiring Black reinsmen with threats, such as "the expensive horses would not be safe."[33]

Into the 1890s, Blacks faced increasing difficulty earning a living in a profession their forebears had helped create. Now that white society was comfortable with white men earning livelihoods as reinsmen, they commanded the lucrative contracts that the premier racing stables had once handed out to Black riders. Prejudice was not all to blame for the shift, according to *Abbott's Monthly* in 1932. The African American newspaper stated that in addition to prejudice, "bronze riders" abandoned the sport because of the infiltration of "big money" as well as scandal. While *Abbott's* did not cite a specific incident, one major instance of bronze rider scandal in 1894 involved New York racing and the Colored Trust. According to the *New York Times* in 1904, this coalition of "negro trainers and owners of horse races, allied by negro jockeys," brought about so much scandal through its gambling operations that turf authorities were forced to act against it.[34]

▬

In spring 1899, reports about Ben Holladay told of him "frisking" as if he were two years old. The troublesome foreleg of last season was "strong and healthy." Yet Holladay went amiss. He was unplaced in his first two starts, the Brooklyn Handicap and Suburban Handicap. He then earned third and second in the next two.[35]

Peter Wimmer could not make sense of it. The horse was healthy, training well, in good temper, and eating daily every bit of twelve quarts of oats and twenty pounds of hay. While Wimmer puzzled over four straight losses, the *New York Tribune* took aim at Fred Taral. Rating his riding in the Brooklyn

Handicap as "99 per cent below par," it also lampooned him as "a mosquito jockey." All four rides on Holladay were "thoroughly discreditable . . . stupid and bungling." Taral was once a top rider, but he should "retire to his road-house and stay there. . . . His usefulness is over." The *Tribune* advised Peter Wimmer to keep Fred Taral off Ben Holladay, but the point was moot. Taral's contractual commitment with Eastin and Larabie was met.[36]

Wimmer sidelined Ben Holladay for July and August. Meanwhile, enthusiastic crowds swarmed the nation's racetracks for summer racing. There was noise in New York City about what a headache it was to reach the venues. The city's first true mode of public transportation had appeared in the 1820s as the horse-drawn omnibus, a large stagecoach seating a dozen passengers. The buses traveled on public transit routes that wound around street blocks. The 1830s introduced the horsecar, a streamlined version of the omnibus moving on metal tracks anchored into the ground. Horseless transportation debuted as steam-powered cable cars in 1888. As the city moved into the 1890s, an estimated 170,000 to 200,000 horses moved 3.5 million New Yorkers. In hand with a large horse population came large quantities of dung and urine. All large metropolitan areas felt the pressing demand for reliable horseless transportation. Train systems and electric streetcars would be the game changers.[37]

Thousands of people arriving by horseless or horse-pulled transportation filed through the entryways at Sheepshead Bay on the afternoon of September 9. The Autumn Cup was on the card. Racegoers' faith in Holladay to pick up the iron-horse banner he had floated a season before was unabated. The three-to-one first choice in the nine-horse field, he would carry top weight of 126 pounds. Wimmer admitted to his friends his skepticism that Holladay could win the two-mile race.[38]

Bangle ripped to the front at flag fall but was quickly outfooted by Latson, with Muskadine lapping at Latson's heels. Holladay strained to join them through the early furlongs, but Henry Spencer fought back with a tight rein, forcing a conservative pace. The fight between those two continued well into the second mile. Spencer then loosened his grip, and Holladay launched into a tear of kangaroo leaps that easily outdistanced the front-runners. His speed picking up, he reeled down the track to defeat his outclassed foes by an eye-popping eight lengths. Spencer mustered every ounce of muscle to rein in his freewheeling mount. Halfway around the course, Ben Holladay's legs finally stopped spinning. Everyone's attention swung to the official time of

3:29, which took down the Sheepshead Bay course record by 2/5 of a second, a record Holladay himself already held, having set it in the 1897 Autumn Cup. Sweeter still, the aging iron horse carried twelve pounds more than he had in the 1897 victory.[39]

Holladay and Henry Spencer followed up the Autumn Cup with runner-up in the Second Special at Gravesend. The next start would be a record setter if they could pull off a third consecutive victory in the Municipal Handicap. On race day, October 14, a cerulean sky shone above a Morris Park racetrack surface in perfect condition. Wimmer was thankful for both. Still, a brutish 130-pound impost stood in the way as well as four contenders under a feathery 106, 110, 110, and 87 pounds. The disparity put some racegoers in a quandary. Holladay was the best horse, but it seemed fantastical that an old iron horse conceding that much weight could win a third Municipal Handicap at a mile and three-quarters. Nevertheless, Holladay was first pick.[40]

The group of five lined up for the starter, who sent them off without delay. Sir Hubert spun to the front; Warrenton and Ben Holladay side by side volleyed behind him. During the first run through the backstretch, Henry Spencer relaxed his custom of holding Holladay under a stiff pull early. Reins loose, the horse passed Sir Hubert, Warrenton, and Laverock. All desperately pummeled the track to keep him in reach. They might as well have chased an express train.[41]

At three lengths ahead, Holladay banked the final turn and swung into the homestretch. The crowd, wanting better views of the horse whose legs whirled like those of a stagecoach team on the fly, jumped from their seats. His lead was six lengths when he reached the wire. And Spencer did not pull him up. Holladay ran another half mile before he had had enough. The time, 3:00 ½, fell short of the 2:59 ¼ record he had set in the Municipal Handicap two years ago. Even so, his performance was unequaled in American turf history three times over—Ben Holladay the only horse, Peter Wimmer the only trainer, and Eastin and Larabie the only owners to have won three Municipal Handicaps, and, astonishingly, in consecutive years.[42]

On Saturday, October 21, Holladay was set to run in the Morris Park Handicap. A bright, sunny sky lighted a racetrack in mint condition. The field would be a more competitive one than on the previous Saturday. Warrenton and Laverock were repeating; Muskadine, Carnero, and Ethelbert were the new faces. Racing secretary Walter Vosburgh socked Holladay with 140 pounds, a panting weight for the strenuous two and a quarter miles. The swift three-year-old Ethelbert received 117, and Vosburgh's allocations for the rest of the field were lighter still. "Mr. Vosburgh is certainly determined that Ben Holladay will not win the long-distance race at Morris Park this afternoon without effort," the *Brooklyn Daily Eagle* declared on race day. Racegoers thought the contest would go to either Holladay or Ethelbert. At post time, wagering slightly favored Ethelbert.[43]

Upon the twirl of the starter's flag, Warrenton and Ethelbert bolted to the front and struck a fast clip for two miles. Through the final quarter where the trailers fired up speed, Warrenton, Ethelbert, Carnero, Laverock, and Ben Holladay were heads apart, to the delight of ten thousand screaming fans. When rounding Holladay through the turn for home, Henry Spencer eased his grip on the reins and chirped *Go!* The horse, pummeling the racetrack even faster, pulled past Ethelbert, and Spencer was certain they had the race won until he spotted a blur blitzing along the rail. Muskadine! Spencer was frantic and shouted, *Faster!* The furious rush of horses and jockeys and colors flashed past the wire with Muskadine, a twenty-to-one long shot and weighted with 106 pounds, eclipsing Holladay, second, and Ethelbert, third.[44]

The thunderstruck racegoers settled down to recount to each other the thrilling action they had just witnessed, saying the race was the best they had seen in years. They would never forget Ben Holladay's monumental effort. Though defeated in the Morris Park Handicap, Holladay earned widespread acclaim, including this from the *Spirit of the Times*:

> Ben Holladay, undoubtedly the best of them all over a cup course, finished his turf career in great style, and although defeated . . . he ran the greatest race of his career; and even with the crusher of 140 pounds to carry over this two-mile and a quarter route, a stronger pace for the last half mile and the stout-hearted Hanover horse would have won. My reason for saying so is that Ben Holladay is possessed of such extraordinary stamina that when thoroughly keyed up as he was in his last effort, he will stand a drive further and keep coming under pressure with more resolute and indomitable courage than most horses I have ever seen race.

Amassing sixty trips to the post during five campaigns, the sixtieth marked his final race. Holladay recorded seventeen wins, nineteen seconds, thirteen thirds, a world record, and three course records. Earnings were slightly more than $36,000. The following April, Peter Wimmer was back at work with the Eastin and Larabie string. After five seasons with Ben Holladay, he admitted that his work without him felt "quite lonely."[45]

◄►

Samuel Larabie and Augustine Eastin sold Ben Holladay to J. B. Haggin in February 1901. The stallion stayed five years at the Elmendorf Farm, another of Haggin's Thoroughbred breeding farms, this one near Lexington. At thirteen years old, Holladay was en route to a new home at the Agricultural and Mechanical College of the State of Mississippi in Starkville, where a new "breeding bureau" was in the works. A photograph of Holladay and the Hutchinson Agricultural Club members who cared for him appeared in the 1907 yearbook, *Reveille.*

Ben Holladay sired numerous outstanding broodmare daughters whose foals defined a new generation of champions. One noteworthy daughter, Ophirdale, is a classic example of a "blue hen," a term rooted in the Thoroughbred racing world that has since bled into other breeds. Blue hen mares produce winner after winner no matter the stallion, which alludes to the mare's own genetic power. Such mares are instrumental in a genetic shift within a breed. Ophirdale taprooted an important line that famously produced Whirlaway, the Triple Crown winner of 1941.[46]

When twentieth-century turf scribes wrote about the wonderful colts and fillies of their era, they sometimes measured them against the greats of the previous century. In October 1920, for instance, a Massachusetts scribe marveled over a big red colt named Man o' War. The upstart colt "seemed to have everything" a racehorse could possibly want. To quantify his statement, the writer chose Domino to emphasize quickness, Hamburg for strength, Henry of Navarre for courage, and Ben Holladay for endurance.[47]

In 1922, Exterminator was on the scene, not in the sensational sense like Man o' War but as a grinding handicap star whose weight-carrying feats ensured him iron-horse status. One admiring New York turf scribe penned, "There is much about the physique of this splendid gelding that suggests Ben Holladay, the champion American cup horse of the late nineties [who won races] at two miles and one quarter, and under heavier burdens than Exterminator has been shouldering. The sort of tasks set before old Ben have not yet been put before Exterminator."[48]

Kinley Mack

"Child of Mist"

During June 16–18, 1896, the city of St. Louis was teeming with Republicans. At hand was the responsibility of selecting a presidential candidate for the November election, with Ohio-born William McKinley as a front-runner. While not a handsome man, McKinley had a prominent forehead, Roman nose, and sharply chiseled mouth that lent him the look of a dignified statesman. McKinley's distinguished service in the Union Army and rank of brevet major appealed to Americans. Republican delegates respected his diverse political experience and exemplary character. Upon the first vote for a presidential nominee on June 18, the delegates unanimously chose William McKinley as their candidate.

The Democrats met in Chicago in July. They chose as their candidate a Nebraska lawyer, William Jennings Bryan. Younger than McKinley and less experienced politically, Jennings was a charismatic orator whose eloquent speeches energized and mesmerized audiences. On November 3, 1896, Americans passed over Bryan in favor of McKinley as their twenty-fifth president. Though McKinley won both the Electoral College and popular vote, his sweep of most of America did not include Montana. Democrats there, it was said, were "plentiful as fleas on a dog's tail."[1]

Montana had at least one Republican in its expanse, the horseman Samuel Larabie, who needed a name for a well-bred colt. In 1896, Larabie sent off his request, McKinley, to the Jockey Club in New York, the official registrar of Thoroughbred horses. Larabie received disappointing news from the club. McKinley had already been granted as a name. Larabie tried President McKinley. That name, too, had been requested and granted. After a bit of transposing, Larabie made his successful request, Kinley Mack.[2]

The Jockey Club, by use of *The American Stud Book*, tracked Thoroughbred bloodlines. The criterion for a genealogically acceptable Thoroughbred horse as decreed by the author, Sanders D. Bruce, called for "an uncontaminated pedigree of five generations." Before the book's existence, horsemen scrutinized and charted pedigrees, but breeding records for American-bred Thoroughbreds were frustratingly sparse and inconsistent. A pedigree registry was first attempted in 1833, but the book by Patrick Nisbet Edgar was as famous for its omissions as its inclusions. Colonel Sanders D. Bruce, a Kentuckian, had spent years researching American Thoroughbred pedigrees. Bruce's first volume of *The American Stud Book* was published in 1873. This accepted registry would expand to multiple volumes, with the Jockey Club assuming the book's publication in 1896.[3]

The details of the day and place where Larabie first laid eyes on the mare Songstress are lost. While Thoroughbreds may be marked with a star, a blaze, and socks, white markings generally do not appear on the body. If Larabie thought he would find a speck of white marring her dark blood bay coat, he was wrong. Songstress was foaled at Kennesaw Stud, Williamson County, Tennessee, in 1886. Smooth lines and curves told of her exquisite English ancestors. Given a turn on the racetrack as a filly, she washed out and was sold to John Mackey, at the time in a partnership with Larabie. Songstress was so striking that Larabie asked Mackey for exclusive ownership of her. Mackey granted his partner's request.[4]

Her service as a Willow Run broodmare stopped temporarily when she was moved to J. B. Haggin's Rancho del Paso, where she was mated to English-bred Islington. Lackluster on the racetrack, Islington in the stud was in full throttle of propagating explosive progeny. Songstress foaled their son Kinley Mack at Rancho in 1896. He was sent to Willow Run where he entangled his legs in a wire fence. The harder he tried to free himself, the more damage to his legs. Because Kinley Mack was sweet tempered, he permitted his caregiver to spend weeks, maybe months, treating his injured legs. Month by month his legs healed. His coltish body lengthened and thickened. The white star shone brightly on his nearly black forehead. At 16.2 hands, Kinley Mack was tall and rangy and stood over a lot of ground.[5]

In May 1898, Peter Wimmer departed Louisville with sixteen Eastin and Larabie Thoroughbreds. Their first stop was Brighton Beach Racecourse on Coney Island, New York. At what point in Kinley Mack's career his trouble-plagued feet began bothering him is unclear, but this might explain why Wimmer would risk losing a beautifully bred two-year-old colt in a claiming race, or "claimer." The entries in claiming races were for sale at a set price, and buyers could purchase a runner until shortly before the race started. Or perhaps Wimmer was put off by the colt's affability. "He is as amiable in his stall and on the track as a four-month-old Newfoundland pup," the *Lexington Daily Leader* stated, adding that a child could lead him "about all day with one finger."[6]

On July 6, 1898, Kinley Mack carried the Eastin and Larabie silks of red jacket, white sash, and blue and white cap for the first time. He could be claimed for $800, but nobody wanted him, and he and eleven other jittery maidens went postward. The poor start favored Rare Perfume, who scrambled ahead of the jumble. She led the race all the way into the home-stretch, where The Gardner swished past her, but The Gardner could not stave off Kinley Mack through the final drive. One New York turf scribe added political banter to his race summary, writing, "The invincibility of the American President was uncouthly emphasized in the second race, when a colt named Kinley Mack beat eleven other maiden two-year-olds. The winner was quoted at 15-to-1 and proved too fast at the finish for The Gardner, whom he beat by a length."[7]

Peter Wimmer's luck held at Saratoga on July 28. Kinley Mack, reaching the post unclaimed, went on to win his race. Wimmer never again risked losing Kinley Mack in a claimer. At the same time, Wimmer also knew better than to look too far ahead, and, as if to affirm his need for restraint, Kinley Mack ran ninth and fourth in the next two starts. He went postward for the Grand Union Hotel Stakes at Saratoga and delivered a solid performance as runner-up. This deep in the season, his proclivity on the track was that of a closer. [8]

The next stop was the Sheepshead Bay Racecourse, set down on Coney Island in 1880. Four years later, the Coney Island Jockey Club lengthened the one-mile dirt course by an eighth of a mile. The Sheepshead Bay venue now boasted America's longest racetrack. A grass course was built, and the grandstand was eventually expanded to three tiers that offered enormous seating capacity, with racegoers spilling onto the rooftop to enjoy views of the bay and the Atlantic. Also on race days, the Sheepshead Bay band played popular tunes. Bracing sea breezes carried the pleasant sounds from inside the music pavilion to the clubhouse and the distant shed rows.[9]

Sheepshead Bay's rival racetrack was Morris Park, and although the latter was regarded as America's most lavish racing venue, racegoers complained of their lack of proximity to the track. Not much of the racing could be seen with the naked eye. The action at Sheepshead Bay could easily be seen from start to finish. Racegoers also liked the smell of the ocean-scented air, and the cries of seagulls wafting over the grounds where stands of beech and maple trees shaded lawns and flower gardens.[10]

Kinley Mack must have liked Sheepshead Bay's salubrious seaside setting. In thirteen days he spun three wins in three starts. Wimmer tried him in the Junior Championship at the Gravesend track on September 18. The race marked his first start in a major event. The field of fourteen edgy, spring-loaded two-year-olds stirred up ninety minutes of chaos at the post before the starter finally got them off. Kinley Mack had an awful start and finished sixth in this final race of his two-year-old campaign.[11]

◼

Optimism for Kinley Mack's future was guarded in spring 1899. His legs and feet always ached from a form of equine osteoarthritis, otherwise known as ringbone. A second ailment, this one unnamed but described as a "peculiar kind," caused the colt's forefeet to bruise easily. Wimmer administered treatment but eventually resorted to specialized aluminum shoes. Grooms stood by with rolls of cotton batting for wrapping the forelegs. Bandaging the legs kept them warm and improved the blood circulation to the feet. All four legs remained wrapped except when the horse exercised or raced.[12]

Ridership during the season would alternate between Fred Taral and Henry Spencer, and Patsy McCue got the call on June 17 at Sheepshead Bay.

Kinley Mack's first race at three years old was an ordinary purse. Competing against eight, McCue and the colt fizzled to sixth. Then they had a good eight days and rebounded with second, second, and first. At Brighton Beach in July, they netted second.[13]

They stayed hot at Saratoga in July and August. They reeled off three wins and in one they successfully carried a career-high impost of 126 pounds. In the six-horse Omnium Handicap on September 2, Kinley Mack, under the field's heaviest impost of 121 pounds, came home fourth. His 1899 season looked pretty good on paper, five wins in ten starts and earnings of $8,470. The Eastin and Larabie Stable overall amassed $31,444, topping the previous high-water mark set one year ago. Yet New York scribes were lukewarm about Kinley Mack. They claimed that he had raced against disproportionate competition and the record was therefore hollow.[14]

◼

On New Year's Day 1900, American horse racing was unrivaled in popularity and drew record-breaking attendance as it bridged the twentieth century. As summer languished in New York City, Chicago, and St. Louis, tens of thousands of people filled the racetrack grandstands weekly. Correspondingly in 1900, the sport of baseball, regarded as America's favorite pastime, drew around thirty thousand fans. Baseball was slumping. As the *St. Louis Republic* pointed out about the two sports in competition in its city, "Operating on the same block [and] on the same street [as the baseball field], with the same transportation facilities, the same distance from the center of city populations, under the same disadvantages of the street-car strike, the Fair Grounds Jockey Club has had the most successful meeting of its career." The *Republic* unable to make sense of it said that the horses and jockeys in competition at Fair Grounds were "the poorest in America," whereas the boys playing baseball were "properly regarded" as America's finest. All summer long, the racehorse at the Fair Grounds had "outdrawn the ball player three to one right down the line." The *Republic* waxed on, "In St. Louis, one can name 100 people offhand who have abandoned baseball to take up golf. . . . Cycling, too, has helped to wean people from the game of the eighties, the game which was the only game, the sight which was the only sight. But racing has been baseball's strongest foe, rival, and most deadly enemy. That it seems to be getting the upper hand no one will deny."[15]

◄►

The twenty-one horses under Peter Wimmer's care at Louisville, Kentucky, in April 1900 combined two stables, those of William C. Whitney and Eastin and Larabie. The arrangement brought together "probably the greatest string of Thoroughbreds trained by one man" and, indeed, would advance fifty-seven-year-old Wimmer to the pinnacle of his career. Wimmer was especially high on Jean Beraud, the prized four-year-old in the Whitney stable. The horse was a terrific two-year-old in 1898, firing off seven consecutive wins before cooling off. Hot again in 1899, Jean Beraud swept up the Withers Stakes before cleaning up at the Belmont Stakes.[16]

Wimmer moved Jean Beraud and Kinley Mack from winter quarters at Churchill Downs to the stables at Sheepshead Bay. The important Brooklyn Handicap would kick off Kinley Mack's campaign with several prestigious events scheduled, and notably, he would face tougher competition than in 1899. Patsy McCue, who was engaged to ride the four-year-old horse, was a top reinsman, but his riding increasingly mirrored his erratic behavior on and off the track. Turf scribes in New York supposed a sunny afternoon for the Brooklyn Handicap at Gravesend and a racetrack perfectly prepared for America's fleetest flyers. The scribes picked their favorites and made predictions on the assumption of a fast track.

That all went out the window on May 24, the day before the race and the day Wimmer moved his horses to Gravesend. Sheets of rain tapped stable roofs for hours. When the downpour quit during the night, the grounds crew jumped from their beds and rushed outside. They hoed and harrowed the racetrack the rest of the night and into the murky sunrise. They could do little to improve the horrible conditions. Weathermen predicted improving conditions throughout Brooklyn Handicap Day, but glancing skyward at low gray clouds, the crew shook their heads doubtfully. By afternoon, dark clouds hung over the track like a funeral pall. Rain fell in sheets. The thirteenth running of the Brooklyn was all but handed over to the mudders, who were unfazed at the prospect of circling a waterlogged, chocolate-dough oval. Unperturbed by losing a shot at the winner's purse worth $7,800, trainer

Andrew Jackson Joyner withdrew his good colt, Ethelbert. Peter Wimmer, fearing Jean Beraud might injure himself on the slippery mud, scratched that valuable colt. Both horses were big favorites.[17]

Twenty thousand spectators spat rude words into the damp, raw wind as they thumbed race programs to hunt up a new candidate on which to bet. The savvy betting men wise to Kinley Mack's achy legs and feet understood the cushioning effect of a racetrack fetlock deep in mud, most likely an advantage for the big bay horse. They were likewise familiar with Raffaello, whose prerace workouts smoked, but too often when looking unbeatable he would turn in a clunker. The six-year-old race mare Imp was last year's Suburban winner, but this season she had lost all five of her starts, though never worse than third. She did whatever was asked of her in the way of speed, athleticism, and heart—except when asked to do it in mud, which she loathed. Meanwhile, the betting ring was operating in chaos. With each scratch, bookmakers refigured prices. The new bets were no sooner registered than word came of another scratch, and with it the crush of men, each trying to reach a stand where bookmaking began anew.[18]

The entries for the Brooklyn Handicap numbered eighteen at sunrise. By 4:10 P.M., at the sound of the bugle, there were nine. The rain poured as Imp, fifth favorite at eight to one and under top weight of 128 pounds, led the wet parade. Weak applause floated from the grandstand. Less was heard for the favorite, Raffaello, under 113 pounds and two to one, and for third favorite Kinley Mack, under 122 pounds and with Patsy McCue on board. The remaining six horses filed onto the track.[19]

The wall of rain obscured the line of vision across the field to where the horses spread out in a horizontal line and waited. Spectators could not see the quick start, nor that Batten was first to poke out his nose. King Barleycorn threw a few strides and poked his nose out in front of Batten's. Knight of the Garter was next in the order, then Imp, then Kinley Mack. Noses separated the five horses.[20]

After the first quarter mile, Knight of the Garter plowed through the slop to pull ahead of King Barleycorn. Over the next quarter mile of slippery surface, spectators saw hardly more than a moving blur as positions changed back and forth. King Barleycorn regained the lead, and Kinley Mack, second, trailed him by a neck. Thereafter, the lead switched between those two, with Imp running third.[21]

Spectators pressed against the rail could hear the dull, frantic under-tone of the front-runners' hooves as they banked the final turn. King Barleycorn pumped the last of his speed and began to fade during the run for the wire. Kinley Mack now led the charge. The jockeys riding the trailers whipped their mounts to keep them close to Kinley Mack's heels spewing mud. Patsy McCue, wanting to glance over the field, looked over both his shoulders for a rear view. It looked good but, unwilling to risk miscalculation because of the rain, McCue stayed folded and still, loos-ened his wrap on the reins, and gave Kinley Mack his head. Legs and feet churning lightning fast drove him. He flashed past the wire one length ahead of the pack. "Kinley Mack wins!" A man at the rail jumped wildly and clapped. Again he yelled, "Kinley Mack wins!" drawing stares from his neighbors. He tried again to rouse them. Once more, "Kinley Mack wins!" Silence. He gave up.[22]

Officials scooped up Patsy McCue and seated him inside the horseshoe decorated with flowers, the sport's version of a throne for the victorious jockey and reserved for America's most important races. McCue was paraded in front of the grandstand, where the dejected crowd gave smatterings of applause. Despite two more races on the card, waves of racegoers seeking relief from the dispiriting weather and sour result of the Brooklyn Handicap emptied from the Gravesend compound.[23]

The next morning the New York Times was howling over the Brooklyn Handicap being in all ways a fiasco. It cursed the rain that forced trainers to scratch the aces, saying that the stripped-down field was slightly better than "a lot of selling platers." The focus of the competing New York Tribune was a race honestly won: "Nothing in the starting, nothing in the riding, nothing in the incidents of the contest, gave Kinley Mack an unfair advantage." Nor was the Brooklyn "a truly great race," the Tribune acknowledged, "not a truly great horse that won it, not a truly great jockey who rode the win-ner." But a solid performance on a racetrack soaked in rain did earn Kinley Mack regard from the Tribune: "He is a child of mist, and never neglect him when the air is drenched, and the ground is soaked."[24]

Four days later, the dry, fast track at Gravesend staged the Parkway Handi-cap. Imp was in command of the six-horse race from the start, with her lead reaching five lengths, and only then did Patsy McCue feel a sense of urgency. His whip sang in the air and cut Kinley Mack's glossy coat. The colt bolted forward but could not gain an inch on Imp, buoyed by the crowd's

Kinley Mack. When this colt began his ascent in eastern racing, Augustine Eastin said, "In time he ought to prove a better horse than Ben Holladay." Photo courtesy of Keeneland Library General Collection.

cheers. The little mare led wire to wire, won her race by two lengths, and set a track record. The *Topeka State Journal*, after screeching at McCue for his "wretched" handling of his mount, ventured that "with a good rider, Kinley Mack would have beaten [Imp] by several lengths."[25]

Accounts of Patsy McCue's early years are contradictory, but all acknowledge Jim Dillon as responsible for lifting the boy from obscurity. As he competed with other newsboys hawking newspapers on a Brooklyn ferry dock, McCue's shouts ticked louder when headlines decreed names of great racehorses and the men who rode them: THE CHAMPION HORSE JOCKEY: FRED TARAL IS SAID TO BE THE BEST RIDER IN THE WORLD. Perhaps McCue thought he could ride a Thoroughbred horse as well as Fred Taral. Maybe a shade better.[26]

Trainers were always looking for small, lightweight boys to take on as apprentices. One day Jim Dillon strode over to the boy and struck up a conversation. The introduction probably happened in 1896, the year McCue turned fourteen. The trainer liked what he heard. McCue quit his newsboy job and moved away from the comfortable home he shared with his aunt after his parents had died.[27]

The boy, who wanted to be a jockey right away, grew bored rubbing down racehorses. One day he vanished. Dillon had no idea where he could be. Somebody had put a bug in the kid's ear about the Bitter Root Stock Farm near Hamilton, Montana, where a millionaire turfman by the name of Marcus Daly operated an extensive Thoroughbred farm. McCue turned up there and was hired as an exercise rider. This was probably in 1897. On weekday afternoons, McCue and the other exercise riders were sent to the public school for classes, but McCue mostly studied hometown girl Stella Parmenter. He was instantly in love.[28]

Even with Stella energizing his life, Patsy McCue was bored stiff with exercising horses, no matter if they were world class. Alcohol helped relieve the tedium. The trainer at the Bitter Root, Matthew Byrnes, tried to keep the boy sober. When that proved pointless, Byrnes purchased a train ticket and shipped McCue back to Brooklyn.[29]

Jim Dillon agreed to take him on as an apprentice jockey. The kid slogged through the lowly claiming races. On the afternoon of August 6, 1898, at Brighton Beach, he got a leg up on Belgravia, trained by Dillon and owned by former heavyweight champ James Corbett. Odds laid on Belgravia ranged from thirty to one, to one hundred to one. Belgravia and McCue were off. Using his hands and chirping to his mount, McCue inspired the colt to rocket from eighth to first and beat nine rivals. McCue rode red hot in November at the Bennings Racecourse in Washington, DC. On the thirtieth, the closing day of the fall meeting at Bennings, McCue piloted five winners in six races. In all of November he rode fifteen mounts, and none finished unplaced. McCue was the "sensation of the year" and at the top of his profession.[30]

He won some credible races early in 1899 before professional troubles started. On May 31 at Gravesend, his mount A.N.B. was four lengths in front and driving toward the finish when McCue looked over his shoulder and began laughing at the trailers. McCue lost his concentration, and so did A.N.B. Jockey George Odom spurred his mount Pirate M. along the inner rail and won the race. On June 14, McCue delivered a "ghastly" ride on Vesuvian, and another one on Little Saint in the Swift Stakes on June 22. In the latter, McCue "committed almost every fault which it is possible for a jockey to commit," the *New York Tribune* declared. Five days later with Nash Turner in the stirrups, Little Saint was, according to the *Tribune*, all "dazzling speed and form" when winning her race. McCue's next suspect ride was astride the reliable race mare May Hempstead. He was astride her for the prestigious Brighton Handicap on July 6, and her performance, according to the *Brooklyn Standard Union*, was "shockingly bad." Over at the *Tribune*, scribes repeatedly reported the sorry ways McCue's mounts "crawled feebly and pitifully" and lampooned him as "misfit McCue" or "Miscue McCue." By mid-July, the newspaper alleged that he was the "pet" jockey of a "cutthroat clique of the shrewdest and most unscrupulous professional gamblers in the United States." With corruption in the sport problematic, the *Tribune* was not wrong to ask, "How long do track officials think it will be before New York stamps out racing if such wrongs go unchecked and unpunished?"[31]

McCue's suspicious riding warranted trips to the stewards' office, but no action was taken. Three months of suspected unethical riding at three racetracks did not slip past the big gun, however. On September 13, 1899, the Jockey Club cited "indifferent or dishonest riding" and suspended McCue indefinitely. The club would refuse to reinstate him until he provided certain facts about his odd and erratic performances. Presumably he cooperated; McCue's license to ride was renewed on May 11, 1900. More than one turfman grumbled about it, and when hearing that McCue was riding for Peter Wimmer, they puzzled over Wimmer's peculiar preference for "that cunning little rascal . . . one of the craftiest rascals ever known on the American turf."[32]

◼

The names of Ethelbert and Jean Beraud hung in the air as favorites for the Suburban Handicap on June 16, 1900. Americans eagerly anticipated the spring classic they had popularized since 1884, the year the Coney Island Jockey Club organized the first running. The mile-and-a-quarter event at Sheepshead Bay consistently attracted first-class racehorses. Peter Wimmer's horse New Jersey–bred Jean Beraud, had been trounced two weeks earlier when matched against America's other premier racehorse, Ethelbert.[33]

In the Ethelbert camp, future Hall of Fame trainer Andrew Jackson Joyner was near the apex of his career. He was, however, already famous on America's racetracks for the rebel yell which he used to cheer his runners in a hard-fought finish. Aside from Ethelbert's defeat of Jean Beraud, Joyner had sent the four-year-old horse to victory in the important Metropolitan

Handicap. Ethelbert was Kentucky bred, but New Yorkers regarded him as a native son by way of ownership, that of Perry Belmont, a New Yorker and son of the late August Belmont I.[34]

Coal-black Imp might be the spoiler, however. The winner of last year's Suburban Handicap, her victory was historic. Imp was the first of her gender to win the Suburban. Her triumph was no fluke; she scored more noteworthy victories and earned honors. Meanwhile, only a handful of turf scribes considered Kinley Mack a contender, though he could win the Suburban on the chance of a misty day and muddy racetrack.[35]

On June 16, the springlike sky in bright shades of blue all but promised Ethelbert a win. In all quarters of New York City and across the nation, nearly everyone believed that speed-loaded Ethelbert would run away with the Suburban and winner's purse valued at $6,800. Swarms of people mobilized toward Sheepshead Bay, as they did every year for the grand race. Private and public conveyances crowded every avenue. Lines of people waited on the docks to board ferries. The trains were full, as were the trolley cars, with bells jangling and clusters of men hanging on from the rear platforms or the steps, and some riding atop the roofs. Wagons, traps, dogcarts, and squads of hacks of all kinds transported commoners to Sheepshead Bay. The wealthiest racegoers rode inside elegant coaches. Some people commuted by automobile, which prompted the *New York Sun* to remark, "This method of reaching the track is growing more popular every day."[36]

Thousands of people funneled through the brass turnstiles at Sheepshead Bay. Ladies of high society strolled the grounds on the arms of escorts whose black attire offset the ladies' butterfly-bright gowns trimmed with flounces and lace. Jaunty feathered hats and fluttering velvet ribbons gave the matrons a fresh, youthful look as they promenaded between the attractions. From the music pavilion, the band's rousing tunes enlivened everyone's step. Gardens of yellow, orange, red, and blue flowers bordering the walkways bounced to sea-tinged breezes, as if nodding the way to the paddock. The lawns never seemed so green.[37]

Chestnuts, blacks, browns, and bays were on view in the paddock. The ten-horse field was superb. In great handicap races like the Suburban, imposts could differ by more than thirty pounds. Thirty-four pounds was the spread for the 1900 contest. The three bay-colored favorites—Ethelbert, Jean Beraud, and Kinley Mack—carried top weights of 130, 127, and 125 pounds, respectively. The coal-black mare Imp shouldered a 128-pound load.[38]

Jockeys abounded. Nash Turner, dressed in silks of vivid blue, waited for a leg up on Jean Beraud. Maroon and scarlet singled out Danny Maher and Ethelbert. A suit of orange and black glistened on Winnie O'Connor, whose black boots clipped as he scooted around restless Imp. Patsy McCue looked dashing in his red jacket with white sash as he stood beside his mount and overheard a well-known turfman remark, "There's Kinley Mack. He won the Brooklyn Handicap, but that was an accident." McCue fired back, "Keep an eye on me just the same."[39]

At four o'clock, the bugler summoned the Suburban field to the racetrack, which was dry on the surface but damp underneath. The jockeys rode their mounts to the post. Spectators watched the flashy silks glinting under the afternoon sun. A wave of thunderous applause welcomed Ethelbert, the six-to-five favorite and looking magnificent. The spectators murmured, "How can they beat him?" Jean Beraud at five to one was next to parade, and then Imp marched past the grandstand. She was at four and a half. The ladies waved lacy handkerchiefs for her. Kinley Mack's entrance enthused shouts from the small contingent of westerners who made the western horse their ten-to-one pick.[40]

The jockeys and mounts circled to behind the barrier. Bits jingled before the barrier torpedoed skyward. The line lurched forward in a false start. Ethelbert roared down the racetrack the farthest, and Danny Maher required a few minutes to wrest the colt back to the line. The second attempt was another false start. Ethelbert again ran a fair distance before Maher, stopping him, rounded him back to the post. Eight minutes had passed since starter Fitzgerald's first attempt. The barrier flew upward a third time. Fitzgerald signaled a fair start. Spectators leaped to their feet. "They're off!"[41]

Imp, Jean Beraud, and Kinley Mack jumped into their strides. Ethelbert, fourth, was boxed in a pocket, and Danny Maher yanked back on the reins to avert a collision and redirect the horse. Those few seconds cost them precious field position, now trailing in seventh. Patsy McCue held Kinley Mack third. Legs whirled in rhythmic strides as the field skipped over the first quarter mile. Jean Beraud inched past front-running Imp and extended his lead to a length through the next quarter.[42]

At three-quarters of a mile, Jean Beraud's advantage over Imp was a neck, and she a neck in front of Kinley Mack. Ethelbert was no better than sixth. Ethelbert's backers were beginning to smell an upset, and they rallied, "Come on!" They yelled louder at the sight of both Kinley Mack and forty-to-one long shot Gulden overtaking Jean Beraud and Imp. Then, as the horses passed the one-mile marker, "There comes Ethelbert!" was the volley of cries. He passed both Jean Beraud and Imp as if they were motionless and now chased front-running Gulden and Kinley Mack. "Whip him, Maher!" came the shouts. Maher was already whipping Ethelbert to ribbons. "Whip him!"

Patsy McCue, glancing over both shoulders, saw the good-sized gap of daylight separating Kinley Mack from Ethelbert and Gulden. Feeling comfortable he had them safely beaten, McCue relaxed his rigid muscles. Kinley Mack in full flight charged toward the finish, where a seething, shouting, jumping sea of humanity pressed itself along the rail. He swept past the wire first, followed by Ethelbert a length and a half behind, Gulden third, Imp fourth, and Jean Beraud sixth.[43]

McCue slowed Kinley Mack down and rounded him back to the portal of people who stood silent and motionless, still in wonder over Ethelbert's definitive defeat. Andrew Jackson Joyner immediately recognized the result as history-making. In the sixteen-year combined histories of the Suburban Handicap and Brooklyn Handicap, Kinley Mack was first to win both crowns in the same year. Samuel Larabie and Augustine Eastin were the first owners, and Peter Wimmer the first trainer. Joyner, a future Hall of Famer, was the first of the trainers to shake Wimmer's hand. Patsy McCue swung off of Kinley Mack. The Sheepshead Bay crew seated him in the floral horseshoe to put him on show in front of the grandstand. Despite most spectators' disappointment with the result, they warmed up to Patsy McCue. He was, after all, a Brooklyn born native son and had smartly piloted Kinley Mack. Bits of applause filtered down to the racetrack. A smile spread across the young jockey's face.[44]

CHAPTER 9

"Two of the Biggest Coon Skins"

Five days after Kinley Mack's historic Suburban Handicap victory, the sport of politics was thrilling crowds of Philadelphians. The Republican National Convention was under way in their city. On June 21, 1900, chairman Henry Cabot Lodge walked to the front of the stage to announce to the delegates that the votes cast for President William McKinley totaled 930, and that this was unanimous. McKinley would be the Republican presidential candidate a second time. The Democrats convened in July in Kansas City. As they had in 1896, they chose as their candidate William Jennings Bryan. McKinley and vice president nominee Theodore Roosevelt launched their campaign against Bryan and vice president nominee Adlai Ewing Stevenson.[1]

Some of the nation's newspapers could not resist mixing up the result of the Suburban with politics. From the *Brooklyn Daily Eagle*, "Kinley Mack, as many have doubtless divined, is a transposed phonetic version of the name of our President, McKinley. Some jokes were negotiated upon the basis yesterday, one Brooklyn Democrat remarking that McKinley would never be a double winner. To which a companion of Republican proclivities replied, 'He will, though. And he won't be a dark horse.'" The *Daily Leader* in Lexington bemoaned Samuel Larabie not only for his Republican leanings but for burdening Kinley Mack with a "particularly absurd" name. Absurd, perhaps, but according to Wisconsin's *Dunn County News*, "There is a winning sound to the name."[2]

The horse should have been an instant turf star in 1900, but too many people resisted the idea of Kinley Mack as a first-class racehorse. Bad weather and a cushy racetrack were advantages in the Brooklyn Handicap, and the spoils thrown to him in the Suburban Handicap were owed to Ethelbert's bad luck. The two false starts were cited, as was Ethelbert's heavy impost, and early in the race he had been pinched in a pocket. The *Daily Inter Mountain* in Butte, sick and tired of national newspapers' constant downplaying of

Montana's best racehorses, quoted a popular Kentucky maxim: "Show me the barn with the most coon skins nailed to it, and I will show you who owns the best coon dog." Kinley Mack, after all, had "nailed two of the biggest coon skins in the woods to his owner's barn."[3]

The *Inter Mountain* might have cringed when Kinley Mack finished seventh in his next race, the Brighton Handicap, but Ethelbert at eighth was worse. One month later, on August 9 at Saratoga Springs, everyone was talking up Ethelbert, who in ten days knocked out back-to-back wins and set speed records. So, on the day of the Beverwyck Handicap, racegoers feverishly wagered on red-hot Ethelbert, but all six of the racehorses, including Kinley Mack, were first class.[4]

The webbed barrier was not in use at the post that afternoon. Starter Caldwell preferred to work in the old style of a flying start. When he dropped the flag, the line of horses faced every which way. Patsy McCue, never expecting the mess could warrant a fair start, pulled up Kinley Mack only to discover that Caldwell had indeed signaled a fair start. Jockey Nash Turner and Ethelbert were even worse off. Ethelbert was facing the wrong way at flag drop. Both Nash and McCue righted their mounts and hastened over the racetrack.[5]

The field was already a long five lengths ahead and moving like lightning. Turner inched Ethelbert to the outside. McCue spotted an opening along the rail and slipped Kinley Mack through. Another avenue opened, and another. They slipped through those. The field swung through the final turn and straightened for the homestretch run. Kinley Mack and Ethelbert were nearly stride for stride when catching front-running Maritmas, and Kinley Mack, pulling slightly ahead of Ethelbert, beat him by the margin of a head. Ethelbert's backers were furious over both the result and starter Caldwell, at whom they screamed, hooted, and hissed.[6]

Two weeks later at Saratoga, Kinley Mack finished third in the Citizen and Merchants Handicap. After making seven straight starts with Kinley Mack, why Patsy McCue missed the latter race is unclear. Turning eighteen years old in 1900, he had been serious about his riding and was consistently winning. He was earning thousands of dollars but also squandering thousands. He would drop $1,000 on baskets of champagne for friends and strangers who were making merry in expensive hotels where he might soak in a Turkish bath. He liked to buy expensive gifts for people, and he donated liberally to charities and charity cases, such as stableboys in need of clothing.[7]

McCue was astride Kinley Mack for the two-mile Autumn Cup on August 29 at Sheepshead Bay. The horse, making his first attempt at two miles, not only showed inordinately wicked velocity as he swished past the furlong poles but won the race in a record 3:27 4/5. The time smashed by 1 1/5 seconds the previous Sheepshead Bay two-mile record set by Ben Holladay. A new track record was struck, and the *Nashville American* took up the fight for legitimacy against resistant turf scribes and turfmen: "No horse has won more distinguished honors during the season of 1900 than Kinley Mack, and few horses have ever received so small a credit for such notable performances. In the year's turf history, the name of the gallant son of Islington will appear most prominently, but he has never achieved the popular favor accorded to Ethelbert, which he beat in the Suburban, nor half that bestowed upon old Imp."[8]

On the eleventh of September at Gravesend, old Imp, Kinley Mack, and McMeekin wheeled into their strides for the First Special. Imp staved off hard-charging Kinley Mack through the backstretch, and McMeekin threw lightning-quick strides. Patsy McCue on Kinley Mack and John Bullman on McMeekin whipped and spurred. Their mounts on a tear over the home-stretch passed the mare, with Kinley Mack holding off McMeekin by a neck at the wire.[9]

Four days later, Ethelbert joined Imp, Kinley Mack, and McMeekin for a run at the Second Special. After one false start, the flag fell downward on the next attempt. Kinley Mack leaped to the front. Imp launched into her mighty stride. McMeekin ran at their tails. Imp pulled slightly ahead of Kinley Mack, and he stuck to her saddle skirts like grim death as she ground out her race.

With the black mare leading and Ethelbert trailing, the field made its second pass through the backstretch. Imp led them into the final turn. Jockeys riding the trailers cocked their whips. Nash Turner lashed Ethelbert. Henry Spencer smacked McMeekin. Patsy McCue swung his whip and batted Kinley Mack. Spencer and McCue heard the quick play of Ethelbert's thudding hooves in a come-from-behind drive, but none could catch Imp. She blew past the wire, with Kinley Mack trailing her by a length, and he half a length in front of Ethelbert, and he two lengths ahead of McMeekin.[10]

The Second Special closed the book on the rivalries. Meeting Imp six times, Kinley Mack outdistanced the future Hall of Fame mare in three races and lost to her twice. Both horses were unplaced in the Brighton Handicap.

In the battle of supremacy against rival Ethelbert, Kinley Mack raced with him four times. Weight spreads between them were never greater than three pounds. Kinley Mack won all four.[11]

All told in 1900, Kinley Mack's record was five for nine, second twice, third once, and he had set a track record in the Autumn Cup. Even so, easterners stuck by Ethelbert as America's best three-year-old of 1900. Their New York horse posted seven wins in thirteen starts and finished runner-up five times. Blame for Ethelbert's losses was well distributed by his backers and New York's turf scribes. They cited trainer Andrew Jackson Joyner, the starters, deliberate misconduct by jockeys, jockeys' faulty rides, and, vaguely, "accidents in contests." The stifling heat inside a stockcar in which the horse traveled was blamed for one loss. Andrew Jackson Joyner probably sighed when he said, "It is useless to keep on making excuses for the horse for it merely makes a man appear absurd." Eastern turf historian Walter Vosburgh, when comparing performances and weight carried, sided with Kinley Mack as "a shade better." The eminent historian also remembered the touchy feet and legs and said that "he had never been a sound horse, and the wonder was he ever accomplished what he did."[12]

On New Year's Eve 1900, a *Boston Globe* headline announced LEADING EVENTS OF THE YEAR. Categorized by month, in May and at number 26: "Kinley Mack Won Brooklyn Handicap." In June at number 16: "Kinley Mack Won Suburban Handicap." And in November: "McKinley and Roosevelt Elected." William McKinley had soundly defeated William Jennings Bryan a second time, but for a second time he had lost the state of Montana.[13]

President McKinley's namesake racehorse warranted this *Evening World* headline on March 25, 1901: A DAY IN THE LIFE OF BRAVE KINLEY MACK, THE CHAMPION OF AMERICAN THOROUGHBREDS. The horse had apparently gained some traction in respect and popularity. Photographs illustrating the article included a side view of "Kinley Mack's intelligent head." The subheadline told of a "Luxurious Rascal Who Eats, Naps, Gallops, Is Groomed and Is Watched by Trainer Wimmer." When breakfast was served, "great eyes pleaded intelligently [and] as plainly as if in human language he was saying, 'Please, hurry. I'm hungry as a bear.'" "Frisky antics" with the grooms kept them hopping as they made his bay coat shine. The *World* had this to say about his racing career: "A cripple, his courage has carried him to victory when his legs were burning as if the bones were white hot iron rods searing the flesh. It was his stout heart, his indomitable gameness that won for him last season the Brooklyn and Suburban Handicaps, two prizes greatly coveted by horsemen."[14]

──

The joy of seeing a champion like Kinley Mack race was one pleasure Samuel Larabie had not experienced. Moreover, since founding his racing stable seventeen years ago, he had seen only three races in which his horses raced. Business matters at the Larabie Brothers Bank and at Willow Run made travel to distant eastern racetracks difficult. Similarly, Augustine Eastin rarely saw the Eastin and Larabie horses compete. In March 1901, Eastin retired from the sport. Larabie chose not to continue without him. Upon hearing this, J. B. Haggin seized the opportunity to purchase the Eastin and Larabie Stable. The value of the lot featuring Kinley Mack, Ben Holladay, the mares Mollie L. and Gypsy, and other horse stock was quoted at between $150,000 and $200,000. The actual price Haggin paid was never revealed but was reportedly the largest in twenty years.[15]

Samuel Larabie and Augustine Eastin as partners had long flouted American horse racing traditions, yet their success was undeniable. For several days in March, multiple tributes to the two turfmen appeared in eastern newspapers. From the *New York Times*: "The former owners, S. E. Larabie, a Montana banker and financier, and Augustus Eastin, a well-to-do Kentuckian . . . have held a place in the public esteem second to that of no man who ever raced horses. In that time, they have had many famous animals, the most noted of which were Poet Scout, Ben Holladay, and Kinley Mack." The *New York Sun* offered: "Be that as it may, no one begrudges the victory of a horse owned by Eastin and Larabie, a firm of true sportsmen, who spared neither ponies nor money in their efforts to breed stake winners for the racing establishment, and who have bred more high classed horses than any racing firm in America within the past dozen years, when it is taken into consideration they own and breed not over fifteen mares."[16]

Peter Wimmer's years of work with Eastin and Larabie were not overlooked. According to *Turf, Field and Farm*, Wimmer's value "has been more manifest year after year, until today there is not a member of his profession more esteemed and whose services are valued more highly than his." Haggin retained Peter Wimmer as trainer for his newly acquired racehorses. In spring 1901 and one week shy of the Brooklyn Handicap, in which Kinley Mack would debut in Haggin's silks, his feet and sliver-thin legs could no longer withstand the violent pounding of moving his half-ton body at a run. He could barely walk because his legs had swelled so badly. Wimmer was kicking himself for having hurried the horse, saying, "It was [the training] which settled his case adversely, for I believe had I gone slowly with him, I should have some good races out of him." There would be no fourth season. After twenty-eight starts, of which Kinley Mack won fifteen, he finished runner-up in six and was third once. His career earnings totaled $36,199.[17]

▸◂

Peter Wimmer and Patsy McCue renewed their association. In June 1901, McCue asked for a few days off to attend the funeral of a fellow jockey. One week passed. Wimmer had no idea where his jockey could be. McCue reappeared on July 4, in time for the high-profile Lawrence Realization Stakes, but he would ride for former mentor Tom Healy. Although McCue's behavior was again erratic, he did not disappoint. His handling of The Parader was "the best The Parader ever got," the *New York Tribune* praised, adding in a fatherly tone, "if he can always ride as he did yesterday, he ought to give more attention to riding and less to things that do not help a boy to ride well." Healy repeatedly tried to keep McCue serious about his riding. When the jockey presented his new bride to Healy in early 1902, the sixteen-year-old Stella Parmenter of Hamilton, she was so delightful that Healy opened his home to the newlyweds until they found one of their own. He hoped Stella would be a steady, calming influence on her husband. A popular young lady in her hometown, she likely outclassed him in education and sophistication. She was genteel and religious and advocated temperance. They could not have been more mismatched.[18]

Stella and Healy kept McCue sober for a brief time. Then, on June 22, 1902, he was astride Hermis, a good colt in perfect condition, for a go at the American Derby. Moments before the start, McCue slipped his foot from a stirrup. Horse and rider left the post late. They were under way until McCue inexplicably pulled Hermis to a stop and quit the race. The trainer, shocked and infuriated, insisted his colt would have won the American Derby had

McCue been sober. McCue's response to the angry trainer was to blame Hermis, who he claimed had gotten himself caught in the webbed barrier. The start was bungled, and because they had so much ground to recover, there was no point in continuing to race. In the next breath, McCue, smirking and flippant, said, "I pulled up because I got tired; a mile and a half was too far for me to ride."[19]

On June 16, 1904, the *New York Sun* reported Patsy McCue "among the missing." Last seen at Morris Park spending his money freely, he turned up in August at Saratoga after convalescing from an unspecified illness. In November, at Elm Ridge Racecourse in Kansas City, reports about McCue's riding there said that "on several occasions [he] tried to go the wrong way on the track after a night of drinking." The next year, 1905, Stella left her husband and returned to Hamilton.[20]

She wrote Patsy in January 1906. He was then seriously ill with tuberculosis. She asked whether she should come to his bedside, but he replied that he was broke and there was little she could do. It is possible that Patsy McCue earned around $150,000 as a professional jockey. As the illness progressed, McCue accepted financial assistance from relatives and the Jockey Club. A cousin arranged for medical treatment in Washington, DC. In a hospital room there, his relatives hung photographs chronicling his glory as a jockey. The pictures cheered him. Twenty-four-year-old Patrick A. McCue sank into delirium and died on May 10, 1906. His body was interred in the Holy Cross Cemetery in Brooklyn.[21]

At about four o'clock in the afternoon on September 6, 1901, at Sheepshead Bay, telegrams and bulletins were on the fly. The city of Buffalo, New York, was hosting a grand event, the Pan-American Exposition. Shots had rung out. Two bullets had pierced William McKinley's chest and stomach. In the days following surgery, President McKinley slowly slipped away. His stomach was unable to properly digest nourishment. The president died the morning of September 14, 1901. He would be the last Civil War veteran to serve as an American president, having fought for the Union Army. He was America's third president to die by the hand of an assassin. Theodore Roosevelt ascended to the presidency as America's twenty-sixth president.

In step with the rest of the grief-stricken nation, the town of Deer Lodge, Montana, designated an official day of mourning. Samuel Larabie was one of the citizens appointed to oversee President McKinley's memorial service on September 19. The honor was shared with neighbors Tom McTague, John Bielenberg, and Conrad Kohrs. America wasted little time before punishing the assassin. On October 29, 1901, the Auburn, New York, state prison put through the electrocution of self-proclaimed anarchist Leon Czolgosz.[22]

▬

The matter of whether Peter Wimmer was naturalized as an American citizen became a problem in spring 1917. In fact, the questionable status of German immigrants numbering in the hundreds of thousands in America became of national concern on April 2, the day America's twenty-eighth president, Woodrow Wilson, asked Congress for a declaration of war against Germany. America entered World War I on April 6. Zeal for the war effort fostered Americanism, or a belief in devotion, loyalty, or allegiance to the United States of America. For instance, the Espionage Act of 1917 and the Sedition Act of 1918 effectively outlawed criticism of America's government leaders and war policies. Extreme anti-German feelings pervaded America during this time.[23]

Peter Wimmer had immigrated with his family to America sometime between 1853 and 1856, according to US Census records. Wimmer placed the year as 1856. Census records are conflicted as to his birth year—1842, 1843, or 1844—and his naturalization status. On February 7, 1918, Wimmer registered with the US Department of Justice as a German alien. Then, on July 12 at the Latonia track, a US marshal arrested the trainer for alleged seditious remarks made against the federal government. Court records document Wimmer's comments: "America did not have a chance to win this war; that President Wilson started the war to protect the Wall Street brokers, who had purchased English and French securities; that President Wilson was a friend of the rich man."[24]

At his federal court trial in Covington, Kentucky, Wimmer admitted making the statements but denied that he had spoken with "malicious intent." The defense attorney argued that his client, as a Confederate States of America veteran, had sworn allegiance to America at the end of the war. Still, on August 15, 1918, Wimmer was found guilty of espionage. He lost his appeal the following year. Seventy-seven-year-old Wimmer received a prison sentence of six months and a $500 fine. Federal prosecutors, however, taking his age and ill health into consideration, concluded that his outbursts were "rather slight." President Wilson unconditionally pardoned Wimmer on September 10, 1920. Wimmer never paid the fine or served time in prison.[25]

All three of his children were at his side when he died on September 27, 1923, in the town of Sheepshead Bay. Three times married and twice widowed, Peter Wimmer was a devoted and "most indulgent" husband and father and, according to the Mississippi *Yazoo Herald*, "loved all kinds of animals, but his favorite was the horse . . . a beautiful, well-groomed horse ready to go."[26]

Samuel Larabie, who loved a beautiful, blooded racehorse, had withdrawn from the American turf in 1901 but continued to breed them and race a few in Helena. The pastime likely wound down upon a land sale of 2,600 acres in June 1910. Two years later, Willow Run Stock Farm no longer existed. The year was a busy one for the sixty-seven-year-old banker. With the assistance of a Seattle architect, Larabie designed a new Larabie Brothers Bank building to replace the one that had existed since 1870. The elegant neoclassical sandstone building opened for business on March 25, 1912. Then, at an August parade that honored Montana's pioneer citizens, Larabie drove a bull team of six hitched to a wagon "gotten up" like the schooners that had crossed the plains.[27]

The scene harked back to 1863, his eighteenth year, when he had driven an ox team out of Council Bluffs, Iowa. Adventure in the West included gold mining. Adventure at one point included being so dirt poor he had to sell his rifle to buy food, and after he borrowed $1,500 to purchase a claim, an avalanche swept away all his improvements. He was now in serious debt, and as he explained his predicament, "I picked my flints and until I could find something to do, I went to washing dishes in a hotel, receiving my board and a small salary. I saved a little money, not much, but every dollar I could get hold of, I put in mining stocks. By and by, the boom came. I was on the right side and in a short time could have bought the hotels where I washed dishes, had I felt so fancied." He was now one of Montana's wealthiest men.[28]

In October, the *Anaconda Standard* published an extensive article extolling Deer Lodge city fathers. Entreaties for a photograph to accompany Larabie's biography fell on deaf ears. The banker had not had a picture taken for a quarter century and "refuses to begin at this time," the *Standard* reported.[29]

Larabie traveled to Lexington in August 1913 to see his friend Augustine Eastin. Enjoying a decades-long friendship, the two men had met in person only twice. Larabie received sad news about John Augustine Eastin the following February. The veteran of the Confederate States of America died of pneumonia on February 20, 1914, at age seventy-nine. A lengthy obituary in the *Thoroughbred Record* recalled the names of the famous racehorses with which he had been associated, and the *Record* eulogized, "It goes without saying that Mr. Eastin will be sorely missed. Acknowledged as one of the best judges of a yearling in Kentucky, his opinion was highly esteemed and leaves a gap it will indeed be hard to fill."[30]

On the morning of April 21, only two months and a day after Eastin had passed, Larabie and his son Charles, after having lunched together, walked back to Larabie Brothers Bank to finish the workday. Samuel was descending the basement stairs when Charles heard his father's loud groan and found him on the basement floor. Samuel Larabie died before the doctor arrived.[31]

Private and public events were either canceled or postponed in honor of the sixty-nine-year-old "backbone" of Deer Lodge. Thirty-nine years married, he and Julia were parents to four daughters and three sons. The funeral services on Sunday, April 26, 1914, had longtime neighbors John Bielenberg and Conrad Kohrs serving as pallbearers. "Never before was there such an outpouring of young and old in Deer Lodge as the gathering which paid its last tribute to the memory of the pioneer banker," the *Anaconda Standard* related. Eighty automobiles and half as many carriages formed the largest funeral procession ever seen in Deer Lodge. Tributes noted how Larabie "delighted in the joy of giving," and how his philanthropy had been central to "beautifying the city."[32]

He was, of course, "a great lover of blooded stock," as the Deer Lodge newspaper *Silver State Post* noted on April 23. America's horse racing journals reported Samuel Larabie's death. The *Thoroughbred Record* mentioned that he raced "many famous horses," and the *Daily Racing Form*, also noting Larabie's prominence on the American turf, listed the names of those horses: Kinley Mack, Ben Holladay, Poet Scout, High Tariff, Julia L., and Montana Regent.[33]

His widow moved to Pennsylvania to be near a daughter. Julia would survive her husband by twenty-two years. On May 9, 1936, Julia Larabie died at the age of eighty. She was returned to Deer Lodge and buried beside Samuel in the Hillcrest Cemetery. In addition to having lovingly attended to Julia, the children, and his horses, Samuel had shepherded the bank he cofounded with William A. Clark and Robert Donnell in 1869. At the time of Samuel's death, the Larabie Brothers Bank held the distinction of being Montana's oldest financial institution. Sadly, like many other American financial institutions during the banking crisis of 1933, Larabie Brothers Bank closed for business on March 4 and never reopened.[34]

▄▄

American horse racing suffered a crisis of its own early in the twentieth century. With racetracks popping up all over the country fast as mushrooms, the sport grew explosively and operated in helter-skelter fashion, to the extreme of blatant corruption. Such criminal elements as race fixing, crooked jockeys, betting scams, and other illegal activity operated surreptitiously despite the Jockey Club acting as a governing authority. The corruption fanned public and government indignation. Antiracing and antigambling Progressives on the march achieved huge victories in 1905 when Chicago and St. Louis banned horse racing. Even in the racing stronghold of New York, reformers successfully lobbied for the passage of the Agnew-Hart Bill in June 1908. Racetrack wagering became illegal, and the new law imposed substantial fines and prison terms for lawbreakers. Stricter antigambling measures were later passed. As gambling revenues dried up, New York racing found it impractical to keep the sport afloat. By 1911, all racetracks in New York had closed. America's West was not immune. Four years later in Montana, passage of the Hayes Bill put an end to racetrack betting. Not all states fell in step with the crusaders, however. Maryland and Kentucky bucked the trend and watched attendance at their tracks skyrocket.[35]

Reaching a peak of 314 racetracks nationally in 1890, the number dipped to 25 in 1908, the year Churchill Downs reintroduced pari-mutuel betting. The machines first appeared there in 1878 but were abandoned by 1890. Pari-mutuel betting now found new life. The beauty of it was eliminating the need for auction pools and bookmakers that could be dishonest. Betting was in the hands of racetrack operators. With the sport's image on the mend and the antigambling frenzy sputtering by 1913, horse racing was righting the ship. All American horse racing would eventually adopt pari-mutuel betting.[36]

The antigambling fanaticism gut-punched America's Thoroughbred breeders. Owners of the great breeding farms dispersed their stock by shiploads to Europe or South America. J. B. Haggin realized the impossibility of marketing young horses on the scale of his Elmendorf Farm's annual production. His "experiment" in 1908 to mitigate losses sent consignments to the Argentine Republic. His agent Matthew Byrnes reported good news of securing "first-class" prices for the first shipment.[37]

Meanwhile, information about how Kinley Mack had fared in the Elmendorf Stud was scant and contradictory. The *Daily Racing Form* judged him successful, but the *Lexington Leader* pegged him as "a total failure." Haggin must have agreed with the *Form*. More practical about horses than he was sentimental, he exported Kinley Mack to the Argentine Republic in 1908. One year later, the *Form* relayed disheartening news from south of the equator. At fourteen years old and under ownership of a Buenos Aires turfman, Kinley Mack was back in training.[38]

Marcus Daly

Copper King

It was said that Marcus Daly could sniff out promising horseflesh as expertly as he could sniff out valuable minerals. Most of the time he relied on horse buying agents scattered across America and overseas to abide by his single order: find the world's best blooded horses and buy them. Price and location were immaterial. These were two advantages of being an extremely wealthy man.[1]

In this way, an agent entered the thick of worldwide bidding to secure the Thoroughbred stallion Ormonde. Bred at the Eaton Stud and owned by England's Duke of Westminster, the stallion was literally royally bred. Ormonde was undefeated in sixteen starts and the winner of the English Triple Crown races. At the garden party the Duke of Westminster hosted at his mansion in honor of Queen Victoria's Diamond Jubilee, Ormonde was a guest of honor. In December 1888, the duke wanted to sell Ormonde, and every turfman in the world wanted to buy him.[2]

The agent for Marcus Daly bid on Ormonde for as long as he thought prudent, stopping at the audacious bid of $85,000 by an Argentine. So, the stallion sailed to Buenos Aires. In short order, the agent was summoned to Daly's office. Perhaps he was permitted to explain to Daly his prudent but futile bidding before the boss began railing at him for disobeying instructions. What was worse, "a greaser" had secured Ormonde for South America.[3]

▬

Legend has it that Marcus's father, Luke O'Daly, once spent his last dollar betting on a racehorse. A farmer in County Cavan, Ireland, O'Daly could not offer his six children much beyond subsistence, but he passed to Marcus his love for fast, beautiful horses. Fifteen-year-old Marcus left Ireland for America and landed at New York Harbor in 1856. A penniless immigrant with little formal education to recommend him, he accepted work as a newspaper boy and errand boy and found a job in a leatherworks factory. For every two dollars Marcus earned, he saved one. The blue-eyed lad grew into a stout, strong man who put muscle into the hustling work of stevedore on the Brooklyn docks. There he heard tales of quick fortunes unearthed in California's northern goldfields. In 1861, Marcus Daly spent his stockpiled dollars on ship passage to Panama, rode a train across the isthmus, and sailed to San Francisco.[4]

Early employment in California included a shovel, but Daly was not shoveling for gold. "Can you dig taters?" a farmer asked him. "Yes, I can," he replied, and he spent three weeks digging potatoes. Those dollars paid his way to the gold diggings in Calaveras County, California. Arriving there, he learned the hand-blistering work of hard-rock mining with shovel and pickax. Daly drifted to the Washoe region in Nevada country. Somewhere in between, his surname shortened from O'Daly to Daly. At the famed Comstock Lode, by way of thorough study of rocks and soils, he became a self-taught "master" in assessing vein structures as well as tunneling, timbering, and blasting. Rising to the rank of shift boss, he made important connections with the captains of the mining industry.[5]

Daly advanced his name as an expert mine manager and appraiser. In Utah at the Alta camp in 1870, he was hired as foreman of the Emma Mine, one of many mines owned by the Walker brothers. Daly was now thirty years old, and relief from spending nearly all his life in male company arrived on a summer day in 1872. During a round of mine inspections, the guests were local mine manager Zenos Evans and his daughter, Margaret. Along the way, Daly jumped into a trench, scooped up a piece of ore, and held it up for his audience. Margaret wanted a closer look, and according to lore, the eighteen-year-old slip of a woman lost her footing and tumbled right into Daly's arms. This was the romantic beginning of a courtship that would unfold into a twenty-eight-year marriage. Marcus and Margaret, or Maggie as he always called her, would raise four children.[6]

News of a camp in the Montana Territory reached the Walker brothers. The silver veins beneath Butte were reportedly as rich as those of the Comstock Lode. The Walkers sent Daly to Butte in the centennial year of 1876. City fathers eager to promote their town hailed Marcus Daly as "the best miner who has ever been in Montana." Daly would say later that the prospects he examined left him generally unimpressed with Butte as a silver camp, but he had an inkling that real value lay in the veins of copper ore. Whether he relayed his hunch about copper to the Walker brothers is open for debate.[7]

In late September, an entourage of Daly, the Walkers, and a mine appraiser returned to Butte. The brothers bought a silver mine, the Alice, and Daly was made a partner. One of the Alice's former owners, Rolla Butcher, took Daly's draft to the Clark and Larabie Bank in Deer Lodge for cashing. It so happened that banker William A. Clark had his eye on the Alice. His intention to buy the mine now upset, Clark allegedly told Butcher that Daly was a fake. Clark refused to honor the draft. This forced Daly to do business with Wells Fargo in Salt Lake City, where Butcher received his money. Daly's friend Ben E. Stack, to whose cabin Daly would go and read the *Irish World* nationalist newspaper, attributed Clark's rascality as laying the groundwork for the well-documented Daly-Clark feud. The two men would remain adversaries and undermine each other at every opportunity for the rest of their lives.[8]

The Alice proved her worth. She was among the most productive silver mines in Butte. With financial security in place, Daly moved his family from Utah to Butte. He continued to poke around properties. He arranged a meeting with Irish miner Michael Hickey, who held the Anaconda Mine in partnership with his brother, Ed, and Charles Xavier Larrabee. When Michael Hickey was soldiering in the Union Army, he read an editorial that told of McClellan's army encircling Lee's force "like a giant anaconda." Hickey did not forget the image that Horace Greeley's words had impressed on his mind. Straightaway, he named the claim he staked in Butte the Anaconda Mine.[9]

The Anaconda was a small affair with a shaft only forty-five feet deep. Daly's offer was to sink it to a depth of ninety feet for a third interest in the property, a proposal Hickey and his partners accepted. At sixty feet, they struck a vein of free-milling silver ore. Daly reported this to the Walkers and proposed that he and the brothers purchase the mine as partners. The Walkers sent a second expert to make an examination, and that report being adverse, the brothers passed on buying the Anaconda. In part because he was ready to strike out on his own, and in part because he was lukewarm about Butte as a silver camp, Daly sold his Alice Mine shares to the Walkers for $30,000. He then turned around and purchased full interest in the Anaconda Mine for $30,000.[10]

Daly now owned a promising mine outright but was capital poor. When he approached the Walker brothers for money to develop the Anaconda, they demurred. Daly next approached George Hearst, whom he had known since the 1860s. In the summer of 1872, they were prospecting in Utah when Daly directed Hearst to a six-foot-long "deep as your shoulders" hole near Park City. Both men thought the hole was worth further examination, and Hearst purchased the claim that would be transformed into the Ontario Mine. "From that $30,000 [purchase of the Ontario], everything else came," Hearst would later write in his memoir, *The Way It Was: Recollections of U.S. Senator George Hearst, 1820–1891.* The Ontario produced millions in silver and was the foundation of his great wealth.[11]

Missouri farm boy George Hearst formed a San Francisco–based mining syndicate with two associates, J. B. Haggin and Lloyd Tevis. These three wealthy men threw in with Marcus Daly. Ownership of the Anaconda Mine was apportioned: Hearst 39 percent, Haggin 26 percent, Daly 25 percent, and Tevis 10 percent. Operations to develop the mine were launched in June 1881. The extracted silver paid handsomely, but within a year the vein was nearly exhausted. One day in 1882 at three hundred feet below ground, the Anaconda's rock-ribbed walls shuddered from intermittent drilling and blasting. A section of rock shattered. The dust cleared. Daly picked up a piece of glance that had fallen to the mine floor. The vein from which it fell looked to be solid copper. His hunch about copper in the Anaconda realized, Daly, awestruck, looked at foreman Michael Carroll and said, "Mike, we've got it!" The discovery marked one of the greatest concentrations of copper in the world.[12]

The timing was perfect. Demand for copper was on the threshold of skyrocketing as electric power infrastructure advanced across the world. Separating ore from copper posed unique complexities, but risk-taking capitalists could make fortunes extracting the mineral. Hastening to California with his brain clicking like a piston, Daly presented his plans to his partners. Most boldly, he wanted to build a state-of-the-art smelting facility to eliminate the expense of shipping copper ore to Swansea, Wales, for smelting, although, as one copper miner said, "They could ship it to hell and back for smelting and still make a profit." Daly wanted to purchase multiple silver prospects and work them for copper. And he wanted a railroad. He envisioned the smelter being linked to the Anaconda Mine. The partners supplied him with a generous budget, and superintendent Daly headed back to Montana to build a massive, multifaceted, integrated copper enterprise.[13]

An early problem was water. A smelting complex on the scale envisioned required huge amounts of water, but the largest sources in Butte were already claimed. Daly found his site twenty-six miles west. Ample supplies of Warm Springs Creek water tumbled through the upper Deer Lodge Valley. Ground was broken for the complex in May 1883. The partners experimented, dealt with vicissitudes, and purchased state-of-the-art equipment regardless of expense. The reduction works, or concentrator, took form and was followed by a massive five-hundred-ton smelter and other infrastructure. By April 1884, the project employed 150 men.[14]

Meanwhile, least enthused about the project was Lloyd Tevis. Early on, he questioned the wisdom of monopolizing investments on a highly experimental smelting plant. During one meeting that became contentious, Tevis moved to levy a "special assessment" to further finance the "experiments." Daly squawked. He had already invested every cent he owned. Tevis suggested to the syndicate's youngest, least experienced, and poorest partner that he relinquish his stock. Haggin, who had not said much, as was typical, drew out a checkbook and began signing blank checks. Handing the book to Daly, he said, "Mark, take that checkbook and use those checks for any purpose you please." Doling out money as unnervingly as that was apparently not unusual, according to a Haggin acquaintance. "I do not mean he invested recklessly or without mature investigation, but when he made up his mind, a few millions, more or less, never moved him from his purpose."[15]

As the "Upper Works" smelting facilities took shape in 1883, Daly made plans to replace the rows of canvas tents with a town. As local lore tells it, Daly pointed to a heap in the distance and said to his friend Morgan Evans, "Main Street will run north and south exactly over the back of that dead cow." Tents gave way to brick or wooden homes forming neighborhoods, a business district, and a first-class hotel named the Marcus Daly. Negotiations with Jay Gould and Sidney Dillon of the Union Pacific Railroad began the following year. Dillon was concerned about investing in a track. If the copper ore in Butte petered out, or if the price of copper fell, Anaconda would become a ghost town. Another Union Pacific representative, Mr. E. H. Wilson, sided with Daly, who repeatedly insisted that volumes of high-grade copper ore would sustain Anaconda and the proposed railroad for one hundred years. On September 7, 1884, the thirty-one-mile Union Pacific-Utah and Northern spur line linked the Upper Works to the Anaconda Mine. The line would transport copper ore for ninety-seven years.[16]

The Anaconda Mining Company invested $4 million in the Upper Works. On September 10, 1884, the *River Press* of Fort Benton announced the inauguration of "the most important and extensive smelting enterprise yet known in connection with the mining history of Montana." Mrs. McCaskell, the wife of superintendent William McCaskell, was escorted to the imposing smelter, where amid rejoicing she applied the match that ignited the first fire. Furnacemen were recruited from Wales, and millmen trickled in from Michigan's copper region. The Anaconda Mining Company was to become the largest single copper producer and metallurgical plant in the world.[17]

Marcus Daly single-handedly turned Butte, Montana, into an
"Irish town." He reportedly brought thousands of Irishmen to the city and hired
them to work in his mines and smelters. An oft-repeated story was of immigrants
being told, "Don't stop in America, go straight to Butte!" Photo courtesy of
Marcus Daly Mansion, Hamilton, Montana.

In 1888, the smoke-belching Upper Works employed 2,400 men. Daly had his hand in other enterprises too, including timber, railroads, coal, and banking. The boss, well on his way to becoming incredibly rich, detested cheap wages, and crews of workmen at the Anaconda Mining Company earned wages ranging from $3.50 to $5.00 per day in 1891. No other company in the region matched those wages. This reflected Daly's belief in good wages, the benefits of which would not only foster a community of permanent skilled labor but also support a prosperous and stable community and tamp down the threat of menacing agitators. For the remainder of his life, Daly would keep a home in his smelter town of Anaconda.[18]

The *Daily Inter Mountain* reported in July 1887 that Marcus Daly had stabled seven Thoroughbred horses in Anaconda. During one visit to a local Thoroughbred horse breeder the previous February, Daly's purchase of Lady Preuitt for $2,500 might have accounted for his first purchase of the Thoroughbred breed. Imported to Montana as a filly from her native state of Kentucky by Colonel William B. Hundley of Helena, Lady Preuitt established herself as a well-known race mare on the Montana racing circuit.[19]

The sport of horse racing came to Anaconda by way of a subscription list circulated for the purpose of building a racetrack on the tract of land Marcus Daly deeded for the venture. Although the subscription list was reportedly "very successful" and shares had been purchased, the one-mile circular course, stables, grandstand, dining room, and bar were financed mostly by Daly's nickel. On August 28, the Anaconda Racing Association held its inaugural meeting at the Anaconda Driving Park. More than one hundred trotters and runners waited restively in the stables. Groups of miners from Butte were a large, boisterous addition to the crowd. The two Daly entries, both Standardbreds, won their respective heats and collected $475 and $500 in winner's purses.[20]

Meanwhile, the Montana Territory marched toward statehood. With the hope of Anaconda being selected as the state capital, the town had to have a newspaper. Much has been written about the founding of the *Anaconda Standard*, and discrepancies abound, but biographers agree that Daly wanted John Durston, former owner-editor of the *Syracuse Standard* in New York, to found and run his newspaper. Durston visited Anaconda at Daly's invitation in 1889.

Durston dinged the town for lacking resources necessary to support a newspaper. Daly was not worried about financial losses, he said, and insisted that his paper would not be a small-town newspaper, but a high-quality regional paper with circulation all over western Montana. Still, Durston declined the offer to publish the paper. Trying a new approach, Daly suggested to Durston that he experience the beehive of activity in Butte, which he envisioned as the principal target of his newspaper. Durston did this, but his mind remained unchanged. Daly asked for one more meeting before Durston departed.[21]

On the appointed day, Durston unfolded a Butte newspaper in the hotel lobby where he waited for Daly. No sooner had he finished reading a brief about Marcus Daly than there the man stood.

"Is it true that you recently paid $4,000 for an untried colt?" Durston asked.

"Yes. I'm fond of horses. I'm going to have a stable that will beat the best."

Durston processed Daly's self-assured response in the sweep of a second. "If you can sink $4,000 in a colt that may or may not grow into a racehorse," Durston said, "I guess you can sink $40,000 into a newspaper that may or may not become a newspaper." Daly's investment was closer to $30,000 before the first issue of the *Anaconda Standard* hit the streets on September 4, 1889, with Durston as editor. Daly and Durston proved a perfect match. According to the Library of Congress, "Historians and journalists alike regard the [*Anaconda*] *Standard* as the icon of Montana newspapers for its sophistication, editorial content, and the influence wielded in state and national politics."[22]

⬛

In January 1891, the Anaconda Mining Company incorporated. Most recently "The Lower Works" was in full operation, handling three thousand tons of copper ore daily. This second smelter lifted America to world leader in copper production. On November 1, 1895, Daly's short narrative about the company's history and the $72 million it invested was published in the *Anaconda Standard*. "This is a vast sum of money," Daly wrote, "and when I consider the changes that have taken place at Butte and at other places in Montana since 1878, I am free to say that personally I take a great deal of pleasure in thinking that the property has been a liberal contributor in the growth and prosperity of Montana."[23]

Regardless of his new title, "Copper King," which he loathed, Daly stayed true to himself, an impoverished Irish peasant who once knew what it was to shovel dirt and swing a pickax. It was not unusual to see him on a street curb engaging with a group of miners. He would borrow a plug of chew and listen to the panoply of Irish brogues. He, too, swapped exaggerations in his low, mellow brogue. But he was also not averse to the material possessions his wealth could afford. He would swap a seat on the curb for an upholstered one in the comfort of his carriage pulled by a pair of matching, high-stepping sorrels. He would use his Copper King stature when it suited him. At the Riverside Siding rail stop, for instance, trains waited for Marcus Daly.[24]

He never ran for public office; he knew he was too unsophisticated. The *Anaconda Standard* was a mouthpiece by which he effectively could, and did, influence state and national affairs. Margaret was said to have helped her husband, still awkward in speech and expression, advance his ability to read and write. More importantly, as Daly pointed out, "When the business magnates of the country cross the continent, they call on me. They respect me in my proper sphere. That is enough satisfaction for a man who started in the world with as little capital as I had."[25]

◼

The Anaconda Mining Company holdings in George Hearst's name were valued at $18 million. Upon his death in 1891, these were dispersed to his widow, Phoebe, and his famous son, William Randolph. The sale of blocks of their shares to the Rothschild banking house four years later forced the Anaconda Mining Company to reorganize and reincorporate as well as adopt a new name, Anaconda Copper Mining Company. Toward the end of the nineteenth century in corporate America, fewer and fewer hands were controlling American industry. The entire petroleum industry, as an example, would emerge as Standard Oil Company. The trend toward consolidation eventually reached copper mining's doorstep, and it is hardly surprising that Anaconda Copper Mining Company came up on the radar.[26]

Daly, the unschooled, rough-hewn hard-rock miner of a passing era, found himself increasingly out of touch with the younger college-trained experts entering the ranks. Anaconda Copper Mining Company was coming around to selling out at the right price, and that price was $23 million, sold to Standard Oil in early 1899. The millions were distributed three ways: $6 million to Daly, $9 million to Haggin, and $8 million to Tevis, who would die a few months later. Daly elected to stick with Standard

Oil. He owned shares and was named company president, but it was a title without chops.[27]

The capitalist investments making Daly richer by the day were in part owed to the only man he ever appeared to be in awe of, James Ben Ali Haggin. Quick-minded, shrewd, and sophisticated, Haggin could upstage his equal in a boardroom, but really he intimidated simply by the way he looked. Swarthy in complexion, dark-eyed, broad through the chest and shoulders,

James Ben Ali Haggin. Everything Haggin did was on a colossal scale. Solely or in partnerships, he owned nearly two million acres of land in the western United States and Mexico. The largest sheep herd on the West Coast was his. A network of mining operations stretched from Alaska to Peru. "Every enterprise which he entered seemed to thrive from the moment it received the impulse of his genius," the *History of Kentucky* notes. Haggin's fortune was dwarfed only by those of John D. Rockefeller and Andrew Carnegie. Photo courtesy of Bradley and Rulofson, photographers, Online Archive of California.

he commanded attention. An interminably stern countenance lent him an even more unnerving appearance.[28]

Haggin's ancestors immigrated to America in 1775 by way of Turkey, Ireland, and England. Born in Harrodsburg, Kentucky, in 1821, James was the son of Terah Temple Haggin and Adeline Ben Ali. He practiced law in Kentucky, then in Natchez, Mississippi, and in New Orleans, before borrowing $500 for passage to San Francisco in February 1850. His law partner in his newly established law firm was brother-in-law Lloyd Tevis. Working as land and corporation attorneys, they acquired a large California ranch through a delinquent loan. Tevis remained a silent partner while Haggin developed the ranch northeast of Sacramento into the Rancho del Paso. With an ability to retain "every impression," Haggin possibly had a photographic mind. If so, he would always remember the American, South American, English, French, and Australian bloodlines he studied. Aside from the traditional Kentuckian's love for a Thoroughbred horse, no other influence accounts for Haggin's affection for the breed.[29]

Rancho del Paso was, simply, huge. When one visitor toured Rancho, he said, "Seven hours of fast driving gives only a dim idea of the vastness of the place." Nearly 1,500 horses gamboled on Rancho at one point in time. Thirty were stallions. Broodmares, horses in training, yearlings, and foals—all of them rambled across the spread's 44,800 acres in the Sacramento Valley. As Haggin himself pointed out, "There was plenty of room for them." The capable superintendent, John Mackey, managed and operated the world's largest horse breeding farm more like a firm than a farm.[30]

Haggin did not operate one racing stable. He operated four. Thoroughbreds and Standardbreds alike were shipped not by the carload but by the trainload. Add to this his ownership of a second breeding farm, the Elmendorf Farm, at Lexington. Ownership of the two overlapped for several years. Upon Haggin's debut in eastern racing in 1885, his gold and blue colors would dominate America's important stakes races into the 1890s. More than his California turf contemporaries George Hearst, Theodore Winters, and Elias J. "Lucky" Baldwin, J. B. Haggin stamped California on the Thoroughbred breeding map.[31]

◼◼

The year Marcus Daly toured Rancho del Paso is uncertain, but he made at least one trip. After seeing all of what Rancho was, Daly aspired to breed blooded horses just as fine in the Bitterroot Valley of Montana. The native Salish and Spokane tribes called the valley "Place of the Bitter Root," referring to the bitterroot plant that grew profusely, and for the same reason explorers Lewis and Clark chose the name "Bitterroot Valley." Daly's introduction to the valley probably happened in the 1860s, with his first entry as leader of a relief party in search of George Hearst, who was heading a timber scouting party. The group had become lost in the "almost unexplored region of the Northwest." Daly and his party found Hearst and his men in the valley's "bottom lands [where] wild grass grew higher than a man's head."[32]

As any capitalist would do, Daly assessed the valley's natural amenities with the centric gaze of exploitation. Lush native grasses could fatten livestock. The valley floor from north to south looked ripe for farming. The eastern Beaverhead Mountains and the western Bitterroot Range bookending the valley were thick with timber. Perhaps as early as that, Daly had speculated about raising horses there. If a horse were to range loose over the low foothills, he would climb up and down and exert himself in the thin air. Volumes of oxygen would pour into his lungs, heart, and muscles. Gravelly mountainsides would make for flinty hooves. Winters were cold, but the air stayed dry and bracing. A Thoroughbred born here and nourished on the bunchgrass would, at lower altitudes, accelerate like the wind and beat any rival on a racetrack. Daly tucked his theory away.

He took ownership of multiple ranches in the Bitterroot Valley, and his landholdings in the country estate of Riverside eventually encompassed twenty-eight thousand acres; the spread was nine miles long and seven miles wide. The existing farmhouse was transformed into a Queen Anne–style mansion with twenty-nine rooms decorated in Victorian grandeur. Riverside was not intended as a solitary retreat; it was to be an opulent but welcoming showplace, with plentiful rooms for guests. Human-made lakes and a swimming pool were built on the grounds. Crews of gardeners manicured flower gardens and lawns, and a horticulturist tended the greenhouses and fruit trees. From the mansion's west-facing porch were views of the Bitterroot Range, cleaved, blue gray, and snow covered. Of all this, Margaret Daly slipped into the role of chatelaine.[33]

In spring 1888, a fleet of carpenters at work on the Riverside grounds marked the founding of the Bitter Root Stock Farm. In the not-too-distant future, Daly would say about the founding, "I have a theory that the state of Montana will produce the best horses of the world and I am testing it. The climate here is cold, but the air is pure, and it increases the lung power of the horses. . . . As to the coldness of the climate and the charge that colts will not grow here in the winter, if this is true, I expect to overcome it by good stabling and good food. Our grass here is better than that of California or Kentucky, and it makes better bones and better feed." The conceived architectural style for his horse farm he blueprinted from Rancho del Paso, tony Kentucky Thoroughbred farms, and aristocratic estates in Ireland. In what seemed a matter of days, a network of two-story red barns and stables arose on the acreage. The farm's multiple departments each had a superintendent. The Thoroughbred and Standardbred departments each had trainers and training centers.[34]

In late summer 1888, a train stopping at Riverside Siding delivered not one or two but rather twenty carloads of horses. The cars were emptied of Thoroughbreds, Standardbreds, and draft horses purchased from Rancho del Paso. Daly's bilateral interest in the Thoroughbred and Standardbred breeds would continue throughout his lifetime, but his preference "hinged on the occasion," according to Ed Tipton, prominent turfman and horse buying agent. "It depended much on whose company Daly was in as to which he gave preference. He generally felt about first to see whether his man was a Thoroughbred man, or devoted to the trotters, before he expressed strongly." Daly's agents made a trip to the neighboring Jefferson Valley, where they purchased eleven Thoroughbreds from Noah Armstrong. Then, in the Deer Lodge Valley, the mares Marietta and Emma Mc were purchased from Tom McTague. At a sale in Butte, an agent purchased a black filly bred by Conrad Kohrs and John Bielenberg. English coach horses and Irish hunters arrived from overseas.[35]

Daly refused to fence with barbed wire and risk injury to his expensive horses. Rows of whitewashed wooden panels five boards high enclosed pastures and paddocks. Lumber for the miles of fence was milled at the Daly sawmills. Nearly all the sawyers in the valley were cutting for him. Mindful of them and the men he employed at his farm, Daly directed his right-hand man, James W. Hamilton, to plat a new townsite for the workers. The boss's newest company town was founded in August 1890 and named Hamilton.[36]

Meanwhile, a syndicate of horsemen was bent on improving the sophistication of Thoroughbred breeding in Montana. The front man was Noah Armstrong, best known for his famed racehorse Spokane. Armstrong owned Spokane's dam, Interpose, and the syndicate understandably wanted Spokane's sire. In December 1890, Armstrong approached J. B. Haggin with a proposal to buy Hyder Ali, already on loan at Marcus Daly's Bitter Root Stock Farm. Armstrong and Haggin struck a $6,000 deal that kept the eighteen-year-old stallion in Montana for good. Upon Hyder Ali's permanency, the clerk responsible for keeping the Thoroughbred records at Bitter Root Stock Farm pulled out his book, *Index: Thoroughbred Stock*, and thumbed to a clean page. He wrote: "Hyder Ali. Bay, black points, small star in forehead, foaled 1871. Bred by A. Welsh, Edenheim Stud, Penn." The syndicate got five years of service from old Hyder Ali before he died on September 5, 1895.[37]

Bitter Root Stock Farm buzzed with the activity of a prosperous town. At its peak in the 1890s, as many as five hundred people cared for 1,200 head of Thoroughbred and Standardbred horses. The superintendents and trainers resided in handsome two-story homes on the Bitter Root grounds. Daly's word was law, or, as his personal secretary remarked, "Many were they who trembled at his approach, and had they been able to foresee his mind, or obtain an inkling of his desires, hastened to do which they supposed to be his will. And he had a way, when apparently taking a liking to a man, of giving him unlimited authority in the matter for which he was responsible." The lower-ranking workforce lived in clusters of cottages. On one occasion, "eight distinguished gentlemen" arrived from Kentucky to take positions as exercise boys. "The gentlemen are dark hued sons of Africa's sunny climate ranging in ages from 8 to 15 years and are neatly uniformed," the *Bitter Root Times* reported in 1893. Duties with the horses were carried out on either an outdoor or indoor track. Eventually there would be two of each. This way, the horses could be comfortably exercised and schooled in the winter. The exercise boys were also schooled, receiving four hours of "study" daily from the resident veterinarian.[38]

Few of America's Thoroughbred breeding farms were so well equipped as to have an equine hospital and a resident veterinarian on the grounds. In 1892, Dr. Morton Edmund Knowles, the state veterinarian of Indiana, was lured away from his job there and hired as the veterinarian for Bitter Root Stock Farm. He designed the hospital and oversaw the construction of a laboratory, quarantine stables, steam bath, "drug" room, and operating room with "strange ropes." The state-of-the art hospital was finished in February 1893. This was nearly one year after a fatal epidemic had killed almost all the Bitter Root foals within days of their birth. More than one veterinarian came to the farm in March 1892 to investigate, but none could isolate the cause. The value placed on the foals lost was estimated at $100,000.[39]

As self-sufficient as the farm was, it was obliged to Kentucky for novelties. One day Daly decided to experiment with grass. Seven hundred acres were tilled under and seeded with bluegrass. That pasture was reserved for broodmares and their foals to see whether they would indeed benefit from bluegrass over native bunchgrass. The final judgment on the experiment goes undiscovered. One farm worker would note decades later that the Bitter Root grew bluegrass "in profusion." Meanwhile, the perfectly appointed farm operated "steadily and frictionless as a marine engine," according to visitors. The systematized, world-class breeding farm that Daly built showcased his wealth and genius as a horseman. It all belied his unsophisticated manner. During the spring thaw, for instance, he traipsed through the paddock avenues unconcerned about his boots spattering muck and being caked with mud.[40]

In October 1891, the boss himself rode the train to New York for the dispersal sale of the Nursery Stud, the breeding farm founded and owned by the late August Belmont I. Newspapers and horse racing journals across America heralded the event as one of a kind because of Belmont, who was a breeding genius. Fierce bidding wars pitted Daly against Haggin, Pierre Lorillard, and other turf icons. Six of the bluest-blooded broodmares on the planet were Daly's at the price of $19,200. These sirens would be the nucleus for the Bitter Root Stud. Each mare was chosen for her bloodlines, and if she had raced, her career was scrutinized. Daly's meticulous care in selecting broodmares ran counter to the views taken by the firm of Antwerp and Lamplighter, compiler of Thoroughbred pedigree tables. The Antwerp tables focused on "the male line in the most prominent horses of the day" in America as well as overseas. Antwerp lamented mares, contending they are a necessary evil, only to serve as material to propagate the breed, and further, mares are never produced per se, for the purpose to serve as broodmares. They are only the sisters of their brothers and the daughters of their sires. Therefore, no consideration will be paid to mares in these tables."[41]

At the time Daly was buying America's best bloodlines for the Bitter Root Stud, another purchase was the 120-acre Aperfield Court in County Kent, England. His extensive knowledge of England's *General Stud Book*, the English model for the *American Stud Book*, was said to surpass most American breeders' familiarity with the *American Stud Book*. Daly spared no expense in securing England's finest broodmares. In reverse, Bitter Root broodmares sailed to Aperfield for "liberal patronage" of England's leading sires. Taking all this in, the nineteenth-century racing historian Lyman Horace Weeks commended Daly for his foresight, writing, "A more notable collection of mares than that which [Daly] has gathered at Bitter Root has seldom, if ever, been seen in the United States. The selection of these mares, whether foreign or native birth, has always been made with special regard to strong winning lines."[42]

Daly, too, followed the common practice of importing highly bred winning stallions to strengthen American-bred bloodstock. When asked why he wanted both English and American blood, Daly was to the point. "I want to breed the best to the best." Montana was the best place to do it, he said, adding, "When you read in the papers of a few years hence that the winners of the Futurity and the Realization were bred by Marcus Daly of Montana, do not be surprised, as the dry, bracing air and rich grasses of Montana are sure to give the youngsters plenty of lung power, with the constitution and conformation, backed by good breeding, to compete with the horses bred anywhere on the face of the globe." After years of contemplating and executing colossal, high-risk, high-gain enterprises, Marcus Daly was ready to relax with the equally vagarious business of breeding winning racehorses.[43]

CHAPTER 11

Montana

Colt of Bones

Horse-buying agents from all corners of America converged at the 1889 Rancho del Paso yearling sale in New York. An agent relied on his experience and knowledge of bloodlines, and whether he liked how a colt or filly was put together. The agent representing Marcus Daly looked over the ninety-six prospects offered. The purchase of Thoroughbred yearlings was always risky. With a gut feeling to also abide by, the agent picked eight.[1]

The yearlings journeyed to their new home in Montana. The four stockcars in which they rode swayed and clattered and snaked northwest through the Rocky Mountains. Dipping into the Bitterroot Valley, the locomotive stopped at Riverside Siding. Railroad men slid the stockcar doors open and handed off the animals to waiting hostlers, who then herded the group a short distance to Bitter Root Stock Farm. There, the record-keeping clerk opened his book, *Index: Thoroughbred Stock*, and recorded eight new entries. One of them read: "Montana. Bay colt, foaled Feb. 13, 1888. White around corner of right hind foot, branded 7. Bred by James Ben Ali Haggin."[2]

Montana was a disappointing example of his breed. His coarse and sharply angular body accentuated an oddly potbellied midsection, and his unnaturally long ears lopped a bit. One day in the future, a famous trainer would take his first look at Montana and say unkindly, "That t'ere old camel." But bloodlines had convinced the agent to pay a premium price of $6,000 for the loose-jointed colt of bones. The hope was that Montana would have a turn of speed like his sire, Ban Fox. That Kentucky bred had peaked to champion two-year-old status in 1885, the year he carried J. B. Haggin's gold and blue. Montana's dam was English-bred Queen, equally as well bred as Ban Fox.[3]

At the farm's training track, colts and fillies described as "graceful, spirited and nervy as young panthers" loped lithely. Not Montana. A ridiculously ungainly gait could trip him up. Everything about him pointed to one of

142

those mistakes that could kill an agent's career, but Marcus Daly, it was said, stood by his agents despite an occasional clunker.[4]

Montana somehow managed to dodge the cull pasture, and in spring 1890 he shipped to New Jersey with seven stablemates. Matthew Byrnes, the trainer, would oversee Marcus Daly's newly fashioned racing stable, Riverside, as well as one owned by J. B. Haggin. The events leading to the Byrnes-Haggin-Daly alliance are unclear, but it is likely that Haggin arranged it, and the deal can be construed as Haggin mentoring Daly in the sport of horse racing.[5]

Byrnes's training center was called Long Branch, so named for the neighboring town. He lived with his wife and two children on a farm nearby known as Chestnut Grove. Both properties were close to the six-hundred-acre Monmouth Park Racecourse, America's largest racing park. The Monmouth Park Association was host to the important Omnibus Stakes, Lorillard Stakes, and Monmouth Cup. Byrnes had once been a jockey and had done a good deal of riding at Monmouth. He would be associated with the park his entire life.[6]

Marcus Daly likely heard the heroic story about his new trainer that had unfolded in 1882. One quiet night, unfamiliar noises in a Monmouth shed row awoke Byrnes. Seizing a pistol, he dashed outside and saw an intruder bolt away from Pizarro's stall. Byrnes for good measure fired above the dim, running figure, who was quickly engulfed in darkness. The stall door's lock had been picked. The intruder most likely had intended to harm the horse.[7]

Byrnes knew better than to hurry Montana in his schooling. He was a big, raw colt, and "we had to be very careful of him" was how Byrnes explained the slow handling. Meanwhile, Montana glowered in his stall like a bull in a pen. And he had turned mean. One of his favorite diversions was to stalk the rats wanting a share of his feed. Mostly he immediately stomped them to death, but sometimes he would let them get into his feed box for a good nibbling. His ears would flatten before he lunged. A snap of his jaws meant certain death. After a killing spree, Byrnes warned the grooms: "[He's] more dangerous than ever and not a safe proposition for an approach." The poor grooms already bore scars and bruises from his vicious bites and kicks.[8]

The racing season of 1890 inched into August. On the twenty-eighth at Monmouth Park, Byrnes sent Montana on parade with the Riverside Stable colors of copper and Irish green. The six-furlong Carteret Handicap was his maiden race. The field of twelve spread out horizontally at the post, and the starter waved his flag. The field bobbed together through early furlongs until Russell, the favorite, spurted to the front and laid out some distance. Just as the crowd was sure Russell had the race sewn up, Montana energized his pace, and clumsy as it was, he could run furiously fast. He pulled even with Russell and those two pounded the ground like thudding hammers on the charge to the wire. By a thrust of his skinny neck, Montana defeated Russell. The risk-taking gamblers cheered wildly for Montana, the thirty-to-one dark horse who stole the race from Russell. The purse paid a nice $8,760.[9]

Montana came to the fight late in the Carteret and stuck with the closer running style three days later in the Futurity Stakes at Sheepshead Bay. Springing from the post and surging into their strides, the burgeoning field of fifteen was nearly even. Montana broke late and had to scramble from thirteenth, but hard running pulled him almost to the front of the pack. He finished a respectable fourth.[10]

Fetlock-deep mud at Sheepshead Bay on September 13 checked Montana's speed, earning him fifth in the Great Eastern Handicap. With only three starts in 1890, the campaign was brief but, importantly, the Carteret Handicap triumph was significant: by winning his first major American horse race, Montana likewise delivered to Marcus Daly his first victory in a major horse race. Daly must have found that gratifying if he was otherwise disappointed in the Riverside Stable. He had invested an estimated $500,000 to finance his inaugural year of racing. The Riverside Stable earned $16,269, of which the Carteret purse accounted for half.[11]

The Daly-Haggin-Byrnes alliance secured jockey Pike Barnes as first-call rider for 1891. Of the arrangement, the *New York Times* predicted a "brilliant opportunity" for the "dusky" jockey to "make a record for himself this season." The statement alluded to the tentative reinsmanship he had demonstrated ever since July 8, 1890, when he raced at Washington Park. Near the end of the Drexel Stakes, Barnes and his mount Santiago thundered directly behind Noretta and jockey Abbas. The race turned disastrous when Noretta stumbled and Abbas, unseated, tumbled to the dirt in the direct path of Santiago. With no chance of escape, Abbas was trampled and killed. The tragedy had Barnes doubly unnerved: feeling responsible for a death was one beast to live with, and then came disturbing accusations that winning the stakes was more important to him than sparing Abbas from being trampled.[12]

On June 5, Barnes angled Montana toward the Morris Park post for the race that would open the colt's three-year-old campaign. Matthew Byrnes was certain Montana could not lose the Withers Stakes. It had looked that way into the last sixteenth, with Montana leading the field but then losing his position to Picknicker. The *New York Tribune* jabbed Barnes for his riding, calling it "anything but brilliant."[13]

They were at Morris Park five days later for the mile-and-a-quarter Belmont Stakes. The *New York Times* endorsed Montana as "the sure thing of the day," and the crowd thought so too, sending him postward as first choice in the six-horse field. The dash from the post had Bermuda first to show in front, with Montana glued to his flank. They clipped at a crisp, rhythmic pace through the first mile. At a quarter mile left to go, Barnes chirped, and Montana bolted past Bermuda like a storm. The eagle-eyed jockeys who trailed watched, waited, hoped for any opportunity to exploit a miscue. Yards of reddish soil still lay ahead, and Barnes, cocksure of an easy victory, began showboating for the grandstand crowd. Montana, flummoxed by the sudden inattention, throttled down. Jockey Snapper Garrison saw this and at once gunned Foxford. In an explosive flurry of speed, that colt cut past Montana and stole the Belmont Stakes.[14]

Pike Barnes's disgrace was a consequence of his disregard for racing's golden rule—*Never stop riding until the race is won.* The *New York Times* bellowed:

> [Barnes] failed to remember, just as hundreds of jockeys have done before him, that Garrison is chain lightning at a finish. So, he kept at his pretty riding for the benefit of the women in the grandstand, and he kept at it just long enough to enable Garrison and Foxford to beat him past the judges by a length. It was a magnificent piece of riding on Garrison's part, a sorry and disgusting bit of work by Barnes, who had a large amount of conceit knocked out of his thick head by his defeat, for he knew, as did everyone on the track, that he had thrown away a race and robbed his employer of a rich stake that should have been his.[15]

Poor Foxford. Barnes's stupidity overshadowed his magnificent performance. The firestorm swirling around Barnes was discussed ad nauseam, and this irritated Foxford owner Charles E. Rand to exasperation. In relief, he proposed a match race, to which Marcus Daly answered, "I'm a newcomer in the East, and I scarcely feel at home yet. It's bad enough to beat me out of the Belmont, but rubbing it in. I will run Montana against Foxford for $10,000 a side. . . . But there is one proviso I make: the winnings must be handed over to the Sisters of Charity."[16]

Rand shut up.

When Barnes and Montana finished fifth in the Thistle Stakes, Barnes had begged for a hard drive down the Sheepshead Bay stretch, but Montana had other ideas and "quit like a steer," as one witness put it. July 1 at Sheepshead Bay was a big day, drawing crowds of racegoers wanting to see the Realization Stakes. The winner's purse at $31,000 was among the American turf's most lucrative, and the five-horse field was deep in talent. If Montana was to defeat powerhouses Potomac and Strathmeath, he would have to run like a deer. Perhaps a different jockey could inspire Montana to fire up enthusiasm and speed.[17]

The colt sizzled under Fred Taral's reinsmanship. Furlongs whizzed by. Montana was running his heart out, but here came a chestnut-colored whirlwind—Potomac. Taral reached back and lashed Montana, and the colt tried harder. From the head of the homestretch to the wire, Montana and Potomac sped in a head-to-head drive, and by a head, or a nose, or an eyelash—depending on who was doing the talking—Montana lost the Realization Stakes to Potomac, or so said the judges. Immediately after the race, Marcus Daly at Sheepshead Bay found Taral and offered him $18,000 to ride for his stable in 1892. Taral said he would think about it, but in the end he would stick with the turfmen engaging him in 1891, Johnny Campbell and A. F. Walcott.[18]

On the day after the Realization, Byrnes and Montana floated on a boat. Byrnes was typically reticent about his work but, electrified by the Realization, told the boat crew that Montana was poised to win the Lorillard Stakes. From captain to stoker, the ship's crew peeled out dollar bills and handed them to Byrnes, entrusting him to make their wagers on July 7 at Morris Park.[19]

Montana's jockey for that big race was Isaac Murphy, conceivably the greatest rider of the nineteenth century. Of the seven horses and jockeys,

Murphy and Montana were a strong team, but bettors liking Strathmeath in the Lorillard made him the seven-to-five favorite. Montana at two to one was second pick, but it was Reckon who jumped cat-quick from the pack. Murphy and Montana dropped to last and stayed there until midrace. Murphy then let slide a slip of rein. Montana, optimizing that weird stride of his, rushed on front-running Reckon and Strathmeath. Legs spun through the final eighth. Tightly bunched Strathmeath, Reckon, Montana, and Pessara knuckled down for a fierce fight. Murphy again relaxed a slip of rein. *Faster!* They bobbed and glided in perfect synchrony, sweeping up four lengths and notching victory over Strathmeath. That winner's purse was worth a cool $17,000.[20]

A Lorillard Stakes victory on the heels of Montana's dramatic performance in the Belmont Stakes garnered volumes of attention. Marcus Daly in his second season of racing was also winning with two-year-olds Tammany and Sir Matthew. He understandably expected more great races from Montana. Instead, the colt went unplaced in four starts. Matthew Byrnes had the horse ready to go, but the *Spirit of the Times* noted that "sickness or some accident generally befell him."[21]

The 1891 season was a disappointment for Pike Barnes. He could no longer ride as if his veins pumped ice instead of blood, since the death of Abbas. And the fear of retribution nagged. As the *New York Times* put it, "It is believed among many horsemen that much of his listless riding was due to the fact he would not go into a crowd because he was afraid some jockey would throw him down and kill him, just as he had been the means of killing Abbas." Barnes was cleared of any malicious act, but new accusations were swirling, alleging that he had fallen in with shady bookmakers paying him to deliberately lose. At least one horseman of good standing, Matthew Byrnes, disputed such claims, attributing the jockey's decline to the depletion of his strength after years of having to make an unnatural weight to ride.[22]

Nonetheless, Byrnes and Marcus Daly searched for a jockey to replace Pike Barnes. The story goes that at an unspecified racetrack in New York in 1891, one of Daly's cronies pointed at Snapper Garrison. Daly surely remembered Garrison's red-hot finish on Foxford in the Belmont Stakes that narrowly defeated Montana, and he likely remembered Garrison's good ride on Montana in the 1890 Futurity. Wanting to size up the jockey more closely, Daly eyed Garrison, walked a circle around him, and in his quaint phraseology remarked, "Whist! But I rather have 'um wid me than agin me."[23]

Garrison had no idea who the man staring at him was. Nor did he know whether he would be relicensed to ride. In midseason 1891, his uncharacteristically bad riding raised suspicions and was alleged to have been criminal, but more serious was illegal betting on horse races. The newly organized Board of Control in New York yanked his license. Snapper Garrison, a favorite with the public, took a fall from grace. Marcus Daly did not care. He needed Snapper Garrison in the pilothouse and engaged the unlicensed jockey at a salary of $12,000. Daly's gamble paid off. Shortly after January 1, 1892, Garrison's license was renewed.[24]

Most nineteenth-century jockeys hailed from rural America, but Edward Henry Garrison was born in good-sized New Haven, Connecticut, on February 9, 1868. Three years of schooling were summarized as "book learnin'." From his work in a blacksmith shop he discovered wonderful things about horses. Garrison seemed a "small, puny-looking lad" according to one writer, but this belied the vivacity of a "wiry little chap with sinews of steel and the courage of a fox terrier and quick as a flash besides." Garrison's quick-as-a-flash work ethic for even menial tasks at a local racetrack impressed "Father Bill" Daly. The exact year and place that their association began is unclear, but it was probably Hartford, Connecticut.[25]

Father Bill was a one-legged trainer famous for schooling racehorses as much as schooling some of America's finest jockeys. He liked nicknames. Ever-restless Garrison was "Jack Snapper." One day at Brighton Beach, a horse had no rider. Father Bill said, "Let Jack Snapper ride him." The clerk recorded "Jack Snapper," and Garrison was "Snapper" the rest of his life.[26]

Father Bill was a harsh taskmaster. When a horse lost a race on account of a boy's "stupidity" or disobedience, all the boys were marched to the racetrack, where Father Bill explained in detail the mishandlings that had led to the loss. Lest the lesson be forgotten, each boy was whipped with a martingale. Garrison reportedly thrived under this strict tutelage. He stayed with Father Bill three years.[27]

Garrison rode toward greatness one nag at a time. They were "mangy cripples," but with Garrison astride, his sleeves rolled up to his elbows and his cap worn backward, the cripples won at long prices. Blessed with intuitive ability to read his mounts' minds and understand their quirks, the left-handed jockey became a favorite with trainers and owners. He could raise the dead with his vigorous use of whip and spur, and this was a hit with the two-dollar and five-dollar betting crowds at Brighton Beach. Garrison as the "Pride of Brighton Beach" rose to celebrity status.[28]

Suited in colorful silks, Garrison cut a dashing figure. His white complexion complemented startling thick dark eyebrows that curved above clear dark eyes. Handsome as a matinee idol, he had moonlighted as an actor on the New York stage. At the racetrack, however, seated on a horse in full stride, Garrison was "positively an eyesore," the *St. Louis Post-Dispatch* bemoaned. "A bump on a log is far handsomer. He has neither seat nor hands, grace nor style. He stands in short stirrups, curls his back like a squirrel, and rides on his horses' neck. His legs are long and just the least bit knock-kneed; his thighs are as strong as the jaws of an alligator and his grip on a horse's withers is like the grip of a vise."[29]

Most jockeys rode with long stirrups and reins. Garrison liked them short. As for riding like a squirrel, Garrison said that crouching over the horse's withers shifted a jockey's weight off his mount's back to the part of its anatomy able to withstand greater strain. Garrison kept his head low and near the animal's neck, and his hands within six inches of the bit. Riding this way cut wind resistance, and he had better control of his mount. As Garrison pointed out, "It don't matter if my style is not handsome, I get there just the same." Although his seat was unconventional, it was not unique to him. In style, he emulated Fred Archer, the great English rider.[30]

Garrison liked to play it close at the finish. He would ride his mount with barely enough effort to win in dramatic flurry, and although a chancy tactic, it did preserve a mount's energy for future races. Watching Garrison ride was to see a mortal man seemingly lift his mount in the air, sail him over the finish, and win by a head, or a nose, or a lip. At Sheepshead Bay on September 20, 1883, Garrison was aboard Dutch Roller for the Great Eastern Handicap. Their desperate, out-of-the-clouds finish in a field of nineteen two-year-olds was reportedly the performance that coined a famous expression in the sports world: "a Garrison finish."[31]

Yet, turning nineteen years old in 1887, Garrison contemplated retirement. He was feeling overwhelmed by constantly having to keep his natural weight of 130 pounds down to a riding weight of at around 110 pounds.[32]

Confronted with the prospect of shedding five pounds overnight, he would start reducing at four o'clock and gulp a heavy dose of "medicine."

Wrapping himself in "flannels and pea-jackets," he ran until he sweated off two pounds. After drinking a bottle of "citrate of magnesia," Garrison soaked in a steam bath and sweated and sweated. Leaving the bath at eleven o'clock in the evening, he walked four miles and went to bed without eating. "I am sick and tired of having to get down to the weight I now ride at," he told an interviewer. "I only eat one meal a day, and that I do not get until my day's work is done. . . . Every day I take an eight-mile spin in heavy sweaters. The first six miles I walk at a brisk pace, and I run the last two as hard as I can. I come in covered with perspiration, and then, no matter how warm the weather is, I have to jump into bed and cover myself with blankets. That is how heavy-weight jockeys reduce in training. I am sick of it." He was sick of it, but in exchange he commanded lucrative contracts for the privilege of riding the world's greatest Thoroughbred horses.[33]

As Garrison's star rose, so did his arrogance, to the degree of distrusting and disregarding trainers' instructions. James Rowe Sr. knew he had Race-land in perfect condition for the 1889 Oriental Handicap. The colt should have won his race, but he did not even place. Rowe was fuming. He dressed down Garrison for deliberately not riding the horse to win. Garrison blamed the horse for having an off day. A row erupted, and owner August Belmont I stuck by his trainer. One week passed. The friction did not lessen. Garrison resigned his post.[34]

His career survived the contretemps, however. J. B. Haggin, who engaged Garrison in 1888, saw no reason not to engage the jockey in 1890, although contract negotiations languished on account of Snapper Garrison's messy personal life. He was dubious as a provider for his wife and two daughters. He was characterized as a high roller and a recklessly heavy plunger who squandered thousands of dollars on a gambling habit. Betting on a boxing match in 1892, he raked in $30,000. Moreover, squabbles over money and property jointly owned with his father-in-law saw the two men repeatedly in and out of court.[35]

Garrison's gregarious nature and the recreational pursuits he loved relieved his troubles. He played cards, shot pool or billiards, and never missed the social season in Washington, DC. On occasion he would moonlight as a starter, bookmaker, or referee of a slugfest in a boxing ring. Garrison himself was a good boxer. And as a first-class wing shot, he enjoyed pigeon-shooting contests in the company of rod and gun club presidents and bookmaker pals. In the fields where quail flew, Garrison hunted over his prized English setter, Prince Charlie.[36]

◨

With the 1892 racing season under way in New York, Snapper Garrison resumed his customary strutting around the racetrack as the man most elegantly dressed. "His vanity remains with him," the *St. Louis Post-Dispatch* observed. "He leaves the jockey room immaculately dressed in the latest Fifth avenue style, white shoes on his feet, Montana shoes he calls them; a posy in his buttonhole, his mustache beautifully curled and waxed, his cane in his gloved hand, his necktie ablaze with diamonds, his watch-chain ornamental with rare charms and his eye searching the for the prettiest girls in the stand."[37]

Garrison would ride Montana. The horse at four years old apparently resembled something of a Thoroughbred. A *Spirit of the Times* writer inspecting the Riverside Stable string wrote flattering things: "[Montana has] grown into a grand, big, handsome animal and has lost the somewhat potbellied appearance. There is a great deal of him, and he is a magnificently muscled colt, who should be as good a racehorse as he has given promise at times of being." Matthew Byrnes picked the Lightweight Handicap at Morris Park for Montana's first start, which would also serve to prep the colt for the Suburban Handicap. With Garrison up, Montana beat five rivals by nearly a length.[38]

Gossip for the Suburban Handicap of 1892 percolated across the country. In New York, the *Evening World* made the claim that even the oldest turfman in America could not remember "such a grand lot of Thoroughbreds together in one race." Any one of the sixteen entries could win it; all were fast and could easily stay the mile-and-a-quarter distance. The jockeys were a fine lot, too. Garrison sat astride Montana, Isaac Murphy astride His Highness, Fred Taral on Pessara, and Willie Simms on Poet Scout. Daredevil Fitzpatrick was aboard Raceland, the winner of the Suburban Handicap one year ago.[39]

The morning of June 18, 1892, dawned drizzly for Suburban Handicap Day. Despite the damp air, the track surface was dry, but it was not fast. A cold sea fog blew in from the Atlantic and shrouded Sheepshead Bay. The weather kept many thousands of people away from the racetrack, but twenty thousand were keen to see which of the racehorses would claim the valuable winner's purse topping out at $17,750.[40]

Montana had smoked in his Suburban prerace trials. Matthew Byrnes stated publicly that if a horse was to defeat him, that animal would have to be blazingly, blazingly fast. The open secret set off a floodgate to the betting shed. The eighty-three bookmakers knew of the open secret, but there was more to be considered than that in the world in which they operated. Byrnes had already won two Suburban Handicap titles, and Snapper Garrison had one to his credit. Bookmakers had to calculate both men into the equation. Not wanting any part of the Byrnes, Garrison, and on-fire Montana triad, the books offered stingy two-to-one odds. Still, Montana and Garrison were a hot ticket.[41]

By the time the saddling bell rang, the original sixteen entries were reduced to eleven. Raceland, the favorite, accepted the field's heaviest load of 124 pounds. Montana carried 117, and the least weighted was Lamplighter with 104. The bugler tapped out "Boots and Saddles." The parade was under way. The ladies, whose colorful summer dresses were hidden by warm heavy capes, rose from their grandstand seats and waved handkerchiefs for their favorites. Some ladies asked their men, "Where is Montana?"[42]

Byrnes had insisted that his horse was too nervous for a parade, a claim scoffed at by some, but the stewards had granted permission for a delayed entry. Moments before the parading contestants reached the post, Montana and Garrison made their theatrical appearance. Even on this gray, gloomy afternoon, Montana's coat shone like polished copper. Garrison, clutching a brand-new whip, shimmered in his suit of copper and green.[43]

An anxious field triggered half a dozen breakaways before the starter sent them off, with most of them breaking cleanly. Montana and Garrison, tenth, were in big trouble already. As Snapper Garrison would remember:

> I was knocked back to almost last position. Montana was a long strider and not smoothly gaited. He floundered and climbed in the run to, and around, the first turn, and whenever I looked through the dust, I could see the field strung out for a hundred yards. Major Domo was leading us a merry dance. Nearing the five-furlong pole, I didn't think I had a chance, but Montana got on his stride and I went after him with the whip. What a licking

I gave him! At every cut he flattened out and fairly flew. In and out through the maze of horses, enveloped in clouds of dust, I shot him, and at every stride I whipped him. At the half-mile pole he was flying. . . .

He picked up one after another of the field in the run around the turn leading to the stretch. At last but two horses were ahead of us. . . . They were so far away it seemed hopeless to try and get them. At the furlong pole I had hopes of catching [Lamplighter] and, although I hated to do it, I went at my horse again with the whip. Under terrific punishment, I got Montana to Lamplighter's tail and there he hung for just a moment. . . .

I never rode a harder finish in my life, and in the last 50 yards we were locked, every man whipping and driving for his life. Neither Lamley, who rode Major Domo, Bergen [*sic*] who was on Lamplighter, nor I could tell which horse had won. . . . Montana

Montana. On February 1, 1892, the future books opened for the Suburban Handicap. Montana was quoted at forty to one. The odds fell to thirty to one in March, then to fifteen to one in April. By race day, he was the two-to-one favorite, owing to a fast and commanding win in the Lightweight Handicap five days before his start in the Suburban. Photo courtesy of *Illustrated American* 11 (July 2, 1892): 358.

was staggering; he was so tired, but I can tell you I was a happy man when I saw my number was up.[44]

Garrison swung off Montana, whom he had whipped for more than three-quarters of a mile. Well-wishers swarmed around the jockey at the dismounting stand, and Montana was led away. Roistering men grabbed him to festoon his jacket with "buds and laurels of any Olympian victor." By evening of Suburban Handicap Day, Garrison and Matthew Byrnes were the nation's most talked-about men and "extolled everywhere where horsemen met," reported the *New York Times*. In Chicago, the *Tribune* related that nobody wanted to talk about anything else. "'Did you back Montana?' everybody asks everybody. Then everybody tells everybody what a wonderful race Garrison rode, for Garrison won just as much as Montana did." Turf scribes and turf historians alike spoke in wonder over Matthew Byrnes. The man had trained three Suburban Handicap winners for three different owners: Pierre Lorillard, J. B. Haggin, and Marcus Daly. Byrnes at age thirty-eight added yet another milestone to an already hefty book of work.[45]

Marcus Daly sent his congratulations by way of telegram. On race day, the order of his day was to conduct inspections of his copper mines. The story goes that Daly tucked his Suburban ticket in the pocket of the suit he hung in the changing house. The inspections wore on underground, and aboveground the changing house caught fire. Daly's winning ticket was now ash. As was his custom, he had made a hefty wager and had every intention of collecting the $40,000 owed him, ticket or not. Then he learned that this was impossible because the bookmaker had died. From one man to the next, in the saloons and pool halls, the story was told and retold, and everyone was roaring with laughter that, for once, Marcus Daly had run out of luck.[46]

Garrison's hefty book of saddling up in 1892 had, at times, turned dangerous. On June 11, Garrison took Shelly Tuttle to the Morris Park post. The fretful colt reared, fell backward, and rolled over, and Garrison was fortunate to escape the horse's full weight. Painfully hurt and unaware that his back had been sprained, Garrison got a leg up and rode Shelly Tuttle to tenth place in the Great Eclipse Stakes. Next, on June 28 at Sheepshead Bay, Garrison no sooner landed Comanche a winner in the Spring Stakes than his chronically underweight body revolted from the strain of whipping a one-thousand-pound animal running flat out. Garrison's couple of coughs worsened into an uncontrollable coughing fit from which he fainted. He was back on his feet in moments and walking the spell off. He then swung into the saddle for two more races, whipping those mounts to third-place finishes. He later revealed that one of his lungs had hemorrhaged.[47]

Montana was back on the racetrack after three weeks of rest that had followed the Suburban. Garrison rode him to fourth place in the Fourth of July Handicap at Monmouth Park. Jockey Daredevil Fitzpatrick and Montana raced on August 9, losing the Champion Stakes before sweeping up a victory in the Comparative Stakes two days later. Garrison missed most of the August racing because he had fallen ill. The hard riding and the methods he relied on to maintain an abnormal weight were compromising his health. He convalesced until August 30, in time for the Twin City Handicap at Sheepshead Bay. He had regained enough strength to deliver a severe whipping, but Montana could not find the power to outstride his rivals and finished third. In the next six starts, with Garrison in the saddle for five, the lone win was in the Labor Day Handicap. Garrison had been sick and his body battered, yet in 1892 he owned the best winning average among all jockeys. Under suspension a year before, he brilliantly reinvented his career.[48]

Expert horsemen were in a conundrum over Montana's twelve starts and nine losses. Opinions were split. The detractors cackled that his victory in the Suburban Handicap was pure luck and advised Marcus Daly to get rid of the horse. Daly did not disagree. "I am not greatly impressed with Montana," he said, "even if he did win the Suburban, thanks to Garrison's grueling finish. . . . He almost invariably disappoints his admirers when great things are expected of him."[49]

The empathetic horsemen attributed Montana's decline to repeated whipping and spurring. One turf authority typified Garrison as "an apostle of the kill or win creed," who during the Suburban "nearly killed Montana." The jockey admitted that he freely plied the whip "so steadily and so effectively in [the Suburban] the good old horse was kept in his stall for two days" and "fairly burned up." The treatment was justified because Montana was a sluggish racehorse needing "a whole lot of urging," and the whip "ringing a steady and cruel song" was an effective tool to get him to do his job. Garrison maintained on the one hand that he "never lashed a racer unless lashing was necessary," but on the other, "a good horse is not a piece of Dresden china, and he ought to be able to stand the gaff." The owners of racehorses, the racegoers, and the press expected jockeys to whip, according to the *Spirit of the Times*, and those who did not were castigated as "sleepy, careless, and at times, worse." Turfman John E. Madden was an exception. The *Atlantic* told the story about Madden giving jockey Winnie O'Connor a leg up on Yankee minutes before the 1901 Futurity. O'Connor asked for a whip. "Well, if you must," Madden said and likely sighed as he walked to a nearby tree in the paddock, stripped off a switch about three inches long, and handed it to O'Connor. The jockey in a huff threw the twig down, directed Yankee to the track, and won the Futurity. O'Connor admitted afterward that Yankee probably would have lost his race had he been whipped.[50]

Montana was in New York with Matthew Byrnes in 1893 but was not raced. Come September, Riverside Stable was mum about why it retired the horse. Racing three seasons, he won six of twenty-four starts and earned $59,050. The Suburban Handicap victory was the pinnacle; he never seemed to be the same horse afterward.[51]

The exercise boys at the Bitter Root Stock Farm had a new stallion to keep fit. Exercise moved from outdoors to the indoor track during the winter. The boys called Montana the "jumper from Jumpersville" because of some of the wild rides he gave them. The roof above the half-mile training track was twenty feet high. When in a playful mood, Montana jumped so high that the boy on his back had to duck his head to keep from hitting the rafters.[52]

For most of the farmworkers, Montana was as welcome as a bad headache. His hell-on-hooves temperament had not improved one bit. With jaws snapping and ears slicked back, his eyes narrowed to slits, Montana menaced the grooms and in one instance sprang at a boy and locked his jaws on the boy's shoulder before dragging him across the yard. Help arrived, and the horse was beaten away, but the kid's shoulder was crushed. The supervisor of the Thoroughbred Breeding and Training Department, Sam Lucas, once understated, "Montana was always in an ugly humor." Lucas grew weary of having to constantly avoid kicks or bites, so he chucked a clod of dry sod squarely into Montana's face. "He then was meaner than ever and never overlooked a possible opportunity to get even," Lucas said. "He was a glutton, and one time I found him choking on his feed as the result of his hungry greed. I swabbed his throat, and I am sure his appreciation of my kindness was the fact that he was always gentle in my hands from then on." Lucas might have saved Montana's life.[53]

The horse was equally unsparing of his own kind. One day a younger stablemate, Tammany, was in a playful mood during exercise and mischievously unseated his rider. Tammany, who wanted to caper some more, made a beeline for Montana, also being exercised. In a blink, Tammany realized he had blundered and backed off, but Montana started a horrible fight. Sinking his teeth into Tammany, he peeled back skin in several places before the handlers pulled him off. Marcus Daly, who expressed the sentiment "Mean. Don't Like Him," kept Montana on the place and even commissioned Henry Stull for Montana's portrait. Said Stull of his subject, "He is not a beauty to look at, by any means."[54]

When Daly eventually wanted to be rid of him, Montana shipped to a California auction in 1899. John Mackey was at the sale, acting on behalf of J. B. Haggin, and bought Montana for $1,000. In this twist of fate, Montana was returned to the place of his birth. His posh existence in the Rancho del Paso Stud was upset in 1905. Haggin, widowed since 1894, had married twenty-eight-year-old Margaret "Pearl" Voorhies. She, too, was a Kentuckian. The couple were returning to their native state and would live in the newly built mansion at Elmendorf Farm.[55]

Rancho del Paso, considered by many to be "the greatest breeding establishment in the world," would be dismantled. On December 4, 1905, at Sheepshead Bay Racecourse, the Fasig-Tipton Company auctioneers began the work of selling more than five hundred horses over four days. Twenty Rancho del Paso stallions, Montana among them, held court on December 7. The sales catalogue included a biography for each stallion. The rundown on Montana's history noted his 1892 Suburban Handicap victory, and the names of twenty money-winning progeny substantiated the statement that "his percentage of winners is very large, and he gets speed, endurance, and good campaigners." J. B. Haggin was at the sale and was apparently unwilling to relinquish all his stallions. Calling out a bid of $71,000, he rocked the sales ring to buy back the one he prized most, sixteen-year-old Watercress. The old man rocked the ring once more with his winning bid of $500 for seventeen-year-old Montana. Haggin now owned the horse a third time. Thereafter, Montana's fate is unknown.[56]

Every hundredth time that Snapper Garrison was asked to name the best horse he ever paraded in the winner's circle, he had to name two. Both horses had carried Marcus Daly's copper and Irish green. Garrison said, "Nothing I have ever ridden approached Montana in courage, although Tammany, which was the greatest horse I ever had leg up on, was a close second in the matter of gameness."[57]

CHAPTER 12

Tammany

One Hundred to One

Of the dozens of Thoroughbred horses arching their finely chiseled heads over paddock fences frosted in snow and ice crystals, Tammany was everyone's favorite at the Bitter Root Stock Farm. Shafts of winter's low-angle amber sunlight deepened his gossamer coat to a golden chestnut, or "the color about which poets sing when they find it in a woman's hair," as described by one romantic.[1]

Four years old in 1893 and recently retired from racing, Tammany was as much a pet as he was an admired champion racehorse. "It made no difference whether his company was a human being or an animal, Tammany would rub his nose in the curls of the little girl who was his frequent visitor and fondle her as gently as her mother," Sam Lucas said. "My small fox terrier puppies frequently found their way into Tammany's paddock. He would pick them up tenderly by the neck and walk with them carefully around his stall. There were few horses like Tammany."[2]

His lineage was rooted in the Tennessee bluegrass of the Belle Meade Plantation near Nashville. Belle Meade master General William H. Jackson ordered the mating of Belle Meade–bred Tullahoma to the stallion Iroquois, bred at the Erdenheim Stud in Pennsylvania. Iroquois had raced with distinction in England, winning the Prince of Wales, the St. Leger, and the crown jewel of English racing, the Epsom Derby. Tullahoma foaled Tammany at the planation in 1889.[3]

The following spring at Belle Meade, turfmen walking the grounds and scrutinizing sixty-one yearlings offered for sale hoped to buy a moneymaker on which to put their colors. At the 1887 sale, for instance, Sam Bryant struck gold with his purchase of a yearling that he raced as Proctor Knott. The agent representing Marcus Daly at the 1890 sale liked what he saw in Tammany and paid $2,500. The colt was sent directly from Belle Meade to Matthew Byrnes at Long Branch. When news of the purchase reached Bitter Root Stock

Farm, the records clerk opened *Index: Thoroughbred Stock* and wrote this entry for the colt he had not yet seen: "Chestnut colt, foaled March 23, 1889. Blaze face to nostril, narrow strip of white from blaze pointing to left eye; left hind foot white above pastern on inside; right hind foot white around coronet. Bred by Belle Meade, Nashville, Tenn."[4]

━

In June 1891, Byrnes was conditioning Tammany, Sir Matthew, and Shellbark for Marcus Daly. Of the three colts, all two-year-old maidens, Byrnes was least impressed with Tammany, but he ran all three at Morris Park on June 6. The crowd of twenty-five thousand filed through Morris Park gates despite cold, damp weather. The big draw was the six-furlong Great Eclipse Stakes, a major event for two-year-olds. A winner's purse of $24,230 awaited the victor. Byrnes and the Riverside Stable boys backed Sir Matthew, and Byrnes urged Hugh John Grant to do the same. But the New York City mayor felt compelled to wager on Tammany despite fluctuating long odds of fifty, sixty, and even one hundred to one.[5]

With the Great Eclipse post parade about to start within minutes, Tammany's jockey was a no-show. Byrnes was scrambling for a replacement. George Miller was available. With that settled, Tammany and Miller were on parade with Shellbark, Sir Matthew, and thirteen more prancing, snorty two-year-olds. Miller rounded Tammany to the post, held the reins tightly, and crouched forward in the saddle. The starter flung his flag. Miller felt the colt lift and cut through the air. From behind Tammany's peaked ears, Miller experienced the thrill of an empty racetrack ahead. Tammany never conceded an inch of dirt to the trailing field, going wire to wire in the Great Eclipse. Sir Matthew finished a disappointing ninth, and Shellbark was fourteenth. Hugh John Grant's winning ticket returned more than $500.[6]

A sensational victory by a dark horse named Tammany was not the only big story to come out of the Great Eclipse. The contest for second place was so tight that it altered American turf history. The judges, unable to determine the placings, had to declare a dead heat and award runner-up honors to *three* horses. Of course, dead heats invariably elicited disputes and controversy. Advocating for an advancing technology known as the "photo finish," *Turf, Field and Farm* stated, "No doubt an instantaneous photograph of the finish between these three would have resulted in a definite decision as to second

Tammany at Tammany Castle. Tammany received his name from his trainer Matthew Byrnes, who chose it in deference to his "good Democrat" boss Marcus Daly, and as a compliment to Daly's good friend Hugh John Grant, mayor of New York City. Photo courtesy of Montana State Historical Society, Helena, Montana.

and third places. . . . The verdict of the camera could not be disputed, and those troublesome affairs, dead heats, would become a thing of the past." Photo-finish technology at the races was first tried in 1881. Camera operators had since continued their experimentation on photographing horses in motion. In one effort, a series of cameras were mounted to a wire and stretched across the racetrack. When tripped, the cameras photographed simultaneous images of the running horse. Photo-finish technology would become a standard tool in twentieth-century horse racing.[7]

At Sheepshead Bay for races on June 29 and August 11, Tammany went unplaced and showed that he could lose. Marcus Daly made the long trip east to watch both Tammany and Montana compete at Morris Park on the afternoon of August 18, 1891. He put $5,000 down on Tammany, second pick, in the Criterion Stakes.[8]

A quick, clean start in the six-furlong Criterion sent Airplant to the lead for four furlongs. Through the fifth, new horses punched through and colors at the field's head clicked like a kaleidoscope. In the last furlong, all seven horses locked like marching soldiers, and the thick, thunderous action must have racked Pike Barnes's nerves, but with hands and voice he urged Tammany through it. They broke clear and Tammany's crisp, open-shut strides put him two lengths ahead of the field before he breezed past the wire first, winning $5,490 in purse money.[9]

Daly presumably wagered on Montana, ready to go in the Omnibus Stakes immediately after the Criterion. Ailing from an inflamed hock, likely aggravated by a long delay at the post, Montana was quickly out of contention and finished tenth. Marcus Daly nonetheless cleaned out the bookmakers of so much cash that detective Robert Pinkerton insisted on personally escorting him back to his hotel.[10]

Three days after the Criterion, Pike Barnes and Tammany earned third in the Select Stakes at Morris Park. This was Barnes's last ride on the colt. In fact, the twenty-year-old would quit the jockey profession in November. He rode for Daly, Sam Bryant, Noah Armstrong, and J. B. Haggin, all of whom paid him well. It was said he would pull wads of greenbacks from his pocket and spend them with the speed of "waters going over the falls at Niagara with a mighty rush." Settling in Chicago, Barnes opened the Keystone Saloon with jockey pal Tiny Williams. Barnes's skills at running a saloon did not correspond to the skills displayed on the back of a running racehorse. Going broke and losing the Keystone, he went to Ohio hoping to make a new life. Barnes contracted tuberculosis and was penniless when he died from the disease in January 1908 at age thirty-seven, leaving behind a job as a barkeep in Columbus. Of all his winning rides, most famous was with Proctor Knott in the 1888 Futurity.[11]

Tammany made his next start on August 29 with George Miller astride for what would be Miller's final ride on the chestnut colt. A field of twenty-two for the Futurity strung out like a cavalry column as it marched to the Sheepshead Bay post. Marcus Daly was said to be eager to win that famed race. He must have been crestfallen when he received the news that Tammany had finished seventeenth.[12]

At the end of each racing season the nation's turf scribes compiled lists. With earnings at $30,070 in 1891, Tammany placed at number nine on the winning horses list. He started in six races and won two and was third once. Byrnes described the colt's movement over a racetrack as "perfect," and in flight, "his legs acted like a pair of shears—open and shut, open and shut." In the wire-to-wire performance that won him the Great Eclipse Stakes, he looked to be a speed horse, but in future races, in the final furlongs, he ripped along in a homestretch charge, showing that he was a closer. Marcus Daly was number six on the winning owners list, accomplishing this in only his second year of eastern racing. His Riverside Stable brought home $79,905. A journalist for *Outing* remarked on the preeminent turfmen recently lost to death or retirement. There was, however, "fresh blood" filling the vacancies, that of Marcus Daly and trainer Matthew Byrnes. The pair of Irishmen was "sure to become most prominent," the journalist enthused.[13]

Matthew Byrnes was born in 1854 and immigrated from Ireland to America with his parents as a young boy. Sharing the same birthday as George Washington, he was fond of saying, "How could I have anything else but luck after being born on the birthday of the liberator of my country?" The graded steps of his turf career included exercising horses for August Belmont I, whose Nursery Stud was then located on Long Island, New York. Graduating to jockey apprentice at age twelve, Byrnes won his first professional race aboard a Belmont-owned Thoroughbred. Byrnes astride Belmont's high-class Glenelg hung up the American track record for a mile and a half. As the number of trips to the winner's circle rose, so did the numbers that registered Byrnes's weight and height. His hope of becoming a great jockey was dashed. He switched to training, a common progression for boy jockeys who grew too tall and heavy for a racing saddle.[14]

After seven years at Nursery Stud, Byrnes moved to one of the nation's most recognized racing stables, the Rancocas, at Jobstown, New Jersey. His position as assistant trainer for tobacco industry tycoon Pierre Lorillard reunited him with his Nursery Stud mentor Jacob Pincus, for whom Byrnes felt "enduring gratitude." Autumn 1880 would prove pivotal. With Pincus overseas, Lorillard asked twenty-six-year-old Byrnes on no less than three occasions to take the job of head trainer, but Byrnes resisted, "appalled by the responsibility involved." Six months later and again without a head trainer, Lorillard insisted: "You must take it."[15]

When "Silent Matt" did not engage with employees or peers, they were not offended. He was simply preoccupied with a horse. His quick and calculated thinking was compared to that of a wolf. One day his dark eyes followed a beauty of a filly, Hiawasse, who at two years old was still so tiny. Lorillard was advised to sell her, but Byrnes appealed to keep her. When she swept the most important stakes for fillies in 1882, Lorillard was indebted to his young trainer. Byrnes also molded Pontiac, his first of three Suburban Handicap winners. Tall and ungainly Wanda seemed to be excluded from certain physical laws, or in Byrnes's words, "She acts as if the ground wasn't good enough for her." Watching her breezy way of barely touching hoof to ground, he thought, "What if she wore aluminum shoes?" This was an expensive proposition at a time when the lightweight metal was almost as valuable as silver. Lorillard bought into Byrnes's thinking and ordered custom-made plates from Tiffany and Company. Fitted in the pricy footwear, Wanda emerged as the Rancocas Stable's principal breadwinner in 1885. Fifty years would pass before American trainers routinely chose aluminum shoes over steel.[16]

Byrnes also pored over Unrest. Lorillard agreed that she was a fine filly, but Dione was better. Byrnes thought not.

"I believe Unrest can give Dione weight and beat her," Byrnes said to his boss.

Lorillard replied, "I'll bet a hundred dollars, no . . . I'll bet you a hat . . . that Unrest can't give Dione a pound."

"All right, sir," Byrnes said, "I'll take Unrest to give Dione twelve pounds."

Lorillard answered, "Very well. There's a party of friends coming here next week. We will show them a race."

With the party looking on, Dione broke first and smoked ahead of Unrest. Lorillard was having a jolly laugh until Unrest smoked Dione through the last furlong. Turning to his trainer, Lorillard acknowledged his mistake, paid his bet, and lit a cigar.[17]

A favorite story about Byrnes that was merrily retold was originally related by a racing secretary. The secretary, who felt pity for the jockeys subjected to Byrnes's intricate instructions, overheard a prerace discussion Byrnes had with Anthony Hamilton. Another well-known trainer, William "Billy"

Matthew Byrnes. Nineteenth-century turf historian Lyman Horace Weeks predicted
that Matthew Byrnes would "go down to posterity as one of the greatest trainers of the
day." By the time Byrnes put away his stopwatch, he had won nearly every noteworthy
stakes in American racing. Accruing sixty years in the sport as a winning trainer, Byrnes
earned a berth in the National Museum of Racing's Hall of Fame. Photo courtesy
of Keeneland Library Hemment Collection.

Lakeland, who was credited with developing Hamilton into a top reinsman,
listened in. As told by the secretary:

> Byrnes gave very minute instruction as to what to do at the
> quarter, the three-eighths, the half and under certain supposed
> circumstances. Hamilton listened in a helpless sort of a way,
> trying his best to understand, but not succeeding very well. When
> Byrnes had finished his instructions, he asked Hamilton:
>   "Now are you sure you understand?"
>   "Yes, sir, I guess so," replied Hamilton.
>   Lakeland was standing close by, chuckling. Byrnes turned to
> him and said:

"Here, Billy, you understand Congo. Just interpret what I've said, will you?"

"Why certainly," answered Billy, and turning to Hamilton, he said: "Get up on that horse and win." Hamilton did as he was told.

The account illustrated Byrnes's devotion to his job, of wanting to ensure that his horse had every chance to win. It also communicated the stereotypical attitudes some white turfmen held toward Black jockeys. But that Byrnes would use the slur "Congo" seems out of character. During summer 1891 when he threw a Salvator Club clambake at Chestnut Grove, the mighty racehorse Salvator, who he trained, was not at the party but his famous Black jockey, Isaac Murphy, was. The champagne flowed, and Murphy partied with luminaries J. B. Haggin, Hugh John Grant, and "half the judicial and political 'somebodies' of New York." Further, when Byrnes had trained Salvator and Firenze, Murphy and Anthony Hamilton were the regular riders who rode those horses to Hall of Fame careers. The two jockeys would earn inductions into the Hall of Fame. Byrnes's inclusion of Murphy at the clambake and defense of Pike Barnes in the aftermath of Abbas's death suggest a high regard for both men.[18]

In April 1892, Byrnes did not need a racetrack or the stopwatch he was rarely without to gauge three-year-old Tammany. A fast set of sound legs, a clean-cut, beautifully proportioned body, an amenable temperament, and a height of sixteen hands all portended a future turf star. Nationally acclaimed Snapper Garrison would repeat as his jockey. This, too boded well for Tammany. On June 4, 1892, racegoers at Morris Park were eager to see the Withers Stakes for three-year-olds. Four of the six horses, Tammany, Patron, Dagonet, and Yorkville Belle, were America's top money earners a season before. Two of the four, Patron and Tammany, took complete command of the race, with Tammany showing off his open-and-shut clip that packed tremendous speed. Three lengths ahead of Patron at the wire, Tammany won the Withers.[19]

Three weeks later at Morris Park, sure bets for the Tidal Stakes were on either Tammany or Patron, but Charade at twenty to one humbled them both. The next morning, New York newspapers were in an uproar, and the

Tribune was all over Snapper Garrison "caught asleep" for overestimating Tammany's speed and underestimating Charade's.[20]

At Sheepshead Bay on July 2, the Coney Island Jockey Club offered six races. Most of the club's work that afternoon was to finalize details for the premier race of the day, the Realization Stakes. The $28,475 winner's share of the purse was the richest an American three-year-old could net in 1892. Of the nine entries, horseplayers backed Tammany as the horse most likely to best manage the mile-and-five-eighths distance despite a track in wretched shape. Storms had pounded it. A handful of players backed Charade, who again would compete as a long shot.[21]

The Pepper, Patron, and Victory were the other big threats waiting to test Tammany like never before. The heavy condition of the track might make Tammany's 119 pounds of impost feel a lot weightier and the distance as far as the stars. To help his horse, Matthew Byrnes sent out stablemate Shellbark as the rabbit. At flag fall, the Riverside pair indeed bookended the field. Shellbark fully exploited his speed through the first mile. After passing that marker, jockey Tod Sloan dropped Shellbark off his pace, leaving Victory and The Pepper to clip along as front-runners. With five-eighths of the track left to cover, Tammany's powerful, precise strides pulled him head-to-head with Victory, and Victory, startled by the intrusion, gave up the race. Tammany now sped after The Pepper, passed him, and without the slightest punishment from Garrison, breezed past the wire and won his race by two lengths.[22]

Byrnes was beaming when he walked to the judges' platform to meet Tammany and Shellbark, already cloaked in velvety blankets of green and copper. The performance was the greatest of Tammany's career, and Shellbark, eighth, ran perfectly as the rabbit. Byrnes was the rare trainer to have won the Realization Stakes twice, the first with Salvator. Marcus Daly had his own claim to making American turf history that day as the first owner to win the Realization Stakes and the Suburban Handicap, with Montana, in the same year. On Daly's home turf of Butte, citizens gone wild emitted raucous yells that "would have made a Comanche blush," the *Anaconda Standard* reported. "The colors of the Riverside Stable, copper and green, were seen on every hand, in buttonholes, on dog collars, on flag staffs in windows and over doors . . . all served to demonstrate the enthusiasm of the crowd over the magnificent victory of the Riverside champion." Celebrations for Tammany and Marcus Daly continued through the night, and if revelers were "a little the worse for wear" the next morning, the occasion certainly justified the performance.[23]

One week later, on July 9 at Monmouth Park, Tammany and Snapper Garrison stormed through the mile-and-a-half Lorillard Stakes at record-setting speed. Upon sealing that victory, worth $17,560, Daly and Byrnes exchanged congratulations for winning the stakes in back-to-back years, and the next round of handshakes were all for Byrnes, three times winning the stakes, with Salvator, Montana, and Tammany.[24]

During that heady time, correspondent Elizabeth A. Thompkins interviewed Byrnes for her feature "Three Famous Trainers." Her coverage of American racing topics impressed the Chicago *Inter Ocean*. This lady writer demonstrated "thorough knowledge of the turfmen and horses of the day." Her work was "to the best standard and very entertaining." The *Inter Ocean* was likewise familiar with the work of another lady turf writer, whose beat was the action at Saratoga, New York. Of that unnamed writer, the *Inter Ocean* remarked, "It is evident from the context of her work that her knowledge of racing is extremely limited. Her ability to indulge in innuendo, in scandalous suggestion, is truly feminine."[25]

Tammany's three months of rest ended on October 8, in time for the mile-and-a-quarter Jerome Stakes at Morris Park. Snapper Garrison was content to keep the colt at the rear of the field while front-runners Yorkville Belle and Julien rolled. When Garrison sensed the filly inching too far ahead, he dug his spurs into Tammany's sides. The colt flew up to Belle, and nearly in unison they passed Julien and then charged down the stretch for home. Belle's jockey Daredevil Fitzpatrick was sure she would shake off Tammany and run away from him, but she was laboring under 122 pounds of weight. Tammany's blazed face reached Belle's saddle girths. At one hundred yards from the wire and still running head-to-head, Garrison and Fitzpatrick redoubled their efforts with spurring and whipping. The filly fought hard to hold every inch of her lead, but Tammany drew past just before the wire and beat her by a scant length.[26]

The colt had won four of five in 1892. His starts were so few, yet he reigned as America's richest three-year-old, earning $72,390. Marcus Daly was number two on the winning owners list, and in a joyous mood in December, he invited everyone in the Bitterroot Valley to the Hamilton community hall for the Tammany Ball, an evening of supper, dancing, and, of course, toasting his champion.[27]

Rather than overwintering his racehorses with Byrnes in New Jersey as was the custom, Daly ordered his racers shipped home for a respite of altitude and pine-scented air. "I have taken all my horses to Montana to find out how the change in climate will affect them," he said. "It may be a costly experiment, but in the end, it may be a blessing to horsemen all over the country, as it may demonstrate that Montana is the long-looked-for climate in which a trainer may begin training early in the spring and have his horses in perfect condition to race at the beginning of the racing season." Of course, the two indoor training tracks ready for use at the Bitter Root would aid the experiment.[28]

Byrnes, too, spent winter 1892 at the Bitter Root. Eastern horsemen had tried to convince him to dissuade Daly from ridiculously wintering a valuable Thoroughbred like Tammany in an environment they perceived as too severe. As Byrnes watched winter's short chilling days lengthen into warmer, longer days, he saw that the horses were better for it and said to the *Bitter Root Times*: "I had serious doubts as to the advisability of the scheme myself, but a trial of Montana wintering has proven conclusively to me that horses winter better here than anywhere else in the United States that I know of." He had come around to the quality of Bitterroot Valley–grown hay and oats, too, and would have no other. Large quantities of Bitterroot feed traveled with the racehorses.[29]

In March 1893, Byrnes and his string of fifteen were en route to New York. A treacherous spring storm in Montana pummeled the train, which stood snowbound for twelve hours. Reaching Washington Park in Chicago, the horses "stood the journey well and suffered no harm," Byrnes told a reporter. "All are rugged, healthy, and high in flesh." Tammany had clocked four thousand miles of train travel in four months, with the blizzard thrown in. Of course, Riverside Stable racehorses traveled more comfortably than did most people. Like other tremendously wealthy turfmen, Marcus Daly purchased custombuilt Arms Palace Horse Cars. Each of the three cars had a name, *Hattie D.*, *Montana*, and *Palfiena*. *Palfiena* afforded comfortable equine accommodations as well as living quarters for the attendants. A fourth car, *Hattie*, reserved for the Daly family, featured bedrooms, parlor, kitchen, and bathroom. Reportedly costing $10,000, *Hattie* was said to be the most luxurious passenger car in America. Yet when Daly traveled without his family, *Hattie* remained parked. "Any old car is good enough for Marcus Daly," he said. A rocking chair, dog, and horses always accompanied him on the train.[30]

Byrnes conditioned Tammany for his four-year-old season until that was upended on June 13, 1893. The horse badly injured his hoof during a workout and forced Byrnes to withdraw Tammany from the Suburban Handicap. This was hugely disappointing. Interest in the race was especially keen that year because Tammany was to meet Lamplighter, the darling of New York racing. With that colt rarely beaten, the wags immediately started in that Byrnes was really dodging Lamplighter. They questioned whether Tammany had at all injured his hoof.[31]

Byrnes focused on healing the severely damaged hoof. Every morning for three months, he walked Tammany to a brook where the horse soaked his feet in the cool, soothing water. The hoof improved but would never be perfect again. Byrnes adjusted Tammany's training regime to include specialized heavy shoes to protect the feet.[32]

September 1893 was unusually dramatic in American horse racing. Pierre Lorillard had retired from the sport a second time. During the dispersal sale of his stock on September 7, Lamplighter was sold to Gottfried Walbaum for $20,000. Lamplighter was a real stunner. Officially a bay in color, his striking bloodlike reddish-brown color beautifully highlighted the black points on his coat. Slightly shorter than Tammany but with a wider girth, the colt was a powerhouse for speed and strength rather than quickness. A wide white blaze ran from the top of Lamplighter's forehead to below his nose, and white stockings covered three legs. Bred at the Spendthrift Stud near Lexington, he was the son of Spendthrift, who famously went undefeated in 1878. Lamplighter's dam, Torchlight, was English bred. Before Walbaum, and before Pierre Lorillard, Lamplighter had first raced for Pennsylvania coal baron Captain Sam Brown.[33]

On the fourteenth, three months after the hoof injury, Byrnes started Tammany in a sweepstakes of little importance. The horse gaily bounced over the Gravesend track and easily won his race. Elated over the performance, an impassioned Byrnes said to R. V. Newton, a well-known Coney Island turfman, "Now let them bring on Lamplighter. People think I've been dodging. I'm ready for Lamplighter anywhere and for any amount." Newton got busy. He telegrammed Gottfried Walbaum. Negotiations began.[34]

As the possibility of a match race took shape, Byrnes was forced to scratch Tammany from the First Special on September 16. He wanted no part of a rain-soaked Gravesend racetrack that might possibly reinjure his horse. Conversely, Green B. Morris, trainer of Lamplighter, elected to run his horse. In hand with Lamplighter's victory came a new round of allegations that Byrnes was still avoiding Lamplighter. Then came even bigger news on September 18—Tammany and Lamplighter were matched.[35]

The Guttenberg Racecourse at North Bergen, New Jersey, received the honor of presenting the most widely anticipated horse race of 1893. Gottfried Walbaum and Marcus Daly each agreed to hang up $2,500 a side on race day, September 28. The Hudson County Jockey Club jumped into the tumult by offering the winner $5,000 in purse money. As more details were related, the horses would carry 122 pounds each. Snapper Garrison would ride Tammany, and Fred Taral would take Lamplighter's reins.[36]

A national rivalry was in full swing. Westerners pointed out to easterners that Tammany had earned more purse money in three seasons than had Lamplighter. Easterners reminded westerners of Lamplighter's record. He had won many more races than Tammany. The two horses had in fact met twice before, as two-year-olds, but neither horse had won. Turf scribes, alert for any scrap of information, were surprised to learn that Green B. Morris was scratching Lamplighter from the Second Special on September 23. Now, said the wags, Morris was deliberately dodging Tammany. Matthew Byrnes stayed the course, starting Tammany over a dry Gravesend racetrack. Without a word of encouragement from Snapper Garrison, Tammany won the Second Special.[37]

Lamplighter arrived at Guttenberg on September 24 with his companion animal, Cora the Collie. With Cora in his stall, Lamplighter showed impeccable manners and bided life calmly, a charming scene. Without Cora, however, Lamplighter raged in a fierce temper. During the Lorillard dispersal sale, for instance, an observer had remarked, "A dangerous horse to those in the vicinity of his heels, and his eyes shone like those of a war horse." As historian Walter Vosburgh told it, Lamplighter was a good racehorse but "unfortunate and eccentric . . . nervous and irritable to such a degree that often his naturally fine turn of speed was quite neutralized. He was not cowardly, but over-anxious, and he had queer notions about being placed on the inside or outside position at the post; while if a horse bumped him during a race, or shut him off, he seemed to lose all sense of the situation."[38]

Tammany arrived at Guttenberg on September 27. Rollicking interplay between the Lamplighter and Tammany factions heated up. The good-natured ribbings that Lamplighter's former trainer J. W. Rogers dished out to Matthew Byrnes led to a friendly wager of $1,000. Snapper Garrison was drumming up bets of his own. He had already made several but wanted more. Now he buzzed Rogers.

"I hear you bet Byrnes $1,000 on the match," Garrison said.

"I have bet $1,000 four or five times in my life. It is a lot of money for anybody who is not a millionaire to risk on a race," Rogers replied.

"I think it is the first time Byrnes bet $1,000, but he has a sure thing as Tammany will beat Lamplighter easily," Garrison said.

"It's almost a sure thing that Lamplighter can beat Tammany," Rogers rejoined.

Garrison laid more bait. "Tammany is a better horse than Salvator."

Rogers bit. Withdrawing his wallet, he pulled out a $1,000 bill. Garrison wrote a check.[39]

▄▄

The nation's most hallowed racetracks were owned and operated by prestigious jockey clubs concerned with the sport's well-being, in addition to making money. Racetracks of the other sort operated as hard-nosed firms that wanted large crowds, dozens of bookmakers, and money. Tracks like Guttenberg.

Operating under the auspices of the Hudson County Jockey Club, Guttenberg was more accustomed to criticism than honored with world-class racing. Guttenberg thumbed its nose at the Board of Control and stuck by practices most racetracks had outlawed. And Guttenberg made money, lots of it, despite low-quality racing that put inexperienced boys on the backs of platers. Equally as bad, the track operated year-round. No matter blinding snowstorms, a frozen racetrack on below-zero days, or fog so dense spectators could not even see the race, the horses went off. Given this, the *Brooklyn Daily Eagle* mocked Walbaum's recent purchase of Lamplighter:

"When the snow begins to fly, Lamplighter will, no doubt, be given a pair of skates and sent circling around the sharp corners with the other knights of the frozen path."[40]

New York racing hated the place. The *World* maintained that since opening day in 1885, the "wretched little racetrack" was the object of "universal ridicule and abuse." It had been "assailed by preachers and powerful newspapers, indicted by Grand Juries, denounced by judges from the bench, and its owners and jockeys outlawed by the other racing associations." Guttenberg grew to be an even bigger sore in 1890 when it sanctioned winter racing for two-year-olds. That just was not done. The *New York Times* called Guttenberg "the veriest travesty on sport" whose nefarious regulars "dared not show their faces in New York City during the daytime for fear of police recognition and arrest." The *New York Tribune* related that regulars were "felons of New York, Brooklyn, Jersey City, Newark and other cities," adding that "never was [there a] more odious and detestable travesty of racing than that which was carried on among the sharpers, the sneak thieves, and the buccaneers of Guttenburg [*sic*]." Snapper Garrison did not think much of the place either, calling it a "roulette wheel" and "sideshow."[41]

Gottfried Walbaum owned Lamplighter, and he owned the Guttenberg racetrack, and he served as the president of the Hudson County Jockey Club. Alternatively known as George or Gus in New York police circles, or blackguard bookmaker "Dutch Fred," Walbaum operated not one but two "disorderly gambling dives" and reportedly "put up a job on his wife" before divorcing her. Given his unsavory character and the ways in which he operated his racetrack, when by-the-book turfmen learned Guttenberg was to host the match, they scratched their heads over why Marcus Daly would allow such a thing. Pointedly asked that question, Daly replied, "I believe in democracy. All men are equal on the turf or under it." Guttenberg was not the only venue in 1893 giving turfmen fits. A St. Louis racetrack that already operated year-round was now running races day and *night*, under the brilliance of recently installed electric lights.[42]

On race day, September 28, 1893, ample sunshine as well as a lightning-fast racetrack boded well for the match race. Lamplighter's final prerace workout two days before was a beauty, and Green B. Morris must have felt confident about his colt's chances when he strolled through the shed rows. Seeing that Tammany was outside his stall having his shoes changed, Morris stopped to watch. He noticed that the set removed looked stouter than the racing plates tapped onto the colt's feet. The full implication of what he was seeing took a few seconds to register before screaming—*Tammany wore heavy, protective shoes during his prerace workouts! And Tammany's prerace time of 2:09 ½ over a mile and a quarter was a smoker. Lamplighter over the identical distance in his final prerace workout reeled off 2:10 ½. How fast could Tammany go when wearing aluminum shoes?* Green threw his arms up in exasperation.[43]

By midmorning, the hordes were catching rides to Guttenberg by ferry, rail, trolley, or horsecar. Some people came by Tally-Ho coaches. Some walked. A line of wagons raised clouds of dust likened to an army on the march. Match races captivated not only the people who lived and breathed horse racing; such contests appealed to nearly all the public. Few people could resist a national event celebrating lightning-fast rival Thoroughbreds with a supporting cast of celebrity owners and jockeys, and big money on the table. Best of all, match races ended arguments: "My horse is faster than your horse." An *Illustrated American* turf scribe observed the scene marking Guttenberg's biggest day ever: "It was a curious procession that passed through the gate of Guttenberg to see the match . . . all sorts and conditions of men and all sorts and conditions of vehicles . . . there were owners of the great racing stables and there were 'touts.' In short, every class was represented—the good that belongs to the turf proper as well as the bad that forms the turf improper."[44]

Streams of people passed through the gates and tramped to the two-thousand-seat grandstand. Thousands swarmed the lawns and fanned across the inner field where excavated dirt heaped in piles resembled newly dug graves. A scribe for the *New York World* clearly detested his assignment. His report led off with distaste for the crowd in which he was forced to mingle. The "unwashed" thousands were shoving, yelling, and pushing "like wild Indians . . . and tramped on each other with reckless freedom and without rebuke." In short, most of the bodies shoulder to shoulder at Guttenberg were "not worthy of the horses," and those who were worthy would certainly never again enter the Guttenberg grounds.[45]

Marcus Daly had pushed aside the matter of business to answer his determination to see at least one race of stature in which his horse raced. Margaret and two daughters had traveled with him. The bookmakers chalked up nine-to-ten odds for both horses. Bettors' frenetic wagering saw $1,000 bills waved in bookmakers' faces. Scores of men with ties to the Tammany Union backed their union's namesake. While Marcus Daly walked unrecognized through the crowded grounds at Guttenberg, professional bettors, or "commissioners," anonymously wagered for him and reportedly plunked down $20,000 on Tammany, which changed the odds to ten to seven. Lamplighter's price was eleven to ten against when the betting closed.[46]

Climbing the stairs to the judges' stand, Daly joined three judges, Gottfried Walbaum, and General William H. Jackson of Belle Meade, the distinguished southerner responsible for breeding Tammany. Tension in the small space magnified upon General Jackson flipping the coin to determine post positions. Lamplighter won the advantageous inside position. Perhaps it was during these unforgettable minutes that Daly made a pledge to himself: *If Tammany wins, I'll build him a castle.*[47]

At 4:16 P.M. the bugler's notes summoned the contestants. Snapper Garrison, glinting in copper and Irish green, pointed Tammany to the sunny racetrack. Matthew Byrnes asked his jockey for one thing: no monkeying around to stage a Garrison finish. Blood bay Lamplighter and Fred Taral made their eye-catching entrance. Taral dazzled in his suit of yellow, red, and white. Whooping and hollering and clapping for America's greatest four-year-olds rose to deafening roars, and Lamplighter hated every bit of it. Forty yards short of the starter's box, he lunged and directed a few kicks at the people who he thought were making the dreadful noise. Taral cajoled him to the post. Tammany was already there, full of buck and play and eager to get going. A handler hung on to the bridle to keep merry Tammany in place. Once the horses settled down, a flash of red sank through the air and Lamplighter leaped like a deer.[48]

His legs were already churning when his feet touched the earth. He had Tammany by a length at first pass of the grandstand. He burned hot as he rounded the turn into the backstretch. Taral glanced over his shoulder and liked what he saw—Tammany and Garrison trailing by about a length. The horses blew by the one-mile marker.[49]

Garrison, curled like a squirrel, hunched even closer to Tammany's ear. They had to roll faster, he said, and Tammany lurched like a machine. By the head of the homestretch, Tammany's driving strides put him head-to-head with Lamplighter. They hit the final furlong. It was now a question of heart. Whose was bigger? Charging over the furlong, Taral felt Lamplighter sag a bit. Cocking the whip, he laid down lashes, first on the right and then on the left. He spurred and desperately urged Lamplighter to stay nose-to-nose with Tammany. But Tammany pumped out greater speed before launching three leaping strides, and suddenly he was ahead of Lamplighter. Spectators on tiptoes roared. "Tammany!" "Tammany!" "Here he comes!" The gap of daylight widened as Tammany peeled off one, two, three lengths. The spectators turned to their neighbors and asked, "By how wide of a margin might Lamplighter lose?" Without touch of whip or spur, Tammany skimmed over the racetrack like an angel flirting with the ground. Garrison, motionless and serious, took Tammany home.[50]

Pandemonium rocked the grandstand. Hats spiraled upward and walking sticks waved without thought of injuring neighbors. Even the backers of Lamplighter were yelling themselves hoarse with cries of "Tammany!" Cheers and yells were said to have gone on fifteen minutes. A noisy swarm of fans leaped over the rail and fanned across the track. Seeing this, Lamplighter slicked back his ears and wanted to fight them. Fred Taral quickly dismounted the angry horse, who was led away to his stall. Taral, stupefied, said, "Why Garrison just galloped along behind me at the great pace we were going, and when we came to the stretch, he passed me as though I was on a selling plater. Make no mistake Lamplighter is a great horse, but he does not compare with Tammany in any sense."[51]

A pushing and shoving horde encircled Tammany, wanting to touch him. He withstood the tumult, as if thinking, *Is all this really necessary?* Nor did he lay back his ears at the reveler yanking on his mane and hacking off a chunk with a penknife. Garrison was crowing, "It was the easiest victory of my life. I have ridden some of the best horses in America, and this one is about the best I ever rode. In no time before or after the race was I in doubt about the result." The fast-moving horde had Garrison and Tammany surrounded and commenced to pull Garrison from his mount. "If 10,000 maniacs gathered from all the asylums in the country had been dumped on the Guttenberg track, their actions would not have been wilder nor their shouts more boisterous than those of the crowd that swooped down upon Garrison and tore him from his horse," one witness said. It was useless for Garrison to beat off the crazed people fighting for souvenirs. By handfuls, they grabbed the flowers adorning the floral horseshoe placed around his shoulders. They then ripped to ribbons his copper-hued jacket.[52]

Clusters of people besieged Gottfried Walbaum, wanting him to speak. "I did not think Lamplighter could be defeated," he admitted. "I never weakened except when I talked with Marcus Daly. He said he traveled 3,000 miles to see his horse win the race and was confident of his ability to defeat Lamplighter." Green B. Morris was gracious, saying, "I am satisfied today's race is the best one I have seen, and I have been racing a heap of years."[53]

Marcus Daly managed to extricate himself from a crush, and when he had room to speak, he said, "I feel extremely happy to own a horse that is capable of defeating such a grand horse as Lamplighter." Turfmen would say they had never seen him so jubilant. Matthew Byrnes accepted congratulations, but he needed to release bottled-up steam. "Some people said I dodged Lamplighter, but this race shows I was willing to meet him anywhere." Byrnes gave Guttenberg a fair shake, saying, "Everything in any way associated with the match has been conducted with the utmost fairness. Everything that could be done to give Tammany an equal chance with Lamplighter was made by Mr. Walbaum and his associates." In fact, the Guttenberg crew had harrowed the track deeper than usual for Tammany, whose hooves were so susceptible to injury on hard surfaces.[54]

When the scribes asked Garrison for a statement, he fired, "I always told you Tammany could beat Lamplighter. I came away with Tammany when I wanted to and had him safe all the way." Daly's thank-you bonus to his winning jockey was $10,000. How much money Daly himself raked in after the race nobody was certain, but Garrison estimated the haul at $100,000.[55]

Meanwhile in Butte, at least one thousand horse-racing fans had gathered in and around a pool hall and waited for hours to hear what the dispatcher sang out in seconds: "Tammany wins easy by five lengths!" Waves of laughter and cheers nearly raised the roof, and one reveler said that the pool hall walls "fairly trembled" in the commotion incited by "lovers of horse racing" and by those "who don't know much about horses but are proud of anything that comes from Montana." The *Hamilton News* granted that Lamplighter was a good racehorse, but so soundly beaten by Tammany he seemed "a Cayuse beside the King of the turf from Montana." The *New York Evening World* likewise granted "King of the Turf" status to Tammany and commended him for a grand performance that put Lamplighter's people in "a cataleptic state from which they awoke hours afterwards and wanted to know how it all happened."[56]

◼

Daly's decision to retire Tammany perfectly sound and unblemished was received by some as unsportsmanlike. Understandably, he wanted the first-class stallion, valued at $50,000, safely installed in the Bitter Root Stud. As Byrnes would point out, "What is the use of keeping him in training? What is there left for a good four-year-old? There are no stakes, nothing but handicaps, and if a man runs his horse honestly in these, the handicappers soon put you out of it by piling up weight."[57]

Tammany earned $117,055 in three seasons of racing. A racehorse reaching six digits in career earnings was rare. More remarkably, he won that kind of money in only fourteen starts, of which he won nine, finished second once, and third once. Not so long ago, in the 1880s, the eyes of the American public had fixated on Miss Woodford. The superlative race mare kept running, and winning, and in her sixth season was the first Thoroughbred of either sex to amass more than $100,000 in earnings. Since her time, the value of purses awarded at major events had skyrocketed. Come 1893, a colt named Domino at only two years old would set a $170,790 single-season earnings record for a horse of any age.[58]

On October 5, Tammany and his stablemate Montana were entrained for the journey from Morris Park to Bitter Root Stock Farm. Daly boarded a passenger train ten days later. While en route to Montana, Daly received good and bad news about Tammany. The horse was home at the Bitter Root but had fallen very sick. The two veterinarians were perplexed; medicine was not helping. The Bitter Root boys resorted to unconventional methods, as Sam Lucas told it: "After nine days of nursing, during which he was fed porter, ale, and champagne, he was on the road to recovery."[59]

◼

In spring 1894, Snapper Garrison rode for Marcus Daly as well as August Belmont II, Gideon Knapp, and J. B. Haggin. The contracts, valued at $23,500, made Garrison America's highest-salaried jockey. But age was creeping up. As with the decline of a champion racehorse, advancing age was no friend of a jockey. Extreme youth and lightness were cardinal. In 1897, Garrison was twenty-nine years old, and when he realized he could no longer ride because of his weight, he wept.[60]

He redirected his fame and popularity into various professions, including trainer, racetrack official, horse-buying agent, and even newspaper columnist. One segment of the autobiographical series "Jockey 'Snapper' Garrison's Own Stories of the Turf" recalled the day at Guttenberg with Byrnes, and Daly. "[We] very well knew that we could lose if Tammany happened to drop dead. Personally, I thought, and still think, Tammany dead could beat Lamplighter alive at a furlong, or a run around the world." Garrison's long association with Montana Thoroughbreds started with Noah Armstrong, who put him atop Spokane, and once he piloted Poet Scout for Samuel Larabie.[61]

On October 26, 1930, Garrison was sixty-two years old when he was hospitalized with uremia, a kidney dysfunction, and other intestinal aliments. He died two days later. "'Snapper' Garrison finished his last stretch and crossed the last wire," the *Brooklyn Times Union* eulogized on October 28. His estate, valued at $1,000, passed to his widow. As far back as 1896, the *New York Times* had warned of Garrison's "worst enemy," the betting ring.[62]

Snapper Garrison picked the Suburban of 1892 as his greatest finish, and, never a humble man, he said the race with Montana was "the greatest race ever run." And the best horse was Tammany, who "knew more about the game than breeders, trainers, riders and officials." In a later interview he would add, "You could take a hair out of his tail and put it in his mouth, and he'd answer just the same as if it were a bit.'"[63]

Racing historians estimate that Garrison rode more than seven hundred winners between 1880 and 1896. He probably earned $2 million. He won a lot of races and rode in a peculiar way, but most memorable was his hell-bent-for-leather finishes won by a mere eyelash. Lucky racegoers who witnessed a Garrison finish regarded it as one of the most extraordinary feats they had ever witnessed in a sport. The phrase inspired multiple "Garrison finish" novels and motion pictures, and perhaps it still had influence in 1955. That year the National Museum of Racing welcomed into its newly conceived

Hall of Fame the inaugural class of champion jockeys. Edward H. "Snapper" Garrison was one of twelve men to get the nod.

As the winter days of 1893 warmed to light frost in the Bitterroot Valley, the Daly family basked in the glory of owning America's most famous racehorse. On a knob near the Daly mansion, ground was broken for a new stable that would house the Bitter Root stallions. Sam Lucas oversaw the stable's design and construction. A brick structure, reportedly "fire-proofed in every detail," took form atop the knob, otherwise known as Tammany Hill. The locals wondered why Lucas wanted two towers and flagstaffs on the roof. Upon its completion, gentle breezes floated the star-spangled banner affixed to one flagstaff, and the Riverside Stable copper and Irish green affixed to the other.[64]

Everyone was welcome to tour Tammany Castle, the result of Daly's pledge on that nerve-racking afternoon at Guttenberg. Verandas, water fountains, and velvet-green lawns beautified the grounds. Marcus Daly himself sometimes greeted parties of visitors. Inside the castle, visitors marveled over chandeliers and state-of-the art provisions. Few of their own homes afforded electricity or modern plumbing. The flooring alternated between carpet and imported cork half a foot thick and prevented the stallions from slipping. Each of the six stalls at eighteen square feet looked more like a living room. Each was plastered, wainscoted, and trimmed in solid oak. All were ventilated and steam heated. The most luxurious stall fitted with velvet-lined walls was Tammany's. The wife of a Daly associate, Mrs. Kate Wellcome, remembered that ordinary flowers were too common for Tammany. "Fresh cut roses were outside his stable door. They stood in a vase close by where he could inhale their fragrance but not eat them."[65]

America's master equine painters came to the farm and set up their easels. In 1893, Henry Cross reached for his palette and produced Tammany's portrait. Henry Stull had his turn and rendered the canvas *The Great $10,000 Match—Entering the Final Furlong*. Stull's work memorialized the showdown at Guttenberg. Manes and tails whip. Muscle and sinew spring and bulge with effort. Tammany is slightly ahead of Lamplighter. The Tiffany and Company craftsman that Daly brought to Anaconda and directed to the Marcus Daly Hotel painstakingly pieced together a mosaic of different shades of hardwood at a conspicuous spot on the barroom floor. The nine-foot-square

Tammany Castle. On September 28, 1899, members of the National Irrigation Congress toured the Bitter Root Stock Farm and Tammany Castle, a luxurious stable named for, and home of, the famed racehorse Tammany. The flag on the flagstaff displayed Daly's racing colors, alternately silver, copper, and green. The stallion Inverness is at right. Photo courtesy of B. C. Buffum Papers (4000055), box 4, item 34, American Heritage Center, University of Wyoming, Laramie.

composite duplicated every line and curve of Tammany's head. Daly never stepped on the picture. It was said he would gaze reverently at the portrait and say, "That's my baby."[66]

He kept Tammany in the Bitter Root Stud for six years. Then, on November 22, 1899, and for reasons unclear other than Daly wanting his pet to have the best chance at proving himself as a quality sire, the stallion was led away from his castle and entrained in the *Hattie D.* His new home would be the McGrathiana Stud in Lexington, among the most lavish and productive Thoroughbred studs in the country. Lamplighter was there, retired from racing since 1895. In sixty-six starts, he had earned around $90,000. Lamplighter was, however, "a losing proposition to owners," according to Walter

Vosburgh, a claim that Gottfried Walbaum backed up when he mused, "My luck turned from the day I bought that horse—everything went against me." No matter the two detractors, turfmen of a later era, 1977, would induct Lamplighter into the National Museum of Racing's Hall of Fame.[67]

Lamplighter's greener pastures were clearly at McGrathiana. Reaching number five on the 1902 winning sires list, the stallion improved to number two in 1903. Four years later, eighteen-year-old Lamplighter was sold to W. R. Shrade, a Missourian with plans to place the horse on stud duty at the state of Missouri's breeding bureau. As for Tammany, he would remain at the McGrathiana Stud until 1901, when he would make a trip north to New York City.[68]

CHAPTER 13

Ogden

"Little Brown Broncho"

At the famed racing town of Newmarket in Suffolk, England, strangers invaded the pen holding several Thoroughbred mares. The men separated the mares from their foals. More commotion arose with *The Manitoba*'s shipmen, who snapped leads to halters and walked the mares aboard the steamer. The journey overseas must have been miserable. For most of the eleven days at sea, the mares rocked with *The Manitoba* as the stormy Atlantic tossed the little steamship around. On October 1, 1894, landfall was the Atlantic Transport Company dock in New York City. All eleven mares purchased by Marcus Daly survived the rough passage.[1]

They were reunited with their foals three weeks later and embarked on the next leg of their journey. Railroad men took charge and entrained the broods. The train rumbled west and through the Rocky Mountains. As legend tells it, at a siding near Ogden, Utah, the locomotive paused for the mare Oriole, pregnant. Oriole foaled her brown colt inside a stockcar. He was named Ogden.[2]

The broods safely reaching the Bitter Root Stock Farm must have made for an especially happy day. In the office of the Thoroughbred department, the clerk opened the ledger *Index: Thoroughbred Stock*. He wrote: "Oriole. Chestnut mare, foaled 1887. [Bred by] Duke of Westminster. Ogden. Brown colt. Foaled April 10, 1894. Few white hairs in forehead."[3]

The story of Ogden's uncommon birth is undoubtedly more interesting and romantic than the factual documentation presented in the *General Stud Book*, England's equivalent of the *American Stud Book*. According to the *General Stud Book*, Oriole lived on an Englishman's estate where she foaled her son on April 10, 1894. The sire was Irish-bred Kilwarlin, representing the best of Irish bloodlines. Six months after the birth, Oriole and her colt were aboard *The Manitoba* sailing for America.[4]

Ogden grew to 15.3 hands and was described as a "good big little horse . . . compact, muscular, with good bone . . . good feet and legs, clean hocks."

Striking black points and black mane and tail accentuated his brown coat beautifully. He was praised for a tractable temperament, and this might have accounted for his lack of gusto on the training track, despite extensive schooling. Underachievers were not tolerated for long at the Bitter Root. Ogden was released into the cull pasture and put up for sale.[5]

At around this time, Marcus Daly was searching for the perfect candidate for his newly conceived western-division racing stable. When and where Daly and Johnny Campbell were introduced is unknown, but in the "nervy little Texan" famous for "springing 'dark uns,'" Daly found his trainer.[6]

The Daly-Campbell association materialized in fall 1895. Campbell had quite a few detractors who criticized him for leaving one racing stable for another within "comparatively few years." His early foray into the sport was like that of many trainers, a jockey who grew too heavy to race. He switched to harness racing and apprenticed as a driver. One story about Campbell making the rounds had him driving the Texas pacer Richball in a heated contest when a dog darted onto the course. Everyone cringed at the spray of dirt, the yelping, and the sight of the dog hobbling away. Everyone expected Richball to lose his stride after striking the dog. But he never wavered an inch. He even won his heat but pulled up lame. His handlers checked his feet. Wedged in a front shoe was the dog's paw, severed slick and clean.[7]

Campbell went back to Thoroughbreds. By spring 1889, he was conditioning runners for the Beverwyck Stable he co-owned with New Yorker Michael Nolan. That year they raced Cassius in the Kentucky Derby, and Cassius finished fifth to Spokane. When the Bluegrass Country puzzled over what had gone terribly wrong with native son Proctor Knott, favored to win the derby, one Tennessee turf scribe wrote: "In the hands of careful men like . . . Johnny Campbell . . . Proctor Knott would be simply invincible."[8]

Campbell settled into his new job training Marcus Daly's horses. As good luck would have it, no one had wanted to pay $250 for Ogden, still sprinting around the cull pasture. In early May 1896, he was among the colts representing the Riverside Stable's western division, which accepted the youngsters' falling short of the high standards that demarcated the eastern division. On occasion the lower-class colts, as late bloomers, warranted a move to the eastern division.[9]

Campbell took the western division to Anaconda. Horsemen from as far as Spokane, San Francisco, and Idaho transported their strings to the smelter town for the races. Four hundred equines converged on the racetrack grounds. The horsemen as well as racegoers congregated at Turf and Daly's saloon on Main Street. Bets were taken at the cashier's window. On big blackboards high on the walls, with a walkway for the marker, horse racing results were written in chalk. Meanwhile, a telegraph operator received dispatches about the races held across the nation, including the odds, the field, and the names of winners. If a race was of national importance, the operator called it as the dispatches came over the wire.[10]

On June 30, 1896, the opening day of the thirty-day meet at the Anaconda Driving Park, newness was everywhere. The Anaconda Racing Association in collaboration with Anaconda city fathers had updated the antiquated racetrack dating to 1888. "The buildings are complete, the track is in splendid condition, the [starting] gates are in working order, the horses are here, and the men are here; all is in readiness for the occasion," said racing secretary Ed Tipton. "Special race trains" from Butte shuttled more fans. Three thousand people crowded the grandstand and lawns. The trove of colorfully dressed ladies was much larger than that seen on an ordinary day at the races. Luminaries such as judges, senators, and racing secretaries from other Montana racing associations were spotted in the crowd, as were banker-horseman Samuel Larabie and cattleman-horseman Conrad Kohrs, making the trip from Deer Lodge. At the starter's box was James B. Ferguson, and although he was a nationally famous starter with career highlights that included Churchill Downs, he was counting on assistance from the newly installed gates, probably made of webbing, for prompt starts.[11]

Riverside Stable had dual entries of Jim Blackburn and Ogden. Prior to the start of the second race, the stable announced its intention to win with Jim Blackburn. Johnny Campbell instructed jockey Frank "Doc" Tuberville to ride Jim Blackburn to that effect. Campbell then turned to jockey Frank Duffy and told him to ride Ogden as the rabbit. Executing Campbell's instructions perfectly, Ogden finished runner-up to Jim Blackburn. After the final race of opening day, racegoers spoke enthusiastically about the refurbished racetrack and "generalship of Manager Tipton." The starting gates worked flawlessly for starter Ferguson, and the queue of races moved "with a precision that was almost military."[12]

Seven races were offered on the July 4 card at Anaconda. Before the start of the first race, Riverside Stable announced its intention to win with Loch Ness. Campbell once again instructed Frank Duffy to ride Ogden as the rabbit. At the end of that trip, Loch Ness and Ogden finished one-two. Ogden made his third start on July 9. No order was given to hold Ogden back, so Duffy, clutching a fistful of coarse black mane, hung on as Ogden jumped out first and his legs pummeled the fast track in a clean, easy sweep. Duffy never stroked him with whip or spur, and Ogden beat his four rivals. Two days later they defeated Loch Ness and his jockey Doc Tuberville by a neck. In his last two races, Ogden ran as a classic speed horse: Sprint to the front. Lead all the way. Win.[13]

The western division's next stop was Butte. A proper racetrack, stables, and spectator benches one mile southeast of town had accommodated horse racing fans since 1878. The local racing club, the West Side Racing Association, so named for Butte's location in the western half of Montana, offered organized meets as early as 1879. Because the association defaulted on a loan in 1895, Marcus Daly, already a large investor in the property, acquired all of it.[14]

Improvements started immediately, including raising the grandstand to three stories and expanding the betting ring. New stables offered larger stalls, and the new paddock had twenty-one roomy stalls with hot and cold water. Jockeys had a private room for dressing and a scales room. A hay barn and shoeing shack were added amenities, as was the new starting gate made of webbing. There were rooms for lunch and wine, and attached to each were toilet rooms. The main bar on the grounds was said to be the equal of those at "any other first-class racetrack." The *Thoroughbred Record* informed the nation's horsemen about the extent of the Montana turf investment. "Nearly $200,000 was spent [in 1896] equipping Anaconda and Butte tracks in a modern way. The Montana racing enterprise is in every way worthy of all classes of owners. It is a fixture of class, value and duration as to attract the best of both the thoroughbred and harness divisions of American racing."[15]

When the West Side Racing Association opened its renovated racetrack on July 20, 1896, for sixty days of racing, miners and professional gamblers, professional men and millionaires with their wives, brothel keepers and their girls, cowboys, farmers, and politicians bumped up against one another in the stands, in the paddock, and in the betting ring. Aside from horse racing, only prizefighting duplicated such a blending of Americans. All ages, races, sexes, rich and poor, gathered around the nation's boxing rings.[16]

Wagering was hotter than ever that summer, and for the umpteenth time Butte upheld its reputation as the hottest betting city in America. This was in part owed to the labor crews operating the mines day and night, and to Marcus Daly, who granted the crews half a day off with pay to attend the races. Women played the horses almost as much as the men. Most who worked for Daly backed the boss's horses because they knew he had high-quality animals and employed good handlers. Miners and smeltermen alike were overheard to say, "Old Marcus, 'e's crazy about harses."

A few workers stuck to native prejudices, however. An Irishman might never make a bet on an English-bred horse, even if it was Daly's. An Englishman might likewise never consider a horse with a speck of Irish blood, or whose colors carried a speck of Irish green.[17]

Ogden made his debut in Butte on opening day. On the strength of his victories at Anaconda, racegoers made him the favorite in the second race. Seasoned horsemen appreciated Ogden's "genuine old-time blood." The colt was popular with the ladies, too: "He looked so cute." Ogden's neck seemed longer than most, and this was an advantage, according to a local scribe. Necks of the kind "sent many of the good ones to victory." The two rival horses, Bill Howard and Tommy Tucker, looked "cumbersome and out of place" alongside Ogden, whose superb form "suggested the thoroughbred of slender, tapering limbs with glossy sinews, arched neck and the proud step."[18]

The three racehorses had to contend with the ferocious, battering wind also bedeviling starter Ferguson, who waved his arms like a windmill to get order in the line. Eleven minutes passed before the webbed starting gate sprang skyward. Horses and jockeys leaped forward and hit the gale head on. All eyes in the grandstand followed the streaking copper and Irish green pulling a length and a half ahead of his two rivals. Ogden with jockey "Brown" astride won his one and only race in Butte, and it marked his final start in Montana. The meeting at Butte continued; money seemed to be everywhere. When sixty days of racing closed, record attendance had brought in more than $1 million in wagers, and the West Side Racing Association had disbursed more than $100,000 in purse money.[19]

Organized racing existed as a circuit in Montana as early as 1882. Racing secretaries with aspirations to improve credibility and standards at their tracks and put them on equal footing with those in the East worked diligently to advance the quality of the meets and increase purse values. For the sport's greater good, personal enmities were laid aside, as happened with Marcus Daly and William A. Clark in 1886. They did not like each other then or later, but both served as officers and trustees for the West Side Racing Association. By 1896, in addition to Butte and Anaconda, the Montana circuit counted courses in Great Falls, Miles City, Glendive, Deer Lodge, Helena, and Missoula. Betting at all tracks was liberal. Butte and Anaconda were nationally famous, but Butte was the citadel. One-fifth of its forty-five thousand citizens with money to spend spent it on the races. World-record times for quarter-, three-eighths, and half-mile distances were set at Butte. It is no wonder that "They're off at Butte!" resonated nationally through pool halls and sporting clubs.[20]

Johnny Campbell and the western division were winning their races. Matthew Byrnes and his eastern division were losing theirs. The topflight two-year-olds Byrnes had selected for eastern racing had flopped, and Marcus Daly's heart was set on winning the Futurity on August 15. He was zero–two in that blue-ribbon contest reserved for two-year-olds. It was late July, and Daly and Byrnes scrambled to make a fresh draft by plucking colts from the western division.[21]

During this time, the Jockey Club received a telegram from Campbell that asked, "See if the colt Ogden is entered for any races in the East and answer." The club replied that he was, and the entries included the Futurity. Conceptualized in 1886, the Futurity had a novel protocol that required turfmen to nominate an entry before it was born. This was done by submitting the name of the mare. Owners who embraced the model paid entry fees to form the purse. The Coney Island Jockey Club as organizer added $10,000 to deliver a very rich stake. Thus, the inaugural Futurity of 1888 had paid an unheard of $40,900 to victorious Proctor Knott, and big money had officially entered American horse racing. The Futurity continued as America's richest and most prestigious event a two-year-old could win. By 1896, the ninth running, the winner's purse was valued at $43,940.[22]

Ogden had matured considerably. He was now an athletic and game racer, and Campbell repeatedly urged Marcus Daly to pluck Ogden from the western string. With that going nowhere, he appealed to his boss to at least visit the track and watch Ogden work. Daly refused. He had great confidence in Matthew Byrnes, who judged Ogden to be too immature for eastern racing. Campbell, now desperate, combed Butte in search of Hugh Wilson, one of the few men who held sway with Daly. Finding him in the Butte Hotel, Campbell got right to the point: "Try and persuade Mr. Daly to let me take Ogden east to run in the Futurity. I know this is a great colt, the best I ever saddled."[23]

The next morning Wilson was at the racetrack, which was shrouded in smog as it usually was. "In those days the Parrot Smelter was down in the valley not far from the track," Wilson said years later. "When Ogden was brought out to work seven furlongs, the smoke from the smelter was so thick a person could hardly discern objects across the track." Campbell loaded Ogden with 125 pounds of tack and jockey and put him to the business of a half-mile workout. The colt needed only forty-eight seconds.[24]

Wilson was now in the delicate situation of compromising Campbell. Not mentioning Ogden's workout and presumably with coaching from the trainer, Wilson urged Daly to send Ogden east for a chance at the Futurity. A few days later, Campbell wore a smile that "could almost be heard." Daly had given in. Campbell's parting words to Wilson were "Have a bet on this colt when he starts in the big race . . . for he will win as sure as he starts." He told his friends to do the same.[25]

Campbell, Ogden, and Doc Tuberville left Butte and journeyed to Saratoga, New York. Despite the comfortable accommodations the *Hattie D.* palace car afforded, at the end of the 2,500-mile trip Ogden was feeling out of sorts. He refused to eat. Campbell offered buckets of milk, which the hungry colt drank greedily.[26]

Selecting the Saratoga Racecourse as the place to condition Ogden was brilliant strategy. From Butte at an elevation of 5,538 feet, they dropped to Saratoga at 440 feet. High-altitude acclimation training was an old strategy used to improve endurance in athletes. Further, at the resort town of Saratoga, racing was on hiatus for the summer. The track was virtually deserted. Campbell worked his brown colt with little observation. During the final workout at Saratoga under a stiff 125 pounds, Ogden knocked out six furlongs very fast. Doc Tuberville was ecstatic. Nothing, he said, short of a Domino could beat Ogden.[27]

Already a veteran of a reinsman's yo-yo life for several years, Tuberville was born possibly near San Francisco. Somebody had described him as a "wezaened [sic] little lad" when the boy was racing horses at California county fairs. At bigger racetracks in San Francisco, Chicago, and St. Louis, Tuberville's engagements alternated between decent mounts and platers. Drifting to the St. Louis Fair Grounds, he got into a jam when he slugged a reporter. That miscue earned him a suspension. Shortly after reinstatement, he swung aboard San Blas, a hundred-to-one long shot in the Mississippi Valley Stakes. They won it. Tuberville secured mounts of higher quality after that race. But two months later he was under investigation for unscrupulous riding. The St. Louis Fair Association exonerated him of any misdeed. Tuberville then drifted to New Orleans, where Johnny Campbell found him, engaged him, and sent him to Montana.[28]

Campbell moved his group to the Sheepshead Bay Racecourse at an elevation near sea level. Matthew Byrnes was already there with his Futurity candidate, Scottish Chieftain. Byrnes was intrigued by the secrecy surrounding Campbell's horse. After inspecting plain, brown, thickset, short-legged Ogden, Byrnes wisecracked that he was a "little brown broncho." Campbell's answer was to propose a friendly bet: if the little brown broncho did not win the Futurity, he would at least finish ahead of Scottish Chieftain. If not, Campbell owed Byrnes a new suit of clothes and vice versa. Byrnes took the bet.[29]

Meanwhile, people were asking Marcus Daly which horse they should play, Ogden or Scottish Chieftain, for the Futurity. As Daly's friend Ben Stack once put it, "Daly was a fine fellow, but you couldn't believe a word he said

about a horse race." Daly was, in fact, a plunger who took full advantage of
eastern prejudices toward western horses as well as people little informed
about horse racing. Campbell's telegrams told of Ogden's phenomenal work,
and Daly, finally coming around to Ogden, disingenuously told those who
asked that in no way was Ogden a better racehorse than Scottish Chieftain.
The askers were similarly unaware of Daly's collusion with private betting
commissioners who anonymously wagered on Ogden on Daly's behalf.
Each time an asker laid money down on Scottish Chieftain, he blundered
right into Daly's scheme. The ruse was working splendidly. Prerace odds for
Ogden soared to 100- to 150-to-1. Bookmakers, meanwhile, waited for the
Daly money backing Scottish Chieftain. So far, they had not seen a nickel.
If anything delighted Daly more than the honor of winning with a horse of
his own breeding, it was delivering a "good drubbing" to the bookmakers,
or "bookkeepers" as he called them, and he detested them.[30]

The morning of August 15, 1896, dawned with a cool, steady breeze across
Sheepshead Bay. The racetrack was dry and fast under a bright blue sky.
The day was glorious, but opinions about the ten entries for the Futurity
were generally that they were "the poorest field in the history of the great
race." Eastern horsemen and scribes alike grumbled more loudly when
unheard-of Ogden dropped into their laps overnight, along with some kid
called "Doc" Tuberville as the jockey. The Sheepshead Bay crowd numbered
only ten to twelve thousand, prompting one New York scribe to bemoan
the "absence of the society element." As it was, that "fashionable racing
set" was "off yachting"; the timing of the race, scheduled two weeks earlier
than in previous years, had caused the shortage of high-society people. New
on the scene was Marcus Daly and his friends as well as a small coterie of
Montana miners who made the trip expressly to see Ogden win the six-
furlong Futurity. As reported by one turf scribe, the miners had "no more
eyes" for the favorite, Ornament, or any other entry than they would for
"a vagrant trio of coyotes on a prairie."[31]

Upon discovering that Ogden and Scottish Chieftain were coupled in the
betting, the miners threw fits. They wanted Ogden straight, no mixing him
up with the other horse. Their protests, pointless, impelled each miner to
state, "I'll bet a hundred on *Ogden*" when registering his bet, and he would

state it as defiantly as had the miner ahead of him. Not one of them would ask for "the Daly Stable," so loyal were they to Ogden. The Riverside Stable pair was well backed at six to two, this in response to Scottish Chieftain's strong performances early in the season, the popularity of his jockey Fred Taral, and, too, Marcus Daly's splendid ruse. Within minutes of the Futurity's start, the bookmakers were surprised by the tremendous plunges of thousands of dollars, and not on Scottish Chieftain but on Ogden. Only then were suspicions aroused, but it was too late for the bookmakers.[32]

The paddock was as busy as the betting shed. Ornament, the betting favorite, was also chief weight carrier, receiving 116 pounds of impost hoisted onto his back. The Riverside Stable pair, at third favorite, accepted 115 pounds for Ogden and 113 for Scottish Chieftain. The lightest weight allocated to the ten-horse field was 105. After saddling, the jockeys astride their high-voltage mounts left the paddock for the racetrack. Ogden and Tuberville on parade passed by the grandstand. Spectators were mum except for the miners who vigorously clapped and shouted their loyalties for Ogden and the state of Montana. The other Riverside entry of Scottish Chieftain and Fred Taral warranted modest enthusiasm from the crowd. Then, Ornament and jockey Tod Sloan, the last pair to make an entrance, roused the entire grandstand into hearty applause and cheers.[33]

The post positions put Ornament alongside the rail. Ogden was positioned next to Ornament, who instantly sidestepped and threw a kick at his neighbor, missed, and threw more. Tuberville was busy turning Ogden this way and that to avoid Ornament's flailing hooves.[34]

Starter James B. Ferguson got something resembling order after twenty-five minutes of kicking, shifting, scrambling, and three false breaks. He snapped his flag. The field bolted into a knitted bunch. Ogden and Ornament were first to the front. Volumes of moist sea-level oxygen poured into Ogden's lungs as he raced, the air feeding his thumping heart and powering his gliding muscles. As the furlong poles were passed, neither Ogden nor Ornament conceded a speck of ground. Tod Sloan was first to strike his whip and lift his spur. Ornament jumped into lightning-quick strides. The crowd jumped up and down and screamed for Ornament, thundering over the homestretch and closing on Ogden. Ornament would do the trick, but next thing his head dropped and his stride unraveled. Sloan fought to regain control of his mount. The crowd wailed at Ogden, sprinting farther ahead.

Not wanting to leave anything to chance, Doc Tuberville touched his colt once with whip and spur. Ogden in a whirl outdistanced Ornament by a length and a half at the moment he hit the wire.[35]

Doc Tuberville whirled his whip over his head. The jubilant miners were cheering, jumping, and yelling amid the thousands of murmurs of, "Who is this Ogden?" "Who is this boy Tuberville?" The judges, discombobulated over which Riverside Stable horse had won, ordered Scottish Chieftain's number hung up on the infield board as the winning number. That colt had finished third, or so everyone thought. Johnny Campbell must have been mystified. Matthew Byrnes, reacting to his colt's number on the board, grabbed Campbell and lifted him into the air, yelling, "Me for the suit, Johnny!" The wrong number was quickly removed and replaced with Ogden's number. Byrnes dropped Campbell "like a hot potato."[36]

Tuberville trotted Ogden back to the judges' stand and dismounted. The perfect ride in a time of 1:10 knocked off a full second from the Sheepshead Bay record for six furlongs. Once that was recorded, racing officials got to the business of honoring the winning jockey in front of a crowd still and silent. Tuberville received a floral wreath around his shoulders, a tradition that roused smatterings of applause from the grandstand. And some cheers drifted to the racetrack. The crowd was softening. He removed his green cap and waved it before being seated in the customary winner's chair adorned with flowers. The Sheepshead Bay band launched into "Hail to the Chief," while over on the lawn, the clan of Montana miners were well into celebrating. They were yelling themselves hoarse and dancing in circles and leading a celebration described as a "war dance." Observing it all, the *New York Times* scribe continued, "The wild Western fashion had taken possession of them. They threw their hats into the air, yelled at the top of their voices, and gave an exhibition of just how very excited men can become over such a thing as a horse race." The ebullient miners kept rollicking, and the scribe enthused, "The friends of Ogden danced and cheered and halloed and hurrahed as no similar coterie of men has ever before done at Sheepshead Bay."[37]

Johnny Campbell and Marcus Daly acknowledged the stream of congratulations coming from all sides as they walked Ogden through the paddock. Horsemen and newspapermen intercepted Daly, who laughed and joked, saying, "I am proud of the colt as he was shipped nearly 2,000 miles to take part in the Futurity and he won it cleverly." In slightly more

Ogden. On August 17, 1896, a Pennsylvania newspaper infused a western slant into its account of Ogden's upset victory in the Futurity: "Like the avalanche which thunders down the side of the mountains which frown upon [Ogden's] home, bearing upon his broad back the western rider, Tuberville, Ogden ran away from the pride of the southwest and the joy of eastern turf men." Photo courtesy of Marcus Daly Mansion, Hamilton, Montana.

than a minute, Ogden's purse money fattened Daly's bank account by $43,940. Daly accepted a bonus of $4,000 as Oriole's owner. Elsewhere on the Sheepshead Bay grounds, the sixty bookmakers sank to their knees. Their losses averaged $2,000, but some lost as much as $25,000. Promissory notes were written, but the books unable to pay "took to the back woods." Daly's own meticulous and cunning coup raked in thousands from the betting ring. The coup was the richest of his life, as well as among the richest in American turf history. Rumors circulated about how much. Daly would eventually reveal to an intimate that the amount of his haul was around $180,000.[38]

The next morning, August 16, the *New York Journal* headline blared OGDEN THE WESTERNER, FIRST. FUTURITY'S GREAT PRIZE TAKEN BY A HORSE OF MYSTERY RIDDEN BY A BOY OF MYSTERY. The *Journal*'s overnight sleuthing demystified some of the mystery. "Ogden is just a plain-looking brown horse, coming out of that nowhere of the West, Montana. Tuberville is just a little earnest-faced, brown-eyed, thin-lipped, soft-voiced person, also from out of the nowhere. But he is a dare-devil horseman, and he has ridden the winner of the Futurity." Newspapers were still printing stories about the Futurity's players two days later. The *Journal* informed its readers about Johnny Campbell, a common subject among turfmen. "It heretofore has been disputed again and again whether Campbell is a good trainer. He has the numberless enemies every successful man makes, and they have never lost a chance to belittle him. They have pointed with glee to the dissolution of the many partnerships Campbell has formed within comparatively few years. . . . Then, with his usual bland smile, he reappears, the originator of a wholly unknown horse that wins the Futurity."[39]

On Ogden's home turf in Montana, five thousand of Butte's citizens were at the races when they learned of the great upset. Celebrations were said to have thrown the town into "the wildest time ever." Across the state, newspapers doubled down on the merits of bunchgrass and ozone. From the *Stockgrowers Journal*, "The winning of the great Futurity stakes by Marcus Daly's colt, Ogden, is another testimonial to Montana grass and Montana ozone. The prediction has been made that Montana would produce world-beaters; the state has won the greatest honors on the American turf, with horses whose names have spread across a continent. They are Montana Regent, Spokane, Montana, Tammany, Senator Grady, and now comes Ogden. . . . The state has Kentucky and American derbies to her credit; also the Suburban and Metropolitan handicaps and a Futurity."[40]

Two weeks later, Ogden and Ornament reversed placings. Ornament, swift and fluid in the Flatbush Stakes, whipped up a lead of three lengths to easily beat Ogden. Ornament, unlike stout and thick Ogden, was a lightly built, sleek colt, following his Arabian ancestry. A blazed face and a lone white hind leg played up a bright chestnut coat. Kentucky bred, Ornament was sired by English-bred Order and was the foal of Victorine. He was a compellingly beautiful animal but repellent in equal measure. Turf scribes wrote about his boorish behavior at the post, things like, "Ornament did not want to go to the post," or "Ornament refused to join the other horses," or "Ornament was obstinate, standing with his head the wrong way of the track." "Cow kicker" was a favorite epithet to make the point that, at every opportunity, he would nail his rivals with kicks. One scribe really intent on making his point wrote "exceedingly erratic disposition," "unruly beast," "faults of disposition," and "failings" in just three sentences.[41]

Ornament and Ogden were cofavorites in the six-furlong Great Eastern Handicap on September 5. Fred Taral, riding for Riverside Stable in 1896, initially resisted accepting Ogden as his mount. Ogden was rightfully Doc Tuberville's for the marquee event at Sheepshead Bay. Tuberville reportedly "felt badly" about the snub. More disheartening for the young jockey, his reinsmanship in the Futurity had been criticized. Marcus Daly rode that bandwagon. On the very afternoon Tuberville delivered the Futurity purse worth $43,940 and a monstrous betting coup of $180,000, Daly stated publicly that Ogden might have performed even better had Fred Taral been in the saddle.[42]

Fred Taral had the ride and directed Ogden to the post. Ornament, keyed up as he always was, sabotaged his start, fell behind quickly, and lost the race early. Ogden thudded homeward to win his race, mindless of the torrential rain and spewing muck. Fred Taral leaped from Ogden's back, wiped away the sand begriming his face, and gasped, "Great Scott, but this is a game colt!"[43]

The Great Eastern closed out Ogden's campaign for 1896. With earnings of $57,425, the colt was America's leading money-winning two-year-old. All told, Riverside Stable's western division cleared $59,150 under Johnny Campbell and outperformed the eastern division, earning $30,605 under Matthew Byrnes. On the days that Marcus Daly opened his personal copies of the Bitter Root *Thoroughbred Stock* catalogue, he jotted notations on the pages, and on Oriole's page: "Best of the imported mares." He even commissioned Henry Stull to paint her picture. The artist would paint Ogden, too, but with Fred Taral in the saddle instead of Doc Tuberville, who had quit Riverside Stable.[44]

❚❚

Tuberville was on the move. At St. Louis Fair Grounds racetrack in 1897, he raced until the stewards ruled him off their track for life. In 1898, he split his time between Oakland, California, and Butte. The following spring, he was in hot water with California racing officials. Tuberville's "peculiar tumble" in one race had him falling off his mount a little too neatly, and the timing of the fall also seemed staged.[45]

His career and life in chaos, Tuberville drifted into the abyss of cheating. At Butte in 1901, Tuberville's dealings with another jockey were construed as a bribe to fix a race. The West Side Racing Association stewards slapped him with a six-month suspension. They smelled something fishy again the next year when Tuberville's mount inexplicably showed "improved form" and won his race by an astonishing six lengths. Endlessly suspicious of everything he did, the stewards ruled him off the track for the rest of the meet. One could never be certain whether a fall to the ground was real or staged. Both battered his body. By October 1908, Tuberville was thirty-one years old, sick, friendless, and broke. Admitted to a charity hospital in New Orleans, he clutched a whip in his hand that was reputed to be the one he used to bat Ogden in the Futurity. Tuberville spoke of Ogden repeatedly, and Frank "Doc" Tuberville "cherished his little rawhide more than anything else," the *Vancouver Daily World* reported, and "hugged the whip to his breast" when dying.[46]

Ogden spent the winter of 1896 at Matthew Byrnes's training center, Long Branch. Byrnes sent the horse to Cape Charles, Virginia, for conditioning before starting as a three-year-old. Everyone who listened to Byrnes talk about the upcoming Withers Stakes on May 15, 1897, heard him say it was as good as won by Ogden, and that Ogden was the highest-class animal ever to come into his hands. Before Ogden, he had trained such champions as Parole, Salvator, Firenze, and Tammany, so the "highest-class" admission was a little surprising.[47]

While Byrnes was uncharacteristically loquacious, Fred Taral as Ogden's regular rider was oddly superstitious. Feeling "hoodooed," he had recently resorted to keeping rabbits' feet on his person to ward the thing off. He was convinced he would lose all his races. The *New York Times* thought it queer for such an "uncommonly intelligent fellow as Taral" to fall for hoodoo "rubbish," adding, "The best way for him to chase away the 'hoodoo' is to forget that it exists and go on about the riding of horses and the winning of races as he has done in seasons past."[48]

The morning of May 15 broke sunny and warm for the Withers Stakes, the season's first major stakes for three-year-olds. Margaret Daly and her daughter "Miss Daly" walked among ten thousand racegoers congregating at Morris Park. With the racetrack surface wet from substantial rain, traction was less than ideal, and the horse possessed of quick speed and strength was the smart bet for the one-mile event. Of the four entries, Ogden, as last season's best two-year-old, was that racehorse, or so thought the racegoers who made him the favorite.[49]

Leaving the post, the field's quick jump into action marked the extent of quickness. Front-running Bannock soon locked into a sleepy pace, more as if he were drawing a hearse in a funeral procession than gunning for a win in an important horse race. Everyone went along for the dawdle. After half a mile of trancelike running, one jockey woke up and urged his colt Octagon to rev up his legs. This roused Taral, who was uncharacteristically indecisive. Attempting to shoot Ogden through an avenue, he would change his mind and pull him back. Despite Taral, Ogden somehow managed to run down Bannock. Taral then chirped for more speed. Nothing. He chirped again. Nothing. Taral fired up the whip. Octagon was coming after them but Ogden refused to try. Taral watched Octagon dart past the wire first, two lengths the winner.[50]

Matthew Byrnes was incredulous. Granted, Ogden was short on his work because of rainy weather in the days before the race. The track was not fast, but neither was it a mud hole. Weight might have slowed Ogden, 122 pounds to Octagon's 119. Fred Taral winced as he said, "I was never so disappointed in my life as I did not think I could lose. I seriously believe I would have given a year of my life to win that race, with Mrs. and Miss Daly looking on." His riding had the *New York Times* baffled but not wordless, describing it as "wholly at sea" and the equivalent of "the veriest novice." And the *Times* wondered why tractable Ogden had sulked. Of course, the horse had been a huge favorite in Montana, and Montanans had backed him with thousands of dollars. The result not only threw them into shock, but "Butte went broke," as put by Henry Stull, who was at the Bitter Root painting horse portraits on the day Ogden lost the Withers. The final two races of the 1897 season were letdowns, going unplaced in the Belmont Stakes on

May 29 and the Broadway Stakes on June 15. Perhaps there was something to Taral's hoodoo after all.[51]

▰

The American turf learned in September 1897 that Marcus Daly and Johnny Campbell had ended their two-year association. Campbell quickly found a new boss in H. L. Frank of Butte. That association would be brief because Frank quickly pulled the plug on his new racing stable, which lost a ton of money. Campbell's career slowly ticked downward. "A few years ago, he was a top-notcher, but this season he has been racing a few horses in Montana with poor success," the *Buffalo Evening News* in New York reported in October 1902. Campbell, who probably never had the respect he deserved in American racing, left his country for opportunities in France. American newspapers occasionally noted his whereabouts, including that he was training horses in Austria in 1907, and in charge of a string in Germany in 1913. Whether Campbell returned to America is unknown, as are the date and place of his death.[52]

▰

Marcus Daly's new trainer was William "Billy" Lakeland, a future Hall of Famer. Lakeland had famously trained Domino, one of America's greatest to ever step on a racetrack. Lakeland was also well known for racing his horses in multiple events in a single day, such as Little Reb during the era of the durable iron horse. Little Reb accomplished the incredible feat of winning three races in a single day and two more the next. Lakeland training for Daly had a good number of first-class Thoroughbreds, and coupled with Lakeland's own talent, the *Boston Globe* rated Riverside Stable as America's "most conspicuous racing stable."[53]

Ridership of Ogden in the 1898 season would be the work of four jockeys, all of them new to the horse. The Brooklyn Handicap at Gravesend on May 28 opened Ogden's campaign. The contest of a mile and a quarter marked Ogden's fifth meeting with Ornament, both of them four-year-olds. The two horses had last competed against each other as two-year-olds. Through the muddy first quarter, front-running Ogden struck the pace until about midway through three-quarters, when his speed sputtered before he sank to seventh, where he finished in the eight-horse race. Two horses, Ornament and Ben Holladay, rushed on as one-two and in that order finished the Brooklyn Handicap.[54]

Ogden picked up a $600 winner's purse at Gravesend before a start in the Suburban Handicap at Sheepshead Bay on June 18, 1898. Weirdly, nearly all eleven horses picked fights at the post, with Ben Holladay kicked in the ribs, and Holladay, infuriated, beelining for Ogden and firing a vicious kick right to Ogden's stomach. This infuriated Ogden, who spun around and assailed Havoc and Tragedian. Ornament was on the attack, too, and so it went. Minutes ticked by. One hour passed. Late afternoon turned to dusk. On the twelfth attempt at a fair start, the battered horses allowed for one perfect moment. The starter, seizing it, sent them off in an excellent start. Ogden sprinted to the lead and had the race in hand until the final one hundred yards where the field made an explosive dash. Ogden finished third, Ben Holladay fifth, and Ornament straggled in, eighth.[55]

Ogden rebounded on June 30 at Sheepshead Bay when he won a nominal purse race. Then came the Long Island Handicap on July 2. The wait at the post wore on because Ornament was "fretful." Once under way, Ogden's thick legs churned and shot his bulk to the front. His shiny black tail rustled like a banner. He had full command of the three-horse race and was never headed. Ornament finished third. Next, at Brighton Beach for three races that would end his 1898 season, Ogden came home a winner in one and runner-up in the other two.[56]

In September, a train chugged into the Hamilton, Montana, depot. Sam Lucas was there to receive Ogden and a second traveler, Hamburg, and took them to Bitter Root Stock Farm where both stallions were honored with quarters in Tammany Castle. The farm soon announced that Ogden had been retired. One day at the Hamilton fairgrounds, townsfolk were treated to the joy of watching Ogden, Hamburg, and Tammany canter over the racetrack for the fun of it. Good times at the Bitter Root ended for Ogden in mid-January 1901. Entrained in a Palace Horse Car, he rode the rails to New York City and was sold to Billy Lakeland for $4,200.[57]

Lakeland told a reporter that seven-year-old Ogden was "still likely to do things." On May 4, 1901, at Morris Park, Lakeland saddled the horse for the one-mile Metropolitan Handicap. Lakeland's time-tested methods could not obliterate the effects of Ogden's age or two-year absence from the racetrack. Ogden finished eighth in his comeback race. Turf scribes felt sorry for him, saying that he was old and spent and "disgracefully beaten" in one of his races at Brighton Beach. Then, on September 2, they went nuts for him all over again.[58]

Lakeland sent out his veteran campaigner not once, but twice on the same card at Sheepshead Bay. Ogden's racing had greatly improved. Appreciating this, the crowd made him top pick in the six-furlong second race. His hot streak of three wins in his last five starts was not unnoticed by the handicapper, who allocated top weight—a 130-pound crusher.[59]

Ogden and jockey Winnie O'Connor ground their way furlong through furlong. Thrusting out that long neck, Ogden won his race by a head, beating five. Returning to the post for the sixth race, he shouldered the top weight of 126 pounds. With O'Connor again as pilot, they now had to outrace four over a mile and a sixteenth, and instead of over dirt, they would have to do it over grass. The crowd, staying loyal to Ogden, backed him as the favorite for the sixth race, but many must have wondered, "Could the plucky old horse do the trick again? And over grass?" [60]

He won it by a length.[61]

That night in New York newsrooms the name "Ogden" was typed into headlines. From the *New York Times*, OGDEN WAS TWICE WINNER, and from the *Sun*, OLD OGDEN'S DOUBLE VICTORY. In the twenty-one-year history of Sheepshead Bay, Ogden was the first racehorse to clinch double victories in a single day.[62]

There was one more race to be run, this one on September 27 at Gravesend. Ogden and O'Connor trotted to the post for the mile-and-sixteenth purse race. Ogden was under 122 pounds, and his two rivals, three-year-old Ethics and two-year-old Fly Wheel, were under 116 and 100 pounds. Fly Wheel had Ogden outgunned by five lengths through the first mile, with Ethics never in contention. Reaching the stretch for home, O'Connor batted his whip. Ogden exploded like a cannonball and landed right at Fly Wheel's saddle skirts. Stamina, however, told in the final drive. Young Fly Wheel could not sustain the blistering pace, and Ogden, carrying the black-and-white silks of Billy Lakeland, defeated Fly Wheel by a solid length.[63]

⬛

Ogden was retired a second time. The *Louisville Courier-Journal* marveled over the stallion's durability at seven years old, "as sound as the day he was foaled." He tallied twenty-eight starts with fifteen wins, eight seconds, one third, and earnings of $59,970. A brilliant sprinter, the little brown broncho was virtually unbeatable at a mile or less, having inherited the speed of his sire, Kilwarlin, but unfortunately not Kilwarlin's stamina. In top form as a two-year-old, Ogden implied greatness, but disappointing losses would outnumber memorable victories. Ogden defeated his bluegrass antagonist Ornament in three of six meetings; they were both unplaced in the Suburban Handicap. Retired in 1899, Ornament had accrued earnings of $99,276, having reached the winner's circle twenty times in thirty-two starts. He was unplaced only twice. Ornament's name appeared on the American leading sires list multiple years. The chaotic chestnut lived the remainder of his life where it began, at the Beaumont Farm in Lexington. He died there on April 26, 1916, at the age of twenty-two.[64]

Lakeland was ready to sell, and John E. Madden thought Ogden would make an attractive stud prospect. His deal with Lakeland in December 1901 secured Ogden for $15,000. The Kentucky turfman moved Ogden to his breeding farm, Hamburg Place, skirting Lexington. Madden purchased the broodmares he would selectively breed to Ogden. He hit his first jackpot in 1906 with the birth of Sir Martin, foaled by Lady Sterling. The chestnut colt, quick to produce results, reigned as America's champion two-year-old colt in 1908. Madden himself stated that Sir Martin was one of the best he ever bred.[65]

In the next stroke of genius, Madden paired Ogden with Livonia. Their black colt was The Finn, foaled in 1912. The Finn was a stakes-winning two-year-old and an even better racehorse at three, winning the Withers Stakes, Belmont Stakes, and other major stakes. The Finn wrapped up his 1915 season as America's champion three-year-old colt. He was again a stakes winner at ages four and five.[66]

⬛

In February 1923, Ogden at twenty-nine years was, according to the *Daily Racing Form*, "still popular, to judge by the fact that his book is full for the coming season at Hamburg Stud." All told, Ogden sired 527 winners, of which 27 were stakes winners. His offspring collectively earned more than $1 million. Curiously, he was never to head the American winning sires list but had a lengthy run on it and was runner-up in 1908 and 1913, third in 1915 and 1916, and fourth in 1914. The gathering and tabulating of statistics on individual Thoroughbred breeders was not started until after World War I, but in the first ten years of such statistics, Madden was at the head of multiple lists, owing in part to Ogden's potent procreation. John E. Madden's legacy as owner, trainer, and breeder would warrant enshrinement into the Halls of Fame at the Harness Racing Museum and at the National Museum of Racing.[67]

Whether he was sentimental about his horses is an open debate, but unquestionably the death of his famous trotter Nancy Hanks in 1915 moved him. He gave the order to bury the mare in a peaceful corner on Hamburg Place. He buried another favorite there, and another, and the quaint cemetery in the shimmering bluegrass grew larger. When Ogden passed on New Year's Eve 1923, Madden gave the order.

CHAPTER 14

Scottish Chieftain

The Wrong Horse

Sam Lucas was never in doubt about Scottish Chieftain. The colt was a good racehorse long before the exciting news of his victory in the 1897 Belmont Stakes reached the Bitter Root Stock Farm. The bay colt had competed against a formidable field of America's crack three-year-olds, and that field had included Ogden, the famous Bitter Root colt. Ogden was the Daly family's favorite racehorse, but Lucas had always preferred Scottish Chieftain, so news of the victory was especially sweet for him.[1]

Lucas supervised the Thoroughbred Breeding and Training Department at the Bitter Root. He would freely admit to anyone that the colts and fillies in his care were his "babies." He looked after them as tenderly as a parent. A native Kentuckian, Lucas was born in Scott County in 1858. Bluegrass Country quickly indoctrinated the boy with its time-honored love for Thoroughbred horses. By age seven, he was exercising Thoroughbreds at Woodburn Farm in Woodford County, Kentucky. At that time, the Woodburn Stud was regarded as America's finest. Lucas dreamed of becoming a jockey until his weight and height, fully six feet as a grown man, put an end to that. Sent to work with the stallions, Lucas had a stroke of luck in caring for Lexington, the greatest Thoroughbred sire the planet had ever seen. Retired from racing as a champion, Lexington was sold to the Woodburn Stud. His name topped the American sires list for sixteen seasons, fourteen in succession, 1861 through 1874. The stallion's genetic impact on the modern American Thoroughbred has yet to be duplicated. When under Lucas's care, Lexington was very old and blind, and fondly called "The Blind Hero of Woodburn."[2]

Lucas was twenty-seven years old when he left Woodburn in 1885 for employment at another famed Thoroughbred institution, the Nursery Stud, recently relocated to Lexington from Babylon, Long Island, New York. Lucas studied bloodlines extensively and honed an intuitive understanding of what made Thoroughbred horses tick. The more he learned about them, the more he loved them. Thoroughbreds were "heaven's creatures," he said, and a stable full of them, well, that was heaven.[3]

The master of Nursery Stud was August Belmont I, who operated in the world of finance as a Manhattan banker. He was conspicuous on the American turf as well as in New York high-society circles. One day in 1866 his friend Leonard Jerome encouraged him to take on a new pursuit. Jerome's brand-new Jerome Park Racecourse outside the Bronx needed a president. Having no background in the sport, Belmont nonetheless stepped into the position. He never looked back. Belmont dedicated his intellect, money, goodwill, and prestige for the betterment of American racing. In the words of the *New York Sun*, "By the close of the very first season of his presidency, Belmont was the autocratic ruler of the club, while [Leonard] Jerome, like the ghost of Don Quixote, stood powerless by his side as one of the vice presidents."[4]

Meanwhile, at racetracks overseas, a Thoroughbred named St. Blaise was reaching the winner's circle in England. Multiple victories in important races included the 1883 Epsom Derby. Then, in his fourth and fifth seasons, St. Blaise no longer showed the verve that had made him a champion. Heeding Sam Lucas's recommendation, on October 13, 1885, Belmont I paid $20,000 for St. Blaise as a stud prospect. Flabbergasted turfmen went so far as to ridicule Belmont I and his new horse.[5]

Five years later, in August 1890, two of St. Blaise's sons, Potomac and Masher, finished one-two in the Futurity. Then, in October, St. Blaise ascended to number one on America's list of winning sires, a triumph August Belmont I lived to see before his death in November. Come December, Belmont's name headed the 1890 winning owners list. Upon St. Blaise's death at age twenty-nine in 1909, his winning progeny had earned nearly $1 million.[6]

■

With the death of Belmont I, Sam Lucas needed a job. Marcus Daly wasted little time wooing him to Montana. Lucas toured the Bitter Root Stock Farm, where familiar sights like beautiful, impeccably bred Thoroughbreds melded with unfamiliar sights like the native bunchgrass below the gray peaks of the Bitterroot Range. The Kentucky horseman's mind whirled: the bunchgrass would cure to yellow and turn white with frost. Snow would fall. Winter in this country was long, cold, and deep. That could not bode well for Thoroughbred horses, at least the kind he was used to. The tour paused at the Bitter Root Stud for introductions to the resident stallions Brown Fox, Silver King, and Child of the Mist. An underwhelmed Lucas summed up his tour in 1890 this way: "I regarded Mr. Daly's prospects for raising good racehorses as poor." Yet something drew him in because he accepted the position of superintendent of Thoroughbred Breeding and Training. He would later admit he had been wrong about the bunchgrass and winter.[7]

Lucas's knowledge of Bitter Root Thoroughbreds' pedigrees and peculiarities soon superseded anyone else's. Horses aside, he liked all animals, and all sorts were under his care. Dozens of dogs lived in kennels grouped around Tammany Castle, and the *Anaconda Standard* mentioned that Lucas loved "a good chicken." During one night at the cockfights, Lucas entered a pair of prized gamecocks. "Put him on the floor so they can see each other and watch them box a round or two," Lucas instructed his friend. The cocks boxed, and fans enjoyed "a boxing that was a beauty."[8]

His extensive knowledge of fowl, dogs, and Thoroughbred horses was an irresistible combination for many people. They would drop in on him at his home on the Bitter Root grounds. Genteel southern manners were foremost. "The man who has not reclined on a bright summer afternoon beneath the shade of the big trees in front of the house and sipped one of Sam's famous toddies while his host discoursed upon horse matters missed a treat that he can never enjoy to such a full extent anywhere else," a Montana newspaper correspondent informed. "It was a wise man who knew when to stop trifling with those toddies. They were too good to leave willingly."[9]

Lucas was otherwise immersed in the business of reinvigorating the farm's anemic bloodstock. He culled the failures and added prepotent studs and broodmares. Miss Darebin from Rancho del Paso was a large brown mare introduced to the broodmare band. Upon her arrival at the Bitter Root, the record-keeping clerk added this entry to *Index: Thoroughbred Stock*: "Miss Darebin. Brown filly, foaled April 14, 1890. Gray spot in forehead, rear hind foot white, branded 106 under mane."

And he wrote an entry for a stallion recently arrived: "Inverness. Chestnut colt foaled 1888, blaze face, both fore pasterns white, a little white on off curb, small black spot on left quarter. Purchased in England for $24,205."

Inverness was literally blue-blooded. He was bred and foaled at the English estate of Lord Randolph Churchill, father of Winston. The chestnut-faced stallion started eight times as a two-year-old and won five races. Imported to America for Marcus Daly in 1890, Inverness injured a leg during the voyage across the Atlantic. The Riverside Stable lost a fine racehorse, but the Bitter Root Stud gained a superbly bred stallion. And Lucas took advantage of it when ordering the coupling of Inverness and Miss Darebin. Perhaps he himself opened the *Index*, thumbed to a clean page, and recorded in a handsome script the arrival of the new colt soon to be his favorite: "Scottish Chieftain. Bay or brown colt. Foaled Feb. 24th, 1894. Faint star."[10]

In spring 1896, Scottish Chieftain was a member of the Riverside Stable eastern division. As such, he traveled in a stockcar to New York, where Matthew Byrnes received the colt. That year Riverside had first call on Fred Taral, who would be Scottish Chieftain's regular rider. Marcus Daly's effort to recruit Taral tracked back five years, to the 1891 Realization Stakes. Marcus

Scottish Chieftain's pedigree card. No known photograph or painting of Scottish Chieftain exists, and without a visual reference, turf historians are left to wonder. Was he charismatic or common looking? Was he an amiable stallion, or did he inherit his sire's savage "man-eater" temperament? Scottish Chieftain must have been good sized because Marcus Daly called him "the big horse." Photo courtesy of Marcus Daly Family Papers, collection 919, box 2, Archives and Special Collections, Mansfield Library, University of Montana, Missoula.

Daly had never forgotten Fred Taral, who took command of Montana, an uninspired colt at the time, and raced him to a head-to-head finish with Potomac. The judges had to confer. In the end, they awarded the victory to Potomac.[11]

Taral eased Scottish Chieftain into his maiden race on May 30 at Morris Park. They finished fifth. They clicked on June 4 at Gravesend, where Scottish Chieftain blazed to the front and easily won that one. At Sheepshead Bay for six starts, they were third in two, scored easy victories in the Spring Stakes and June Stakes, and then crashed in the Great Trial Stakes, coming in tenth in a twelve-horse field. They rebounded as runner-up in the Pansy Stakes. In these early races, during the final furlongs when uncorking blasts of his fastest, hardest running, Scottish Chieftain was a textbook closer. At Brighton Beach on August 10, they had a horrible start, but Taral landed the colt fifth. On the eve of the Futurity, August 14 at Sheepshead Bay, Scottish Chieftain had a decent shot at it, especially with Fred Taral in the irons, or so said the turf scribes. But the race did not go well. Scottish Chieftain was balky at the post, and this cost them a clean fast start, but Taral managed to ride him to fifth. Nevertheless, Riverside Stable had prevailed in the Futurity, with Ogden taking a turn in the winner's circle.[12]

⬛

Fred Taral spent the off-season in New York City. He gravitated to the sport of boxing, as did many jockeys. Spotted in pugilists' corners, he would sound the gong as timekeeper. On occasion he would referee a bout. Taral incorporated the punching bag into his training regime, and his valet, Cheeky George, was said to "go some with the mitts." Taral spent long nights patronizing the casinos and was reportedly a "heavy plunger" in craps. He palled around with heavyweight champion John L. Sullivan, also an avid gambler. They were, of course, conspicuous for their fame as well as their lopsided statures that begged for comment—they were, as Sullivan liked to joke, "Big and Little casino."[13]

Born in Peoria, Illinois, in 1867, Fred Taral had the opportunity to study all sorts of horses in the livery stable owned by his father. The family relocated

to Harper, Kansas, in 1880, to be proprietors of a hotel. Fred grew bored with his job as desk clerk and ran away.[14]

His independence at age fourteen took him to the Oklahoma Territory. There, from behind sets of half-wild mustang ears, he navigated the "bush tracks" on Indian reservations or elsewhere in the middle of nowhere. Rookie jockeys learned on the fly, riding a fractious mount in one race and then a broken-down nag in the next. At these homemade bush tracks, the main rule was that there were no rules. This way, things would stay uncluttered: no licensing, no regulations about fouls or anything like that. The jockeys themselves enforced racetrack justice. All knew that if they committed a foul, they would be fouled right back. The conniving veteran jockeys, many at the rock bottom of their careers, taught the rookies things about racing they would never learn anywhere else.[15]

Bush tracks were the lowest form of American horse racing. In the home-made bleachers, quarrels would erupt, or worse. It was not unheard of for such disputes to lead to murder, as happened in 1886 in Oklahoma. Two men in hotheaded disagreement over a race drew Winchesters and, at only three feet apart, fired. One fell dead and the other was mortally wounded.[16]

Fred Taral went north to Chicago to advance his career. On an unknown day at Washington Park, trainer Lew Elmore put the kid on a Thoroughbred named Loupe and the kid won his first professional race. Still at Washington Park on July 30, 1886, throwing a leg over Della Beach, Taral rode the 150-to-1 long shot to victory.[17]

Whether astride a dark horse or a favorite, Taral usually won. Turfmen liked the way the kid rode, his short body and taut limbs compactly pressed over his mount's withers. His seat was firm and solid, even graceful, and hands of "steel and velvet combined" kept time with his mount's rhythm. In those early years of his riding, he honed an innate sense for timing and exploiting weaknesses in rival horses and jockeys. Turfmen joked that if Taral were mounted on a Kentucky mule against a field of Thoroughbreds, they would "back the mule and trust Taral to land him a winner." They marveled over him again in 1894. That year Fred Taral won the Brooklyn, Suburban, and Metropolitan Handicaps, known collectively as the New York Handicap Triple Crown. He was first to accomplish the feat.[18]

Taral perfected whipping to an art form. As one witness observed, "I have seen Taral change his whip from the right to the left hand, when hemmed in so that he could not use his right hand at all, never dropping his horse's head for a part of a second, which would have cost him the race, and win by an eyelash or lip."[19]

Fred Taral whipped the hell out of his mounts. At the sight of the little man dressed in racing silks, his greatest mount, Domino, exploded in a fury. Getting a leg up was impossible for Taral unless handlers blindfolded the horse or laid a blanket over his head. Good racehorses "hated certain jockeys," Taral once said, and "horses tremble[d] when some particular jockeys approached to mount them. The animals remembered hard punishment the boys gave them in some preceding race," just as he himself had done with Domino. But in Taral's mind, he and Domino were on friendly terms: "I could get everything there was out of them." On "friendly terms" must have been light-years away from Domino's thinking.[20]

He was fierce with the whip and spur but an amiable person who endeared himself to the racetrack hierarchy from stableboy to owner. They called him the "Dutchman," which harked back to his German heritage. It was said that Taral would sooner ride a horse for a poor owner or an unlucky man than for a millionaire if he believed he could win for the poor man and help him along. When losing a race, he reportedly "suffered very much." Everyone involved in the American turf had respect for "straight as a string" Taral, whose "honest blue eyes mirrored the integrity of his character." Early in his career he rode for turfman Dan Honig, who liked him immediately:

> In fact, nobody could dislike him. He was so good-natured and willing to do anything you asked him. . . . Taral did well with me, and when it came time to go east, Johnny Campbell offered him a salary of $2,500. I had told Taral that I would give him $1,000. When he told me about Campbell's offer, I said to him: "No, you sign with him. He has a larger stable and you will have greater opportunities to make money." But Taral said he would work for me for $1,000 if I would only say the word. I urged him to go where he could do the best and he went. Taral was as honest as the day was long. . . . The public had absolute confidence in Taral, and he never for one moment, abused it. If ever a soul of honor sat in a saddle, he was one.[21]

His good judgment lapsed at least once. Taral violated the rules of racing when he accepted "a present" of $500 during the season of 1895. The Jockey Club's September 1896 judgment stated, "Owing to Taral's universally accepted good character, he is reprimanded by the stewards, and ordered to refund the money received by him in violation of the rules and all jockeys are warned that the penalty for accepting presents under Rule 150 will be strictly enforced."[22]

Taral was arguably America's best jockey in the 1890s. The year-to-year contracts he signed increased by thousands of dollars, and an annual income ticked upward of $40,000. His home was the comfort of a New York City mansion. He was a model husband and father. The habit of plunging in craps aside, he was considered a "thrifty young man," as told by the *Daily Racing Form*. Taral's diverse investments included several farms and houses, milk routes, grocery stores, and saloons, in addition to "several fast horses and some fine hunting dogs." The *Form* continued, "As a crack shot, an expert boxer, a good pool and billiard player and a clever athlete, he manages to extract some amusement from life during the winter when he isn't starving to keep himself down to riding weight." Taral himself said of his profession, "Riding is as easy as rolling along in a carriage, it's the starvation that hurts."[23]

Reengaged by Riverside Stable in 1897, Fred Taral reported for duty for the Withers Stakes, the season's first major race in New York. Both Matthew Byrnes and Marcus Daly badly wanted to win that one. With two eligible three-year-olds in Scottish Chieftain and Ogden, the stable elected to start Ogden only. After an impressive 1896 with Ogden, the hope for his kickoff race was to deliver a good pummeling to the Withers competition. But no— sulking through the race, he refused to exert himself.[24]

Ogden's reputation as a crack three-year-old was now dubious. The Daly family stood by him, and their loyalty might have complicated things for Byrnes, expected to pick the right horse for the May 29 Belmont Stakes. During the prerace trials, Byrnes watched Ogden sputter while Scottish Chieftain streaked over the oval like a sudden wind. He was the superior colt, but Byrnes knew how badly Ogden needed the Belmont Stakes. The one mile and three-eighths distance over the slightly hilly Morris Park course proved a tough test for three-year-old mettle, and for this reason the Belmont was regarded as a classic event. The prestige accorded to a Belmont Stakes winner was comparable to that reserved for a Futurity or Realization Stakes winner. Owning a Belmont Stakes title was more important to turfmen than the purse money; the 1897 victor would collect a modest $3,200.[25]

On the morning of the race, Byrnes opened a telegram from Marcus Daly. The contents instructed Byrnes to wager $500 on Ogden. By late morning at Morris Park, Byrnes posted an official announcement stating that Riverside Stable intended to win the race with Odgen. It is plausible the telegram swayed Byrnes to pass over Scottish Chieftain. But importantly, the matter was settled: Ogden was the right horse to win the Belmont Stakes.[26]

He would need help, however, and Scottish Chieftain would make the perfect rabbit. Byrnes's preparation included changing jockeys. He put Fred Taral astride Ogden and top reinsman Joe Scherrer astride Scottish Chieftain. The Westchester Racing Association offered six races that afternoon, with the Belmont Stakes third on the card. The glorious day glowed with sunshine, the temperature was comfortably cool, and several thousand people gathered at Morris Park.[27]

August Belmont II had his heart set on not only winning the race named for his father but also winning it in consecutive years. Since the death of his father, he had stood at the helm of the family's Nursery Stud racing and breeding empire. Belmont II's intuitive sense about breeding winners and knowledge of bloodlines matched those of his father. John E. Madden said that Belmont II was the best breeder of Thoroughbreds America had ever known. The masterpiece, Man o' War, was yet unseen. That colt would not race until 1919.[28]

The two colts that represented the Nursery Stud in the 1897 Belmont Stakes were Don de Oro and Octagon. The pair was coupled in the betting and the race favorite. Scottish Chieftain and Ogden, also coupled, elicited a strong following as the second choice. The turf writers liked Don de Oro and Octagon but were equally high on Scottish Chieftain, or "The Chieftain," as they were now calling him. The "lengthy, racing-looking colt" had impressive prerace workouts to recommend him, and the allocated 115-pound impost was manageable. Identical poundage was put on the backs of Horoscope and On Deck. Heavier allotments were distributed to Octagon, 122 pounds, and 125 for both Don de Oro and Ogden.[29]

The six Belmont Stakes hopefuls pranced over the course baked dry and fast. Scottish Chieftain and Don de Oro acted balky at the post, but the delay to compose them was brief. All horses walked forward. The flag snapped. All broke cleanly. Don de Oro immediately thrust himself into the lead and rounded the first turn crisply, as did Scottish Chieftain, ready for the chase. The next three racers did not manage the turn as skillfully. Octagon and Horoscope jammed into Ogden, who was knocked nearly from his feet. He regained his footing and Fred Taral tried desperately to move him closer to the pack now far ahead, but the distance would be too much. With Ogden the first horse beaten, Matthew Byrnes's rabbit strategy was already off the rails.[30]

Scottish Chieftain was still hot on Don de Oro's tail. Octagon was trying to catch them, but at midrace, he could not yet outstride Scottish Chieftain. Joe Scherrer wondered about Ogden and Taral. Glancing around to locate them and not finding them, Scherrer realized that if Riverside Stable was to win the prize, Scottish Chieftain would have to do it. Scherrer urged. *Go!* Under this gentle coaxing, the colt lengthened his stride even more before hurtling himself at Don de Oro, gassed from running flat out for a mile and a quarter. In one, two, three strides, Scottish Chieftain picked off Don, but On Deck rolled up alongside to challenge. Scherrer would not have it. He flattened his body over The Chieftain's neck and spoke low and sweet—*Faster!* The colt sprang like a released arrow slipping through the air. His advantage over On Deck lengthened, and soon Scottish Chieftain was the only thing in the space from the final furlong pole to the wire. The colt's swift time of 2:23 ¼ set a course record. On Deck finished second, Octagon third, Horoscope fourth, Don de Oro fifth. Although Fred Taral never gave up, Ogden was last.[31]

The trip around the oval had not gone exactly as Matthew Byrnes planned, but he did not mind winning with the wrong horse. Byrnes hurried over to Scherrer and the colt, already immersed in the intoxicating gaiety of the winner's circle. Byrnes sang out, "Bring that cup and let the horse have a drink out of it. He deserves it." The "cup" was really a silver trophy commissioned by August Belmont from Tiffany and Company. Mr. Belmont graciously presented the lustrous trophy to Margaret Daly, whose husband was in Montana.[32]

Sam Lucas of the Bitterroot Valley was the genius responsible for The Chieftain's existence. The horseman's popularity swelled to even greater proportions, or, as put by the *Anaconda Standard*, "Sam Lucas seems to have grown several inches taller . . . his smile has spread all over his face since he got the telegram announcing the result of the race. And he isn't a bit selfish in his pleasure either." The *Western News* effused, "Sam Lucas who bred and always had a warm spot for the Chieftain . . . [was] immensely pleased. The victory was especially gratifying from the fact that the great three-year-old was bred and raised on the Bitter Root stock farm—a genuine product of the Bitter Root ozone and bunch grass." All of Montana swelled in pride for their native son.[33]

Scottish Chieftain was American horse racing's newest turf star. Expectations were high. Weight was piled on. Under imposts of 126 and 130 pounds and competing against top three-year-old competition, he finished runner-up twice and unplaced three times. The *Daily Racing Form* of June 15 noted that two of the races on soft ground had caused problems for the "exceptionally long strider," who "slipped and sprawled into defeat." Fred Taral and Joe Scherrer had alternated as riders. At the close of 1897, the Belmont Stakes accounted for Riverside Stable's only victory in a major eastern race that season. Marcus Daly was grievously disappointed.[34]

Daly's extensive involvement in eastern racing had reached seven years. When asked a few years earlier whether he viewed racing as merely a millionaire's luxury or whether he expected to make money, he answered like the capitalist he was:

> Of course, I expect to make money out of them. No one in Montana goes into luxuries of that kind for the fun of the thing, and if I really thought I could not make a profit out of my stables, I would sell them tomorrow. . . . My farm is run on the same business principles as are the mines and smelters. Everything is systematized and kept in book shape. Every saddle and bridle is charged, and if a halter strap is broken it has to be brought back before a new one can be given out. I know to a cent what everything costs, and I keep two sets of books, one of my racing and the other of my breeding stables. I have weekly reports, and I know just exactly on what horses I am making and on what I am losing.[35]

Yet national newspapers and racing journals continued to trivialize his involvement as a hobby and perpetuate the general belief that his love for the sport was a simple extension of being fond of swift, beautiful horses.[36]

Marcus Daly indeed loved high-class, high-priced Thoroughbred race-horses and had committed hundreds of thousands of dollars to them but grew weary of supporting them merely to look at them. On September 1, he ordered all his racehorses returned to the farm. The *Hattie D.* and *Palfiena* cars clattered east, were filled with racehorses, and clattered back. Shake-ups at the Bitter Root continued. Daly opted not to renew trainer Johnny Campbell's contract. The nation's turfmen were asking, "Has Daly quit the turf?" Rumors swirled that he had. When quizzed about his leanings by an unnamed New York newspaper, Daly responded, "My immediate reasons for withdrawing from the Eastern turf are that there is not a horse in my stables that can win a high-class race, and there is no prospect that any horses that I now own will prove winners of stake events for which they are nominated." He continued, "A racing stable in the east is expensive. To run for big stakes means keeping a large number of horses in training. So far it has cost me about $500,000 for the experiment, and I have come to the conclusion, taking all things into consideration, the game is not worth the candle."[37]

Nor had Daly disentangled himself from his work. "For several years past, I have expected and hoped that circumstances would allow me to spend the racing season in the east," he said. "The pressure of business does not lessen, hence I cannot continue the hope of seeing my horses work and run."[38]

On November 9, the *Salt Lake Tribune* reported more startling news at the Bitter Root. Daly and Matthew Byrnes had ended their seven-year association, and Byrnes had then announced his intention of quitting his profession altogether. He was already aboard an eastbound train.[39]

On April 11, 1898, Byrnes debuted as a starter at Bennings Racecourse in Washington, DC. The stewards there admired his work. After fulfill-ing that commitment, he worked the flag at Saratoga. By the end of July, complaints had piled up over his inability to start even the smallest field of veteran horses. Byrnes's second season as a starter began inauspiciously at Montgomery Park in Memphis. A slipshod start in the second race on April 11 left a horse at the post. The fifth race was worse; four horses were left behind. Byrnes's bungling played into the hands of the bookmakers and turfmen who were unhappy with the Memphis Jockey Club for selecting Byrnes in the first place. Byrnes resigned his post the next day. Saratoga welcomed him back, but within two weeks he felt it necessary to resign his post there. The most common complaint about his work was too much leniency: "The boys jolly him at the post, and their excuses for pulling up and not breaking are accepted in perfect good faith."[40]

Falling back on his true love, Byrnes trained and raced his own small strings until taking his talent overseas in 1903. The "language of the natives" was the stumbling block to finding success at a Hungarian nobleman's racing stable. He returned to America and trained for various turfmen. In 1908, he was back with J. B. Haggin as a horse-buying agent.[41]

By 1930, Byrnes had returned to his hometown of Eatontown, New Jersey, and was regaled as the "pioneer trainer of Eastern New Jersey." He had been tightening saddle girths around horse bellies since the age of eleven or twelve. It is a rare gift for a trainer to get his hands on a Hall of Fame horse. Matthew Byrnes trained three: Parole for Pierre Lorillard, and both Firenze and Salvator for J. B. Haggin. No wonder onlookers pointed out Byrnes "one hundred times a day" before they whispered, "There's the man who trained Salvator." When asked over the years to name the best horse he ever trained, Byrnes swayed from one champion to the next. He admitted as much, once saying, "I did say at one time that Tammany was as good as Salvator. I firmly believe that he is, if not better, but Salvator is not on the turf and Tammany is, so that question is matter of judgment." And when he had Ogden, Ogden was better than Tammany or Salvator. Byrnes's final word on the subject came in August 1932. The best he had ever trained was Salvator and the best mare was Firenze. Byrnes spent his final years at Long Branch, New Jersey, where he succumbed to pneumonia on March 19, 1933, at age eighty. His own induction into the Hall of Fame in 2011 was predated by the three champions he trained: Salvator in 1955, Firenze in 1981, and Parole in 1984.[42]

After having turned his back on eastern racing's high-stake thrills in September 1897, Marcus Daly reversed his decision that December and practically began his turf career anew. Thoroughbred horses arrived from the Eastin and Larabie Stable, Nursery Stud, Rancho del Paso, and Belle Meade Plantation, and from turfman John E. Madden of Kentucky, he bought Hamburg.[43]

The brown colt was born and bred in 1895 at Elmendorf Farm in Lexington. The farm was then under the ownership of Con Enright. Madden purchased

Hamburg, the son of Hanover and Lady Reel, as a weanling for $1,200. Robust and fiery, Hamburg had obvious talent but was a rough one to handle, even for a gifted horseman like Madden. The colt wanted to go his own way and fought one exercise rider after another. The riders, as they slid from his back to the dirt, grabbed fistfuls of his mane, leaving it raggedy looking, like something moths had eaten. He grew to sixteen hands, and to power his huge hindquarters and huge gaskins, he had the appetite of two horses. Madden conditioned the colt into America's two-year-old champion of 1897.[44]

Hamburg conquered his competition over long distances with the ease of a sprinter. Handicappers allocated 127- to 135-pound imposts to slow him down. It made little difference. He just kept winning. To carry so much weight and concede twenty-five to as many as forty pounds to his rivals and win was an astonishing feat for a three-year-old, let alone a two-year-old. Turfmen compared Hamburg to half brother Ben Holladay, another Herculean who accepted severe imposts as an everyday thing. They talked up Hamburg as possibly the greatest two-year-old America had ever seen.[45]

On September 11, 1897, Hamburg was under 135 bone-crushing pounds and giving away eleven to forty pounds to thirteen rivals. Delayed at the post for more than half an hour, the two-year-old won the Great Eastern Handicap by one length. Madden returned Hamburg to the paddock, where, as he liked to tell it, "A thick-set man with a stubby mustache came up and said, 'Young man, do you own that colt?'

'That depends,' I replied, 'whether you want to buy or attach him.'

'I would be pleased to buy him,' said my caller, who was Marcus Daly. 'What is the price?'

'$45,000.'

'Rather steep,' he remarked.

'Not for this kind.'"[46]

John E. Madden was the most formidable horse trader America's turfmen had to brave. In addition to scrupulous study of bloodlines, he abstained from alcohol and never gambled. These underpinned a discriminating eye for horseflesh, and he was intuitively wired for breeding, training, and trading. He got offers for Hamburg but was not anxious to sell. On December 11, 1897, three months after Hamburg's magnificent performance in the Great Eastern, rumors of a private sale leaked. Madden reportedly was negotiating with Billy Lakeland, but nobody knew for whom Lakeland was acting. Then, oddly, no turfman had come forth the next morning professing to own Hamburg. Since a flick of Hamburg's ear generated volumes of news copy, New York racing went wild with speculation. Neither Madden nor Lakeland was talking, so the names of America's foremost horsemen were bantered about as the buyer: William C. Whitney, James R. Keene, Foxhall Keene, J. B. Haggin, Marcus Daly, Pierre Lorillard, and Daly's New York agent W. L. Powers. Haggin's agent John Mackey floated the possibility that Hamburg had not been sold after all.[47]

"The Hamburg Mystery," as the imbroglio was called, generated hysteria in every corner of America's racetracks. The mystery dragged on for days and was blamed for loss of "sleep and brain tissue." Then, the night of December 22, turfmen of a stoic nature sighed in relief upon W. L. Powers announcing that Marcus Daly now owned Hamburg.[48]

The price paid was the next sensation. Everyone wanted to know how much. More than thirty years earlier, Leonard Jerome had paid $40,000 for a sire prospect named Kentucky. The figure stood as the American record price for a two-year-old until Madden reportedly demanded $40,001 for Hamburg so that he would surpass Jerome's record. Marcus Daly obliged, and, as Madden told it, "He handed a Wells Fargo draft for $40,000 and a silver dollar." Madden reportedly used the draft to buy property near Lexington where he would establish his breeding farm, Hamburg Place.[49]

When the calendar year flipped to 1898, Daly must have been anxious but excited for Riverside Stable's fresh start with its three-year-old turf star. At Morris Park on May 26, Hamburg was decked out in the copper and Irish green for the first time. Daly probably felt good about Hamburg's chances of following up Scottish Chieftain's triumph in last year's Belmont Stakes. Alas, even with skilled Fred Taral in the saddle, Hamburg was trounced. He finished a distant third, as many as ten lengths behind victorious Bowling Brook. In Hamburg's defense, the track was heavy, and he was fat and out of condition.[50]

If Daly was alarmed about the colt and his trainer Billy Lakeland adjusting to each other, his worry was short-lived. Lakeland had Hamburg sleek, conditioned, and winning within weeks. Rapid-fire victories in three races included a romp through the Realization Stakes. That victory was exceptional: Marcus Daly was America's first turfman to win the event twice, first winning with Tammany in 1892.[51]

That historic event was unfortunately tainted by shabby treatment of Fred Taral. The stink started with jockey Tod Sloan, who wanted to ride Hamburg in the Realization. Even though Taral was contractually engaged as Hamburg's rider, W. L. Powers granted Sloan's request to ride Hamburg, leaving Taral without a mount.[52]

That episode was not the first in which Taral was set down in favor of Sloan. Four days earlier, Taral was to ride Ogden in a purse race until Powers granted Sloan's wish to ride that colt. Again, Taral had no mount to ride. To sit Taral down twice called into question either his honesty or ability or both. Powers insisted the switch to Sloan in no way reflected negatively on Fred Taral. Rather, the change was made for Ogden's sake, who, according to Powers, "seems to fret and worry when [Taral] is on his back." Sloan and Ogden won their race.[53]

Taral weathered the first snub quietly, but after two snubs in four days, he was fuming. He struck back by standing in front of Powers and ripping up his contract. Powers released Taral from any obligation and handed over a check for salary owed, but not before asking the jockey to reconsider. Taral's riposte was an emphatic *No*. The racing public, with whom he was immensely popular, supported his actions. His peers supported him, too. Many of them had been hurt by Tod Sloan's wheedling to secure mounts not his to ride.[54]

Taral's career was winding down by 1898, and in 1903, his dominance in American racing waning, he shipped overseas with his close friend Johnny Campbell. There, after eight seasons of riding, Taral had recorded more victories in Europe than any other jockey. The day he hung up his silks for good in 1909, he had won nearly all of American racing's greatest events. His uncommonly lengthy career covered twenty-seven years. A pronounced association with Montana racehorses and turfmen included Scottish Chieftain, Hamburg, Montana, and Ogden. When riding for Samuel Larabie, he sat astride Julia L., Poet Scout, Ben Holladay, and Kinley Mack. Taral piloted many acclaimed champions to the winner's circle and picked Domino as his greatest mount. Domino's superiority over all others was largely owed to Taral whipping the daylights out of him. Taral went on to reinvent himself as a trainer, even going abroad and conditioning racehorses for the Crown Prince of Germany until the outbreak of World War I, when he returned home.[55]

The financial sense Taral exemplified as a young man was misdirected later in his life. Little of his fortune was left for his family upon his death on February 13, 1925. He died from pneumonia at age fifty-eight in New York. Thirty years later, the National Museum of Racing examined Fred Taral's contributions to the American turf. The achievements and accolades supporting his induction into the Hall of Fame were many, and the statistic of 1,437 career victories in 5,000 races was a good place to start. Fred Taral was inducted in 1955.[56]

⬛

On July 30, 1898, in the three-horse field for the Brighton Cup, the entries Ogden and Howard Mann were supposed to present something of a challenge for Hamburg over the forever distance of two and a quarter miles. Jockey Tod Sloan had only to sit quietly on Hamburg's back. Before the half mile was covered, Hamburg led Howard Mann and Ogden by a sixteenth of a mile, and by this margin won his race. In justice to Ogden, second, he was a sprinter, never a stayer across long distances. The racetrack was damp with rain, too, and Ogden had been under 130 pounds to Hamburg's 112. Ogden's most ignominious defeat stood as the most extraordinary victory of Hamburg's career.[57]

Marcus Daly retired Hamburg sound of body and wind on August 8, 1898. Had he opted to race the colt a third season, eager handicappers would have been waiting with monstrous imposts. Daly's focus on Hamburg shifted from the racetrack to the stud barn:

> I have great hopes he will prove to be a great sire. . . . He is yet an experiment, but I am determined, so far as I am able, to leave nothing undone to make this possible. I have secured twelve mares from England, after considerable time and expense, and along bloodlines, which, I believe will produce great stock if Hamburg proves to have the indispensable quality of prepotency, without which, of course, nothing good can come. The horse, however, has practically cost me nothing. I paid $40,000 for him and he won $52,000 in the season I ran him.

A record of sixteen wins in twenty-one starts amassed $60,380 in career earnings. Hamburg never finished a race unplaced; only five horses ever finished ahead of him. Tod Sloan, who rode many exceptional racehorses, gave this pointed tribute: "Hamburg was the only great horse I ever rode."[58]

⬛

While future Hall of Famer Hamburg racked up a winning season in 1898, four-year-old Scottish Chieftain was stringing together a winning season of his own in his native Montana. In July he was two for two in Butte and in a third race earned third. After a month-long break in August, his campaign moved to Anaconda. There, on September 5, he took down the Labor Day Handicap by a neck. The victory, worth $5,000, marked the fattest purse of his career. In the Copper City Handicap five days later, he was runner-up. Then, at Great Falls for three starts, he finished first, second, and fifth. His earnings of $7,080 made the season his richest. With the horse entered in several important eastern races for 1899, Scottish Chieftain was sent to Billy Lakeland in New York but for unknown reasons was scratched from all. In fact, The Chieftain never raced again. After three seasons on the track, twenty-four starts netted eight wins, five times second, and three times third. Career earnings totaled $14,475. Horse racing journals of the 1890s were consistent in judging him "a good racehorse."[59]

In autumn 1898, Scottish Chieftain returned to the Bitterroot Valley, where, perhaps, Sam Lucas met the train at the Hamilton depot. Lucas's health had been in decline. If Hamiltonians were unaware of his situation, the *Western News* related on January 10, 1900, that Lucas, "seriously afflicted with stomach trouble," had suffered a relapse that confined him to his bed for two days. Two weeks later, the *Western News* broke the story of his impending departure from Bitter Root Stock Farm. "Mr. Lucas . . . says he will go back to Kentucky and buy a nice little farm and home for Mrs. Lucas and the children and a few good brood mares, a couple of good racehorses and some game chickens for himself and settle down. Mr. Lucas regrets to leave . . . and only does so in the hope that he may better his health and prospects."[60]

All of Hamilton was invited to the farewell gala, covered extensively by the *Western News*. The stage of the Lucas Opera House was tastefully decorated with evergreens, including a big streamer inscribed "Farewell Sam." The five hundred people who came for the farewell were entertained with music by the Hamilton orchestra and "O'Brien & McCauley's giant phonograph." Everybody who shook Lucas's hand bid him and his family "Godspeed and unbounded happiness and prosperity to come." Lucas took the stage and said to his well-wishers: "Dear Friends, I do not know what to say on this occasion or how to thank my friends for the beautiful watch, except that I love you all and it almost breaks my heart to leave you all . . . I feel the people of Montana are the best people on earth. So I won't say good-bye . . . for I am coming back . . . to meet all of you again."[61]

Lucas continued to surround himself with horses. In his care in 1905 were twenty-nine stallions and four mares he personally delivered to Japan for service in the Russo-Japanese War. On his return trip to Kentucky, a stopover in the Bitterroot Valley reacquainted him with old friends. "He notes many changes since he left here five years ago," the *Western News* reported. "However, he is still of the opinion the Bitter Root is the most beautiful and best valley on earth." Two years later, Lucas returned to Butte without his family. He found work in the mines. He went broke, and the once-famous horseman eroded to a "broken, disconsolate hanger-on at pool and bar rooms." He sank farther into oblivion, becoming a vagrant repeatedly in trouble with the law for selling "moonshine" and taking part in scuffles. Sam Lucas died on a charity hospital cot on March 28, 1929. He was seventy-three. Marcus Daly Jr. paid for the funeral expenses and the interment at Holy Cross Cemetery in Butte.[62]

At the Bitter Root Stock Farm on September 29, 1899, a large sale commenced. The Montgomery Ranch in Madison County, Montana, purchased several horses. A few of them, two broodmares and Scottish Chieftain, who was possibly in New York with Lakeland at the time of the sale, were shipped by train to their new home on December 15. The Chieftain would have at least one more home, with Wellington D. Randall, a western turf associate of Marcus Daly's. The horse would sire at least one good offspring in Lady Chieftain. She raced on the Butte and Anaconda tracks as "a handsome and speedy daughter of the famous Scottish Chieftain."[63]

Scottish Chieftain ran the race of his life on May 29, 1897. Yet, oddly, the rare distinction of being a Belmont Stakes winner sank into oblivion in his home state. More than a century would pass before this was rectified, in February 2015, when Montanans honored their native son with an induction into the Montana Cowboy Hall of Fame and Western Heritage Center.

CHAPTER 15

End of an Era

Marcus Daly trailblazed the West's mining and smelting industries and founded the world's largest copper-producing company. By 1900, at age fifty-eight, his once-vigorous body was withering. Constant exposure to noxious dust and fumes had weakened his heart, and a kidney disorder known as Bright's disease grew acute. Daly's team of physicians urged scaling back on his work and advised against maintaining a racing stable. He complied. Small consignments of his horses shipped to auction houses in New York. This marked the early diminution of Bitter Root Stock Farm.[1]

Against his physicians' recommendation, Daly traveled to Nauheim, Germany, to soak in the mineral water baths reputed to cure illnesses. The outcome was not what he had hoped for. Upon returning to New York in September 1900, he was sick and experiencing fainting spells. Advised that his death was imminent, he chose to prepare for it in his suite at the Netherlands Hotel rather than at the Bitter Root or the Daly home on Fifth Avenue. The four children came to New York to comfort their father and mother. Daly lapsed in and out of consciousness during the last week of his life and at times was delirious. He spent the last Saturday visiting with J. B. Haggin. The two men talked quite a while. Soon after Haggin departed, Daly lapsed into unconsciousness. At four o'clock in the morning on November 12, 1900, Daly roused and spoke to Margaret and the children. He died four hours later. He left to his family a fortune estimated at $25 million.[2]

◄►

When the news of his death reached Montana, a hush fell over Anaconda. The smelters and city businesses were closed. Hundreds of mourners attended memorial services, with hundreds turned away because the churches could not accommodate everyone. John Durston was still editor at the *Anaconda*

Standard. His November 13 eulogy focused on Daly's inspiring tenacity: "If things appeared to go wrong, he never permitted himself to be swerved from his purpose. If serious and unexpected obstacles blockaded the way, he never turned back. If reverses came . . . he never was dismayed. He was always the man who took the hopeful view in presence of emergencies; it often fell to his lot to be the one to inspire all others with pluck. . . . His own homely phrase was: 'Of course, I have guessed wrong a good many times, but my average is pretty good.'"[3]

Hundreds of obituaries appeared elsewhere in Montana and highlighted Daly's contributions as a Montanan. The multiple enterprises he founded employed thousands of men "at the best wages known, thereby enabling them to make happy and contented homes for their families," the *Ravalli Republican* wrote. As for generosity, the *Bozeman Chronicle* stated simply, "His secret and unostentatious charity and helpfulness was felt in a thousand ways that the world never heard of."[4]

Butte was also draped in black. On the hills to the north, flags on the mine hoists floated at half-mast. Butte's population of "colored" citizens, according to the *Anaconda Standard*, "feel they have lost a great friend of the race in the death of Mr. Daly, as he has always championed their cause and kept them at work in his hotels, farm, and smelters. They are not unmindful of it, and highly appreciate his good will for their interests."[5]

Obituaries appeared in the national newspapers. The *Detroit Tribune* opened its tribute in respect to Daly's heritage by noting that he was "Irish, and all that the word implies. His veins were full of red blood, his nerves were like electric wire." The *Seattle Post-Intelligencer* focused on his industry: "He did not sit in an office in New York and direct operations by wire. He was always on the ground, exercising real superintendence and giving personal attention to details, whether they related to mine, mess house or smelter. He grew up with the Anaconda property and today it represents what his care, calculation and hard work have brought about." In Washington, DC, the Copper King was "intimately and favorably known to the public men of the capital city for years. He has long had scores of friends among the distinguished leaders of both great political parties. Expressions of deep sorrow at his untimely death were heard on every hand today."[6]

On the morning of November 15 inside St. Patrick's Cathedral in New York, three thousand mourners paid their respects to the Daly family during funeral services. Pallbearers included longtime friend John W. Mackay from the Comstock days, former New York mayor Hugh John Grant, and, of course, Haggin. Marcus Daly's body was interred temporarily in the Mackay mausoleum in Green-Wood Cemetery, Brooklyn, until the Daly mausoleum was completed. Disappointed by the news, Montanans had hoped that the family would return his body to the state that had done so much for him and for which he had done so much.[7]

The nation's horse racing and sporting journals printed eulogies. The final statement in the *Thoroughbred Record* homage was, "To all his various interests, Mr. Daly is a great loss, but none will feel his absence so keenly, and no industry will have so hard a time to replace him, as the thoroughbred horse business of America." *Turf, Field and Farm* expressed a similar sentiment. "At Bitter Root Farm, Ravalli County, Montana, he bred thoroughbreds and trotters, never hesitating at expense to secure prepotent strains of blood, and successes in this field were more gratifying to him than in any other domain of thought or activity." The tribute ended with, "Mr. Daly was a man of strong convictions and earned the reputation as a resolute fighter. His loss will be severely felt in the business world, but it is as a breeder and turfman that his death is widely deplored." Beyond the immediacy of Daly's death, turf historian Hamilton Busbey wrote in 1907 that Marcus Daly "helped Montana before the world by demonstrating that its grass and climate were favorable to the growth of the highest type of domestic animals, and that the lung expansion which attended growth in open pastures was such as to sustain inherited speed. Before the establishment of the Bitter Root Farm, the popular impression was that Montana might grow indifferent cattle, but not race horses of high class."[8]

The sport would advance in Montana without its most influential turfman, as the 1901 founding of the Montana Jockey Club illustrated, with Hugh Wilson as president. Butte's old-timers remembered Wilson as the man to persuade Daly to try Ogden in the 1896 Futurity. In Butte on Labor Day, September 2, 1907, on North Main Street, cords were drawn from the American flag covering a memorial statue. From atop a huge base, a larger-than-life bronze figure of Marcus Daly looked across Butte. But he was horseless. The oversight dismayed an old-time miner who said, "Arrah, they should have put him astride a big, phite harse. Marcus was always wild about harses!"[9]

▬

The Bitter Root Stock Farm began winding down operations. With neither Margaret nor the children sharing Daly's passion for blooded horses, trainloads of them were en route to New York. On December 23, 1900, upon the departure of broodmares from the Hamilton depot, a pall sank over the town. And it fell again, at twilight on January 17, 1901, when handlers herded eighty-three Thoroughbreds to the depot. Ogden and Hamburg were entrained, and one by one the remaining horses were loaded into seven Palace cars. This final shipment was said to be the most valuable collection of horses the West had ever seen. Hamiltonians who gathered to bid them farewell watched the train chug into darkness that "kindly shut the sad scene from view," the *Rocky Mountain Husbandman* rued. "The last of the Bitter Root thoroughbreds, a gallant and stalwart race, moved out of the city, rolled down the valley and sped eastward to New York, never to return." The dissolution of the Bitter Root Stock Farm was now complete.[10]

The train was headed for New York City. The Fasig-Tipton Company headquartered at Madison Square Garden would take charge. Fasig-Tipton specialized in the sale of high-class blooded horses. Of Daly's breeding operation, the firm said, "America and England have contributed their choicest strains of blood to make the Bitter Root Stock Farm the foremost breeding establishment in the world." One hundred eighty-five Bitter Root horses would pass through the sales ring on January 30 and 31, 1901. The *Thoroughbred Record* predicted "the greatest sale of thoroughbreds ever held in the Western hemisphere will be consummated." The *Breeder and Sportsman* noted, "Only one such event, the dispersal of the late August Belmont's immense breeding establishment ten years ago compares with the coming sale."[11]

With that kind of promotion, people with only marginal interest in horses streamed through the Madison Square Garden doors on the snowy night of January 30. The event was not merely a horse sale but a must-see-and-be-seen-at affair within New York society circles. The well-to-do arrived dressed and groomed as if attending a seasonal ball. The rest of the assemblage included the middle classes, bookmakers, "tattered" stable hands, and "loudly dressed touts of the African origin," as put by one fashion-conscious observer.[12]

The Fasig-Tipton Company had prepared for a full house. Even so, few of the seven thousand people could station themselves near the ring. People were also densely aswarm at the auctioneer's stand. Seeing this, auctioneer William Easton called on policemen for assistance. The men in blue cleared a pathway for J. B. Haggin, John Mackey, John E. Madden, J. W. Rogers, William C. Whitney, Billy Lakeland, Charles Reed, Peter Wimmer, Matthew Byrnes, W. L. Powers, James R. Keene, and other well-known turfmen warranting ringside seats.[13]

Seven Bitter Root stallions led off the evening's festivities at eight o'clock. The eminent horse of the night, Hamburg, was first to be sold. Cheers erupted when a handler led him into the sales ring. At six years old, he looked imperious as ever. With all eyes riveted on him, Hamburg "fairly laughed at the crowd, fooling with his muzzle, full of play and good spirits," wrote one of the many turf scribes at the Garden. The stallion was once a superlative racehorse, but his lot as a sire was an open question. His first crop of foals

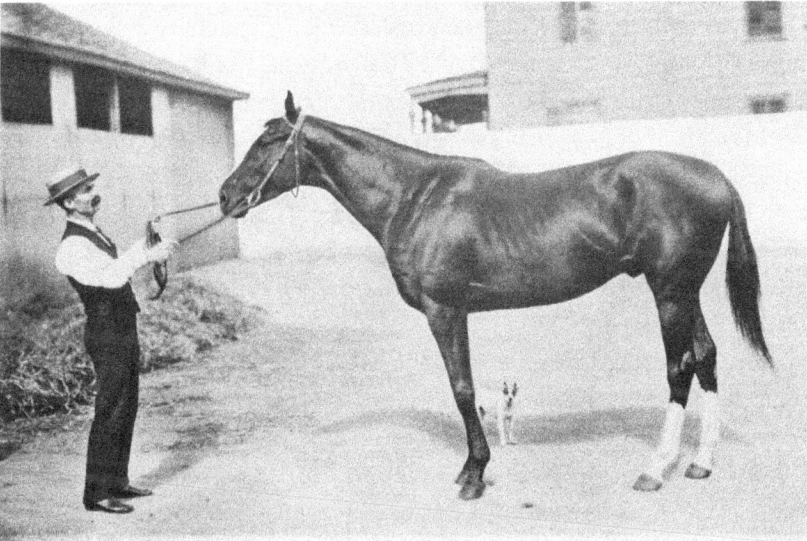

Hamburg with his trainer William "Billy" Lakeland. Hamburg was a sweet-tempered stallion and a favorite with Bitterroot Valley locals, who characterized him as "wise" and "without vicious traits." Photo courtesy of Keeneland Library General Collection.

had dropped, but they were yet yearlings. Hamburg had proven his virility, however, since thirty-one broodmares waiting for their moment in the ring were pregnant with his foals.[14]

Auctioneer Easton talked up Hamburg for ten minutes, mostly recalling how the stallion had mowed down the competition in one rich stakes after another. Easton looked over the sea of humanity and asked for a bid. The crowd hushed for the expected breakneck bidding, but there was only silence. Each horseman positioned around the circle waited for his neighbor to shout first. "$40,000!" came the cry from John E. Madden. Madden had handled Thoroughbred horses numbering in the thousands and always maintained that Hamburg was the greatest he had ever seen. John Mackey and J. W. Rogers seesawed the price to $50,000. Mackey upped it to $51,000. Rogers, $55,000. Mackey, $56,000. Madden rejoined, $57,000. Mackey, $58,000. Madden, "$60,000!" Silence. Even Hamburg stopped trying to nip the top of his handler's cap. Easton slammed the hammer. Madden's bidding was not on behalf of himself but for William C. Whitney.[15]

Marcus Daly had hoped for Hamburg to be a great sire, and "if that is realized, I will feel I have done something for the American thoroughbred, which is the purpose that has inspired me." Under Whitney's ownership, Hamburg reigned as America's top winning sire in 1905. All told, his twenty-seven stakes winners included the wonderful fillies Hamburg Belle and Artful, and Artful was destined for the Hall of Fame. She packed 130 pounds in one 1901 race and sped to a six-furlong straightaway record that stood for decades. Many of Hamburg's daughters were successful broodmares, with Adriana taprooting the line to produce twentieth-century legend Bold Ruler as well as Native Dancer, television's first Thoroughbred horse celebrity. Both sons were illustrious sires in their own right. Reaching the age of twenty in 1915, Hamburg died at the Whitney farm. He received his berth in the Hall of Fame in 1986.[16]

Thirteen-year-old Inverness had to follow all that. He had produced a Belmont Stakes winner in Scottish Chieftain but was otherwise undistinguished in the stud. This had peeved Daly, who once threatened to geld him and use him as a saddle horse. Madden, however, was convinced Inverness could still turn a trick on a broodmare. He shouted, "$100." Silence. Inverness was his.[17]

A chestnut stallion with a crooked white blaze was next to go under the hammer. Tammany had traveled to Madison Square Garden from the

McGranthiana Stud in Lexington. He had been in the stud since 1894, and his only offspring to win a high-profile race was Tokalon, who on May 21, 1906, as a twenty-five-to-one dark horse, stole the Brooklyn Handicap from the cracks. Strenuous efforts on the part of Easton did not spark any great enthusiasm. Michael Murphy, a Pennsylvania oil baron, gave the high bid of $4,000. Tammany lived the rest of his life at Murphy's stud farm near Philadelphia, dying there in May 1906 at age seventeen. The details of his death were not disclosed.[18]

The bidding opened at $1,000 for Ogden, the Futurity champion of 1896. As with Hamburg, Ogden's first foal crop were yearlings and his quality as a sire was anyone's guess. Increments of $100 and $500 jumped the price to $4,000. His former trainer Billy Lakeland bumped it to $4,200. Ogden was his.[19]

The next series of stallions to pass through the ring were Isidore, The Pepper, and Bathampton. Then, starting alphabetically, one by one broodmares were led into the ring. Forty-five were sold by the time auctioneer Easton called it a night.[20]

Lakeland's first night as Ogden's new owner started off well-intentioned. Outside Madison Square Garden, snow continued falling. Lakeland had the stallion blanketed and hooded from feet to ears before sending him into the wintry night. A Black stableboy was paid five dollars to walk Ogden down winding roads that led to Sheepshead Bay where a stall was waiting. Lakeland went home and waited for word of Ogden's safe arrival.[21]

The night grew later. No word came. Lakeland grew anxious. No longer able to stand the silence, he dispatched messengers in different directions. No word came. At daybreak he was unable to stand his idleness, but before he left home to search for his missing horse, the telephone rang. A police sergeant asked, "Have you bought a horse?" The sergeant explained that a policeman on street patrol had found a shivering horse standing over a boy asleep on a corner. The intoxicated boy was taken to the police station. Ogden was in custody, too, at the station stable where nice policemen were feeding him oats. Forthwith, Lakeland was on his way to the station. Once things were settled there, he personally oversaw Ogden's transfer to Sheepshead Bay.[22]

The auction resumed on January 31 at two o'clock. Miss Darebin, dam of Scottish Chieftain, took her turn in the auction ring. She sold back to her breeder, J. B. Haggin, for $3,600. Oriole, dam of Ogden, sold for $1,000 to a

New York turfman. Haggin bid on nearly every mare and secured twenty-nine of them. The likes of John E. Madden, James R. Keene, and W. L. Powers found it completely useless to bid against him. The sale progressed into evening, and Haggin got a good share of the two- and three-year-olds. At the conclusion of day two, Haggin was the principal buyer of the Bitter Root Thoroughbreds.[23]

Haggin's strong patronage had to have been sentimentally tinged, since he had mentored "Mark" Daly like a son. And like Mark, James Ben Ali Haggin loved a blooded horse. He would breed them until the day he died, at ninety-one years old, on September 12, 1914. Haggin heirs inherited an estate of at least $50 million. Neither his three children nor his second wife, Pearl, was interested in breeding horses. And so, on October 28, 1915, at the Elmendorf Farm, a public auction dispersed all ninety-seven of Haggin's horses.[24]

Haggin would posthumously reach one more pinnacle in the sport he loved. During ceremonies at the National Museum of Racing on August 5, 2022, Haggin was feted as a "Pillar of the Turf." This highest honor is reserved for America's greatest turfmen. Within this select group, James Ben Ali Haggin once again rubbed shoulders with August Belmont I, August Belmont II, William C. Whitney, and James R. Keene.[25]

Two more auctions in 1901 sold more Bitter Root stock. One offered forty-one Thoroughbred broodmares, yearlings, and foals brought over from Daly's English stud, Aperfield Court. The third and final sale dispersed 227 Standardbreds. All told, 369 horses sold for $728,755. According to Fasig-Tipton, the sale was the best on record in America given the number of horses sold.[26]

The bloodlines of several of Marcus Daly's Bitter Root horses would supercharge future turf stars. Two of them were Sysonby and Regret, and Assault would capture the 1946 Triple Crown. But none could trump Colin. A true anomaly is an undefeated horse, and Colin ran the table, fifteen for fifteen across the 1907 and 1908 racing seasons. Like Colin had, the great Man o' War would race two seasons only. With twenty wins in twenty-one starts, turfmen quickly heralded Man o' War as America's greatest racehorse of all time. Hall of Fame jockey Joe Notter, who helped Colin along to a Hall of Fame career, disagreed. He offered this standard reply: "Man o' War was great but remember—Colin *never* lost a race." Perhaps Colin's greatest honor came from James Rowe Sr., his Hall of Fame trainer. Rowe always considered Colin to be the masterwork of his career. He asked for only three words on his epitaph. "He trained Colin."[27]

⋈

As the stables and paddocks emptied at the Bitter Root, Margaret Daly kept one racehorse at home because her husband had wanted it that way. She honored Marcus's request that Senator Grady live out his life at the Bitter Root. Neither she nor anyone else in her late husband's inner circle knew the reason why. Lounging in the paddock on a summer's day in 1909, Senator Grady needed some good hard running, or so thought some of the Bitter Root boys. They hatched a plan to enter the chestnut in a three-hundred-yard dash at the Hamilton fairgrounds. Senator Grady was marvelous! He ran as if twenty months old instead of twenty years. His lead was so huge he looked to be the only horse in the race. The boys raced the grand old Senator twice more. Margaret received the news sternly. Rounding up the conspirators, she told them the Senator deserved peace. She ended her scolding: "Promise me this will never happen again." They nodded and no one lost his job.[28]

Women in Hamilton admired Margaret, and many baby girls were named for her. Marcus had "doted on his Maggie" until the day he died. She was at the farm on July 10, 1941, when she became ill. Margaret died peacefully on July 14 at age eighty-eight. The *Ravalli Republican* reported a community "saddened by the sudden loss of one of its most distinguished citizens." After funeral services in Hamilton, Margaret's body was sent to Green-Wood Cemetery in Brooklyn and interred next to Marcus and two of her adult children already in repose in the Daly mausoleum. She was survived by two daughters.[29]

The Riverside estate passed to the Daly children and was abandoned. The boarded-up mansion fell into disrepair. Tracts of acreage were sold. One day in 1986 a group of Hamilton citizens wanting to save the Daly home mobilized to form the Daly Mansion Preservation Trust. The Montana legislature agreed to forgive $400,000 of $600,000 in inheritance taxes due on the estate. The trust would deliver the $200,000 balance. Room by room the home was restored to its former magnificence and 46.6 acres around it were preserved. Public tours of the historic estate began in 1987. Tammany Castle survives as a private home.[30]

▬

With Marcus Daly dead in 1900, and Noah Armstrong withdrawn from horse racing, and Samuel Larabie leaving the sport in 1901, Montana as a presence in American horse racing would not outlast the three turfmen. Perhaps there was simply not a horseman with both the inclination and money who wanted to enter the speculative business of operating a high-class racing stable that would have to travel back and forth for East Coast racing. Nevertheless, elsewhere in America new generations of twentieth-century turfmen either sustained dynasties or founded new ones as they turned out crops of fast, leggy colts and fillies.

As it stands today, Noah Armstrong, Samuel Larabie, and Marcus Daly were once looked upon as iconoclastic for importing expensive blooded horses to high-altitude valleys alternately covered in bunchgrass or snow. The men had an extraordinary run. For fourteen years, 1886 to 1900, the nation's eminent turfmen, turf scribes, and sporting publications repeated the names of the Armstrong-Larabie-Daly famed flyers that had emerged from "that nowhere in the West." The swift horses won the biggest prizes, shaped historical events, and were fodder for local lore as well as sources of regional pride. At home, on both coasts, and everywhere in between they outraced the East for the winner's circle.

Acknowledgments

From article to book, the journey has taken fourteen years of my life. When I decided to write about three frontiersmen and their racehorses, Molly Holz, the editor of the Montana Historical Society's magazine, *Montana, the Magazine of Western History*, asked for the story that became "In the Winner's Circle: How Montana Thoroughbreds Upset the Nineteenth Century's Racing Establishment." She then urged me to develop the article into a book. Molly directed me to Dr. Charles E. Rankin of the University of Oklahoma Press. I am grateful to Dr. Rankin, who acquired the book in 2015. Molly and Dr. Rankin have my enduring gratitude.

I had to write my first book proposal. I consulted multiple "How to Write a Nonfiction Book Proposal" books. They did not always agree on the best way to structure a winning book proposal. One night after going from book to book to book, I was frozen in fear. I was probably writing the proposal all wrong; would I lose my shot at writing a book for OU Press? I could no longer write a word. When I telephoned my mother, Rae Melin, I unloaded my fears of blowing my chance. She settled me down, and her simple words, "Write it how you want to write it," made crystal clear what I needed to do. The "how to" books went back on the bookshelf. I listened to my heart and gut instincts, and I wrote. Leave it to a mother to help deliver a successful book proposal.

During my multiple journeys through the great state of Montana, many people assisted me with my research as I expanded the "Winner's Circle" article into this book. In providing thank-yous here, I hope I have not missed listing someone for his or her contribution. Any such oversight is not a lack of appreciation.

I thank Darlene Gould at the Marcus Daly Mansion in Hamilton for letting me spend hours in the basement where I researched archival documents. My thanks to the Ravalli County Museum and Historical Society, also in Hamilton, where I spent hours combing through vertical files and microfiche. In Twin Bridges, I thank Joy Day at the Twin Bridges Historical Association, and Patricia Darling; in Deer Lodge, the Reverend Teresa Kendall of the First Presbyterian Church, the Grant-Kohrs Ranch National Historic Site, and the William K. Kohrs Memorial Library; in Dillon, the Beaverhead County Museum; in Missoula, the Maureen and Mike Mansfield Library at the University of Montana; and in Butte, the Butte–Silver Bow Public Archives.

In Helena, a special thank-you to the late Ellen Baumler of the Montana Historical Society. She was an author, a researcher, and a storyteller who embodied what it means to be a dedicated historian advocating the importance of history. From the time I began research for the "Winner's Circle" article to the near completion of this manuscript, Ellen always willingly shared her knowledge about early Montana horse racing, even after her retirement in 2018.

Research for my book took me to the Keeneland Library in Lexington, Kentucky, dedicated to all things Thoroughbred. There I had access to volumes of the *American Stud Book*, *General Stud Book*, *Goodwin's* and *Kirk's* turf guides, sporting journals, and, of course, lots of wonderful books about racehorses. My connection with the staff at this incredible resource has exceeded ten years. Cathy Schenck, Betsy Baxter, Becky Ryder, Katie Farmer, Roda Ferraro, and Kelly Coffman have assisted me immensely. In March 2020, my long-awaited three weeks of research there ended after only six days, when the COVID-19 pandemic shut down Lexington and the rest of America. That abrupt end was a huge disappointment. The many high points in those six days included meeting Becky Ryder, Katie Farmer, and Roda Ferraro. The Keeneland librarians continued to help me write my book remotely.

Other people who were instrumental have encouraged me in their own way, beginning with my dear friend Judy McKernan. One day in the 1990s, she surprised me by handing me assorted writers' magazines. This was her way of encouraging me to become a writer. She's never stopped urging me forward.

My husband of twenty-three years, Kris Moser, steadfastly supported my career as a freelance writer. He expertly edited my work until his passing in September 2013 by suicide. My life was upended. Work on this project stopped. I attempted to resume work on it in November but found that I could not. Another attempt in January produced the same result. One morning in May I awoke to sunshine spilling into the bedroom. From the window, I saw blue sky, pine trees, and a verdant valley of native grass. It was then that I missed my robber barons and racehorses. As the months passed and I wrote their stories, I healed, but I still miss my first editor. I am grateful to still be a part of the lives of Kris's four children, Barbara Brugger, Mary Catherine Conger, Michael Moser, and Matthew Moser.

On my home turf in Montana, Kelly Anne Terry, the former director of the Lewistown Public Library, helped me develop the Winner's Circle PowerPoint program I presented to the Montana Board of Horse Racing in 2015. I thank the board members for being interested in my project as well as connecting me with Bob Curran of the Jockey Club in New York. In Lewistown, author Arnon Hurwitz critiqued every chapter of my book and offered fresh views. I am indebted to journalist Charlie Denison, who critiqued every chapter, some more than once. I thank him for his unflagging enthusiasm as my book progressed. My dear friend Carol Marsh never failed to ask, "How is the book coming?" She would listen and smile as I related the most recent tribulations. After an afternoon hiking with Carol and then getting back to work on the book, tackling the tribulations was easier.

The late Katherine Carey of Iowa began breeding Standardbreds in the 1950s. She was well known for her extensive knowledge of pedigrees. Katherine provided me with books, clippings, and other historical material about Standardbred and Thoroughbred horses. One out-of-print text has been invaluable to have on hand, Ada Powell's *Copper, Green and Silver*. I will always be grateful to Katherine for parting with it.

Wyoming author Gayle Irwin never puts down her pen but found the time to arrange an annual writers' retreat for the two of us. I thank her as well as Kevin and Judy Lund for providing me with hours of uninterrupted time to write in the quiet beauty of a Wyoming ranch.

Colorado historian Carolyn Bowra shares my passion for historical subjects and research. When all my efforts failed and I was stuck, I sent her an SOS and she jumped in and began researching. Our successes and rabbit holes are about even. I owe Carolyn many margaritas.

South Dakota author Diane Diekman read this manuscript twice. Her honest critiques, knowledge of the nuts and bolts of writing, and willingness to share her experience of writing biographies of country and western singers for the University of Illinois Press have been invaluable. We met through the splendid online Internet Writing Workshop, which I joined in 2003. The other members of the nonfiction group who faithfully critiqued chapters are Paul Fein, Sheri McGregor, Janaki Lenin, Ellen Dreyer, and the late Gary Presley and Mona Vanek.

An influential teacher I must mention is Mr. Walter Janda, who taught American literature at the junior high school in my hometown of Broomfield, Colorado. I credit him with instilling my love for books. His gentle demeanor and enthusiasm for the classics drew me in. He offered three or four titles students could choose from and were expected to read every couple of weeks. I remember Conrad Richter's *The Light in the Forest* as one of my choices.

I do not think it is possible for an author to have had a finer editorial team than the one selected for my book. I thank Amy Hernandez, Laurel Anderton, Helen Robertson, Upuli DeSilva, and especially I thank senior acquisitions editor Alessandra Jacobi Tamulevich.

My family has always encouraged me to research and write. They gave me good-natured ribbing, too, because completing my book was taking *forever.* They are my mother Rae Melin, my late father Tom Melin, Hiltrud Melin, Tracey Stockert, Sharon Melin, Anna Frisby, Deb Miller, and Lisa Roy. My ever-supportive aunt, the late Shari McCrory, helped me through difficult losses in 2013 and 2017. Her belief in angels eased my sorrow.

From article to book, I researched and wrote nearly every day. The work was at times frustrating, monotonous, and lonely. Through it all, my sentinel, the late Liza Jane Moser, has had my enduring gratitude.

Notes

Chapter 1

1. Ellen Baumler, "Montana State Fairgrounds Racetrack," National Register of Historic Places Registration Form, section 8, p. 2, 5, State Historic Preservation Office, Helena, MT (hereafter SHPO); "Early Montana Races," *Helena (MT) Independent*, March 23, 1890.
2. "An Old Turfman," *Anaconda (MT) Standard*, August 29, 1895.
3. Baumler, "Montana State Fairgrounds Racetrack," section 8, p. 5; "Early Montana Races."
4. "Sixty Miles for $2,000!," *New North-West* (Deer Lodge, MT), November 18, 1870; "Montanians in New York," *Helena (MT) Weekly Independent*, February 9, 1888; "A Novel Horse Race," *New North-West*, November 4, 1870. For an in-depth account of the historic Sixty Miler, see Catharine Melin-Moser, "The Sixty-Miler," *Montana Quarterly*, Fall 2021.
5. "Longest Race Ever Run in This Country," *Great Falls (MT) Tribune*, November 25, 1904; "Sixty Miles for $2,000!"; "Here It Is," *New North-West* (Deer Lodge, MT), March 7, 1890.
6. "Sixty Miles for $2,000!"; "Novel Horse Race."
7. "Sixty Miles for $2,000!"
8. "Sixty Miles for $2,000!"
9. "Sixty Miles for $2,000!"; Melin-Moser, "Sixty-Miler," 62.
10. "Eleventh Annual Fair," *Butte (MT) Weekly Miner*, September 14, 1880.
11. "Bunch Grass," *New North-West* (Deer Lodge, MT), June 10, 1871.
12. "The Great West," *New North-West* (Deer Lodge, MT), May 11, 1872.
13. "Tammany at His Home," *Anaconda (MT) Standard*, July 10, 1897. According to various sources, Montana's cool-season grasses have a high protein content of 15 percent, and warm-season grasses 6 to 12 percent, depending on the species. Low protein content for cool-season grasses is 5 percent and for warm-season grasses, 4 to 8 percent.
14. Conrad Kohrs, *Conrad Kohrs: An Autobiography* (printed by Conrad Kohrs Warren, Deer Lodge, MT: Platen Press, 1977), 18, 38, 42; *Progressive Men of the State of Montana* (Chicago: A. W. Bowen, n.d.), 258.

15. "Territorial News," *Helena (MT) Independent*, August 27, 1876; "Cariboo," *Helena Independent*, September 12, 1876; "First Thoroughbred Colt Foaled in Montana," *Helena (MT) Daily Herald*, April 3, 1878.

16. Kohrs, *Conrad Kohrs*, 72.; "Regent," *New North-West* (Deer Lodge, MT), March 28, 1879; "Lady Lancaster," *American Stud Book*, vol. 1, rev. ed. (New York: Sanders D. Bruce, 1884), 615 (hereafter *ASB*); "Butte's Famous Race Track Passes into History," *Anaconda (MT) Standard*, December 19, 1915. Sportswriter George S. Klotz states that John Bielenberg imported Regent to Montana, per the article "Deer Lodge Firm Maintained One of the Most Successful Stables of Thoroughbred Racers in History of the Turf," *Anaconda (MT) Standard*, January 1, 1922. Conrad Kohrs and John Bielenberg's ranch survives to this day as the historic Grant-Kohrs Ranch National Historic Site, operated by the National Park Service.

17. "Spokane's Native State," *St. Paul (MN) Globe*, January 27, 1890; "Montana Blooded Stock," *Rocky Mountain Husbandman* (Diamond City, MT), April 25, 1878; "Equine Jottings and Gleamings," *Farmer's Magazine and Kentucky Livestock Monthly*, January 1882, 93–94; "Thoroughly Thoroughbred," Jockey Club, 3–4, accessed May 1, 2018, https://www.jockeyclub.com/pdfs/thoroughly_thoroughbred .pdf (site discontinued). Kentucky bluegrass is a cool-season grass. Depending on the location, the high protein content can range from 15 to 20 percent.

18. "Thoroughly Thoroughbred"; William H. P. Robertson, *History of Thoroughbred Racing in America* (New York: Bonanza Books, 1964), 16.

19. Robertson, *History of Thoroughbred Racing*, 16, 22, 26–28, 87–88; Thomas L. Altherr, ed., *Sports in North America: A Documentary History*, vol. 1, *Part I, Sports in the Colonial Era, 1618–1783* (Gulf Breeze, FL: Academic International Press, 1997), 263.

20. "Endurance of Montana Horses," *Rocky Mountain Husbandman*, December 27, 1883.

21. "Live Stock," *Rocky Mountain Husbandman* (Diamond City, MT), April 3, 1884; "Montana a Superior Horse Country," *Rocky Mountain Husbandman* (Diamond City, MT), May 22, 1884.

22. "This Is the Home of Monarchs of the Turf," *Anaconda (MT) Standard*, December 18, 1898; "Ogden, the Westerner, First," *New York Journal*, August 16, 1896; "Marcus Daly's English Farm at Aperfield, Kent County," *Daily Inter Mountain* (Butte, MT), December 21, 1900.

Chapter 2

1. "Straight Tips on Races," *Helena (MT) Independent*, July 2, 1891.

2. "Noah Armstrong," Armstrong Family Bible; Noah Armstrong renounces Canadian citizenship, State of Minnesota, County of Blue Earth, witnessed June 14, 1855; "Hannah Howd," https://www.glendalemontana.com/names-data base; "Noah Armstrong," https://www.glendalemontana.com/noah-armstrong; Noah Armstrong land deed, Fairbault, MN, August 10, 1859. The "Hannah Howd" biography notes the date of marriage "in about 1854." However, the

"Noah Armstrong" biography notes 1855 as the year of the marriage. All www
.glendalemontana.com material was originally accessed on June 19, 2017. As
of August 29, 2021, this website was discontinued. Printouts of the web pages
cited are in the author's possession.

3. James McClellan Hamilton, *History of Montana: From Wilderness to Statehood*
(Portland: Binsford and Mort, 1970), 211. The article "The Duty of the Hour,"
Great Falls (MT) Tribune, August 3, 1889, expands on Armstrong's boom-
and-bust mining venture in Montana to include that he "struck it rich" and,
after a short absence, returned to Minnesota, where he "dazzled us all by what
appeared at the time to be great wealth. He had made $60,000. Then he went
back to Montana and lost it all, but after prospecting around awhile again, he
struck a vein of metal which brought him $250,000."

4. Muriel Sibell Wolle, *Montana Pay Dirt: A Guide to the Mining Camps of the Treasure
State* (Denver: Sage Books, 1963), 187; Michael A. Leeson, *History of Montana,
1739–1885: A History of Its Discovery and Settlement, Social and Commercial Pro-
gress, Mines and Miners, Agriculture and Stock-Growing, Churches, Schools and
Societies, Indians and Indian Wars, Vigilantes, Courts of Justice, Newspaper Press,
Navigation, Railroads and Statistics, with Histories of Counties, Cities, Villages and
Mining Camps* (Chicago: Warner, Beers, 1885), 487. Leeson states that the original
discoverer of silver in the region is credited to William Spurr, locating the Forest
Queen lode in 1872.

5. Wolle, *Montana Pay Dirt*, 187–88.

6. "Noah Armstrong," https://www.glendalemontana.com/noah-armstrong;
"Spokane," https://www.glendalemontana.com/spokane.

7. Wolle, *Montana Pay Dirt*, 188, 190; Leeson, *History of Montana*, 487.

8. *More History of Beaverhead County, 1800–1997*, vol. 2 (Dillon, MT: Beaverhead
County History Book Association, 1997), 1021.

9. "Noah Armstrong," https://www.glendalemontana.com/noah-armstrong; *More
History of Beaverhead County*, 41, 1021. The article "Territorial Items," *New
North-West* (Deer Lodge, MT), April 21, 1876, notes the purchase of two smelters.
The articles "Horseback Notes," *Butte (MT) Miner*, July 24, 1877, and George B.
Conway, "History and Romance Told of Beaverhead County's Yesterdays," *Dillon
(MT) Tribune*, December 18, 1925, as well as *More History of Beaverhead County*
state that a twenty-ton smelter was erected. This was possibly in addition to a
forty-ton smelter.

10. Helen Clark, "A Whopper of a Ghost Town and Whale of a Horse," *Ghost Town
Quarterly*, Spring 1989, 46; "Hecla Residence," National Register of Historic
Places Registration Form, section 8, pp. 2–3, SHPO; Conway, "History and
Romance."

11. Wolle, *Montana Pay Dirt*, 192.

12. Leeson, *History of Montana*, 482; "Territorial News," *Helena (MT) Independent*,
October 7, 1876; "Territorial," *New North-West* (Deer Lodge, MT), December 5,
1879; Conway, "History and Romance"; Susan Nardinger, *Spirit Horse of the*

Rockies (Great Falls, MT: Spirit Horse Enterprises, 1988), 17–18; *More History of Beaverhead County*, 1023; "Glendale Gatherings," *Dillon (MT) Tribune*, September 26, 1885. Wolle states in *Montana Pay Dirt* (192) that Glendale's population in 1881 was seven hundred.

13. Hecla Consolidated Mining Company Articles of Incorporation and "Hecla Consolidated Mining Company," www.glendalemontana.com/hecla-consolidated-mining-company; Leeson, *History of Montana*, 482; "Hecla Residence," section 8, p. 3.

14. "Hecla Residence," section 8, p. 3; Hecla Consolidated Mining Company Articles of Incorporation; Nardinger, *Spirit Horse*, 15.

15. "Hecla Consolidated Mining Company."

16. Michael P. Malone and Richard B. Roeder, eds., *Montana: A History of Two Centuries* (Missoula: University of Montana, 1976), 146, 158; "Bryant Mining District," Montana Department of Environmental Quality, accessed September 12, 2017, https://www.deq.mt.gov.

17. "Spokane," https://www.glendalemontana.com/spokane; Armstrong Family Papers, 3–4 (hereafter AFP), SHPO; "Kentucky Horse Stock," *Cincinnati Enquirer*, April 22, 1880; "Spokane's Fortunate Owner," *Ottawa (ON) Journal*, June 20, 1889; "William Hillhouse Raymond," *Progressive Men of the State of Montana* (Chicago: A. W. Bowen, n.d.), 811–12. Susan Nardinger, in *Spirit Horse* (20), states that Armstrong turned his business affairs over to his son-in-law, Charles W. Turner.

18. AFP, 3.

19. AFP, 1–2; Nardinger, *Spirit Horse*, 21.

20. AFP, 5–6.

21. AFP, 4–6; Chere Jiusto and Christine Brown, *Hand Raised: The Barns of Montana* (Helena: Montana Historical Society Press, 2011), 98–99; AFP, 7.

22. AFP, 3–6.

23. Frank Quinn, "Bronco Buster Joe Redfern Will Be Listening to Big Derby, Remembering 'His' Colt Spokane," *Montana Standard* (Butte), April 25, 1954; AFP, 7.

24. "Life in Racing Stables," *Helena (MT) Independent*, June 25, 1891; Mary Simon, *Racing through the Century: The Story of Thoroughbred Racing in America* (Irvine: CA, BowTie Press, 2002), 114.

25. Hilary N. Steinmetz, "Rancho del Paso, the World's Largest Thoroughbred Farm" (master's thesis, California State University, 2009), 11, https://scholars.csus.edu/esploro/outputs/graduate/Rancho-Del-Paso-the-worlds-largest/99257830994201671#file-0; "A Jockey Suspended," *San Francisco Examiner*, January 2, 1889.

26. "Equine Jottings and Gleamings," *Farmer's Magazine and Kentucky Livestock Monthly*, January 1882, 93–94; "Local News," *Helena (MT) Independent*, April 4, 1882; "Montana Matters," *Helena Independent*, October 18, 1882; Harry P. Mawson, "His Majesty the Thoroughbred," *Munsey's Magazine*, August 1900, 592.

27. "Talk about Spokane," *Louisville (KY) Courier-Journal*, May 20, 1889. Charles Armstrong states that his father anticipated "a profitable investment" from horse breeding and racing (AFP, 3). Charles never referred to the undertaking as a hobby. However, newspaper accounts trivialized the venture as a hobby, and other sources noting his pursuit of horse racing as a hobby include Wolle in *Montana Pay Dirt* (207) and Nardinger in *Spirit Horse* (20). Montana horse racing historian Ellen Baumler attributes her "hobby" reference to Homer Faust's article "Spokane, a Montana Horse, Won Famous Race," *Circle Banner*, May 19, 1932. See Baumler's "Montana State Fairgrounds Racetrack," section 8, p. 4, SHPO. The Faust statement is chronologically the earliest "hobby" reference the author found.
28. "A Montanaian Abroad," *Rocky Mountain Husbandman* (Diamond City, MT), February 15, 1883; "Catina," *ASB*, vol. 4, 136; "Racing Colors," *Goodwin's Official Annual Turf Guide for 1888* (New York: Goodwin Bros.,1888), cxiv (hereafter *Goodwin's*, followed by the year); "Lord Raglan," *Louisville (KY) Courier-Journal*, June 5, 1883; "Once Again's Victory," *Inter Ocean* (Chicago), May 4, 1889; *Goodwin's 1883*, 31.
29. "The Horse," *Breeder's Gazette*, May 19, 1887, 795; "The Derby," *Louisville (KY) Courier-Journal*, May 24, 1883; "The History of Churchill Downs," year 1883, accessed January 3, 2018, http://www.churchilldowns.com/visit/about/churchill-downs/history (site discontinued); "The Kentucky Derby," *St. Paul (MN) Globe*, May 24, 1883; *Goodwin's 1883*, 44–45; William H. P. Robertson, *History of Thoroughbred Racing in America* (New York: Bonanza Books, 1964), 109.
30. "History of Churchill Downs"; "The Horse," *Breeder's Gazette*, May 19, 1887, 795; Brian Bouyea, "Aristides: The Original Kentucky Derby Hero," National Museum of Racing and Hall of Fame, accessed July 15, 2019, https://www.racingmuseum.org/blogs/aristides-original-kentucky-derby-hero#:~:text=Aristides%20earned%20a%20purse%20of,Belmont%20Stakes%20to%20stablemate%20Calvin.
31. *Goodwin's 1883*, 44–45.
32. "Died," *Dillon (MT) Tribune*, July 14, 1883; "Charles Armstrong," https://www.glendalemontana.com/names-database; "Harry C. Armstrong," Find a Grave, accessed June 29, 2017, https://www.findagrave.com/memorial/33725660/harry-c-armstrong. Susan Nardinger surmises in *Spirit Horse* that Armstrong's entry into horse breeding and racing was to relieve his grief over the deaths of family members. "Here, at the Glendale cemetery, we discovered the reason for Noah's immersion into his hobby, horse racing" (xv). Presumably, she is referring to the deaths of the three grandchildren and the later death of his wife, Hannah, in 1885. The author's research confirmed Armstrong's purchase of Thoroughbreds as early as 1880, and he raced Lord Raglan in 1882. Thus, Lord Raglan's entry into the sport preceded the 1883 deaths of the grandchildren and the 1885 death of Hannah.

33. "Third Race," *Spirit of the Times*, August 18, 1883, 75; "Brief Items," *Helena (MT) Independent*, October 17, 1883; "Brief Items," *Helena Independent*, December 30, 1883; "Montana Condensed," *Dillion (MT) Tribune*, January 5, 1884.

34. "A Fine Stud of Racers," *Helena (MT) Weekly Herald*, September 4, 1884.

35. "Interpose," *ASB*, vol. 4, 240; "Spokane's Sire," *Times-Democrat* (New Orleans), July 19, 1889. Charles Armstrong states incorrectly that Grey Cloud was foaled at Doncaster Ranch. See AFP, 4.

36. *Goodwin's 1884*, 675–76.

37. "Montana," *Montana Standard* (Butte), April 2, 1885; *Goodwin's 1885*, 65, 125, 236–37, 239, 241, 243, 285–86, 287, 289–92, 295–96, 297, 299; *Goodwin's 1886*, 191–92, 200, 213, 411, 429; AFP, 4; "The Grand Circuit," *Burlington (VT) Free Press*, July 18, 1887; John H. Davis, *The American Turf: History of the Thoroughbred, Together with Personal Reminiscences by the Author, Who, in Turn, Has Been Jockey, Trainer and Owner* (New York: John Polhemus, 1907), 117, accessed July 15, 2019, https://babel.hathitrust.org.

38. "Spokane's Birthplace," *St. Paul (MN) Globe*, September 2, 1889; "Proud of the Victorious Horse," *Chicago Tribune*, June 23, 1889. A handful of articles, such as "Spokane Victorious," *Yellowstone Journal* (Miles City, MT), June 25, 1889, state incorrectly that Armstrong purchased Interpose at an auction following the death of General Richard Rowett. Rowett died on July 13, 1887. Interpose foaled her colt Spokane in 1886.

Chapter 3

1. "Interpose," *ASB*, vol. 6, 540.

2. "Talk about Spokane," *Louisville (KY) Courier-Journal*, May 20, 1889; "A Spirit Horse," *Louisville Courier-Journal*, May 19, 1889.

3. "A Great Stock Farm," *Helena (MT) Independent*, January 31, 1890; Frank Quinn, "Bronco Buster Joe Redfern Will Be Listening to Big Derby, Remembering 'His' Colt Spokane," *Montana Standard* (Butte), April 25, 1954; "Horses and Horsemen," *Helena Independent*, April 2, 1890; "Their Final Race," *Star Tribune* (Minneapolis), March 2, 1890.

4. "Billy and Jean Dingley," *History of Beaverhead County, 1800–1920*, vol. 1 (Dillon, MT: Beaverhead County History Book Association, 1990). 171; "Willie P. Dingley," 1880 Census, Butte City, Deer Lodge County, Montana, HeritageQuest Online, accessed June 14, 2018, https://www.heritagequestonline.com/hqoweb /library/do/login; *Goodwin's 1885*, 65, 287, 295, 297, 299; *Goodwin's 1886*, 191, 200, 213; "William Post Dingley," *Dingley-Huff Newsletter No. 10*, Dingley-Huff vertical files, Beaverhead County Museum, Dillon, MT.

5. Helen Clark, "Montana's Winner of the Kentucky Derby," *Western Horseman*, November 1959.

6. "Going to Conquer," *Great Falls (MT) Tribune*, March 14, 1888. In *Spirit Horse* (35), Nardinger states that Spokane was shipped to Memphis for formal training in spring 1887. The author's research determined that formal training began

at Doncaster and moved to St. Louis in 1888. See "Sporting Notes," *St. Louis Globe-Democrat*, March 7, 1888, and "Horses at the Fair Grounds," *St. Louis Globe-Democrat*, April 15, 1888.

7. "Lucky Baldwin's Luck," *Chicago Tribune*, July 6, 1888; *Goodwin's 1888*, 232.

8. "Proud of the Victorious Horse," *Chicago Tribune*, June 23, 1889; "Horses and Horsemen," *Daily Independent* (Helena, MT), November 10, 1890.

9. *Goodwin's 1888*, 434, 497; "Cold, but Exciting," *Cincinnati Enquirer*, October 3, 1888.

10. *Goodwin's 1888*, 504–5.

11. *Goodwin's 1888*, 511; "Turf Notes," *St. Louis Globe-Democrat*, November 12, 1888.

12. "The Sporting World," *Memphis Avalanche*, November 11, 1888; *Goodwin's 1889*, 90. The article "The Montana Horse," *Great Falls (MT) Leader*, July 3, 1889, states that Hundley trained Spokane in 1889. All other sources the author consulted state that Rodegap was the trainer. The article "Sulky and Saddle," *Daily Alta* (San Francisco), May 22, 1889, reported Spokane's height at fifteen hands, three inches.

13. *Goodwin's 1889*, 90. According to *Goodwin's 1889*, Strideaway was raced by the Islip Stable. Presumably that Strideaway was not the Strideaway Conrad Kohrs purchased in 1877, in addition to Regent.

14. "The First Futurity," *Cincinnati Enquirer*, September 2, 1909; "A Vivid Description," *Memphis Daily Appeal*, May 15, 1889; "Knott Pulled Double," *Louisville (KY) Courier-Journal*, May 3, 1889.

15. "Sam Bryant Lucky at Last," *Chicago Tribune*, September 5, 1888; Margaret Lindsley Warden, *The Belle Meade Plantation*, ed. and rev. Robert D. Cross (Nashville: Belle Meade Plantation, 2018), 13, 30; "Belle Meade," *Nashville Banner*, April 30, 1887; "Proctor Knott," *Cincinnati Enquirer*, September 5, 1888. The price Sam Bryant paid for Proctor Knott varies among sources. For $175, see "Winner of First Futurity," *Daily Racing Form*, September 10, 1920; for $340, see "Sam Bryant Lucky at Last"; for $425, see "Proctor Knott Dead," *Daily American* (Nashville), August 7, 1891. The figure of $450 is the most repeated. See "Happy Tennesseans," *Louisville (KY) Courier-Journal*, September 4, 1888; "Proctor Knott," *New York Times*, December 21, 1888; and "Proctor Knott," *Cincinnati Enquirer*, September 5, 1889.

16. "Tallapoosa," *ASB*, vol. 6 (1889), 685; Hamilton Busbey, *Recollections of Men and Horses* (New York: Dodd Mead, 1907), 255, accessed January 17, 2018, https://books.google.com; "Knott for the Suburban," *New York Sun*, March 16, 1890.

17. "Proctor Knott First," *Louisville (KY) Courier-Journal*, September 4, 1888; *Goodwin's 1888*, 390–91.

18. *Goodwin's 1888*, 390–91; "Veitch Column: Futurity Stakes Has Storied Past," *Troy (NY) Record*, October 17, 2017, https://www.troyrecord.com/2017/10/17/veitch-column-futurity-stakes-has-storied-past/; *Goodwin's 1888*, 328; "Sam Bryant Lucky at Last"; William H. P. Robertson, *History of Thoroughbred Racing in America* (New York: Bonanza Books, 1964), 138.

19. "Sam Bryant Lucky at Last"; "How Proctor Knott Lives," *New York Times*, December 25, 1888.

20. *Goodwin's 1889*, 132. Interestingly, the author found only one source addressing Proctor Knott's weight advantage: "Proctor Knott Defeated," *New York Times*, May 10, 1889.

21. Walter S. Vosburgh, *Racing in America, 1866–1921* (New York: Scribner Press, 1922), 143.

22. "Derby Day," *St. Louis Globe-Democrat*, May 27, 1888; Edward Hotaling, *The Great Black Jockeys: The Lives and Times of the Men Who Dominated America's First National Sport* (Rocklin, CA: FORUM, 1999), 221; Larry K. Menna and Thomas L. Altherr, eds., *Sports in North America: Sports in the Progressive Era, 1900–1920* (Gulf Breeze, FL: Academic International Press, 1998), 417.

23. John E. Kleber, *The Encyclopedia of Louisville* (Lexington: University Press of Kentucky, 2015), 329, accessed November 2, 2019, https://books.google.com /books?id=pXbYITw4ZesC&q=pari-mutuel#v=snippet&q=pari-mutuel&f =false; James C. Nicholson, *Racing for America: The Horse Race of the Century and the Redemption of a Sport* (Lexington: University Press of Kentucky, 2021), accessed March 8, 2024, https://www.google.com/books/edition/Racing_for _America/-E_mDwAAQBAJ?kptab=editions&gbpv=1; Hotaling, *Great Black Jockeys*, 221. Sources vary as to whether Oller's first name was Joseph or Pierre.

24. "Royal Derby," *Louisville (KY) Courier-Journal*, May 10, 1889; "West Point's Graded School," *Mississippian* (Jackson, MS), May 22, 1889; "Knott Again Defeated," *Inter Ocean* (Chicago), May 15, 1889.

25. "The Two Thousand," *Daily American* (Nashville), May 2, 1889; Dave Kindred, "Until the Derby, 'You Ain't Never Been Nowheres,'" *Washington Post*, May 8, 1983, accessed January 15, 2018, https://www.washingtonpost.com/archive/sports /1983/05/08/until-the-derby-you-aint-never-been-nowheres/c7587775-f385-4cc2 -b748-abede8e3f87b/.

26. John L. O'Connor, *History of the Kentucky Derby, 1875–1921* (New York: Rider Press, 1921), 44–45; *Goodwin's 1889*, 132; "Royal Derby"; "First Futurity."

27. "Royal Derby."

28. "Royal Derby."

29. Samuel L. Boardman, *Handbook of the Turf: A Treasury of Information for Horsemen* (New York: Orange Judd, 1894), 247; "How to Start Horses," *Helena (MT) Independent*, July 13, 1890.

30. Ron Hale, "History Challenge: Racing's Most Bizarre Episodes," *Daily Racing Form*, August 29, 2013, accessed September 19, 2018, https://www.drf.com/news /history-challenge-racings-most-bizarre-episodes; "Tips on the Derby," *Chicago Tribune*, June 25, 1898.

31. For additional reading about the history of horse race starting, see William E. Burke, "The Evolution of the Stall Gate," *National Turf Digest*, April 1930; G. F. T. Ryall, "How about Starting Gates?," *Polo*, November 1935, 14; Steve Haskin,

"'They're in the Gate,'" *Thoroughbred Record*, September 1989, 981; Jim Harmon, "The Man Who Gave Racing a Fresh Start," *Sports Illustrated*, October 29, 1990, accessed April 28, 2019, https://vault.si.com/vault/1990/10/29/the-man-who-gave-racing-a-fresh-start-in-1939-clay-puetts-electric-starting-gate-revolutionized-the-sport.
32. "Royal Derby"; "Record Derby," *Louisville (KY) Commercial*, May 10, 1889.
33. "Royal Derby"; "Record Derby"; O'Connor, *History of the Kentucky Derby*, 46.
34. *Goodwin's 1889*, 132; "Armstrong's Ultimatum," *St. Paul (MN) Globe*, May 12, 1889.
35. "King of the Turf," *Helena (MT) Independent*, May 15, 1889; "Spokane's Great Victory," *Daily Inter Mountain* (Butte, MT), May 13, 1889; "Spokane's Triumph," *Weekly Herald* (Helena, MT), May 16, 1889; "Armstrong at 'Em!," *Madisonian* (Ennis, MT), May 18, 1889; "Montana Pride," *Helena (MT) Independent*, May 15, 1889; Homer Faust, "Spokane, a Montana Horse, Won Famous Race," *Circle Banner*, May 19, 1932; Quinn, "Bronco Buster Joe Redfern."
36. "Proctor Knott Defeated."
37. "Royal Derby"; "The Race of the Day," *San Francisco Examiner*, May 10, 1889. According to "Royal Derby," Spokane's victory was "popular" despite Proctor Knott's "fame."
38. "Louisville," *Spirit of the Times*, May 18, 1889.
39. "Jockey Mounts in 1889," *Goodwin's 1889*, cxxxvii.
40. "The Turf," *Louisville (KY) Courier-Journal*, April 20, 1890.

Chapter 4

1. "Talk about Spokane," *Louisville (KY) Courier-Journal*, May 20, 1889; Susan Nardinger, *Spirit Horse of the Rockies* (Great Falls, MT: Spirit Horse Enterprises, 1988), 65–66.
2. *Goodwin's 1889*, 135; "Sackcloth and Ashes," *Daily American* (Nashville), May 15, 1889; "Blue Wing's Gossip," *Daily American*, May 20, 1889; "They Can't Beat Him," *Louisville (KY) Courier-Journal*, May 15, 1889.
3. "They Can't Beat Him"; "Sackcloth and Ashes"; *Goodwin's 1889*, 135.
4. "Sackcloth and Ashes."
5. "Sam Bryant's String," *Louisville (KY) Courier-Journal*, May 19, 1889; "Blue Wing's Gossip"; *Goodwin's 1889*, 173; "The Spring Races," *St. Louis Post-Dispatch*, May 30, 1889.
6. "The Owner of Spokane," *Helena (MT) Independent*, June 2, 1889.
7. "Champions of the Turf," *Chicago Tribune*, June 11, 1889.
8. "Banneret Takes a Mile," *Chicago Tribune*, June 20, 1889; "About Spokane's Race," *Helena (MT) Independent*, June 29, 1889.
9. "The Western Turf," *Louisville (KY) Courier-Journal*, June 24, 1889; "Proctor Knott's Departure," *Louisville (KY) Courier-Journal*, June 19, 1889; *Goodwin's 1889*, 240–41.

10. Nardinger, *Spirit Horse*, 73; "Spokane's New Clothes," *Louisville (KY) Courier-Journal*, June 21, 1889.

11. "Strathmeath Won the Great American Derby," *Chicago Tribune*, June 21, 1891.

12. *Goodwin's 1889*, 241.

13. "Proctor Not First," *Louisville (KY) Courier-Journal*, June 23, 1889; "Spokane the Victor," *Chicago Tribune*, June 23, 1889.

14. "Spokane the Victor"; "Western Turf"; "Proctor Not First."

15. "Proctor Not First"; "Proud of the Victorious Horse," *Chicago Tribune*, June 23, 1889.

16. "Western Turf."

17. "Great Spokane," *Memphis Daily Appeal*, June 23, 1889; "Spokane," *Louisville (KY) Courier-Journal*, June 23, 1889, 12.

18. "Spokane's Owner Interviewed," *Rocky Mountain Husbandman* (Diamond City, MT), January 16, 1890, found in the Noah Armstrong Vertical Files, Montana Historical Society, hereafter MHS; "Another Derby Account," *Louisville (KY) Courier-Journal*, June 25, 1889; Helen Clark, "Montana's Winner of the Kentucky Derby," *Western Horseman*, November 1959.

19. "Kentucky Derby Winner," *Montana Magazine*, May–June 1998, 48.

20. "Won by Proctor Knott," *Chicago Tribune*, July 5, 1889; "Bryant Has Recovered," *Louisville (KY) Courier-Journal*, June 25, 1889.

21. "Won by Proctor Knott"; *Goodwin's 1889*, 273.

22. *Goodwin's 1889*, 301.

23. "Our Great State," *Great Falls (MT) Tribune*, July 15, 1889.

24. "Turf Topics," *Helena (MT) Independent*, July 30, 1889; *Goodwin's 1889*, 438.

25. "Fast Horses Sold," *Wichita (KS) Daily Eagle*, September 3, 1889; "Knott for the Suburban," *New York Sun*, March 16, 1890. The Scoggan name alternately appears as Scoggin or Scroggan, but Scoggan is the spelling in *Goodwin's Turf Guide*. In addition to George Scoggan, the names of Hiram Scoggan and O. M. Scoggan are occasionally mentioned in connection with Proctor Knott. See "Proctor Knott Sick," *Fort Worth (TX) Daily Gazette*, July 29, 1891, and "Fast Horses Sold."

26. *Goodwin's 1889*, 456; "Exile Finishes First," *Chicago Tribune*, September 4, 1889.

27. "Talk of the Turf," *San Francisco Chronicle*, December 22, 1889; "Montana Horse News," *Helena (MT) Independent*, May 4, 1890.

28. George Brown Tindall and David E. Shi, *America: A Narrative History*, vol. 2 (New York: W. W. Norton, 1993), 500–501.

29. "The Great Northwest," *Anaconda (MT) Standard*, July 17, 1890; "Has Changed Trainers," *Helena (MT) Independent*, October 24, 1889. The article "Another Spokane," *Helena (MT) Independent*, May 16, 1891, 5, implies that Armstrong and Hundley renewed their association.

30. "Spokane's Owner Interviewed"; "Among the Horses," *River Press* (Fort Benton, MT), April 16, 1890.

31. "The Turf," *Louisville (KY) Courier-Journal*, April 20, 1890; "Sport of All Authority," *Brooklyn (NY) Daily Eagle*, May 25, 1890; *Goodwin's 1890*, 207.

32. "Hotel Handicap," *Cincinnati Enquirer*, June 8, 1890; "A Queer Proceeding,"
Daily American (Nashville), June 8, 1890; "Pulsifer Not Satisfied," *Inter Ocean*
(Chicago), June 19, 1890; "Potomac Raked in the Pot," *Inter Ocean* (Chicago),
August 31, 1890.

33. For detailed information about the fire and blistering procedure, see "The
Veterinarian," *Kansas Farmer* (Topeka), September 1, 1886, and "Treatment
for Bone Spavin," *Pacific Rural Press* 54, no. 6 (August 7, 1897), accessed September 27, 2020, https://cdnc.ucr.edu/?a=d&d=PRP18970807.2.5&srpos=2&e=
-------en--20--1--txt-txIN-%22treatment+for+bone+spavin%22-------; "Stories
and Comment," *Daily American* (Nashville), September 2, 1890; "Turf Notes,"
Philadelphia Inquirer, September 22, 1890.

34. "Proctor Knott in Good Form Again," *Indianapolis Journal*, May 16, 1891; *Goodwin's 1891*, 191, 223–24, 249; "Dr. Nave Beats Proctor Knott," *Chicago Tribune*,
June 3, 1891.

35. *Goodwin's 1891*, 393, 397; "Proctor Knott Dies at Saratoga," *Chicago Tribune*,
August 7, 1891; "Proctor Knott Dead," *Daily American* (Nashville), August 7,
1891; "General Sporting News," *Daily American*, August 17, 1891.

36. "The Brighton Beach Races," *Turf, Field and Farm*, July 4, 1902; "A Noted Turfman Is Passing Away," *Louisville (KY) Courier-Journal*, June 1, 1902; "Will Run
in the Derby," *Chicago Tribune*, June 20, 1889.

37. *Goodwin's 1890*, 291, 295, 302; "Spokane and Nevada," *Helena (MT) Independent*,
June 27, 1890.

38. "Proud of the Victorious Horse"; "The Turf"; "Lost to the Turf," *Seattle Press
Times*, October 15, 1891; "Spokane in the Stud," *Seattle Post-Intelligencer*, December 1, 1891.

39. "Noah Armstrong Home," *Helena (MT) Independent*, November 13, 1890;
"Spokane," American Classic Pedigrees, accessed April 17, 2020, http://www
.americanclassicpedigrees.com/spokane.html; "Batten, Rush, and Spirituelle,"
Chicago Tribune, October 1, 1899.

40. "The Armstrong Sale," *Butte (MT) Weekly Miner*, April 23, 1891; "Hamilton," *Helena (MT) Independent*, April 25, 1891; "About the City," *Anaconda
(MT) Standard*, April 23, 1891; "A Fine Property," *Dillon (MT) Tribune*, April 6,
1900; "Octogenarian Dies at Home of His Son," *Seattle Post-Intelligencer*,
April 22, 1907; "Charles Armstrong," Department of Health, Death Index,
1907–1960, Washington State Archives, accessed December 16, 2019, https://
www.digitalarchives.wa.gov; "City Brevities," *Semi-Weekly Miner* (Butte, MT),
June 6, 1885.

41. Homer Faust, "Spokane, a Montana Horse, Won Famous Race," *Circle Banner*,
May 19, 1932; Nardinger, *Spirit Horse*, 143–44; Grace Roffey Pratt, "Montana's
Kentucky Derby Winner," *Western Horseman*, January 1976; Ralph Bidwell,

"Spokane, Montana's Lone Derby Winner," *Great Falls (MT) Tribune*, May 7, 1977; Nardinger, *Spirit Horse*, 144.

42. "Land and Stock," *Semi-Weekly Interior Journal* (Stanford, KY), December 2, 1898; "Spokane Sells for $100," *New York World*, November 30, 1899; "Thoroughbreds," *Official Catalogue: Annual Horse Show*, vol. 16 (November 1900), 103–4, accessed August 14, 2019, https://www.google.com/books/edition/Official _Catalogue/zk4CAAAAYAAJ?hl=en&gbpv=1&dq=Sixteenth+annual+horse +show+official+catalouge+Spokane&pg=PA104&printsec=frontcover; "The Awards," *New York Tribune*, November 21, 1900; "The Thoroughbred," *Turf, Field and Farm*, November 22, 1901, 1129.

43. "News Offerings of Mount Holly," *Camden (NJ) Daily Courier*, December 3, 1904.

Chapter 5

1. Noel V. Bourasaw, "Charles Xavier Larrabee, Montana Copper King and Investor behind Fairhaven and Sedro," part 1, *Skagit River Journal*, accessed July 14, 2013, http://www.skagitriverjournal.com/wa/whatcom/fairhavensth/pioneers /pre1900/larrabee/larrabee01-bio1.html. Michael Leeson states in *History of Montana* (1078) that Larabie left Omro in 1864.

2. Bourasaw, "Charles Xavier Larrabee"; "Territorial News," *Helena (MT) Weekly Herald*, August 21, 1873; Leeson, *History of Montana*, 1078.

3. Leeson, *History of Montana*, 1078; "Death of a Montana Pioneer," *Great Falls (MT) Tribune*, January 6, 1892.

4. Leeson, *History of Montana*, 1078; Michael P. Malone, *Battle for Butte: Mining and Politics on the Northern Frontier, 1864–1906* (Seattle: University of Washington Press, 1981), 14; "Old Friends of Sen. Clark Welcome Him Back to Butte," *Butte (MT) Miner*, November 16, 1913; *Larabie Brothers Bank, 401 Main*, pamphlet, S. E. Larabie Vertical Files, MHS; "Larabie Brothers Bankers, Inc.," *Silver State* (Deer Lodge, MT), September 18, 1919.

5. "Kleinschmidt & Denuee," *New North-West* (Deer Lodge, MT), August 12, 1870; "Death of a Montana Pioneer"; "Donnell & Co.'s Bank," *New North-West*, December 23, 1870; Leeson, *History of Montana*, 1078.

6. "Married," *Helena (MT) Weekly Herald*, March 4, 1875; "Fine Stock," *New North-West* (Deer Lodge, MT), July 9, 1875; "Items," *Helena Weekly Herald*, May 27, 1875; "Personal," *New North-West*, January 5, 1877.

7. "Butte Items," *Helena (MT) Independent*, March 3, 1877; "Notice of Dissolution of Partnership," *Butte (MT) Daily Miner*, May 27, 1884; "An Old Firm Dissolved," *Helena Independent*, January 6, 1890; "C. X. Larrabee Called by Maker," *Daily Missoulian* (Missoula, MT), September 17, 1914. The sequence of events involving the partners' banking activities varies slightly among the sources cited.

8. "Pioneer Banker Stricken; Death Comes Suddenly," *Silver State* (Deer Lodge, MT), April 23, 1914.

9. 1880 US Census for Deer Lodge County, MT, roll 742, p. 179A, Enumeration District 012, https://www.heritagequestonline.com/hqoweb/library/do/login; Leeson, *History of Montana*, 562.

10. Leeson, *History of Montana*, 551; "Deer Lodge and the Deer Lodge Valley," This Is Montana, University of Montana, accessed February 18, 2022, https://www.umt.edu/this-is-montana/columns/stories/deerlodge.php.

11. "Montana Blooded Stock," *Rocky Mountain Husbandman* (Diamond City, MT), April 25, 1878; "Christine," *ASB*, vol. 4, 139; "High Bred Horses," *Daily Inter Mountain (Butte, MT)*, March 15, 1890.

12. "Gypsy," *ASB*, vol. 6, 502; "A Trainer's Notes about Racing," *New York Tribune*, October 30, 1891; "Horse Notes," *New North-West* (Deer Lodge, MT), July 2, 1886.

13. "Territorial Fair," *Bozeman (MT) Avant Courier*, October 3, 1878. The First Territorial Fair was held in 1868 at Madam Cody's track in Helena. The *Helena Daily Independent* referred to the fair of September 23, 1878, as the Ninth Territorial Fair, held at the Lewis and Clark County fairgrounds. Construction in 1870 of the Lewis and Clark County fairgrounds, where the fair was moved to, accounts for the use of "Ninth." Also see Baumler, "Montana State Fairgrounds Racetrack," section 8, p. 5, SHPO.

14. "Territorial Fair," *Helena (MT) Weekly Herald*, September 26, 1878.

15. "Montana," *West Shore* 9 (February 1, 1883): 40; George S. Klotz, "Deer Lodge Once Had One of Greatest Racing Stables in America That Swept the Country with Notable Gallopers," *Three Forks (MT) News*, August 8, 1922; "Fine Stock," *Helena (MT) Independent*, August 5, 1883.

16. "Prominent Turfman Dies at Lexington," *Daily Racing Form* (Chicago), February 22, 1914, https://drf.uky.edu/catalog/1910s/drf1914022201/drf1914022201_1_5#q=%22Eastin%22#fq=55_s%3A%221910s%22fq%5B%5D=63_s%3A%221914%22fq%5B%5D=64_s%3A%2202%22fq%5B%5D=65_s%3A%2222%22. The article quotes Eastin as saying that Larabie mentioned Bonnie Australian and Vice Regent, both foaled by Christine and sired by Regent, and both good racehorses, as examples of why Christine might do even better as a broodmare if bred to Thoroughbred stallions in Kentucky. Eastin's statements cannot be accurate, as neither horse would have been racing in 1882, the probable year that he met Larabie. Vice Regent was not foaled until 1882, and Bonnie Australian did not race until 1883. "Eastin & Larabie Quit the Turf; Great Horses Which They Raced," *Nashville American*, April 7, 1901.

17. "Christine," *ASB*, vol. 5, 203; "Eastin & Larabie Quit."

18. "Eastin & Larabie Quit"; "Daly's Great String," *Chicago Tribune*, March 16, 1893; "Horse Transactions," *New North-West* (Deer Lodge, MT), November 5, 1886; The Arms Palace Horse and Stock Car Company catalogue (Chicago, 1889), accessed July 31, 2022, https://archive.org/details/cataloguearmspalooarms/page/n1/mode/2up.

19. "Sporting Notes," *Memphis Avalanche*, February 13, 1887; "Montana Regent," *Weekly Yellowstone Journal* (Miles City, MT), August 21, 1886; *Goodwin's 1886*, 68–69, 98, 100, 127–28, 131–32; "A Rattling Record of Sports," *Helena (MT) Independent*, July 31, 1886. The article "Still Another," *New North-West* (Deer Lodge, MT), October 22, 1886, states that Lee Paul was training Montana Regent. Further, "Sale a Marker in Turf History," *Democrat and Chronicle* (Rochester, NY), March 13, 1901, states that Peter Wimmer developed and handled Eastin and Larabie Thoroughbreds as early as Montana Regent. The author found no sources supporting such a claim. Her earliest source for Wimmer joining the Eastin and Larabie Stable is "Notes of the Turf," *Daily Racing Form* (Chicago), January 19, 1897.

20. *Goodwin's 1886*, 212–13, 245–46, 344–45; "Montana Regent."

21. "Personal," *New North-West* (Deer Lodge, MT), October 29, 1886; *Goodwin's 1887*, cxxi; "Latonia's Second Day," *Cincinnati Enquirer*, October 3, 1886; *Goodwin's 1886*, 418.

22. "Friday, October 8, 1886," *Daily Inter Mountain* (Butte, MT), October 8, 1886; *Goodwin's 1886*, 422; Joseph Durso, "On Horse Racing: Run Rabbit Run, but May the Great Horse Win," *New York Times*, July 14, 1992, accessed March 3, 2022, https://www.nytimes.com/1992/07/14/sports/on-horse-racing-run-rabbit -run-but-may-the-great-horse-win.html.

23. "Friday, October 8, 1886."

24. "Friday, October 8, 1886"; "The Races at Latonia," *Memphis Daily Appeal*, October 8, 1886; *Goodwin's 1886*, 422; Klotz, "Deer Lodge Once Had One of Greatest Racing Stables."

25. *Goodwin's 1886*, 409–10, 426; "Noteworthy Turf Notes," *New York Sun*, February 6, 1887; "Miscellaneous," *National Tribune* (Washington, DC), February 10, 1887.

26. "Montana Regent," *New North-West* (Deer Lodge, MT), October 29, 1886; "John D. Morrisey," *Indiana State Sentinel* (Indianapolis), April 13, 1887. The article "Horse Notes," *New North-West*, December 23, 1887, states that Montana Regent sold for $8,500. The author found only two references as to whether the partners raced for pleasure only or for profit. Klotz states in "Deer Lodge Once Had One of Greatest Racing Stables" that Larabie "simply bred and raced for the sport in it." On the other hand, upon retiring the Eastin and Larabie racehorse Ben Holladay in 1899, trainer Peter Wimmer remarked that to race the horse another season "would not be profitable." See "Starting Must Be Improved," *Nashville Banner*, November 24, 1899. *Goodwin's 1887*, 47, 61, 78–79, 82; "Turf Notes," *St. Louis Globe-Democrat*, March 25, 1888; "Story of a Rough-Hewn Millionaire," *Fisherman and Farmer* (Edenton, NC), January 11, 1889; "Items and Inquiries," *National Live-Stock Journal*, September 25, 1888, 614, https://www.google.com/books/edition/National _Live_Stock_Journal/b9I1AQAAMAAJ?hl=en&gbpv=1; "Track Talk," *Daily American* (Nashville), December 19, 1888; *Goodwin's 1888*, 633; *Goodwin's 1889*, 51, 52, 635. *Goodwin's Turf Guides* for 1888 and 1889 state that Montana Regent raced for A. P. Mulcahy. The author could not find additional information about

the arrangement. "Westchester Meeting," *San Francisco Examiner*, May 31, 1890. The *Daily Democrat* of Huntington, Indiana, states that Montana Regent was pronounced "perfectly sound" for racing in 1891, but his name is not listed in *Goodwin's* for 1891.

27. "Julia L.," *ASB*, vol. 6, 566; "Notes from the Northwest," *Breeder's Gazette: A Weekly Publication Devoted to the Interests of Livestock Breeders* 19 (January 14, 1891): 31; "Julia L.," *New North-West* (Deer Lodge, MT), July 27, 1888.

28. According to "Poor Racing," *Cincinnati Enquirer*, May 13, 1888, John McFadden was training Julia L. The author could not find additional information about McFadden as her trainer. *Goodwin's 1888*, 91, 139, 208–9; "Julia L. Wins at Chicago," *New North-West* (Deer Lodge, MT), July 6, 1888.

29. "MacBeth's Great Finish," *Chicago Tribune*, July 1, 1888; *Goodwin's 1888*, 208–9, 244, 432, 495; "A Fast Three-Quarters," *Chicago Tribune*, July 15, 1888.

30. "A Montana Winner," *Helena (MT) Independent*, July 4, 1888; "Montana Flyers," *Bozeman (MT) Weekly Chronicle*, July 18, 1888. For more examples of "Montana horse," see "Personal," *New North-West* (Deer Lodge, MT), October 29, 1886; "Spokane's Triumph," *Weekly Herald* (Helena, MT), May 16, 1889; "Montana Horse Wins," *Ravalli Republican* (Stevensville, MT), September 22, 1897; "Owned in Deer Lodge," *Butte (MT) Miner*, October 24, 1897; "Mayor Harrison a 'Regular,'" *Butte Miner*, October 24, 1897; "Pertinent Paragraphs," *Billings (MT) Weekly Gazette*, November 5, 1897; "Ben Is a Great Horse," *Anaconda (MT) Standard*, June 27, 1899. An excellent example of the sense of regional ownership is presented in "Suburban Handicap," *St. Louis Republic*, June 16, 1900.

31. "Julia L. Disabled," *Kentucky Leader* (Lexington), April 8, 1889; "Crowned," *Louisville (KY) Courier-Journal*, May 7, 1895. The *American Stud Book* lists Julia L. as Halma's dam. Eastin stated incorrectly that Julia T. was Halma's dam.

32. "Hamilton's Bad Tumble," *New York Times*, June 27, 1891; "Proud Perkins," *Louisville (KY) Courier-Journal*, May 7, 1895; "Racing in the West," *Spirit of the Times*, June 7, 1890, 861; "Horses and Horsemen," *Helena (MT) Weekly Independent*, May 29, 1890.

33. *Black Horsemen of the Kentucky Turf* (Lexington: Kentucky Horse Park, 2018), 7, 11; Charles E. Trevathan, "No More Negro Riders," *Chicago Tribune*, April 1, 1900.

34. "Boys," *Cincinnati Enquirer*, July 1, 1899; "'Monk' Wins Six Races," *Chicago Tribune*, July 11, 1891.

35. Larry K. Menna and Thomas L. Altherr, eds., *Sports in North America: Sports in the Progressive Era, 1900–1920* (Gulf Breeze, FL: Academic International Press, 1998), 414; "Sporting," *Pittsburg (PA) Press*, March 2, 1891; "Jockey Fred Taral," *Burlington (VT) Free Press*, March 10, 1891.

36. Pellom McDaniels, *The Prince of Jockeys: The Life of Isaac Burns Murphy* (Lexington: University Press of Kentucky, 2013), 227; Allen Sangree, "The Making of a Jockey," *Ainslee's Magazine*, June 1901, 400; "Riders of Race Horses," *Brooklyn (NY) Daily Eagle*, September 14, 1890.

37. "Hamilton's Bad Tumble."

38. "Daly's Big Offer," *Helena (MT) Independent*, July 10, 1891; "Boys."

39. "Julia L.," *ASB*, vol. 6, 566; "Pretty Good," *New North-West* (Deer Lodge, MT), November 25, 1893.

40. *Goodwin's 1894*, vol. 2, 78, 202–3, 205, 246, 348, 351, 357, 358–59, 482; *Goodwin's 1895*, vol. 1, 221, 224; John H. Davis, *The American Turf: History of the Thoroughbred, Together with Personal Reminiscences by the Author, Who, in Turn, Has Been Jockey, Trainer and Owner* (New York: John Polhemus, 1907), 92, accessed July 15, 2019, https://babel.hathitrust.org; Lyman Horace Weeks, *The American Turf: An Historical Account of Racing in the United States* (New York: Historical Company, 1898), 386; "Soup Perkins Was the Last," *Los Angeles Times*, September, 17, 1911. The article "Proud Perkins," *Louisville (KY) Courier-Journal*, May 7, 1895, states that Perkins's mother, father, sister, and cousins were present at Churchill Downs for the Kentucky Derby.

41. *Goodwin's 1895*, vol. 1, 270; "Crowned"; Davis, *American Turf*, 92; "Soup Perkins Was the Last."

42. *Goodwin's 1895*, vol. 1, 277, 338–39, 431; "Oakley Gossip," *Cincinnati Enquirer*, July 12, 1895; *Goodwin's 1897*, vol. 1, 414–15, 445; "Halma," Kentucky Derby Charts 1875–2007, accessed February 13, 2020, https://www.kentuckyderby.com.

43. "World of Sport," *Morning Herald* (Lexington, KY), July 31, 1897; "Valuable Horse," *Star-Gazette* (Elmira, NY), July 11, 1901; "Halma Arrives from France," *New York Times*, September 11, 1906.

44. "Halma, Horse of His Day, Dead," *Daily Racing Form* (Chicago), June 18, 1909, accessed May 5, 2020, https://drf.uky.edu/catalog/1900s/drf1909061801 /drf1909061801_1_3.

45. "In the World of Sport," *Anaconda (MT) Standard*, November 10, 1891.

46. "Horse Notes," *New North-West*, July 2, 1886. "Eastin & Larabie Quit the Turf" states that the selling price for Gypsy as a filly was $150.

47. "Longfellow," National Museum of Racing and Hall of Fame, hereafter, NMRHF, accessed November 24, 2023, https://www.racingmuseum.org/hall-of-fame /horse/longfellow-ky; Walter S. Vosburgh, *Racing in America, 1866–1921* (New York: Scribner Press, 1922), 86, 87; Davis, *American Turf*, 76.

48. "Horse Notes," *New North-West* (Deer Lodge, MT), December 23, 1887.

Chapter 6

1. "Christine," *ASB*, vol. 5, 203; "Gypsy," *ASB*, vol. 6, 502; Frank Freidel, *Our Country's Presidents* (Washington, DC: National Geographic Society, 1966), 35.

2. "How Poet Scout Was Named," *Buffalo (NY) Enquirer*, October 13, 1891; "Notes," *Helena (MT) Independent Record*, September 11, 1891. The *Enquirer* is the only source the author found stating that Larabie and Crawford were acquainted.

3. "He's a Race Horse," *Louisville (KY) Courier-Journal*, May 19, 1891.

4. *Goodwin's 1890*, 294–5, 355, 360, 451–52; "He's a Race Horse."

5. "He's a Race Horse."

6. *Goodwin's 1891*, 189, 192.

7. "He's a Race Horse"; *Goodwin's 1891*, 192. Monk Overton was contractually engaged in 1891 to ride for Hardy Durham and Ed Corrigan. Presumably, he was permitted to freelance when not engaged to ride Durham or Corrigan mounts.

8. "Taking Another Derby," *Chicago Tribune*, May 24, 1891.

9. "About the Turf," *Gazette* (Montreal, Canada), October 15, 1891; "Big Day at Morris Park," *New York Sun*, October 11, 1891; "Suburban Handicap," *Livestock Record*, June 24, 1892, 498.

10. "Taking Another Derby"; *Goodwin's 1891*, 218.

11. Mawson, "His Majesty the Thoroughbred," 594; "Ornament Beats Ogden," *New York World*, August 30, 1896; Samuel L. Boardman, *Handbook of the Turf: A Treasury of Information for Horsemen* (New York: Orange Judd, 1894), 53.

12. Katherine C. Mooney, *Race Horse Men: How Slavery and Freedom Were Made at the Racetrack* (Cambridge, MA: Harvard University Press, 2014), 40; Harry P. Mawson, "His Majesty the Thoroughbred," *Munsey's Magazine*, August 1900, 594.

13. "Death of High Tariff," *Kentucky Leader* (Lexington), June 22, 1891; "High Tariff," *Cincinnati Enquirer*, May 28, 1891; *Goodwin's 1891*, 221.

14. *Goodwin's 1891*, 332–33; "The Great American Derby," *Daily Press* (Topeka, KS), June 18, 1891.

15. "The Race of the Year," *Inter Ocean* (Chicago), June 21, 1891; "High Tariff No More," *Anaconda (MT) Standard*, June 21, 1891; "Pictures of the Day," *Chicago Tribune*, June 21, 1891; "At the Clubhouse," *Inter Ocean*, June 25, 1893.

16. *Goodwin's 1891*, 332–33; "Strathmeath Won the Great American Derby," *Chicago Tribune*, June 21, 1891.

17. *Goodwin's 1891*, 332–33; "High Tariff No More."

18. "High Tariff No More"; "The Race of the Year."

19. "Grief of a Race Horse," *Helena (MT) Independent*, August 26, 1891; "General Sporting Notes," *Chicago Tribune*, August 19, 1891.

20. *Goodwin's 1891*, 379; "At Washington Park," *St. Louis Globe-Democrat*, July 5, 1891; "Topics of the Turf," *San Francisco Chronicle*, July 5, 1891.

21. *Goodwin's 1891*, 386; "'Monk' Wins Six Races," *Chicago Tribune*, July 11, 1891; "Remarkable Riding Feats in This Country and England—Only Six Jockeys Ever Won Full Card in One Day," *Daily Racing Form* (Chicago), December 13, 1916, accessed October 6, 2020, https://drf.uky.edu/catalog/1910s/drf1916121301 /drf1916121301_3_1#q=%22Overton%22#fq=55_s%3A%221910s%22fq%5B%5D=63 _s%3A%221916%22fq%5B%5D=64_s%3A%2212%22fq%5B%5D=65_s%3A%2213%22; Henry Brown, "They're Off!," *Abbott's Monthly*, February 1932, 7.

22. William H. P. Robertson, *History of Thoroughbred Racing in America* (New York: Bonanza Books, 1964), 7, 15, 149; "The Thoroughbred," *Turf, Field and Farm*, September 20, 1901, 913.

23. Mooney, *Race Horse Men*, 229; "A Great Racing Year," *Rocky Mountain Husbandman*, April 25, 1890; Robertson, *History of Thoroughbred Racing*, 174–75; Vosburgh, *Racing in America*, 43.

24. *Goodwin's 1891*, 559–60; "A Splendid Struggle," *New York Sun*, August 19, 1891; "Wants to Run It Over," *Chicago Tribune*, June 22, 1891; "Two Wonderful Fillies," *New York Tribune*, October 11, 1891; "Montana News," *Fergus County Argus* (Lewistown, MT), September 17, 1891.

25. "Curt Gunn's Good Race," *Chicago Tribune*, September 18, 1891; *Goodwin's 1891*, 672; "Big Day at Morris Park."

26. Ryan Goldberg, "A History of Drugs in Racing," *Thoroughbred Daily News*, May 2, 2013, accessed July 17, 2022, www.thoroughbreddailynews.com; Mark Shrager, *The Great Sweepstakes of 1877: A True Story of Southern Grit, Gilded Age Tycoons, and a Race That Galvanized the Nation* (Guilford, CT: Lyons Press, 2016), 16.

27. "Sporting Gossip," *Anaconda (MT) Standard*, September 20, 1891; "Poet Scout's Fast Run," *Chicago Tribune*, October 11, 1891; *Goodwin's 1891*, 748.

28. *Goodwin's 1891*, 748; "Big Day at Morris Park"; "The New-York Club Races," *New York Times*, October 11, 1891.

29. "Mr. Belmont's Prize," *New York Sun*, August 31, 1890.

30. *Goodwin's 1891*, 748.

31. "Big Day at Morris Park"; *Goodwin's 1891*, 748.

32. "How Poet Scout Was Named"; "Notes," *Helena (MT) Independent*, September 11, 1891; "Two Wonderful Fillies"; "Poet Scout's Fast Run."

33. "The New-York Club Races"; "Poet Scout's Hickory," n.p., n.d., S. E. Larabie Vertical Files, MHS.

34. "Track Talk," *Butte (MT) Weekly Miner*, February 11, 1892; *Goodwin's 1892*, 285–86, 414–15. The Decoration Handicap was Monk Overton's last race on Poet Scout. After retiring from racing in 1901, he became a trainer. Overton died penniless on March 28, 1935. The article "At the Races," *Kentucky Leader* (Lexington), April 5, 1935, hailed Overton as "one of the ace Negro jockeys, out ranked only by Isaac Murphy."

35. "Poet Scout," *New York Evening World*, July 12, 1892; "A Splendid Struggle"; *Goodwin's 1892*, 509.

36. "A Victory for Poet Scout," *New York Times*, July 13, 1892; *Goodwin's 1892*, 509.

37. "A Victory for Poet Scout"; *Goodwin's 1892*, 509; "Palmy Days When Montana Horses Were Best on Any Track Recalled by Races," *Helena (MT) Independent*, July 12, 1937.

38. "Poet Scout Fouled," *Chicago Tribune*, August 7, 1892; "At Monmouth Park," *Indianapolis Journal*, August 7, 1892; *Goodwin's 1892*, 617.

39. *Willow Run Stock Farm Catalogue 1888*, Samuel Larabie Vertical Files, MHS; "The Poet Scout Catalogue for 1893," *New North-West* (Deer Lodge, MT), March 25, 1893; "Track Talk," *St. Louis Post-Dispatch*, November 28, 1892.

40. *Goodwin's 1893*, vol. 1, 400–401; *Goodwin's 1893*, vol. 2, 51, 72–73, 77, 303, 305–6, 436, 441; "Heads Apart," *Cincinnati Enquirer*, October 4, 1893.

41. Edward Gardner Jones, *The Oregonian's Handbook of the Pacific Northwest* (Portland: Oregonian Publishing Co., 1894), 536.
42. *Goodwin's 1895*, vol. 1, 273, 278, 472; *Goodwin's 1895*, vol. 2, 164; "For Benefit of Monument Fund," *Butte (MT) Miner*, July 21, 1904.
43. "Poet Scout's Varied Career," *Great Falls (MT) Tribune*, December 13, 1902; "Meeting Will Be a Great Success," *Butte (MT) Miner*, June 28, 1898; "The Races Are On," *Butte Miner*, July 3, 1898; "A Splendid Opening for the Butte Races," *Anaconda (MT) Standard*, July 3, 1898; "A Terrific Explosion," *Anaconda Standard*, July 9, 1898; *Goodwin's 1898*, vol. 2, 99, 102.
44. "Mackay [sic] to M'Tague," *Anaconda (MT) Standard*, August 24, 1898.
45. *Goodwin's 1901*, vol. 2, 218, 220, 307–9; *Goodwin's 1902*, vol. 2, 411, 413; "Poet Scout's Varied Career."
46. "Picnic of the United Irish Societies," *Anaconda (MT) Standard*, July 25, 1904; "Eastin & Larabie Quit the Turf," *Nashville American*, April 7, 1901; "Big Crowd at Picnic," *Butte (MT) Inter Mountain*, July 25, 1904.

Chapter 7

1. Noel V. Bourasaw, "Charles Xavier Larrabee, Montana Copper King and Investor behind Fairhaven and Sedro," part 1, *Skagit River Journal*, http://www.skagitriverjournal.com/wa/whatcom/fairhavensth/pioneers/pre1900/larrabee/larrabee01-bio1.html; Robert G. Athearn, ed., review of "The Saga of Ben Holladay: Giant of the Old West," *Montana, the Magazine of Western History* 10, no. 2 (Spring 1960): 53; J. V. Frederick, *Ben Holladay: The Stagecoach King* (Glendale, CA: Arthur H. Clark, 1940), 177, 190–91, 217, 260–61.
2. "Mollie L.," *ASB*, vol. 6, 788. For sources citing Montana as Ben Holladay's foaling place, see Baumler's "Montana State Fairgrounds Racetrack," section 8, p. 2, SHPO, and Dave Walter, title unknown, *Montana Magazine*, May–June 2006, 96; "Track Gossip," *Morning Herald* (Lexington, KY), September 12, 1897; "Notes of the Turf," *Daily Racing Form* (Chicago), November 3, 1899; "Three Priceless Foals," *Butte (MT) Miner*, October 4, 1903.
3. *Goodwin's 1895*, vol. 1, 271, 473; *Goodwin's 1895*, vol. 2, 64, 90, 137, 167, 295, 299, 449, 484, 559, 567.
4. "Notes from the Paddock," *Kansas City Times*, September 28, 1896; "Jockey Mounts in 1895," *Goodwin's 1895*, vol. 2, ccxlvii; *Goodwin's 1896*, vol. 1, 232–33, 236–37, 313–14, 319, 370, 435–37, 441; "Ben Holladay," *Louisville (KY) Courier-Journal*, September 25, 1896; *Goodwin's 1896*, vol. 2, 32, 99, 133, 168, 409, 412, 455–56, 462, 535, 546.
5. "Notes of the Turf," *Daily Racing Form* (Chicago), January 19, 1897; "Peter Wimmer Registers," *Louisville (KY) Courier-Journal*, February 8, 1918; "About Jean Beraud," *Buffalo (NY) Commercial*, June 20, 1900; "Peter Wimmer Was a Soldier," *Pittsburg (PA) Press*, November 30, 1902; Frank W. Thorp, "A Day in the Life of Brave Kinley Mack, the Champion of American Thoroughbreds," *New York Evening World*, March 25, 1901.

6. "Fatherland," *Weekly Democrat* (Natchez, MS), January 2, 1889; "Peter Wimmer Was a Soldier."

7. "Morris Park's Wind-Up," *New York Times*, October 23, 1898; "Oakley Gossip," *Cincinnati Enquirer*, June 19, 1896.

8. "Gossip of the Turf," *Daily Racing Form* (Chicago), March 2, 1899; "Peter Wimmer Was a Soldier."

9. *Goodwin's 1897*, vol. 2, 212, 219, 370, 372–73.

10. "Hamburg Is a Marvel," *New York Sun*, September 12, 1897; *Goodwin's 1897*, vol. 2, 378.

11. *Goodwin's 1897*, vol. 2, 378.

12. "Hamburg Is a Marvel"; *Goodwin's 1897*, vol. 2, ccxxiii, 379; "Surprises at Sheepshead," *New York Times*, September 12, 1897.

13. *Goodwin's 1897*, vol. 2, ccxlvii, 419, 540, 546; "Ben Holladay's Victory," *New York Times*, October 24, 1897; "Ben Holladay's Record," *New York Sun*, October 24, 1897; "At Morris Park," *Spirit of the Times*, October 30, 1897; Samuel L. Boardman, *Handbook of the Turf: A Treasury of Information for Horsemen* (New York: Orange Judd, 1894), 247.

14. "Ben Holladay's Record"; "A Montana Horse," *Daily Inter Mountain* (Butte, MT), October 29, 1897.

15. John Dizikes, *Yankee Doodle Dandy: The Life and Times of Tod Sloan* (Lincoln: University of Nebraska Press, 2004), 73–75; "Gossip of the Sporting World," *Nashville Banner*, May 28, 1898; "Autumn Days at Gravesend," *Turf, Field and Farm*, September 17, 1897, 362.

16. William H. P. Robertson, *History of Thoroughbred Racing in America* (New York: Bonanza Books, 1964), 152.

17. *Goodwin's 1898*, vol. 1, 347, 443, 580; "W. C. Whitney's Racers," *St. Paul (MN) Globe*, July 10, 1898.

18. *Goodwin's 1898*, vol. 1, 585; "Races at Sheepshead Bay," *New York Times*, August 30, 1898; *Goodwin's 1898*, vol. 2, 319, 351; "Racing," *Brooklyn (NY) Citizen*, September 6, 1898.

19. Walter S. Vosburgh, *Racing in America, 1866–1921* (New York: Scribner Press, 1922), 32–33; "New Westchester Track," *New York Times*, May 12, 1889; "The New York Club Races," *New York Times*, October 11, 1891.

20. Lyman Horace Weeks, *The American Turf: An Historical Account of Racing in the United States* (New York: Historical Company, 1898), 454.

21. "Ben Holladay Likes Mud," *St. Louis Globe-Democrat*, October 9, 1898; "Ben Holladay Best Handicap Horse," *Brooklyn (NY) Times Union*, October 10, 1898; "May Not Start," *Nashville Banner*, April 17, 1899. The article "The Racetrack," *New York Tribune*, October 9, 1898, claims that trainers who wanted liberal odds laid on the horse "industriously and diligently" circulated the story that one of Ben Holladay's legs "had filled to so appalling an extent that he could not possibly win the Morris Park Special."

22. "Gossip of the Horsemen," *New York Times*, October 10, 1898; *Goodwin's 1898*, vol. 2, 475.

23. "Racing," *Brooklyn (NY) Citizen*, October 16, 1898.

24. "The Morris Park Races," *New York Times*, October 16, 1898; *Goodwin's 1898*, vol. 2, 537–38.

25. *Goodwin's 1898*, vol. 2, 565; "Game Ben Holladay's Great Performance," *Brooklyn (NY) Daily Eagle*, October 23, 1898.

26. "Morris Park's Wind-Up"; "Game Ben Holladay's Great Performance."

27. "Morris Park's Wind-Up."

28. "Morris Park's Wind-Up"; "Notes by M. T. G.," *Breeder's Gazette*, December 7, 1898, 565; "Ben Holladay's Glorious Race," *New York Journal*, October 23, 1898.

29. "They're of the Royal Line," *Anaconda (MT) Standard*, December 18, 1898; George S. Klotz, "Deer Lodge Firm Maintained One of the Most Successful Stables of Thoroughbred Racers in History of the Turf," *Anaconda (MT) Standard*, January 1, 1922. Samuel Larabie tried to sell Ben Holladay at the end of 1898 according to "Larrabe Is Here," *Morning Herald* (Lexington, KY), November 22, 1898, and "Lexington Sales," *Nashville American*, November 24, 1898.

30. "Promising," *Cincinnati Enquirer*, March 1, 1899.

31. "Promising."

32. "No More Negro Riders," *Chicago Tribune*, April 1, 1900.

33. Katherine C. Mooney, *Race Horse Men: How Slavery and Freedom Were Made at the Racetrack* (Cambridge, MA: Harvard University Press, 2014), 227.

34. Henry Brown, "They're Off!," *Abbott's Monthly*, February 1932, 6; Steven A. Riess, "The American Jockey, 1865–1910," *Transatlantica*, February 2011, 6, accessed September 29, 2020, https://journals.openedition.org/transatlantica/5480.

35. "Gossip of the Turfmen," *New York Times*, April 30, 1899; "Ben Holladay's Last Year," *Brooklyn (NY) Times Union*, April 25, 1899; *Goodwin's 1899*, vol. 1, 469–70, 622–23, 635; *Goodwin's 1899*, vol. 2, 25.

36. "Race Track and Stable Gossip," *Anaconda (MT) Standard*, April 16, 1899; "The Racetrack," *New York Tribune*, May 28, 1899; "The Racetrack," *New York Tribune*, July 2, 1899; "The Racetrack," *New York Tribune*, September 10, 1899.

37. Águeda García de Durango, "New York, Manure and Stairs: When Horses Were the Cities' Nightmares," *Smart Water Magazine*, June 9, 2019, January 1, 2023, https://smartwatermagazine.com/blogs/agueda-garcia-de-durango/new-york-manure-and-stairs-when-horses-were-cities-nightmares.

38. *Goodwin's 1899*, vol. 2, 335; "The Racetrack," *New York Tribune*, September 10, 1899.

39. "Windup at Sheepshead," *New York Sun*, September 10, 1899; "Races at Sheepshead," *New York Times*, September 10, 1899; "Ben Wins the Autumn Cup," *Spirit of the Times*, September 16, 1899; *Goodwin's 1899*, vol. 2, 335; *Goodwin's 1897*, vol. 2, 378–79.

40. *Goodwin's 1899*, vol. 2, 366–67, 466–67.

41. "Holladay's Great Record," *New York Times*, October 15, 1899; "Ben Holladay's Handicap," *Brooklyn (NY) Daily Eagle*, October 15, 1899.

42. "Holladay's Great Record"; "Post and Paddock Notes," *Standard Union* (Brooklyn, NY), October 16, 1899; *Goodwin's 1899*, vol. 2, 467; *Goodwin's 1897*, vol. 2, 540.

43. *Goodwin's 1899*, vol. 2, 504; "Racing Gossip," *Brooklyn (NY) Daily Eagle*, October 21, 1899.

44. "Wise Folks Wins," *Philadelphia Inquirer*, October 23, 1899; "Morris Park Racing," *New York Times*, October 22, 1899; *Goodwin's 1899*, vol. 2, 504.

45. "Wise Folks Wins"; "The Whitney Stable," *Spirit of the Times*, November 4, 1899. Turf writer Kelston incorrectly identifies the Metropolitan Handicap as Holladay's final race, in which he carried 140 pounds. "Carter Handicap," *Illustrated Buffalo (NY) Express*, April 15, 1900.

46. "Ben Holladay Sold to Breeding Bureau," *San Francisco Examiner*, December 23, 1906; "Hutchinson Agricultural Club," *Reveille*, vol. 3 (Starkville: Agricultural and Mechanical College of the State of Mississippi, 1907), 151.

47. "The Marvel of the Turf," *Berkshire Eagle* (Pittsfield, MA), October 2, 1920.

48. "Exterminator May Eclipse Record for Winnings Registered by Star Son of Fair Play and Mahuba," *Press and Sun-Bulletin* (Bingham, NY), June 3, 1922.

Chapter 8

1. Frank W. Thorp, "A Day in the Life of Brave Kinley Mack, the Champion of American Thoroughbreds," *New York Evening World*, March 25, 1901.

2. "Gossip of the Turf," *Daily Racing Form* (Chicago), March 2, 1899; "How Kinley Mack Got His Name," *Chicago Tribune*, June 17, 1900; "Why Ethelbert Lost the Suburban," *St. Louis Republic*, June 24, 1900.

3. S. D. Bruce, *The American Stud Book* (New York: Sanders D. Bruce, 1873); William H. P. Robertson, *History of Thoroughbred Racing in America* (New York: Bonanza Books, 1964), 33; Walter S. Vosburgh, *Racing in America, 1866–1921* (New York: Scribner Press, 1922), 46–47.

4. "Golden Rod Stake," *St. Louis Post-Dispatch*, July 7, 1900; "Songstress," *ASB*, vol. 6, 966.

5. "Race Track and Stable Gossip," *Anaconda (MT) Standard*, November 27, 1898; "Stakes Winners," *Breeder and Sportsman*, June 2, 1900, 437; "Famous Horses of California," *San Francisco Chronicle*, December 30, 1900; "Autumn Races at Sheepshead Bay," *Turf, Field and Farm*, September 8, 1899, 913; "Eastin & Larabie Quit the Turf," *Nashville American*, April 7, 1901. "Stakes Winners" states that Islington was standing at the Robinson Farm, owned by "Mr. Robinson of Tulare county," and that Songstress was sent there for breeding to Islington. Some sources consulted by the author state that Kinley Mack was foaled elsewhere than California. For instance, "The Eastin & Larabie Stable Quit the Turf; Great Horses Which They Raced," *Nashville American*, April 7, 1901, states that Kinley Mack was foaled at Elmendorf Farm.

6. *Goodwin's 1898*, vol. 2, 51; "Kinley Mack," *Daily Leader* (Lexington, KY), June 28, 1900. The article "Sports and Sportsmen," *New York Tribune*, August 30, 1900, complained that Wimmer "sedulously disseminated the fiction that Ben Holladay had four lame legs and a lame backbone." Wimmer's "fiction" about Ben Holladay, according to the *Tribune*, was being repeated with Kinley Mack. The *Tribune* insisted Kinley Mack's legs were "sounder and stronger than those of the Eiffel Tower and [have] never been near the verge of breaking down."

7. *Goodwin's 1898*, vol. 2, 51; "Ornament in Front," *New York Sun*, July 7, 1898.

8. *Goodwin's 1898*, vol. 2, 169, 175, 237, 251; "Another Stake for Matanza," *Chicago Tribune*, August 21, 1898.

9. Vosburgh, *Racing in America*, 27–28; "Suburban Is an Upset," *New York Sun*, June 19, 1898; "The Suburban, Also, Goes to Kinley Mack," *Brooklyn (NY) Daily Eagle*, June 17, 1900; "Walks about the City," *Brooklyn Daily Eagle*, August 25, 1889.

10. "Suburban Is an Upset."

11. *Goodwin's 1898*, vol. 2, 301, 320, 353–54, 377; "W. Overton Is Again Left," *Chicago Tribune*, September 14, 1898.

12. Francis Trevelyan, "Sloane Going to England," *New York Journal*, September 9, 1898, 11; "Betting," *Buffalo (NY) Times*, February 18, 1900; "Autumn Races at Sheepshead Bay"; Thorp, "Day in the Life of Brave Kinley Mack."

13. *Goodwin's 1899*, vol. 1, 621–22, 629, 633, 637; *Goodwin's 1899*, vol. 2, 54.

14. *Goodwin's 1899*, vol. 2, 160–61, 167, 226, 302, 306. "Successful as Usual," *Butte (MT) Miner*, November 20, 1899. Kinley Mack's earnings were calculated based on figures in *Goodwin's*.

15. "Baseball Appears to Be Outdone by Horse Racing," *St. Louis Republic*, August 5, 1900.

16. "Runners for the East," *St. Paul (MN) Globe*, April 9, 1900; "Flyers Get Trials of Brooklyn," *St. Louis Republic*, May 25, 1900; *Goodwin's 1898*, vol. 1, 349, 354, 410, 449, 525, 531, 588; *Goodwin's 1899*, vol. 1, 370–71, 461–62.

17. "Brooklyn Handicap," *Buffalo (NY) Enquirer*, May 26, 1900; "Starters for the Brooklyn Handicap," *New York Evening World*, May 25, 1900; "Great Handicap for Kinley Mack," *Chicago Tribune*, May 27, 1900; "Dark Horse," *Daily Leader* (Lexington, KY), May 27, 1900; *Goodwin's 1900*, vol. 1, 451.

18. "Kinley Mack Lands Brooklyn Handicap," *Brooklyn (NY) Daily Eagle*, May 27, 1900; "Yellow Tail Was Beaten," *St. Louis Globe-Democrat*, May 29, 1900; "Imp," NMRHF, accessed May 14, 2020, https://www.racingmuseum.org/hall-of-fame /horse/imp-oh; *Goodwin's 1900*, vol. 1, 218, 245, 373, 379, 397–98, 451; "Imp Ran and the Others Also Ran," *Chillicothe (OH) Gazette*, May 13, 1900.

19. *Goodwin's 1900*, vol. 1, 451.

20. "Dark Horse."

21. "Dark Horse."

22. "Kinley Mack Lands Brooklyn Handicap"; "Great Handicap for Kinley Mack."

23. "Brooklyn Handicap Won by Kinley Mack," *New York Times*, May 27, 1900. The article "The Making of a Jockey," *Ainslee's Magazine*, June 1901, 402, offers a photograph of Patsy McCue seated in the floral horseshoe following the 1900 Brooklyn Handicap. Accessed December 7, 2019, https://www.google.com/books/edition/Ainslee_s_Magazine/DYoXAQAAMAAJ?hl=en&gbpv=1.

24. "Brooklyn Handicap Won by Kinley Mack"; "Kinley Mack's Brooklyn," *New York Tribune*, May 27, 1900.

25. "Imp Ran and the Others Also Ran"; *Goodwin's 1900*, vol. 1, cxxiv, 456–57; "Sporting News," *Topeka (KS) State Journal*, June 14, 1900.

26. "The Champion Horse Jockey," *San Francisco Chronicle*, September 20, 1896; Harry N. Price, "When Patsy M'Cue Won Fame and a Fair Bride," *Washington Post*, May 13, 1906; "A Newsboy Jockey," *Philadelphia Inquirer*, January 1, 1899.

27. Price, "When Patsy M'Cue Won Fame."

28. Price, "When Patsy M'Cue Won Fame"; "West Ahead of East," *Anaconda (MT) Standard*, January 11, 1897; "Patsy McCue Well Known to Bitter Root People," *Anaconda Standard*, May 13, 1906.

29. "Horses and Horsemen," *Butte (MT) Miner*, February 25, 1901; "Butte's Great Race Track Passes into History," *Anaconda (MT) Standard*, December 19, 1915.

30. "Belgravia at Thirty to One," *San Francisco Call*, August 7, 1898. Belgravia also raced as Belgrave. "Patsy M'Cue Begun in Butte," *Butte (MT) Inter Mountain*, May 19, 1906; *Goodwin's 1898*, vol. 2, 202; "Bennings Meeting Ended," *St. Louis Globe-Democrat*, December 1, 1898; "A Newsboy Jockey."

31. "Jockeys of the Year," *New York Times*, May 28, 1899; "Purse Races at Brooklyn," *New York Times*, June 1, 1899; "Yesterday at Gravesend," *Brooklyn (NY) Standard Union*, June 15, 1899; "The Racetrack," *New York Tribune*, June 1, 1899; "The Racetrack," *New York Tribune*, June 23, 1899; "Imp Springs a Surprise," *Brooklyn Standard Union*, July 7, 1899; "The Racetrack," *New York Tribune*, July 12, 1899; "The Racetrack," *New York Tribune*, July 16, 1899.

32. "Mesmerist's Fleet Dash," *Brooklyn (NY) Daily Eagle*, August 31, 1899; "M'Cue Suspended," *Buffalo (NY) Courier*, September 4, 1899; "Jockey McCue Reinstated," *Brooklyn (NY) Times Union*, May 11, 1900; "The Scandals Excite Talk," *New York Tribune*, August 11, 1900.

33. *Goodwin's 1900*, vol. 1, 462, 584; "Carrie C.," *ASB*, vol. 7, 139.

34. "Contemporary Views," *Wilmington (NC) Morning Star*, May 30, 1921; *Goodwin's 1900*, vol. 1, 373; "Maori," *ASB*, vol. 7, 641.

35. Vosburgh, *Racing in America*, 170; "Suburban Handicap," *St. Louis Republic*, June 16, 1900.

36. "Banastar Wins," *New York Sun*, May 28, 1899; "Imp's Suburban," *New York Sun*, June 18, 1899; "Kinley Mack Wins," *New York Sun*, June 17, 1900.

37. *Goodwin's 1900*, vol. 1, 584; "Suburban Day," *Illustrated American* 11 (July 9, 1892): 357; Wallace T. Hyde, "Suburban Handicap Our Greatest Race," *Daily Leader* (Lexington, KY), June 12, 1898; "Suburban Is an Upset."

38. *Goodwin's 1900*, vol. 1, 584.

39. "Kinley Mack Wins."
40. "Kinley Mack Wins"; "How the Race Was Won," *New York Times*, June 17, 1900; *Goodwin's 1900*, vol. 1, 584.
41. "Kinley Mack Wins"; "Suburban Won by Kinley Mack," *New York Times*, June 17, 1900.
42. "Kinley Mack Wins."
43. "Kinley Mack Wins"; *Goodwin's 1900*, vol. 1, 584.
44. "Kinley Mack Wins"; "Suburban Won by Kinley Mack"; "Hildago's Gossip," *Breeder and Sportsman*, December 28, 1901; "Imp's Sister, Scioto," *Democrat and Chronicle* (Rochester, NY), March 28, 1902.

Chapter 9

1. "Closing Day of the Convention," *Chicago Tribune*, June 22, 1900; "Bryant Nominated," *Kansas City Gazette*, July 6, 1900.
2. "What's in a Name, Even It Be Transposed?," *Brooklyn (NY) Daily Eagle*, June 17, 1900; "Kinley Mack," *Daily Leader* (Lexington, KY), June 28, 1900; "Right in the Ring," *Dunn County News* (Menomonie, WI), June 22, 1900.
3. "Horses and Horsemen," *Daily Inter Mountain* (Butte, MT), June 30, 1900.
4. *Goodwin's 1900*, vol. 2, ccv, 75, 158–59, 238; "Kinley Mack Won the Beverwyck," *Philadelphia Inquirer*, August 10, 1900.
5. "Saratoga Races," *Evening Star* (Washington, DC), August 10, 1900; "Start Beats Ethelbert," *New York Sun*, August 10, 1900.
6. "Start Beats Ethelbert"; *Goodwin's 1900*, vol. 2, 238; "Kinley Mack Wins at Saratoga," *Chicago Tribune*, August 10, 1900.
7. "Saratoga Races," *Scranton (PA) Republican*, August 24, 1900; *Goodwin's 1900*, vol. 2, 312; "Horse Jockey's Great Spenders," *Knoxville Sentinel*, February 17, 1908; "Death First at the Wire," *Washington Post*, May 12, 1906.
8. *Goodwin's 1900*, vol. 2, 347; "Kinley Mack's Cup Race," *New York Times*, August 30, 1900; "Kinley Mack's Claim to Large Honors," *Nashville American*, September 1, 1900.
9. "Commando Cantered In," *New York Times*, September 12, 1900; *Goodwin's 1900*, vol. 2, 406.
10. *Goodwin's 1900*, vol. 2, 412; "Imp Wins Another Race," *New York Times*, September 16, 1900.
11. Walter S. Vosburgh, *Racing in America, 1866–1921* (New York: Scribner Press, 1922), 175.
12. "Ethelbert Beaten Again," *New York Tribune*, September 9, 1900; "Racing," *New York Tribune*, August 10, 1900; "Sports and Sportsmen," *New York Tribune*, September 16, 1900; "Kinley Mack's Suburban," *New York Tribune*, June 17, 1900; "Ethelbert and Jean Beraud," *Kansas City Star*, June 2, 1900; "This Racing Year," *St. Louis Post-Dispatch*, November 7, 1900; Vosburgh, *Racing in America*, 175.
13. "Leading Events of the Year 1900," *Boston Globe*, December 31, 1900.

14. Frank W. Thorp, "A Day in the Life of Brave Kinley Mack, the Champion of American Thoroughbreds," *New York Evening World*, March 25, 1901.

15. George S. Klotz, "Deer Lodge Once Had One of Greatest Racing Stables in America That Swept the Country with Notable Gallopers," *Three Forks (MT) News*, August 8, 1922; "Eastin Will Retire," *Buffalo (NY) Review*, March 13, 1901; "Sale of Kinley Mack," *New York Times*, March 12, 1901; "Sale a Marker in Turf History," *Democrat and Chronicle* (Rochester, NY), March 13, 1901.

16. "Sale of Kinley Mack"; "Pioneer Banker Stricken, Death Comes Suddenly," *Silver State Post* (Deer Lodge, MT), April 23, 1914.

17. "Handicap Cracks at the Bay," *Turf, Field and Farm*, February 15, 1901; "J. B. Haggin Returns to the Turf," *Brooklyn (NY) Daily Eagle*, March 12, 1901; "Gossip of the Turf," *Daily Racing Form* (Chicago), July 25, 1901; "Eastin & Larabie Quit the Turf; Great Horses Which They Raced," *Nashville American*, April 7, 1901.

18. "Jockey McCue Is Missing," *Chicago Tribune*, June 12, 1901; "The Racetrack," *New York Tribune*, July 5, 1901; "Hamilton," *Ravalli County Democrat* (Hamilton, MT), March 5, 1902. The author found no evidence of McCue riding for Peter Wimmer after McCue disappeared in 1901.

19. "Horses and Horsemen," *Baltimore Sun*, June 26, 1902; "Eastern Derby Colts Go Home," *Chicago Tribune*, June 23, 1902; "City Park," Cincinnati Enquirer, January 3, 1909; "Explain Their Defeat in the Derby," *Chicago Tribune*, June 24, 1902.

20. "Gossip of the Racetrack," *New York Sun*, June 16, 1904; "Saratoga Race Track," *Philadelphia Inquirer*, August 6, 1904; "Topics of the Turf," *Kansas City Star*, November 11, 1904; "Patsy M'Cue Well Known to Bitter Root People," *Anaconda (MT) Standard*, May 13, 1906.

21. Price, "When 'Patsy' McCue Won Fame and a Fair Bride"; "Patsy McCue, Famous Jockey, Dead," *Western News* (Hamilton, MT), May 16, 1906; "Death at Wire," *Washington Post,* May 13, 1906.

22. "Memorial Services in Honor of the Dead," *Anaconda (MT) Standard*, September 18, 1901.

23. Justine Robles, "Americanism: Keep Americanism Alive!," VFW Auxiliary, accessed January 15, 2023, https://vfwauxiliary.org/americanism-keep-americanism-alive/.

24. US Census, 1880, Yazoo City, Mississippi, 38, accessed March 21; US Census, 1900, Brooklyn Ward 31, Kings, New York, 11; US Census, 1910, Brooklyn Ward 31, Kings, New York, 13; US Census, 1920, Manhattan Assembly District 9, New York, New York, 1B, accessed April 5, 2022. Census information accessed through HeritageQuest Online, https://www.heritagequestonline.com/hqoweb/library/do/login. "Peter Wimmer Registers," *Louisville (KY) Courier-Journal*, February 8, 1918; "Wimmer Held," *Lexington (KY) Leader*, July 12, 1918; Wimmer v. United States, Caselaw Access Project, Harvard Law School, accessed March 21, 2021, https://cite.case.law/f/264/11/.

25. "Peter Wimmer Guilty," *Thoroughbred Record*, August 17, 1918; "Appellate Court Matters," *Cincinnati Enquirer*, November 6, 1919; "To Prison for Espionage,"

Kansas City Star, March 12, 1920; "President Pardons Kentucky Horseman," *Hartford (KY) Republican,* September 10, 1920; *Amnesty and Pardon for Political Prisoners: Hearings Before a Subcommittee of the Committee on the Judiciary, United States Senate, Sixty-Sixth Congress, Third Session* (Washington, DC: US Government Printing Office, 1921), 192, accessed April 6, 2022, https://books .google.com/books/about/Amnesty_and_Pardon_for_Political_Prison.html ?id=3gkvAAAAMAAJ.

26. "Peter Wimmer Dies at Sheepshead Bay," *Yazoo (MS) Herald,* October 15, 1923.

27. "Deer Lodge News," *Butte (MT) Miner,* June 6, 1910; *Larabie Brothers Bank, 401 Main,* pamphlet; "Deer Lodge News," *Butte Miner,* March 23, 1912; "Sluice-Box Honor Arouses Pioneers," *Anaconda (MT) Standard,* August 23, 1912.

28. "Larabie Dies," *Salt Lake Telegram,* April 22, 1914; "Eastin & Larabie Quit the Turf."

29. "S. E. Larabie," *Anaconda (MT) Standard,* October 13, 1912.

30. "Famous Racers Will Be Seen in Kentucky," *Lexington (KY) Herald,* August 22, 1913; Ray O'Loughlin, "Montana Livestock Sketches, Larabee Brothers Follo," 5, S. E. Larabie Vertical Files, MHS; "Death of Mr. J. A. Eastin," *Thoroughbred Record,* February 28, 1914, 107.

31. "Prominent Pioneer Dies," *Spokane Chronicle,* April 24, 1914.

32. "In Deer Lodge," *Anaconda (MT) Standard,* April 26, 1914; "Tribute of a Friend to Late S. E. Larabie," *Anaconda Standard,* April 23, 1914; "Hundreds Attend Funeral," *Anaconda Standard,* April 27, 1914; "Pioneer Banker Stricken."

33. "Pioneer Banker Stricken"; untitled, see "A telegram was received," third column, *Thoroughbred Record,* April 25, 1914; "S. E. Larabie Dies in Montana," *Daily Racing Form* (Chicago), April 23, 1914.

34. "Larabie Rites Set for Wednesday," *Montana Standard* (Butte), May 12, 1936; "S. E. Larabie Dies in Montana"; "Pioneer Banker Is Laid to Final Rest," *Silver State Post* (Deer Lodge, MT), April 30, 1914; "Closed Deer Lodge Bank Pays Dividends," *Great Falls (MT) Tribune,* September 16, 1943.

35. William H. P. Robertson, *History of Thoroughbred Racing in America* (New York: Bonanza Books, 1964), 194–97; Mary Simon, *Racing through the Century: The Story of Thoroughbred Racing in America* (Irvine: CA, BowTie Press, 2002), 30; Steven A. Riess, ed., *Sports in America from Colonial Times to the Twenty-First Century: An Encyclopedia* (New York: Routledge, 2015), 457; Edward Hotaling, *The Great Black Jockeys: The Lives and Times of the Men Who Dominated America's First National Sport* (Rocklin, CA: FORUM, 1999), 327.

36. Robertson, *History of Thoroughbred Racing,* 196.

37. "Good Horse Market," *Salt Lake Tribune,* November 22, 1908.

38. "How Kinley Mack's Sire Died," *Daily Racing Form* (Chicago), November 18, 1908; "Peter Wimmer an Old-Time Turfman," *Lexington (KY) Leader,* August 8, 1920; "Noted Kinley Mack among the Thoroughbreds Purchased by Argentine," *Oregon Daily Journal* (Portland), June 19, 1910; "Kinley Mack Again in Training," *Daily Racing Form* (Chicago), February 25, 1910.

Chapter 10

1. "Marcus Daly's Breeding Venture," *Daily Racing Form* (Chicago), December 6, 1907.

2. Mary Fleming, *A History of the Thoroughbred in California* (Los Angeles: Sinclair, 1983), 17–19.

3. "Turf Notes," *Kansas City Gazette*, December 28, 1888. Ormonde's purchase price varies among reports. See "The Turf of Brazil," *St. Joseph (MO) News-Press*, November 2, 1894; "The Passing of Ormonde," *Nashville Banner*, October 17, 1900; C. C. Goodwin, *As I Remember Them* (Salt Lake City: Salt Lake Commercial Club, 1913), 273–74; Fleming, *History of the Thoroughbred*, 19.

4. "Millionaires' Dress," *Fall River (MA) Daily Globe*, November 12, 1891; *Progressive Men of the State of Montana* (Chicago: A. W. Bowen, n.d.), 16; Michael P. Malone, *Battle for Butte: Mining and Politics on the Northern Frontier, 1864–1906* (Seattle: University of Washington Press, 1981), 18. The Marcus Daly Mansion website states that Lucas O'Daly fathered eleven children. See "History of Marcus Daly," accessed November 14, 2021, https://www.dalymansion.org/history-and-preservation. Ed Tipton, who was a close associate of Daly's, is quoted in "Marcus Daly's Breeding Venture," *Daily Racing Form* (Chicago), December 6, 1907, as saying that O'Daly was a "country gentleman in Ireland and thoroughbred breeder." All other sources the author consulted stated that O'Daly was an impoverished farmer. US Census, 1900, Anaconda, Deer Lodge County, Montana, 79, accessed October 18, 2021, HeritageQuest Online, https://www.heritagequestonline.com/hqoweb/library/do/login; C. P. Connolly, "The Story of Montana," *McClure's Magazine*, September 1906, 455; "Some Newly Told Tales," *Ravalli County Democrat* (Hamilton, MT), January 2, 1901; Marcus Daly Mansion Archives, Hamilton, MT; "History and Preservation," Marcus Daly Mansion, https://www.dalymansion.org/history-and-preservation.

5. Frank G. Carpenter, "The Copper King," *Deseret Weekly* (Salt Lake City), May 13, 1893, 658; "Death of Marcus Daly," *New York Times*, November 13, 1900; Connolly, "Story of Montana," 458; Malone, *Battle for Butte*, 19; Michael P. Malone and Richard P. Roder, "Mining," *Montana, the Magazine of Western History* 25, no. 2 (Spring 1975): 27.

6. Malone, *Battle for Butte*, 19; Marcus Daly Mansion website, "History of Marcus Daly."

7. "On Anaconda Hill," *Anaconda (MT) Standard*, November 3, 1895; Michael Malone and Richard Roder, eds., *Montana: A History of Two Centuries* (Seattle: University of Washington Press, 1976), 153; Malone, *Battle for Butte*, 25.

8. Malone, *Battle for Butte*, 20; B. E. Stack, "Origin of the Clark-Daly Feud," 1933, Marcus Daly Vertical Files, MHS. Author Michael Malone states in *Battle for Butte* (83) that "Stack's account has two major weaknesses. On the one hand it is vintage 'oral history,' subject to fabrication and unsupported by hard evidence. On the other, it fails to dovetail with the fact that Daly made part of the original

purchase of the Alice lode from the Clark and Larabie Bank directly, which hardly indicates an obstructionist attitude on the part of Clark."

9. "They Drove the Stakes," *Anaconda (MT) Standard*, December 16, 1900; Connolly, "Story of Montana," 457–58.

10. "They Drove the Stakes"; Malone, *Battle for Butte*, 25; C. B. Glasscock, *The War of the Copper Kings* (New York: Grosset and Dunlap, 1966), 69. For George Hearst's account of the Anaconda Mine, see his memoir, *The Way It Was: Recollections of U.S. Senator George Hearst, 1820–1891* (Hearst Corporation, 1972), 23–24. Author Matthew Bernstein writes of the account in his book *George Hearst: Silver King of the Gilded Age* (Norman: University of Oklahoma Press, 2021), 150.

11. Matt J. Kelly, *Anaconda: Montana's Copper City* (Anaconda, MT: Soroptimist Club, 1983), 7; Hearst, *The Way It Was*, 20.

12. Malone, *Battle for Butte*, 27–28.

13. Gilbert Rogin, "The Right Man in the Right Place—at Last," *Sports Illustrated*, November 13, 1967, accessed January 12, 2023, https://vault.si.com/vault/1967/11/13/the-right-man-in-the-right-placeat-last; Malone, *Battle for Butte*, 27.

14. Helen Fitzgerald Sanders, *A History of Montana*, vol. 1 (Chicago: Lewis Publishing, 1913), 710–11; "The Output of Butte," *Butte (MT) Miner*, August 23, 1883; "Personal," *New North-West* (Deer Lodge, MT), April 25, 1884.

15. "When Haggin Came to Daly's Rescue," clipping, n.d., no periodical name, Marcus Daly Vertical Files, MHS; "James B. Haggin Dies at Newport, R.I.," *Thoroughbred Record*, September 19, 1914.

16. "Copper King Marcus Daly Sighted over Dead Cow When Planning Main Street of Anaconda in 1883," *Great Falls (MT) Tribune*, July 13, 1958; Patrick F. Morris, *Anaconda, Montana: Copper Smelting Boom Town on the Western Frontier* (Bethesda, MD: Swan, 1997), 37; Malone, *Battle for Butte*, 31. Daly would eventually build his own railroad in 1894, the Butte, Anaconda and Pacific Railway, to carry his ore. See Malone, *Battle for Butte*, 41.

17. "The Anaconda Smelter," *River Press* (Fort Benton, MT), September 17, 1884; Carroll Van West, "Marcus Daly and Montana: One Man's Imprint on the Land," *Montana, the Magazine of Western History* 37 (Winter 1987): 61; "First National Bank of Anaconda, Mont.," *Anaconda (MT) Standard*, August 8, 1891, 6; Hugh Daly, *Marcus Daly of Montana: A Biography* (privately printed, 1934), 4; "The Mining History of Butte and Anaconda," Discover Mining History with the Mining History Association, accessed October 19, 2021, www.mininghistoryassociation.org/ButteHistory.htm.

18. "The Anaconda," *Idaho Semi-Weekly World* (Idaho City), December 21, 1888; Van West, "Marcus Daly and Montana"; "Mining Interests," *Lincoln (NE) Journal Star*, March 11, 1891; "Marcus Daly," in *Progressive Men of the State of Montana*, 17; "Death of Marcus Daly."

19. "Home Notes," *Daily Inter Mountain* (Butte, MT), July 1, 1887; "House," *Butte (MT) Semi-Weekly Miner*, February 23, 1887; "Veritas," ASB, vol. 4, 494; "The Coming Fair," *Helena (MT) Independent*, September 17, 1881.

20. "Anaconda Notes," *Butte (MT) Weekly Miner*, April 14, 1888; "Montana Men and Things," *Daily Inter Mountain* (Butte, MT), May 16, 1888; "Anaconda Racing Association Articles of Incorporation," May 1, 1888, Butte–Silver Bow Public Archives, Butte, MT; "On the Square," *Butte Weekly Miner*, August 29, 1888; "First Annual Meeting of the Anaconda Racing Association," *Butte Weekly Miner*, August 22, 1888; "Smelter City Races," *Helena (MT) Independent*, August 29, 1888.

21. Morris, *Anaconda, Montana*, 78; Glasscock, *War of the Copper Kings*, 112.

22. Glasscock, *War of the Copper Kings*, 112–13; John Palmer Fought, "John Hurst Durston, Editor: The Anaconda Standard in the Clark-Daly Feud" (master's thesis, Montana State University, 1959), 15–16, accessed December 26, 2021, https://scholarworks.umt.edu/etd/5031; "About the *Anaconda Standard*," Library of Congress, accessed August 5, 2021, https://chroniclingamerica.loc.gov/lccn/sn84036012.

23. "Anaconda Mining Company Articles of Incorporation," January 14, 1891, Butte–Silver Bow Public Archives; Morris, *Anaconda, Montana*, 103; "On Anaconda Hill."

24. "Sports of All Sorts," *Anaconda (MT) Standard*, October 11, 1893. For "Copper King" references, see Lyman Horace Weeks, *The American Turf: An Historical Account of Racing in the United States* (New York: 1898), 179; "Montana Wins the Suburban of 1892," *Anaconda Standard*, May 21, 1911; "A Broken Hoof," *Cincinnati Enquirer*, July 2, 1891; "Women on the Turf," *Inter Ocean* (Chicago), August 17, 1891; "Turf Topics," *Nebraska State Journal* (Lincoln), August 23, 1891; "Histories of Winners," *San Francisco Chronicle*, June 19, 1892; Carpenter, "Copper King," 658; "The Winners on the Turf," *New York Sun*, October 16, 1893; Glasscock, *War of the Copper Kings*, 104; "Fleet-Footed Steeds," *Butte (MT) Miner*, August 21, 1885.

25. Malone, *Battle for Butte*, 80; Daly, *Marcus Daly of Montana*, 11; *Anaconda Copper Etchings Diamond Jubilee, 1883–1858* (Anaconda Diamond Jubilee Corp., 1958), 17, accessed December 2, 2021, https://babel.hathitrust.org.

26. Malone, *Battle for Butte*, 45–46; Malone and Roder, *Montana: A History of Two Centuries*, 158.

27. "Marcus Daly's Sale of His Anaconda Interests," *Evening Express* (Los Angeles), June 17, 1899; Malone, *Battle for Butte*, 137. Malone states in *Battle for Butte* (135) that John D. Rockefeller was not involved with Standard Oil's "copper caper" and in fact disapproved of it.

28. John Lindsay, *Amazing Experiences of a Judge with an Autobiography and Tribute to Marcus Daly* (Philadelphia: Dorrance, 1939), 76, accessed November 15, 2021, https://babel.hathitrust.org.

29. "James Ben Ali Haggin," in *History of Kentucky* (Chicago: S. J. Publishing, 1928), 570–71; Ronald Parsons, "James Ben Ali Haggin and His Thoroughbreds" (research paper, California State University, May 26, 2000), 4–5.

30. "Haggin Is King of All Horsemen," *Philadelphia Inquirer*, July 13, 1903; "Purchase of Rancocas Brings Old Times to Mind," *Brooklyn (NY) Daily Eagle*, March 14, 1920; Kent Cochran, "California's Original Breeding Industry," *Thoroughbred of California*, June 1962, 795; William H. P. Robertson, *History of Thoroughbred Racing in America* (New York: Bonanza Books, 1964), 143.

31. S. E. Moffett, "James Ben Ali Haggin," *Cosmopolitan* 33 (June 1902): 166; Robertson, *History of Thoroughbred Racing*, 144–45.

32. "Daly's Horses," *Quad-City Times* (Davenport, IA), December 8, 1892. For versions of the Hearst rescue and Daly's introduction to the Bitterroot Valley, see Weeks, *American Turf*, 179; Edward B. Reynolds, "Horse Racing in Montana," *Roundup (MT) Record-Tribune*, August 22, 1940; "Tammany at His Home," *Anaconda (MT) Standard*, July 10, 1897; Kelly, *Anaconda: Montana's Copper City*, 7. George Hearst does not mention the incident in his memoir, *The Way It Was*. Darlene Gould, Daly Mansion executive director, Hamilton, MT, in an email message to the author on September 7, 2022, stated that the Daly mansion does not have an accepted version of the year of Daly's first entry into the valley.

33. Kathleen Cook and Lon Johnson, "Riverside," National Register of Historic Places Registration Form, section 8, p. 1, section 7, pp. 1–2, SHPO; Carpenter, "Copper King," 658; Ada Powell, *The Dalys of the Bitter Root* (privately printed, 1989), 31–32.

34. Carpenter, "Copper King," 658.

35. "Mr. Daly's Stable," *Daily Inter Mountain* (Butte, MT), August 20, 1888; "Marcus Daly's Breeding Venture"; "McTague Retires," *Anaconda (MT) Standard*, July 7, 1896; "Black Filly," *Catalogue of Thoroughbreds, Property of Kohrs and Bielenberg* (1896), no. 19, on file at the Grant-Kohrs Ranch National Historic Site, Deer Lodge, MT; Powell, *Dalys of the Bitter Root*, 41. Daly's ownership of Standardbred horses and his racing of them is traced back to at least April 1886, about a year before he purchased Lady Preuitt. See "Local Matters," *Butte (MT) Miner*, April 28, 1886. At the Marcus Daly Mansion Archives, see the entries for local purchases, Oklahoma, Fairview, Fernleaf, Fairweather, Bozeman, Lavic, Tuckahoe, Marietta, and Emma Mc, inside the Bitter Root Stock Farm ledger titled *Index: Thoroughbred Stock*.

36. "The Montana Race Horse," *Daily Inter Mountain* (Butte, MT), October 28, 1891. For detailed descriptions of the Bitter Root Stock Farm and its operation, see also "Daly's Future Home," *Tacoma Daily Ledger*, February 4, 1900; "Horse Racing in Montana"; "Training Thoroughbreds," *Western News* (Hamilton, MT), January 16, 1895; Powell, *Dalys of the Bitter Root*, 21.

37. "Sporting Notes," *Inter Ocean* (Chicago), December 10, 1890; "Items of Interest," *Breeder's Gazette*, December 3, 1890, 426; "Hyder Ali," *Index: Thoroughbred Stock*; "Good Stock Wanted," *Anaconda (MT) Standard*, December 5, 1895.

38. "Daly's Future Home"; Ada Powell, *Copper, Green and Silver* (privately printed, 1993), 1, 4; "The Montana Race Horse"; Lindsay, *Amazing Experiences of a Judge*, 77; Powell, *Dalys of the Bitter Root*, 47; "From the Racetrack," *Star Gazette*

(Elmira, NY), October 31, 1892; "Sporting World," *Anaconda (MT) Standard*, February 10, 1895.

39. "Morton Edmund Knowles," *Journal of the American Veterinary Medical Association* 63, n.s. 16 (April 1923): 671, https://books.google.com; "Marcus Daly's Veterinary Hospital," *Thoroughbred Record*, March 2, 1895; "Fatal Epidemic among Colts," *San Francisco Examiner*, March 27, 1892; "Hospital for Horses," *Anaconda (MT) Standard*, February 6, 1893.

40. "Daly's Future Home"; "Tammany at His Home," *Anaconda (MT) Standard*, July 10, 1897; Carpenter, "Copper King," 658; "Haynes Has Devoted Life to Turf," *Lexington (KY) Herald*, February 26, 1931.

41. "Sale of the Belmont Stud," *New York Times*, October 17, 1891; Francis Trevelyan, "The Status of the American Turf," *Outing*, March 1892, 476, https://www.google .com/books/edition/Outing/Q6vQAAAAMAAJ?hl=en&gbpv=1&dq; "Valuable Books for Horsemen," *Turf, Field and Farm*, February 17, 1899, 174; Antwerp and Lamplighter, *Modern Pedigrees* (New York: Metropolitan Job Printing, 1895), 6, on file at the Keeneland Library, Lexington, KY.

42. "Marcus Daly's English Stud Farm," *Thoroughbred Record*, September 9, 1899; "Sports of All Sorts"; "Marcus Daly's Purchases," *Helena (MT) Weekly Independent*, October 2, 1890; Weeks, *American Turf*, 193. The year that Daly bought Aperfield Court is unclear.

43. "Daly's Horses," *Quad-City Times* (Davenport, IA), December 8, 1892.

Chapter 11

1. "Haggin in Good Luck," *Daily Examiner* (San Francisco), July 2, 1889.

2. "Marcus Daly's Horses," *Helena (MT) Weekly Herald*, July 25, 1889; "Montana," *Index: Thoroughbred Stock*; "Queen," *ASB*, vol. 6, 104.

3. Walter S. Vosburgh, *Racing in America, 1866–1921* (New York: Scribner Press, 1922), 152; "Haggin in Good Luck"; "Horses and Horsemen," *Daily Inter Mountain* (Butte, MT), July 15, 1891.

4. Ada Powell, *Copper, Green and Silver* (privately printed, 1993), 115–16; "Marcus Daly's Breeding Venture," *Anaconda (MT) Standard,* December 6, 1907.

5. "The Running Turf," *Cincinnati Enquirer*, March 17, 1890. Ada Powell, in *Copper, Green and Silver* (ix), stated that "it is believed" Marcus Daly raced Thoroughbreds on eastern tracks as early as 1889, but *Goodwin's Turf Guide* for 1889 had no listing for Daly or Riverside Stable.

6. "Pneumonia Fatal to Matt Byrnes," *Asbury Park Press* (NJ), March 20, 1933.

7. Walter Vosburgh, *Cherry and Black: The Career of Mr. Pierre Lorillard on the Turf* (printed for Pierre Lorillard, 1916), 76.

8. "At Old Monmouth," *New York World*, March 9, 1891; "Turf King: Fast Horses Bred in the Bitter Root," *Powder River Examiner* (Broadus, MT), November 18, 1921.

9. *Goodwin's 1890*, 504; "It's a Brilliant Finish," *New York World*, August 29, 1890.

10. *Goodwin's 1890*, 534–35; "Mr. Belmont's Great Prize," *New York Sun*, August 31, 1890.

11. "Head's Apart," *New York Evening World*, September 13, 1890; *Goodwin's 1890*, 557; "The Season's Winners," *Daily American* (Nashville), October 24, 1890; "Sporting," *Pittsburg (PA) Press*, December 2, 1890.

12. "Racing News and Notions," *New York Times*, March 16, 1891; "Racing News and Notions," *New York Times*, November 9, 1891.

13. *Goodwin's 1891*, 243; "Picknicker in the Lead," *New York Tribune*, June 6, 1891.

14. "The Belmont Foxford's," *New York Times*, June 11, 1891; *Goodwin's 1891*, 271.

15. "Belmont Foxford's."

16. "Mr. Daly Is a True Sportsman," *New York Sun*, June 13, 1891.

17. *Goodwin's 1891*, 327; "His Highness's Prize," *New York Sun*, June 30, 1891.

18. *Goodwin's 1891*, 331; "Potomac Won," *Brooklyn (NY) Daily Eagle*, July 2, 1891; "Daly's Big Offer," *Helena (MT) Independent*, July 10, 1891; "A Great Racing Year," *Topeka State Journal*, March 26, 1891; "The Closing Days," *Louisville (KY) Courier-Journal*, October 12, 1891.

19. "Montana Canters Home," *Chicago Tribune*, July 8, 1891.

20. *Goodwin's 1891*, 368; "Montana," *New York Evening World*, July 7, 1891.

21. *Goodwin's 1891*, 559–60, 702, 714, 748; "Rejoicing at Anaconda," *Spirit of the Times*, June 25, 1892, 945.

22. "Racing News and Notions," *New York Times*, November 9, 1891.

23. "Stable Gossip," *Boston Globe*, July 11, 1892.

24. "Jockey Garrison's Disgrace," *New York Evening World*, June 26, 1891; "'Snapper' Garrison to Be Reinstated," *Middletown (NY) Times-Press*, January 6, 1892; "Stars of the Turf," *Bremen (IN) Enquirer*, May 15, 1891; "News of the Week," *Champaign County News* (Champaign, IL), January 9, 1892.

25. Lyman Horace Weeks, *The American Turf: An Historical Account of Racing in the United States* (New York: 1898), 376; F. G. Smith, "'Snapper' Garrison," *Wallace's Monthly*, April 1893, 127; "Two Men Who Have Been Famous in the Turf World," *Lakin (KS) Investigator*, March 6, 1901; "'Snapper Garrison,' Famous Jockey, Dies of Heart Attack," *Democrat and Chronicle* (Rochester, NY), October 29, 1930.

26. William H. P. Robertson, *History of Thoroughbred Racing in America* (New York: Bonanza Books, 1964), 168; Smith, "'Snapper' Garrison," *Wallace's Monthly*, 127.

27. Smith, "'Snapper' Garrison," *Wallace's Monthly*, 127.

28. "Five Famous Jockeys," *St. Louis Post-Dispatch*, November 28, 1889; W. C. Vreeland, "Snapper Garrison, Daredevil Finisher, Greatest Jockey in U.S.A," *Brooklyn (NY) Daily Eagle*, October 29, 1930.

29. "'Snapper' Garrison as an Actor," *Inter Ocean* (Chicago), March 5, 1894; "Five Famous Jockeys."

30. Vreeland, "Snapper Garrison, Daredevil Finisher"; "Nubs of News," *Breeder's Gazette*, December 30, 1886, 990; "Snapper Garrison's Ways," *St. Louis Dispatch*, December 14, 1892. Tod Sloan popularized the crouched style of riding later known as the "monkey crouch" or "monkey on a stick."

31. For articles describing Garrison's riding style and close finishes, see "Speedy Fortunes," *St. Paul (MN) Globe*, July 23, 1893; "Snapper Garrison's Ways"; "Snapper Garrison," *Evening Star* (Washington, DC), August 6, 1892; "'Snapper' Garrison Noted Jockey, Dies in Hospital at 62," *Brooklyn (NY) Times Union*, October 28, 1930. The *Times Union* incorrectly states 1886 as the year of the Great Eastern Handicap with Dutch Roller.

32. Richard Sowers, *The Kentucky Derby, Preakness and Belmont Stakes: A Comprehensive History* (Jefferson, NC: McFarland, 2014), 42.

33. "Snapper Garrison," *Cincinnati Enquirer*, June 20, 1890; "Items and Inquires," *National Livestock Journal*, September 25, 1888, 614.

34. "Belmont, the Millionaire Turfman, Fires Snapper Garrison," *Record-Union* (Sacramento), September 20, 1889; "Six Races at Gravesend," *Chicago Tribune*, September 19, 1889; "Garrison Resigns," *St. Louis Dispatch*, September 25, 1889.

35. Weeks, *American Turf*, 376; "Is Jockey Garrison Broke?," *New York Sun*, January 2, 1890; "Walks about the City," *Brooklyn (NY) Daily Eagle*, August 3, 1890; "The Belmont Foxford's," *New York Times*, June 11, 1891; "General Sporting Miscellany," *Star-Gazette* (Elmira, NY), September 10, 1892; "Quarreled," *New York Evening World*, January 1, 1890; The US Census, 1900, Brooklyn Ward 31, Kings, New York, 7, and US Census, 1910, Brooklyn Ward 31, Kings, New York, 10, record Garrison's wife's name as Sadie. The US Census, 1920, Brooklyn Assembly District 21, Kings, New York, 4, records it as Sarah. The US Census, 1930, Brooklyn Assembly District 21, Kings, New York, 1B, records it as Anna. All four censuses accessed September 29, 2019, at HeritageQuest Online, https://www.heritagequestonline.com/hqoweb/library/do/login. Garrison's death certificate lists "Sarah" as the name of his wife.

36. "Snapper Garrison," *Evening Star* (Washington, DC), August 6, 1892; "Done to Defeat Union," *Chicago Tribune*, July 6, 1891; "Foot Ball and Calvinism," *Allentown (PA) Leader*, November 3, 1893; "Garrison as a Starter," *St. Louis Globe-Democrat*, December 3, 1893; "General Sporting Notes," *Indiana State Sentinel* (Indianapolis), January 7, 1891; "Mike Leonard Defeats Henry Mick in a Six Round Go," *Brooklyn (NY) Daily Eagle*, April 13, 1892; "Matters of Sporting Notes," *New York Evening World*, February 14, 1891; "A Bad Day for Favorites," *Gazette* (Montreal, Canada), August 25, 1890; "Snapper Garrison," *San Francisco Chronicle*, November 11, 1893.

37. "Snapper Garrison's Ways."

38. "The Riverside String," *Anaconda (MT) Standard*, April 21, 1892; *Goodwin's 1892*, 375–76.

39. "Montana," *New York Evening World*, June 18, 1892; "Garrison and Montana," *New York Times*, June 19, 1892; *Goodwin's 1892*, 414–15.

40. "Garrison and Montana"; "Post and Paddock," *Spirit of the Times*, June 25, 1892, 948; *Goodwin's 1892*, 414–15.

41. "The Suburban Handicap," *Live Stock Record*, June 24, 1892; "Garrison and Montana"; *Goodwin's 1892*, 414–15.

42. *Goodwin's 1892*, 414–15; "Garrison and Montana."

43. "Garrison and Montana"; "Suburban Day," *Illustrated American*, July 9, 1892, 359.

44. "When Marcus Daly's Crack Colt, Montana, Won the Suburban Handicap in Driving Finish," *Powder River Examiner* (Broadus, MT), October 28, 1921.

45. "Suburban Day," 359; "Garrison and Montana"; "Montana's Game Race," *Chicago Tribune*, June 19, 1892.

46. "Rejoicing at Anaconda," *Spirit of the Times*, June 25, 1892; "When Marcus Daly Was Turf King; Fast Horse Raised in Bitter Root," *Powder River Examiner* (Broadus, MT), November 18, 1921; C. B. Glasscock, *The War of the Copper Kings* (New York: Grosset and Dunlap, 1966), 163.

47. "The Turf," *New York Evening World*, June 29, 1892; "Garrison Very Ill," *Brooklyn (NY) Daily Eagle*, August 7, 1892.

48. *Goodwin's 1892*, cccv, 503, 619–20, 716, 719, 746, 754, 863–64, 889, 892; "Garrison Very Ill"; "Lamplighter," *New York Evening World*, August 31, 1892.

49. "Daly's Horses," *Quad-City Times* (Davenport, IA), December 8, 1892.

50. "Snapper Garrison's Ways"; "Montana Wins the 1892 Suburban," *Anaconda (MT) Standard*, May 21, 1911; "New York, Saturday, August 23, 1890," *Spirit of the Times*, August 23, 1890, 190; Peter Burnaugh, "Thoroughbred and Blackguards: Inside the Sordid World of Horse Racing," *Atlantic*, July 1925, accessed January 7, 2018, www.theatlantic.com.

51. "Gone East," *Bitter Root Times* (Hamilton, MT), March 18, 1893; "Montana, Marcus Daly's Famous Horse," *Bitter Root Times*, September 23, 1893; "Two Men Who Have Been Famous in the Turf World."

52. "Marcus Daly's Racers," *Daily Independent* (Helena, MT), December 26, 1892.

53. Glasscock, *War of the Copper Kings*, 163–64.

54. "Turf King"; *Thoroughbred Stock*, Bitter Root Stock Farm catalogue, September 1896, archives, Daly Mansion, 15; "Marcus Daly's Investments," *Salt Lake Tribune*, January 16, 1893; "Tammany at His Home," *Anaconda (MT) Standard*, July 10, 1897.

55. "Horses at Auction," *Los Angeles Times*, December 30, 1900.

56. "Rancho Del Paso Stud Sale," *Thoroughbred Record*, October 28, 1905, 274; "Montana," *Great Dispersal Sale of the Entire World-Renowned Rancho Del Paso Thoroughbred Stud*, accessed April 13, 2019; https://www.google.com/books/edition/Great_Dispersal_Sale_of_the_Entire_World/NooCAAAAYAAJ?hl=en&gbpv=1; "Stallion Watercress Is Sold for $71,000," *New York Times*, December 8, 1905.

57. "When Marcus Daly's Crack Colt, Montana, Won the Suburban Handicap in Driving Finish," *Powder River Examiner* (Broadus, MT), October 28, 1921.

Chapter 12

1. "Tammany Is King," *New York World*, September 29, 1893.

2. "Turf King: Fast Horses Bred in the Bitter Root," *Powder River Examiner* (Broadus, MT), November 18, 1921.

3. "Tullahoma," *ASB*, vol. 6, 1025; "Iroquois," *ASB*, vol. 4, 320; "Tammany," *Dispersal Sale of the Entire Bitter Root Stud*, no. 3 (New York: Fasig-Tipton, 1901).

4. "Tammany," *Index: Thoroughbred Stock*; "The Belle Meade Sale," *Daily American* (Nashville), April 25, 1890. The Salt Lake City *Deseret Weekly* quotes Marcus Daly as saying he paid $10,000 for Tammany, but all other sources state $2,500. See "The Copper King," *Deseret Weekly*, May 13, 1893, 658.

5. "Tammany's Big Winning," *Anaconda (MT) Standard*, June 10, 1891; *Goodwin's 1891*, 244; "Tammany Wins at Racing," *New York Times*, June 7, 1891; "Tammany at Westchester," *New York Tribune*, June 7, 1891; "And Tammany Won," *Anaconda Standard*, July 3, 1892.

6. "Tammany's Big Winning"; *Goodwin's 1891*, 244; "Tammany at Westchester." The jockey George Miller who is mentioned in chapter 12 is not the same George Miller mentioned in chapter 1.

7. "Tammany Wins at Racing"; *Goodwin's 1891*, 244; "Photographing Finishes," *Rocky Mountain Husbandman*, March 24, 1892; Mary Karmelek, "Winning in a Snap: A History of Photo Finishes and Horse Racing, *Scientific American*, May 7, 2013, accessed October 1, 2022, https://blogs.scientificamerican.com /anecdotes-from-the-archive/winning-in-a-snap-a-history-of-photo-finishes -and-horse-racing.

8. *Goodwin's 1891*, 327–28, 497, 559; "Rey Del Rey the Winner," *New York Times*, August 19, 1891; "Rey Del Rey's Race," *Inter Ocean* (Chicago), August 19, 1891.

9. "Rey Del Rey," *New York Evening World*, August 18, 1891; *Goodwin's 1891*, 559.

10. "Rey Del Rey's Race"; *Goodwin's 1891*, 559; "Montana Turfman," *Great Falls (MT) Tribune*, June 24, 1892.

11. "Racing News and Notions," *New York Times*, November 9, 1891; "Pike Barnes near Death," *Buffalo (NY) Times*, June 29, 1905; "Jockey Pike Barnes Dead," *Washington Post*, January 11, 1908.

12. *Goodwin's 1891*, 562–63, 596–97.

13. "Winnings of Great Horses in 1891," *Tribune Almanac and Political Register for 1892*, 240, accessed November 11, 2022, https://books.google.com; W. C. Vreeland, "Purchase of Rancocas Brings Old Times to Mind," *Brooklyn (NY) Daily Eagle*, March 14, 1920; "Leading Winning Owners in 1891," *Tribune Almanac and Political Register for 1892*, 240; Francis Trevelyan, "The Status of the American Turf," *Outing*, April 1892, 39.

14. Lyman Horace Weeks, *The American Turf: An Historical Account of Racing in the United States* (New York: 1898), 301; "Rejoicing at Anaconda," *Spirit of the Times*, June 25, 1892; "Death Comes to Matthew Byrnes," *Thoroughbred Record*, March 25, 1933; "Jacob Pincus," *Thoroughbred Record*, May 4, 1918, 252; "Another American Outfit," *Baltimore Sun*, January 5, 1903; "Chestnut Grove Sold," *Red Bank (NJ) Register*, December 22, 1920.

15. Weeks, *American Turf*, 301; Walter Vosburgh, *Cherry and Black: The Career of Mr. Pierre Lorillard on the Turf* (printed for Pierre Lorillard, 1916), 73.

16. "Tammany at His Home," *Anaconda (MT) Standard,* July 10, 1897; "Sporting," *Los Angeles Daily Times,* March 1, 1897; Vosburgh, *Cherry and Black,* 74, 122, 124–25; "Rightful Place," *Thoroughbred Times,* August 6, 2011.

17. Vosburgh, *Cherry and Black,* 114.

18. "Why Stakes Are Reduced," *Brooklyn (NY) Daily Eagle,* January 2, 1898; "Post and Paddock," *Spirit of the Times,* August 30, 1890, 226.

19. "The Riverside String," *Anaconda (MT) Standard,* April 21, 1892; "Bishop Hero a Winner," *Helena (MT) Independent,* October 26, 1893; *Goodwin's 1892,* 334; "Tammany Won the Withers," *New York Tribune,* June 5, 1892.

20. *Goodwin's 1892,* 420; "Upsets in a Series," *New York Tribune,* June 24, 1892.

21. *Goodwin's 1892,* 463–64; "News of the Horse World," *Buffalo (NY) Commercial,* July 1, 1892; "And Tammany Won."

22. "Tammany's Realization," *New York Tribune,* July 3, 1892.

23. "Tammany's Realization"; "Copper and Green Win," *Anaconda (MT) Standard,* July 3, 1892.

24. *Goodwin's 1892,* ccxxv, 507.

25. "Women on the Turf," *Inter Ocean* (Chicago), August 17, 1891.

26. *Goodwin's 1892,* 872; "Tammany Wins Once More," *New York Times,* October 9, 1892; "Fought Every Inch," *San Francisco Chronicle,* October 9, 1892.

27. "Winnings of Great Horses in 1892," *Tribune Almanac and Political Register for 1893,* 242, https://books.google.com; "Leading Winning Owners in 1892," *Tribune Almanac and Political Register for 1893,* 241; "A Grand Tammany Ball," *Anaconda (MT) Standard,* December 3, 1892.

28. "Daly's Horses," *Quad-City Times* (Davenport, IA), December 8, 1892.

29. "Gone East," *Bitter Root Times* (Hamilton, MT), March 18, 1893; "Bitter Root Oats Did It," *Anaconda (MT) Standard,* October 7, 1893.

30. "Daly's Great String," *Chicago Tribune,* March 16, 1893; "On Short-Distance Horses," *Inter Ocean* (Chicago), March 18, 1893; "Notes," *Helena (MT) Independent,* June 21, 1891; Ada Powell, *Copper, Green and Silver* (privately printed, 1993), 104; "Horse Car That Cost $40,000," *Dollar Weekly News* (Wilkes-Barre, PA), July 12, 1902; Frank G. Carpenter, "The Copper King," *Deseret Weekly* (Salt Lake City), May 13, 1893, 658; "Death of Marcus Daly," *New York Times,* November 13, 1900; Ada Powell, *The Dalys of the Bitter Root* (privately printed, 1989), 81.

31. "Tammany in a Bad Way," *Evening Star* (Washington, DC), June 14, 1893; Vreeland, "Purchase of Rancocas."

32. "Salvator, Tammany, Grady," *Anaconda (MT) Standard,* February 4, 1894.

33. "Lamplighter for $20,000," *New York Evening World,* September 7, 1893; "Tammany Is King"; "Torchlight," *ASB,* vol. 6, 121.

34. *Goodwin's 1893,* vol. 1, 331; "Talk of the Turf," *New York Evening World,* September 15, 1893. Newspaper reports about the sequence of events that transpired between Byrnes, Newton, and Walbaum vary. For examples, see "Tammany

Is in Fine Form," *New York Tribune*, September 15, 1893; "Rudolph Shows His Form," *New York Sun*, September 15, 1893; "Sporting World," *Brooklyn (NY) Citizen*, September 15, 1893.

35. "Highland Wins Well," *Chicago Tribune*, September 17, 1893; *Goodwin's 1893*, vol. 2, 333; "The Crowd and the Sport Poor," *New York Tribune*, September 17, 1893; "Talk of the Turf," *New York Evening World*, September 15, 1893.

36. "Tammany and Lamplighter," *Brooklyn (NY) Daily Eagle*, September 16, 1893; *Goodwin's 1893*, vol. 2, 463. Newspaper accounts of the day frequently spelled the name "Guttenburg," but *Goodwin's Turf Guide* spelled it "Guttenberg."

37. *Goodwin's 1891*, 562, 596; "Tammany Is in Fine Form"; *Goodwin's 1893*, 367.

38. "Thursday's Big Match," *New York Tribune*, September 25, 1893; "Tammany, King of the Turf," *New York Sun*, September 29, 1893; Vosburgh, *Cherry and Black*, 145.

39. "The Lamplighter-Tammany Match," *New York Tribune*, September 18, 1893; "A Trainer's Notes on the Turf," *New York Tribune*, September 23, 1893. At the time, 1893, it was illegal for jockeys to bet on a horse race at racetracks operating under the Board of Control. See "The Turf," *Tribune Almanac and Political Register for 1892*, 238, accessed November 11, 2022, https://www.google.com/books/edition /The_Tribune_Almanac_and_Political_Regist/nhwXAAAAYAAJ?hl=en&gbpv =1&dq=An+order+by+the+Board+of+Control+that+jockeys+should+not+bet &pg=RA2-PA238&printsec=frontcover. Garrison stated in "A Trainer's Notes on the Turf" that he could legally bet on the match race since Guttenberg did not operate under the rules of the Board of Control.

40. Steven A. Riess, *The Sport of Kings and the Kings of Crime: Horse Racing, Politics, and Organized Crime in New York, 1865–1913* (Syracuse, NY: Syracuse University Press, 2011), 107, 109–10; William H. P. Robertson, *History of Thoroughbred Racing in America* (New York: Bonanza Books, 1964), 194; "Among the Horsemen," *Brooklyn (NY) Daily Eagle*, September 18, 1893.

41. "Tammany Is King"; Riess, *Sport of Kings*, 108, 110; "Hudson County's Degradation," *New York Times*, November 4, 1893; "Tammany Shows Up Lamplighter," *Anaconda (MT) Standard*, June 18, 1911.

42. "Hudson County's Degradation"; "Daly, the Copper King," *Cambridge City (IN) Tribune*, January 3, 1901; Robertson, *History of Thoroughbred Racing*, 194.

43. "Lamplighter's Speedy Trial Spin," *New York Tribune*, September 27, 1893; "Gravesend's Dull Sport," *New York Tribune*, September 27, 1893; "Salvator, Tammany, Grady."

44. "Tammany, King of the Turf"; "Tammany the Winner," *Morning Post* (Camden, NJ), September 29, 1893; "Lamplighter Defeated by Tammany," *Illustrated American*, October 14, 1893, 475.

45. "Tammany Is King."

46. "Tammany, King of the Turf"; "Tammany Wins the Race," *New York Tribune*, September 29, 1893.

47. "Tammany Wins the Race"; Powell, *Dalys of the Bitter Root*, 44.
48. "Tammany Is King"; "Talks with Racing Men," *New York Tribune*, September 29, 1893; "Tammany Wins the Race."
49. "Tammany Is King."
50. "Easy for Tammany," *Helena (MT) Independent*, September 29, 1893; "Tammany the Winner"; "Tammany Is King"; *Goodwin's 1893*, vol. 2, 463. The article "Easy for Tammany" states that Garrison "cut Tammany ruthlessly," whereas "Tammany Is King" states, "Garrison does not have to raise his whip or lift his spur."
51. "Tammany Shows Up Lamplighter"; Tammany Wins the Race"; "Gossip of the Turf," *New York Evening World*, September 29, 1893; "Tammany the Peer," *Boston Post*, October 1, 1893.
52. "Gossip of the Turf"; "Tammany at His Home," *Anaconda (MT) Standard*, July 10, 1897; "Tammany Is King."
53. "Talks with Racing Men."
54. "Talks with Racing Men"; George S. Klotz, "Sportsman Tells of Famous Horses in Daly Stable and Betting Coup," *Helena (MT) Daily Independent*, March 26, 1933.
55. "Talks with Racing Men"; "Tammany Shows Up Lamplighter."
56. "Cheering Tammany's Victory," *Anaconda (MT) Standard*, September 29, 1893; "Bitter Root Oats Did It"; "Gossip of the Turf," *New York Evening World*, September 29, 1893.
57. "Tammany's Withdrawal," *Butte (MT) Miner*, October 19, 1893; "Lamplighter and Tammany," *San Francisco Chronicle*, September 30, 1893; "Gossip of the Turf," *New York Evening World*, October 9, 1893.
58. "Great Money Winners," *Daily Racing Form* (Chicago), November 22, 1906.
59. "Daly's Racers Coming," *Helena (MT) Daily Independent*, October 6, 1893; "Tammany Sick," *Yellowstone Journal* (Miles City, MT), October 18, 1893; "Montana State News," *Daily Inter Mountain* (Butte, MT), October 3, 1893; "Turf King."
60. "Death of Snapper Garrison," *Blood-Horse*, November 8, 1930, 1323; "Snapper Garrison, Noted Jockey, Dies," *Brooklyn (NY) Daily Eagle*, October 28, 1930; John H. Davis, *The American Turf: History of the Thoroughbred, Together with Personal Reminiscences by the Author, Who, in Turn, Has Been Jockey, Trainer and Owner* (New York: John Polhemus, 1907), 103.
61. "Death of Snapper Garrison"; "Tammany Shows Up Lamplighter."
62. "'Snapper' Garrison Noted Jockey, Dies in Hospital at 62," *Brooklyn (NY) Times Union*, October 28, 1930; "Snapper Garrison Left His Widow Only $1,000," *Brooklyn (NY) Daily Eagle*, November 4, 1930; "Requital Won the Prize," *New York Times*, July 12, 1896; "Garrison, Edward H.," Standard Certificate of Death, Department of Health of the City of New York, October 28, 1930. The death certificate does not record a date of birth but gives his age as sixty-one. Lyman

Horace Weeks notes Garrison's birth date as February 6, 1868, in his book *The American Turf* (376). Some newspaper accounts state that his death was heart-related.

63. "Snapper Garrison Recalls Famous and Exciting Finishes," *Ottawa (ON) Journal*, November 22, 1919; "How Lucky Baldwin Was Always Lucky," *Anaconda (MT) Standard*, June 4, 1911.

64. "Copper King's Paradise," *Daily Republican* (Monongahela, PA), March 6, 1900; "Sam Lucas, Gentleman," *Anaconda (MT) Standard*, January 28, 1900.

65. "Daly's Future Home," *Tacoma (WA) Daily Ledger,* February 4, 1906; Beth Wohlberg, "Marcus Daly's Famous Racers to Join the Ponies on a Carousel," *Missoulian* (Missoula, MT), October 24, 1999; Harriet Miller and Elizabeth Harrison, "Marcus Daly's Western Champions," *Western Horseman*, March 1958; Gregory Daschle, "For the Love of Tammany," *Spur*, January–February 1986, 62; Ellen Baumler, "Montana State Fairgrounds Racetrack," National Register of Historic Places Registration Form, section 8, p. 4, SHPO; Helen Clark, "Lonely Grave Contains Remains of Two Colorful Sports Figures," *Great Falls (MT) Tribune*, September 18, 1966.

66. "An Outsider's View," *Anaconda (MT) Standard*, January 18, 1893; "In the World of Sports," *St. Louis Globe-Democrat*, December 18, 1893; "About the City," *Anaconda Standard*, May 12, 1897; H. Minar Shoebotham, *Anaconda: Life of Marcus Daly, the Copper King* (Harrisburg, PA: Stackpole, 1956), 161–62.

67. "Hamilton Happenings," *Anaconda (MT) Standard*, November 22, 1899; "Milton Young Buys Lamplighter," *Thoroughbred Record*, September 7, 1895; Robertson, *History of Thoroughbred Racing*, 145–46; Vosburgh, *Racing in America*, 158.

68. Thomas B. Merry, *The American Thoroughbred* (Los Angeles: Commercial Printing House, 1905), 125; "Horse Lamplighter," *Muncie (IN) Evening Press*, November 29, 1907.

Chapter 13

1. "Imported Stock Here," *New York Sun*, October 2, 1894; "All from England," *Great Falls (MT) Tribune*, October 7, 1894. The *Great Falls Tribune* article lists ten mares purchased by Marcus Daly.

2. "Marcus Daly's Lot Goes West," *Chicago Tribune*, October 25, 1894. The *Chicago Tribune* states that twelve mares were purchased. Joe H. Palmer, *Names in Pedigrees* (Lexington: The Blood-Horse, 1939), 413.

3. "Oriole," *Index: Thoroughbred Stock*; "Ogden," *Index: Thoroughbred Stock*.

4. Betsy Baxter, archives technician, Keeneland Library, email message to author, June 25, 2013. *General Stud Book*, v. 17, August 1892, 453, 880.

5. Palmer, *Names in Pedigrees*, 419; "Blood That Tells," *Anaconda (MT) Standard*, January 1, 1897; George S. Klotz, "Marcus Daly's Great Coup When Ogden Won the Futurity at Sheepshead Bay," *Great Falls (MT) Tribune*, February 24, 1907.

6. "Ogden's Big Surprise," *New York Sun*, August 16, 1896; "Butterflies or Waltzer?," *New York World*, August 25, 1894.

7. "Campbell Again Shows in Front," *New York Journal*, August 17, 1896; "Won with a Dog in His Foot," *Buffalo (NY) Enquirer*, January 5, 1904.

8. Klotz, "Marcus Daly's Great Coup"; "Blue Wing's Gossip," *Daily American* (Nashville), May 20, 1889.

9. "Going to California," *Anaconda (MT) Standard*, July 28, 1897.

10. "Off for Anaconda," *Ravalli Republican* (Hamilton, MT), May 6, 1896; "All's in Good Shape," *Anaconda (MT) Standard*, June 29, 1896; Matt J. Kelly, *Anaconda: Montana's Copper City* (Anaconda, MT: Soroptimist Club, 1983), 32.

11. "All's in Good Shape"; "Big Crowds in Town," *Anaconda (MT) Standard*, June 30, 1896; "On the Opening Day," *Anaconda Standard*, July 1, 1896; "Track Notes," *Anaconda Standard*, July 1, 1896.

12. "On the Opening Day"; *Goodwin's 1896*, vol. 2, 278.

13. "Rare Royal Racing," *Anaconda (MT) Standard*, July 5, 1896; *Goodwin's 1896*, vol. 2, 279–80; "Off of a Hay Cart," *Anaconda Standard*, July 10, 1896.

14. "Turf Matters at Butte," *Butte (MT) Weekly Miner*, August 20, 1878; "Minor Items," *Daily Miner* (Butte, MT), August 31, 1879; "On a Suit against the West Side Racing Association," *Butte (MT) Miner*, December 10, 1895; "Articles of Incorporation," Abstract of Title to the Daly Addition to the City of Butte, 11, Butte–Silver Bow Archives, Butte, MT.

15. Richard Gibson, "Daly Played Big Part in Butte's Racing Scene," *Montana Standard* (Butte), July 4, 2016; "Goodwin's Western Turf Notes No. 7," *Turf, Field and Farm*, July 2, 1897; "Season Opens at Butte," *Butte (MT) Miner*, July 21, 1896; "The Montana Racing Circuit," *Thoroughbred Record*, March 20, 1897.

16. C. B. Glasscock, *The War of the Copper Kings* (New York: Grosset and Dunlap, 1966), 165.

17. "Butte's Place in the Athletic World," *Anaconda (MT) Standard*, December 20, 1896; "Montana and Its Racing," *Daily Racing Form* (Chicago), September 12, 1896; "Goodwin's Western Turf Notes No. 7"; Workers of the Writers' Program of the Work Projects Administration in the State of Montana, *Copper Camp: Stories of the World's Greatest Mining Town, Butte, Montana* (New York: Hastings House, 1944), 131; Glasscock, *War of the Copper Kings*, 162; H. Minar Shoebotham, *Anaconda: Life of Marcus Daly Copper King* (Harrisburg, PA: Stackpole, 1956), 147.

18. "Season Opens at Butte."

19. "Season Opens at Butte"; *Goodwin's 1896*, vol. 2, 311; "Butte's Place in the Athletic World."

20. Untitled article, see "The Montana Racing Circuit . . . ," first column, *Rocky Mountain Husbandman*, August 17, 1882; "Montana Racing Circuit," *Rocky Mountain Husbandman*, January 6, 1891; "Meeting West Side Racing Association," *Butte (MT) Weekly Miner*, December 15, 1886; *Goodwin's 1896*, vol. 2, cclxxiv; Shoebotham, *Anaconda*, 163.

21. George S. Klotz, "Marcus Daly's Part in American Turf History," *Anaconda (MT) Standard*, January 18, 1920.

22. Walter S. Vosburgh, *Racing in America, 1866–1921* (New York: Scribner Press, 1922), 168; *Goodwin's 1896*, vol. 2, 251.

23. "Ogden's Race and Victory Referred To," *Anaconda (MT) Standard*, August 4, 1907.

24. "Ogden's Race and Victory."

25. The article "Ogden's Big Surprise," *New York Sun*, August 16, 1896, states that Johnny Campbell and Marcus Daly figured Ogden as a possible ringer in the Futurity, and with that race in mind, they purposely orchestrated Ogden's two losses at Anaconda to relieve him of a high weight penalty in the Futurity. Hugh Wilson's firsthand account is the wrinkle in the *Sun's* claim. His 1907 retelling of Ogden's trip to the Futurity, "Ogden's Race and Victory Referred To," makes no mention of Campbell and Daly as conspirators of a betting coup. Wilson was a close friend of Daly's and reportedly had influence over him. It would seem that Wilson, as an influential friend, would have imparted information about Daly and Campbell if the conspired coup was fact. As it was, Ogden's impost of 115 pounds for the Futurity was three pounds less than the high-weight 118-pound impost he carried in two of his Anaconda races.

26. "Livingston News," *Anaconda (MT) Standard*, July 29, 1896; Palmer, *Names in Pedigrees*, 415.

27. Klotz, "Marcus Daly's Great Coup"; "Story of the Race," *Anaconda (MT) Standard,* August 21, 1896.

28. "M'Coy Is a Great Man," *Anaconda (MT) Standard*, March 31, 1899; "Requital a Crackerjack," *Morning Times* (Washington, DC), August 24, 1896; "San Blas 100 to 1," *Cincinnati Enquirer*, June 7, 1895; "Tuberville under Ban," *St. Louis Post-Dispatch*, August 10, 1895; "Track Talk," *St. Louis Post-Dispatch*, August 17, 1895; "Ogden's Big Surprise."

29. Klotz, "Marcus Daly's Great Coup."

30. Glasscock, *War of the Copper Kings*, 162; W. C. Vreeland, "Purchase of Rancocas Brings Old Times to Mind," *Brooklyn (NY) Daily Eagle*, March 14, 1920; George S. Klotz, "Sportsman Tells of Famous Horses," *Helena (MT) Independent*, March 26, 1933.

31. "Ogden's Futurity," *New York World*, August 16, 1896; "Ogden Wins a Futurity," *New York Times*, August 16, 1896. "Won by Ogden," *Altoona (PA) Tribune*, August 17, 1896, states a crowd size of twelve thousand.

32. *Goodwin's 1896*, vol. 2, 251; "Ogden Wins a Futurity"; "Ogden's Big Surprise."

33. *Goodwin's 1896*, vol. 2, 251; "Ogden Wins a Futurity."

34. "Ogden's Big Surprise"; "Marcus Daly's Great Coup."

35. "Another Account of the Race," *Anaconda (MT) Standard*, August 16, 1896; "Ogden's Big Surprise"; "Ogden Wins a Futurity"; *Goodwin's 1896*, vol. 2, 251. Newspaper reports vary as to post positions for the Futurity.

36. "Ogden the Westerner, First" *New York Journal*, August 16, 1896; Klotz, "Marcus Daly's Great Coup."

37. *Goodwin's 1896*, vol. 2, 251; "Ogden's Big Surprise"; "Ogden the Westerner, First"; "Ogden Wins a Futurity."

38. "Talk about Turf Affairs," *New York Tribune*, August 17, 1896; *Goodwin's 1896*, vol. 2, 251; Klotz, "Sportsman Tells of Famous Horses"; "Story of the Race"; "Marcus Daly's Great Coup."

39. "Ogden the Westerner, First"; "Campbell Again Shows in Front."

40. "Ended with a Flourish," *Butte (MT) Miner*, August 16, 1896; "Ogden's Race and Victory"; "Great Is Montana Grass," *Anaconda (MT) Standard*, September 12, 1896.

41. "Ornament's Flatbush," *New York Sun*, August 30, 1896; *Goodwin's 1896*, vol. 2, 287; Victorine, ASB, v. 7, 1070; "Requital Won the Prize," *New York Times*, July 12, 1896; "Ogden's Big Surprise"; Klotz, "Marcus Daly's Great Coup"; "The Futurity Field for Saturday," *Detroit Free Press*, August 12, 1896.

42. "Ogden's Great Eastern," *New York Sun*, September 6, 1896; "Ornament Beats Ogden," *New York World*, August 30, 1896; "Honor to the West," *Anaconda (MT) Standard*, August 16, 1896.

43. *Goodwin's 1896*, vol. 2, 293; "Ogden's Great Eastern."

44. "West Ahead of East," *Anaconda (MT) Standard*, January 11, 1897; *Thoroughbred Stock* sale catalogue, September 1896, 65; "A Painting of Ogden," *Anaconda (MT) Recorder*, May 19, 1897.

45. "Doc Tuberville Is Off for Life," *San Francisco Examiner*, July 13, 1897; "M'Coy Is a Great Man"; "Persons Ruled Off," *Daily Racing Form* (Chicago), September 23, 1899.

46. "Judges Regard Riding with Suspicious Eye," *Daily Inter Mountain* (Butte, MT), July 29, 1902; "Old-Time Jockey," *Cincinnati Enquirer*, October 14, 1908; "Friendless Jockey Dies Hugging Whip He Used in Big Race," *Vancouver (BC) Daily World*, October 30, 1908.

47. "Horse Talk," *Anaconda (MT) Standard*, October 14, 1896; "Gossip of the Turf," *San Francisco Chronicle*, February 13, 1897; "A Defeat for Ogden," *New York Sun*, May 16, 1897; Francis Trevelyan, "Gossip of the Turf," *New York Journal*, May 17, 1897.

48. "Octagon Won the Withers," *New York Times*, May 16, 1897.

49. "Big Three Year Old Race," *Brooklyn (NY) Daily Eagle*, May 15, 1897; "A Defeat for Ogden"; "Ogden Is Defeated by Octagon," *Chicago Tribune*, May 16, 1897; *Goodwin's 1897*, vol. 1, 289–90.

50. "Ogden Is Defeated by Octagon"; "Octagon Won the Withers"; *Goodwin's 1897*, vol. 1, 289–90.

51. "A Defeat for Ogden"; *Goodwin's 1897*, vol. 1, 290, 366–67, 443; "Ogden's Defeat," *Daily Inter Mountain* (Butte, MT), May 12, 1897; "Octagon Won the Withers"; "Montana Has the Belmont," *New York Tribune*, May 30, 1897.

52. "Senator Bland," *Anaconda (MT) Standard*, September 15, 1897; "Devotee of the Turf," *Butte (MT) Miner*, September 15, 1897; "Gossip of the Montana Races," *San Francisco Call*, September 11, 1898; "Gossip of the Runners," *Buffalo (NY)*

Evening News, October 3, 1902. "Horse Notes," *Daily Inter Mountain* (Butte, MT), November 16, 1897, states that Johnny Campbell managed Daly's "Anaconda ranch." Adding more confusion to Campbell's status with Daly is "Do Fast Work at Gravesend," *Chicago Tribune*, March 12, 1898, stating that Campbell "will handle Mr. Daly's Northwestern string," but the author's research showed that Campbell trained for Frank in 1898. See "On the Track," *Anaconda (MT) Standard,* June 6, 1898. The author was unable to ascertain where and when Johnny Campbell died.

53. "Marcus Daly and Some of His Horses," *Boston Globe*, January 31, 1898; "William Lakeland," NMRHF, accessed July 10, 2018, https://www.racingmuseum.org /hall-of-fame/trainer/william-lakeland.

54. *Goodwin's 1898*, vol. 1, 443.

55. *Goodwin's 1898*, vol. 1, 451–52, 580; "Historical, and Costly Kicking Match," *Brooklyn (NY) Citizen*, June 19, 1898.

56. *Goodwin's 1898*, vol. 2, 1, 5, 77, 168, 203; "Won in a Hard Drive," *Philadelphia Inquirer*, July 3, 1898.

57. "Gossip of the Montana Racers"; "Hamilton Happenings," *Ravalli Republican* (Stevensville, MT), September 7, 1898; "Hamilton Happenings," *Ravalli Republican*, October 12, 1898; "W. C. Whitney Buys Hamburg," *Spirit of the Times*, February 2, 1901, 72.

58. "Sale of Hamburg Get Occurs on May 24," *Anaconda (MT) Standard*, May 10, 1901; "Big Handicap, Banastar's," *New York Tribune*, May 5, 1901; *Goodwin's 1901*, vol. 1, 438; "Favorites Lost in Mud," *New York Times,* August 1, 1901.

59. *Goodwin's 1901*, vol. 2, 152, 182–83, 185, 190, 346, 438.

60. *Goodwin's 1901*, vol. 2, 348, 350; "Ogden Was Twice Winner," *New York Times*, September 3, 1901.

61. "Ogden Was Twice Winner."

62. "Ogden Was Twice Winner"; "Old Ogden's Double Victory," *New York Sun*, September 3, 1901.

63. *Goodwin's 1901*, vol. 2, 473; "Favorites Beaten, Ring Is Hard Hit," *Brooklyn (NY) Daily Eagle*, September 28, 1901.

64. "Madden Buys Ogden," *Louisville (KY) Courier-Journal*, December 17, 1901; Palmer, *Names in Pedigrees*, 412; Edward L. Bowen, "Ornament," *Blood-Horse*, July 23, 1973, 2674. Bowen states on page 2673 that Ornament made thirty-four starts, and on page 2674 states thirty-two starts.

65. Palmer, *Names in Pedigrees*, 419–20; "Madden Buys Veil to Mate with Ogden," *San Francisco Call*, January 21, 1909; "Lady Sterling," *ASB*, vol. 10 (New York: Jockey Club, 1910), 599; "Crack Racers," *Cincinnati Enquirer*, December 21, 1908.

66. "Livonia," *ASB*, vol. 11 (New York: Jockey Club, 1914), 352.

67. "Ogden a Successful Sire," *Daily Racing Form* (Chicago), February 7, 1923, 11; William H. P. Robertson, *History of Thoroughbred Racing in America* (New York: Bonanza Books, 1964), 208; Palmer, *Names in Pedigrees*, 420; "John E. Madden," NMRHF, accessed December 15, 2018, https://www.racingmuseum

.org/hall-of-fame/trainer/john-e-madden; "John E. Madden," Harness Racing Museum and Hall of Fame, accessed December 15, 2018, https://harnessmuseum .com/content/john-e-madden.

Chapter 14

1. "The Chieftain," *Western News* (Hamilton, MT), June 2, 1897.
2. "Sam Lucas, Gentleman," *Anaconda (MT) Standard*, January 28, 1900; William H. P. Robertson, *History of Thoroughbred Racing in America* (New York: Bonanza Books, 1964), 76–77; J. Keeler Johnson, "Lexington: Great Racehorse, Outstanding Sire," April 16, 2020, America's Best Racing, https://www .americasbestracing.net/the-sport/2020-lexington-great-racehorse-outstanding -sire.
3. "Sam Lucas, Gentleman"; Lyman Horace Weeks, *The American Turf: An Historical Account of Racing in the United States* (New York: 1898), 222; "St. Blaise for Mr. Belmont," *Baltimore Sun*, October 13, 1885. The original Nursery Stud, founded by August Belmont I, was located on Long Island, New York. According to turf historian Edward L. Bowen in his book *Legacies of the Turf: A Century of Great Thoroughbred Breeders*, vol. 1 (Lexington: Blood-Horse Publications, 2003), 40, Belmont I became convinced of Kentucky's soil, climate, and other advantages and reestablished the Nursery Stud near Lexington in 1885. "Trainer of Daly Racing Stars Is Called to Death," *Montana Standard* (Butte), March 29, 1929.
4. J. Keeler Johnson, "August Belmont II: The Man Who Bred Man o' War," *The Sport*, June 4, 2018, https://www.americasbestracing.net/the-sport; Robertson, *History of Thoroughbred Racing*, 104.
5. "Turf King: Fast Horses Bred in the Bitter Root," *Powder River Examiner* (Broadus, MT), November 18, 1921; "The Turf," *Stock-Farm* (Lexington, KY), November 12, 1885.
6. "Mr. Belmont's Great Prize," *New York Sun*, August 31, 1890; "Belmont's St. Blaise Dead," *New York Times*, October 16, 1909. St. Blaise came under a series of owners after Belmont I, including Charles Reed, J. B. Haggin, and August Belmont II, who returned St. Blaise to the Nursery Stud at Lexington, where the stallion died.
7. "Turf King."
8. "Daly's Future Home," *Tacoma Daily Ledger*, February 4, 1900; "Flags and Ballots," *Anaconda (MT) Standard*, November 2, 1896.
9. "Sam Lucas, Gentleman."
10. "Miss Darebin," *Index: Thoroughbred Stock*; "Inverness," *Index: Thoroughbred Stock*; "Inverness," *Dispersal Sale of the Entire Bitter Root Stud*, No. 2; "In the Field of Sport," *Anaconda (MT) Standard*, November 23, 1890; "Blood That Tells," *Anaconda Standard*, January 1, 1897; "Scottish Chieftain," *Index: Thoroughbred Stock*; "Miss Darebin," *ASB*, vol. 7, 712.
11. "Daly Employs Taral," *Buffalo (NY) Evening News*, February 5, 1898; "Daly's Big Offer," *Helena (MT) Independent*, July 10, 1891; "Potomac Won," *Brooklyn (NY) Daily Eagle*, July 2, 1891.

12. *Goodwin's 1896*, vol. 1, 297, 358; *Goodwin's 1896*, vol. 2, 2, 6, 8, 10–13, 209, 251; "The Turf," *Standard Union* (Brooklyn, NY), August 14, 1896.

13. "Gossip About the Sports," *Brooklyn (NY) Daily Times,* December 5, 1896; "The Coming of George Dixon," *Scranton (PA) Tribune,* November 15, 1894; "How Some Jockeys Train," *New York Sun,* May 4, 1896; "Pugilistic Points," *Detroit Free Press,* March 11, 1899; "Current Sport Chat," *Illustrated Buffalo (NY) Express,* March 25, 1900; "Speedy Fortunes," *St. Paul (MN) Globe,* July 23, 1893. The article "A Famous Jockey," *Buffalo (NY) Courier,* November 15, 1894, states that Taral "never gambles."

14. Weeks, *American Turf,* 374.

15. "Fred Taral," NMRHF, accessed July 4, 2018, https://www.racingmuseum.org /hall-of-fame/jockey/fred-taral; "Anything Goes in the Bush," *Sports Illustrated,* October 31, 1966, accessed December 14, 2023, https://vault.si.com/vault/1966 /10/31/anything-goes-in-the-bush.

16. "Shooting at a Horse Race," *Cheyenne Transporter* (Darlington, OK), April 15, 1885.

17. "Jockey Fred Taral," *Burlington (VT) Free Press,* March 10, 1891; *Goodwin's 1886,* 216. Another version of Taral's early years on racetracks appears in "Greatest of Jockeys," *Buffalo (NY) Courier,* January 1, 1896. The article puts Taral in Louisville in 1877, hired as an exercise rider for "Mr. Labold" and under the tutelage of trainer John McGinty. Taral would have been ten years old.

18. "How Jockeys Ride and Win," *Philadelphia Inquirer,* September 13, 1896.

19. Robertson, *History of Thoroughbred Racing,* 167; "How Jockeys Ride and Win."

20. Peter Burnaugh, "Thoroughbred and Blackguards: Inside the Sordid World of Horse Racing," *Atlantic,* July 1925; Kent Hollingsworth, *The Kentucky Thoroughbred* (Lexington: University Press of Kentucky, 2011), 68; "Views of a Jockey, Fred Taral Writes of Horses and Their Riders," *Logansport (IN) Pharos-Tribune,* May 6, 1896.

21. "Speed Shakespeare II," *Brooklyn (NY) Daily Eagle,* July 8, 1896; "Greatest of Jockeys"; John Dizikes, *Yankee Doodle Dandy: The Life and Times of Tod Sloan* (Lincoln: University of Nebraska Press, 2004), 87; "Fred Taral Always Enjoyed the Confidence of the Public," *Buffalo (NY) Times,* March 4, 1900.

22. "Grannan Is Ruled Off," *New York World,* September 29, 1896; "Grannan v. Westchester Racing Ass'n," Caselaw Access Project, Harvard Law School, accessed February 21, 2020, https://cite.case.law/nys/44/790/.

23. "Taral, Noted Rider of the 90's Dies," *New York Times,* February 14, 1925; "Jockey Fred Taral," *Aspen (CO) Daily Times,* April 11, 1893; "The Closing Days," *Louisville (KY) Courier-Journal,* October 12, 1891; "Gossip of the Turf," *Daily Racing Form* (Chicago), March 15, 1899; "How Some Jockeys Train." According to "Speedy Fortunes," *St. Paul (MN) Globe,* July 23, 1893, "thrift" was not one of Taral's "stronger characteristics."

24. "Octagon Won the Withers," *New York Times,* May 16, 1897; *Goodwin's 1897,* vol. 1, 289–90.

25. "Marcus Daly's Belmont," *New York Sun*, May 30, 1897; "In Furious Style," *Anaconda (MT) Standard*, May 30, 1897; *Goodwin's 1897*, vol. 1, 366–67; Larry K. Menna and Thomas L. Altherr, eds., *Sports in North America: Sports in the Progressive Era, 1900–1920* (Gulf Breeze, FL: Academic International Press, 1998), 413. In the history of the Triple Crown series, the inaugural running of the Belmont Stakes in 1867 predated the Preakness Stakes by six years and the Kentucky Derby by eight.

26. "In Furious Style"; "Montana Has the Belmont," *New York Tribune*, May 30, 1897.

27. "Marcus Daly's Belmont."

28. For an overview of August Belmont II, see chap. 3 of Edward Bowen, *Legacies of the Turf: A Century of Great Breeders*, vol. 1 (Lexington: Blood-Horse Publications, 2003); and Mark Simon, "Pillar of the Turf: August Belmont II Was an American Original," *Daily Racing Form* (Chicago), August 2, 2013.

29. *Goodwin's 1897*, vol. 1, 366–67; "In Furious Style."

30. "Marcus Daly's Belmont"; "In Furious Style"; "Scottish Chieftan," *Thoroughbred Record*, June 5, 1897.

31. "Fox Keene's Clever Ride," *New York Times*, May 30, 1897; "Another Account," *Anaconda (MT) Standard*, May 30, 1897; *Goodwin's 1897*, vol. 1, 367.

32. "Montana Has the Belmont," *New York Tribune*, May 30, 1897; untitled article, see "The meeting at Morris Park . . . ," second column, *Turf, Field and Farm*, May 28, 1897, 385.

33. "Hamiltonians," *Anaconda (MT) Standard*, June 1, 1897; "The Chieftain."

34. *Goodwin's 1897*, vol. 1, 440, 502; *Goodwin's 1897*, vol. 2, 36–37, 271, 318; "Notes of the Turf," *Daily Racing Form* (Chicago), June 15, 1897; "Marcus Daly May Retire," *Thoroughbred Record*, September 6, 1897.

35. Frank G. Carpenter, "The Copper King," *Deseret Weekly* (Salt Lake City), May 13, 1893, 658.

36. For "hobby" references, see "Hon. Marcus Daly," in *Progressive Men of the State of Montana* (Chicago: A. W. Bowen, n.d.), 15; "Mr. Daly Is a True Sportsman," *New York Sun*, June 13, 1891; "Two Famous Men Who Have Been Famous in the Turf World," *Lakin (KS) Investigator*, March 6, 1901; "Marcus Daly—Copper King," *Thoroughbred Record*, September 10, 1898, 127; "Rivalry of Clark and Daly," *Inter Ocean* (Chicago), February 4, 1900.

37. "Daly Leaves the Turf," *Butte Miner*, September 11, 1897; "Has Daly Quit the Turf?," *Butte (MT) Miner*, September 6, 1897.

38. "Daly Leaves the Turf," *Butte Miner*, September 11, 1897.

39. "Matt Byrnes and J.J. Moran Retire from the Bitter Root Ranch," *Butte (MT) Miner*, November 8, 1897; "Daly Leaves the Turf." Byrnes would act as a horse-buying agent for Daly in 1897; see "The Hamburg Mystery," *New York Times*, December 15, 1897.

40. "On the Turf," *Buffalo (NY) Commercial*, April 12, 1898; "Troxler's Fall Causes Regret," *Daily American* (Nashville), March 12, 1899; "Poor Starting Mars the

Sport," *Daily American*, April 12, 1899; "Starter Byrnes Resigns," *Chattanooga Daily Times*, April 12, 1899; "Racing at Saratoga," *New York Times*, August 3, 1900; "Bardella's Fast Race," *Brooklyn (NY) Daily Eagle*, August 14, 1898; "Poor Work with the Flag," *Brooklyn Daily Eagle*, August 17, 1899.

41. "Turf News and Gossip," *Brooklyn (NY) Daily Eagle*, March 5, 1900; "Holtman Signs for the Season," *San Francisco Chronicle*, February 14, 1904; "Many Good Horses for Oakland Races," *Anaconda (MT) Standard*, September 16, 1908.

42. "Byrnes Returns East after Racing Season," *Daily Record* (Long Branch, NJ), March 18, 1930; "Women on the Turf," *Inter Ocean* (Chicago), August 17, 1891; "Talks with Racing Men," *New York Tribune*, September 29, 1893; Francis Trevelyan, "Gossip of the Turf," *New York Journal*, May 17, 1897; "Death Comes to Matt Byrnes," *Thoroughbred Record*, March 25, 1933.

43. "Hamburg," *Index: Thoroughbred Stock.*

44. "Lady Reel," *ASB*, vol. 7, 527; "Hamburg," NMRHF, accessed October 7, 2016, www.racingmuseum.org/hall-of-fame/hamburg; Walter S. Vosburgh, *Racing in America, 1866–1921* (New York: Scribner Press, 1922), 173; J. Keeler Johnson, "A Lofty Place in History for Hamburg," *The Sport*, July 3, 2017, accessed March 5, 2018, https://www.americasbestracing.net/the-sport/2017-lofty-place-history-hamburg.

45. "Surprises at Sheepshead," *New York Times*, September 12, 1897.

46. *Goodwin's 1897*, vol. 2, 378; "Hamburg Wins, Ornament Defeated," *Thoroughbred Record*, September 10, 1897; W. H. Gocher, "John E. Madden," *Indianapolis Star*, November 10, 1929.

47. Robertson, *History of Thoroughbred Racing*, 206; "People Talked About," *Leslie's Weekly*, March 10, 1898, 147, https://www.google.com/books/edition/Frank_Leslie_s_Illustrated_Newspaper/Vcc4AQAAMAAJ?hl=en&gbpv=1&dq=%22Madden%22+%22Harry+Reed%22+%22Robert+Steele%22&pg=PA147&printsec=frontcover; "What Lakeland Says," *Daily Leader* (Lexington, KY), December 11, 1897; "The Hamburg Mystery," *New York Times*, December 15, 1897.

48. "Gossip of the Runners," *New York Sun*, December 27, 1897; "Hamburg Will Race Here," *New York Times*, December 22, 1897.

49. W. C. Vreeland, "John E. Madden Record Breeder and Salesman," *Brooklyn (NY) Daily Eagle*, November 5, 1929.

50. *Goodwin's 1898*, vol. 1, 415–16; "Bowling Brook's Belmont," *New York Times*, May 27, 1898; Ada Powell, *Copper, Green and Silver* (privately printed, 1993), 31.

51. *Goodwin's 1898*, vol. 1, 522, 586; *Goodwin's 1898*, vol. 2, 7.

52. "Racing at Sheepshead," *New York Times*, July 1, 1898.

53. "Racing at Sheepshead"; "Jockey Fred Taral Roasts Tod Sloan," *Buffalo (NY) Enquirer*, July 5, 1898; *Goodwin's 1898*, vol. 2, 1.

54. "Racing at Sheepshead"; "Peep O' Day the Winner," *Brooklyn (NY) Daily Eagle*, July 2, 1898; "Jockey Fred Taral Roasts Tod Sloan."

55. "Racing Men Sail Abroad on Saturday," *New York Evening World*, February 5, 1903; Richard Sowers, *The Kentucky Derby, Preakness and Belmont Stakes: A Comprehensive History* (Jefferson, NC: McFarland, 2014), 46; "Taral Quits Saddle," *San Francisco Call*, May 8, 1909; "Taral, Noted Rider of the 90's Dies."

56. "Taral, Noted Rider of the 90's Dies"; "Fred Taral," NMRHF, accessed July 4, 2018, https://www.racingmuseum.org/hall-of-fame/jockey/fred-taral.

57. *Goodwin's 1898*, vol. 2, 168.

58. "Marcus Daly on Racing," *Chicago Tribune*, April 9, 1899; "News and Gossip of the Running Turf," *Brooklyn (NY) Daily Eagle*, January 28, 1901; "Hamburg," NMRHF, accessed March 15, 2018, https://www.racingmuseum.org/hall-of-fame/horse/hamburg-ky.

59. *Goodwin's 1898*, vol. 1, 100–101, 139; *Goodwin's 1898*, vol. 2, 383, 386, 461, 463; "Race Track and Stable Gossip," *Anaconda (MT) Standard*, February 4, 1898; "Race Track and Stable Gossip," *Anaconda Standard*, March 23, 1899; "Inverness," *Dispersal Sale of the Entire Bitter Root Stud*, No. 2.

60. "Bitter Root Brevities," *Western News* (Hamilton, MT), January 10, 1900; "Sam Lucas," *Western News*, January 24, 1900.

61. "Presented with a Watch," *Western News*, January 31, 1900.

62. "Sam Lucas, Once Noted as Race Horse Trainer, Dies," *Anaconda (MT) Standard*, March 29, 1929; "Bitter Root Brevities," *Western News* (Hamilton, MT), August 9, 1905; "Sam Lucas is in Town," *Western News*, November 22, 1905; Darleen Gould, Daly Mansion executive director, Hamilton, MT, email message to author, September 27, 2016; "The City in Brief," *Western News*, November 12, 1912; Workers of the Writers' Program of the Work Projects Administration in the State of Montana, *Copper Camp: Stories of the World's Greatest Mining Town, Butte, Montana* (New York: Hastings House, 1944), 242; "Vagrant Once Had Important Post," *Anaconda Standard*, December 14, 1920; "Heavy Fine Imposed," *Anaconda Standard*, November 16, 1909; "Famous Trainer Dies Here," *Montana Standard* (Butte), March 30, 1929; "Butte Death Notices," *Montana Standard*, March 31, 1929. The article "Trainer of Daly Racing Stars Is Called to Death," *Montana Standard*, March 30, 1929, states that Lucas had resided in Butte "since 1902." Sources suggest that from 1900 through at least 1905 Lucas also split his time between Kentucky and New York. For a New York reference, see "Bitter Root Brevities," *Western News*, August 9, 1905. The 1910 US Census lists Sam Lucas as living in Kentucky with his sister. The 1920 US Census lists him in Silver Bow County, Montana, as a boarder.

63. "The Local Field," *Ravalli Republican* (Hamilton, MT), December 15, 1899; "Race Track and Stable Gossip," *Anaconda (MT) Standard*, March 5, 1899; "Randall, Former Turf King, Dead," *Great Falls (MT) Tribune*, October 13, 1917; "All Ready for the Big Celebration," *Anaconda Standard*, July 4, 1907.

Chapter 15

1. "Marcus Daly," *Boston Globe*, November 12, 1900; "Announcement," *Dispersal Sale of the Entire Bitter Root Stud, 1901* catalogue (n.p.: Fasig-Tipton Company); "Metropolitan Notes," *Thoroughbred Record*, July 7, 1900, 2; "Marcus Daly's Horses Sold," *New York Times*, July 4, 1900.

2. "Marcus Daly Is Dead," *Butte (MT) Miner*, November 13, 1900; "Peacefully Comes Death to Its Waiting Victim," *Anaconda (MT) Standard*, November 13, 1900; "Death of Marcus Daly," *New York Times*, November 13, 1900.

3. "In Anaconda," *Anaconda (MT) Standard*, November 16, 1900; "Marcus Daly," *Anaconda Standard*, November 13, 1900.

4. "Marcus Daly," *Ravalli Republican* (Hamilton, MT), November 16, 1900; Ada Powell, *The Dalys of the Bitter Root* (privately printed, 1989), 86.

5. "A Day of Sorrow in Butte," *Anaconda (MT) Standard*, November 16, 1900; "Far and Wide Spreads a Wave of Sorrow," *Anaconda Standard*, November 13, 1900.

6. "The Best of Friends," *Anaconda (MT) Standard*, November 18, 1900; "Death of Marcus Daly," *Seattle Post-Intelligencer*, November 13, 1900; "In Washington," *Anaconda Standard*, November 13, 1900.

7. "Marcus Daly's Funeral Today," *New York Tribune*, November 15, 1900.

8. "Death of Marcus Daly," *Thoroughbred Record*, November 17, 1900; "Death of Marcus Daly," *Turf, Field and Farm*, November 16, 1900, 1270; Hamilton Busbey, *Recollections of Men and Horses* (New York: Dodd, Mead, 1907), 248, accessed January 7, 2021, https://babel.hathitrust.org/cgi/pt?id=nyp.33433066617501&view =1up&seq=316&q1=Bitter+Root+Farm.

9. "Montana Turfmen Organize a Jockey Club and the Copper State Will Have a Long Season of Racing," *San Francisco Call*, January 5, 1901; "Monument to Marcus Daly Unveiled," *Western News* (Hamilton, MT), September 4, 1907; Workers of the Writers' Program of the Work Projects Administration in the State of Montana, *Copper Camp: Stories of the World's Greatest Mining Town, Butte, Montana* (New York: Hastings House, 1944), 130, 303.

10. "Brood Mares Leave," *Ravalli County Democrat* (Hamilton, MT), December 26, 1900; "Last of the Stallions," *Anaconda (MT) Standard*, January 18, 1901; Ada Powell, *Copper, Green and Silver* (privately printed, 1993), 136.

11. "Announcement," *Dispersal Sale of the Entire Bitter Root Stud, 1901* catalogue; see W. H. Gocher, *Fasig's Tale of the Turf with Memoir* (Hartford, CT: privately printed, 1901), 164; "Dispersal Sale of the Bitter Root Stud," *Thoroughbred Record*, January 26, 1901, 55; "Daly Sale Catalogue," *Breeder and Sportsman*, January 5, 1901.

12. "Whitney Buys Hamburg," *New York Times*, January 31, 1901.

13. "Whitney Buys Hamburg," *New York Times*; "Whitney Buys Hamburg," *New York Sun*, January 31, 1901.

14. "The Marcus Daly Sale," *Spirit of the Times*, February 9, 1901; "W. C. Whitney Buys Hamburg," *Spirit of the Times*, February 2, 1901.

15. "Hamburg Brings $60,000," *New York Tribune*, January 31, 1901; "W. C. Whitney Buys Hamburg."

16. "Marcus Daly on Racing," *Chicago Tribune*, April 9, 1899; "Famous Racer Dies on Farm," *Evening Sun* (Baltimore), September 11, 1915; "Hamburg," NMRHF Portraits, "Hamburg," http://www.tbheritage.com/Portraits/Hamburg/html, accessed March 5, 2018.

17. "Ogden's Big Surprise," *New York Sun*, August 16, 1896; "W. C. Whitney Buys Hamburg."

18. "W. C. Whitney Buys Hamburg"; *Goodwin's 1906*, vol. 1, 527; "Tammany," *Thoroughbred Record*, December 9, 1933, 344; "Spirited Bidding for Blooded Stock," *Philadelphia Inquirer*, June 17, 1917.

19. "W. C. Whitney Buys Hamburg."

20. "W. C. Whitney Buys Hamburg."

21. "A Race Horse Was Arrested," *Buffalo (NY) Enquirer*, February 20, 1901.

22. "News and Gossip of the Running Turf," *Brooklyn (NY) Daily Eagle*, January 31, 1901; "A Race Horse Was Arrested."

23. "W. C. Whitney Buys Hamburg"; "Sale a Marker in Turf History," *Democrat and Chronicle* (Rochester, NY), March 13, 1901; "Bitter Root Stud Sale," *Thoroughbred Record*, February 2, 1901; "The Marcus Daly Sale."

24. "James B. Haggin Dies at Newport," *Thoroughbred Record*, September 19, 1914; "James Ben Ali Haggin," NMRHF, accessed September 26, 2022, https://www.racingmuseum.org/hall-of-fame/pillar/james-ben-ali-haggin; "The Passing of Elmendorf Stud," *Thoroughbred Record*, September 11, 1915, 126; "The Haggin and Clay Dispersal Sales," *Thoroughbred Record*, October 30, 1915, 208.

25. "James Ben Ali Haggin," NMRHF, accessed September 26, 2022, https://www.racingmuseum.org/hall-of-fame/pillar/james-ben-ali-haggin.

26. Untitled article, see "On the Atlantic Transport Line . . . ," third column, *Turf, Field and Farm*, September 20, 1901; "High Prices for Trotters," *New York Sun*, November 27, 1901; Gocher, *Fasig's Tale of the Turf*, 163–65.

27. Mary Simon, *Racing through the Century: The Story of Thoroughbred Racing in America* (Irvine: CA, BowTie Press, 2002), 42–43, 34.

28. "Hamilton Was Host to All Western Montana," *Western News* (Hamilton, MT), July 7, 1909; "Senator Grady Wins," *Missoulian* (Missoula, MT), July 18, 1909; Powell, *Copper, Green and Silver*, 40.

29. Muriel Sibell Wolle, *Montana Pay Dirt: A Guide to the Mining Camps of the Treasure State* (Denver: Sage Books, 1963), 181; Ellen Baumler, "Marcus Daly's Romance," September 11, 2013, accessed November 9, 2021, http://ellenbaumler.blogspot.com/2013/09/marcus-dalys-romance.html; "Hold Funeral Services for Mrs. Daly, 88," *Ravalli Republican* (Hamilton, MT), July 17, 1941.

30. *The Historic Estate of Copper King Marcus Daly*, pamphlet, Marcus Daly Mansion; Don Erdman, "Daly Mansion Acquisition Timeline 1984–1986," Marcus Daly Mansion Archives.

Index

Italicized references indicate illustrations.

www.ingramcontent.com/pod-product-compliance
Lightning Source LLC
Chambersburg PA
CBHW020445100426
42812CB00036B/3454/J